T0319776

TRANSPORT MATTERS

Edited by
Iain Docherty and Jon Shaw

Foreword by
John McTernan

First published in Great Britain in 2019 by

Policy Press
University of Bristol
1-9 Old Park Hill
Bristol
BS2 8BB
UK
t: +44 (0)117 954 5940
pp-info@bristol.ac.uk
www.policypress.co.uk

North America office:
Policy Press
c/o The University of Chicago Press
1427 East 60th Street
Chicago, IL 60637, USA
t: +1 773 702 7700
f: +1 773-702-9756
sales@press.uchicago.edu
www.press.uchicago.edu

© Policy Press 2019

British Library Cataloguing in Publication Data
A catalogue record for this book is available from the British Library

Library of Congress Cataloging-in-Publication Data
A catalog record for this book has been requested

978-1-4473-2955-8 hardback
978-1-4473-2956-5 paperback
978-1-4473-2958-9 ePub
978-1-4473-2957-2 ePDF

The right of Iain Docherty and Jon Shaw to be identified as editors of this work has been
asserted by them in accordance with the Copyright, Designs and Patents Act 1988.

Cover design by Liam Roberts

Printed and bound by CPI Group (UK) Ltd, Croydon, CR0 4YY

To our friends and colleagues, especially at ScotRail and Great Western Railway, who keep the transport system working day and night, and welcome us into the real world whenever we venture out from the ivory tower.

Contents

List of figures, tables and boxes

Figures

Tables

Boxes

List of abbreviations

ACTRA	Advisory Committee on Trunk Road Assessment
AONB	Area of Outstanding Natural Beauty
AST	Appraisal summary table
ATIS	Advanced Traveller Information System
AV	Autonomous vehicle
BBAF	Better Bus Area Fund
BCR	Benefit–cost ratio
BEIS	Department for Business, Energy and Industrial Strategy
BEV	Battery electric vehicle
BGS	British Geological Survey
BUG	Bus users' group
CABE	Commission for Architecture and the Built Environment
CAV	Connected and autonomous vehicle
CBA	Cost–benefit analysis
CBD	Central business district
CBI	Confederation of British Industry
CEBR	Centre for Economics and Business Research
CfIT	Commission for Integrated Transport
CIHT	Chartered Institute of Highways and Transport
CM	Collaborative mobility
CO_2	Carbon dioxide
CCC	Committee on Climate Change
CPRE	Campaign to Protect Rural England
DAD	Decide, announce and defend
DCLG	Department for Communities and Local Government
DCMS	Department for Culture, Media and Sport
DEFRA	Department for Environment, Food & Rural Affairs
DEM	Digitally enabled mobility
DfT	Department for Transport
DoE	Department of the Environment
DoT	Department of Transport
DP	Deliberative polling
DRT	Demand-responsive transport
DTI	Department of Trade and Industry
EEA	European Environment Agency
ENIAC	Electronic Numerical Integrator and Computer

ETM	Electronic ticket machine
EV	Electric vehicle
FCEV	Fuel-cell electric vehicle
GIS	Geographic information system
GOS	Government Office for Science
G-PaTRA	Green Passenger Transport in Rural Areas
GPN	Global production network
GVA	Gross value added
HEFCE	Higher Education Funding Council for England
HEV	Hybrid electric vehicle
HFC	Hydrogen fuel cell
HGV	Heavy goods vehicle
HiAP	Health in All Policies
HITRANS	Highlands and Islands Transport Partnership
HSR	High-speed rail
HS1	High Speed 1
HS2	High Speed 2
HS2AA	High Speed 2 Action Alliance
ICE	Internal combustion engine
ICT	Information and communication technology
IEA	International Energy Agency
IPCC	Intergovernmental Panel on Climate Change
ITF	Integrated Transport Forum
ITF	International Transport Forum
ITRACT	Improving Transport and Accessibility through New Communication Technologies
ITS	Intelligent Transport System
ITSO	Integrated Transport Smartcard Organisation
KPI	Key performance indicator
LAG	Local action group
LIDAR	Light Detection and Ranging
LRT	Light rapid transit
LSTF	Local Sustainable Transport Fund
MAA	Moving annual average
MaaS	Mobility as a service
MAMBA	Maximised Mobility and Accessibility of Services in Regions Affected by Demographic Change
MAMCA	Multi-actor, multi-criteria analysis
MC(D)A	Multi-criteria (decision) analysis
MoT	Ministry of Transport
MP	Member of Parliament
NGO	Non-governmental organisation

NHS	National Health Service
NIC	National Infrastructure Commission
NIMBY	Not in my back yard
NO_x	Oxides of nitrogen
NO_2	Nitrogen dioxide
NPV	Net present value
NRPS	National Rail Passenger Survey
NTM	National Traffic Model
NTS	National Travel Survey
ONS	Office for National Statistics
PHEV	Plug-in hybrid electric vehicle
PJP	Personalised journey plan
PM	Particulate matter
PPM	Public performance measure
PTAL	Public Transport Accessibility Level
PTI	Planning time index
PTP	Personalised travel plan
PWC	Price Waterhouse Coopers
RHTM	Regional Highway Traffic Model
RRL	Road Research Laboratory
RSBC	Royal Society for Blind Children
RSPH	Royal Society for Public Health
RSSB	Rail Safety and Standards Board
RT	Right-time performance
RTPI	Royal Town Planning Institute
SACTRA	Standing Advisory Committee on Trunk Road Assessment
SAE	Society of Automotive Engineers
SDI	Sustainable Development Indicators
SEU	Social Exclusion Unit
SMMT	Society of Motor Manufacturers and Traders
SNP	Scottish National Party
SRA	Strategic Rail Authority
SRN	Strategic Road Network
SUV	Sports utility vehicle
TEE	Transport economic efficiency
TfL	Transport for London
TfN	Transport for the North
TfWM	Transport for the West Midlands
TNCs	Transportation network companies
TOC	Train Operating Company
TRRL	Transport and Road Research Laboratory

TSC	Transport Systems Catapult
TSGB	Transport Statistics Great Britain
UNFCCC	United Nations Framework Convention on Climate Change
UTF	Urban Task Force
WebTAG	Web-based Transport Appraisal Guidance
WEB	Wider economic benefit
WHO	World Health Organization
WLTP	Worldwide Harmonised Light Vehicle Test Procedure
WTP	Workplace travel plan

Notes on contributors

Iain Docherty and **Jon Shaw** have written and/or edited six books together on various aspects of transport, travel and mobility.

Iain is Dean of the Institute for Advanced Studies at the University of Stirling. His research interests focus on the links between public administration, institutional change and city and regional competitiveness. He is the theme lead on transport and infrastructure for the *Productivity Insights Network*, a major ESRC initiative created to give non-economists the opportunity to explain why economists have consistently failed to crack the UK's resilient productivity puzzle. Iain is also working with various colleagues contributing to this book on the policy and governance issues surrounding the development of 'smart' mobility and autonomous vehicles, a research agenda that will probably keep all of us in publications for the rest of our research careers. Keen train traveller yet also (much to Glenn Lyons' disgust ☺) a secret petrolhead, Iain can be found on Twitter cataloguing the increasing difficulty of simply walking around thanks to the idiocy of British drivers, using the hashtag #militantpedestrian.

Jon is Professor of Geography at the University of Plymouth. In addition to his books with Iain, he wrote *Competition, Regulation and the Privatisation of British Rail* and co-edited *All Change* and the *Sage Handbook of Transport Studies*. His research has focused mainly on mobility policy and strategy, although of late he's enjoyed being involved in projects on jogging and the accessibility of disabled people from micro-level perspectives. Jon is the Deputy Chair of the European Platform for Transport Sciences, Chair of the Scientific Advisory Board of *econex Verkehrsconsult* and a member of the Great Western Railway Stakeholder Advisory Board. He has also been a Specialist Adviser to the House of Commons' Transport Committee. Although, unlike Iain, he's not a petrolhead (it would be a bit difficult to claim anything otherwise with a 56 plate Fiesta) and has a quite reasonable disposition as a pedestrian, he's never entirely managed to put sustainable transport into practice, retaining at least for the time being silver status with British Airways.

Jillian Anable is Professor of Transport and Energy at the Institute for Transport Studies at the University of Leeds. She is an expert in travel behaviour, climate change and energy policy, with particular emphasis on the potential for demand-side solutions. Her current research focuses on the market transformation and decarbonisation of vehicle markets using regulatory and fiscal policy and the evaluation of the impacts of sustainable transport interventions.

Stewart Barr is Professor of Geography at the University of Exeter. His research interests focus on sustainable development, behavioural change and environmental policy. He has undertaken a wide range of research projects exploring the ways in which publics engage with environmental change, and the challenges and opportunities for promoting behavioural shifts in the context of climate change mitigation. In the field of transport and mobility, his research focuses on the connections between policy, place and practice, which have formed the basis of his latest book, *Geographies of Transport and Mobility* (Routledge).

Christian Brand is an interdisciplinary environmental scientist, physicist and geographer with over 20 years' research experience in academic and consultancy environments. He is Associate Professor of Transport, Energy and Environment at the University of Oxford's Environmental Change Institute and Transport Studies Unit, and Acting Director of the TSU. Christian's research interests revolve around the development and use of low carbon scenarios and transitions pathways, the role of active travel in meeting public health and climate change goals, and interdisciplinary issues in transport, energy and climate change policy. He is the author of 50 peer reviewed journal papers and over 30 book chapters and technical reports, and has been principal or co-investigator on research projects worth over £20 million.

Kiron Chatterjee is Associate Professor in Travel Behaviour at the Centre for Transport and Society at the University of the West of England, Bristol. His research seeks understanding of the way in which people travel and how this is influenced by the transport system and social, economic and technological change. He has a particular interest in using longitudinal data to understand changing travel behaviour over the life course and has pioneered the use of biographical data collection methods. He is currently investigating how commuting influences personal wellbeing, reasons for the declining car use of young adults, how cycling can be facilitated in later life and the design and evaluation of sustainable transport interventions.

Julie Clark is a Senior Lecturer in the School of Media, Culture and Society at the University of the West of Scotland and is an

Associate Director of the ESRC Doctoral Training Partnership at the Scottish Graduate School for Social Science. Her field of interest is the relationship between policy, health and wellbeing, with particular reference to the role of transport and social inclusion. She gained a doctorate in Urban Studies at the University of Glasgow for her mixed methods investigation of the relationships between social inclusion and car ownership, and has project managed the multi-strand research project *GoWell: Studying Change in Glasgow's East End* since it began in 2012. Julie's applied, policy-relevant research has been recognised with a Research Council UK Award for Research Impact and a Sir Peter Hall Award for Wider Engagement.

William (Billy) Clayton is a Senior Lecturer in the Centre for Transport and Society at the University of the West of England, Bristol. He is a member of the teaching team on UWE's BA Geography, MSc Transport Planning, and MSc Transport Engineering and Planning programmes. He is also an active researcher, involved in a number of projects related to sustainable transport, autonomous (driverless) vehicles, cycling, public transport, new mobile technologies and travel, transport mapping and transport evaluation. Billy is the author of numerous academic papers, articles and reports.

Tom Cohen is a Senior Fellow at UCL's Centre for Transport Studies in London. He entered the academic world after a decade in transport consultancy, obtaining a doctorate that involved the development of a novel form of participatory budgeting. Tom's long-standing enthusiasm for the meaningful involvement of citizens in transport decision making arises from broader interests in transport justice and the way transport policy is made. He has wide experience of citizen participation as both practitioner and researcher and this has taught him to seek a path between cynicism and utopianism. Tom teaches transport policy, transport behaviour change and street design. His current research centres on the governance of automated vehicles.

Angela Curl is a Senior Lecturer in the Department of Population Health at the University of Otago – Christchurch, New Zealand. Her research interests are focused around understanding diverse experiences of transport and mobility and how these intersect with the built environment to influence health and wellbeing. She has a focus on older people's mobilities as a key interface between research in transport and health. Angela is a geographer by training and has experience across disciplinary boundaries, having worked in departments of Geography, Urban Studies, Landscape Architecture and Population Health, and as a transport planning practitioner.

David Dawson is Lecturer in Transport Management and Resilience at the University of Leeds. Interested primarily in sustainable and resilient transport systems, his interdisciplinary background has enabled him to engage with research on sustainable transport transitions and long-term climate and flood resilience. He has worked on multiple research grants and undertaken independent research fellowships engaged with transport practitioners both nationally and internationally. David has also worked with government departments and provided expert evidence for policy makers on the management of resilience across the transport sector.

Dan Durrant is Lecturer in Infrastructure Planning at UCL's Bartlett School of Planning. He conducted his doctoral research at Bartlett's OMEGA Centre in Megaprojects and Development, in which he studied HS2 and the role of different local, regional and national civil society organisations in responding to the issues generated by the project. Dan's research interests include the role of civil society in the decision-making processes of infrastructure projects. In particular he focuses on the way civil society provides spaces for deliberation, the development of institutions that might improve the quality of decision making, and the ability of a wider range of interests to shape the planning and development of infrastructure and the delivery of projects.

Phil Goodwin is Emeritus Professor of Transport Policy at University College London and the University of the West of England. He was formerly a transport planner at the Greater London Council, a Director of the Port of Dover, Director of the Transport Studies Unit at the University of Oxford and at UCL, and a Professor at UWE. He was a member of the Standing Advisory Committee on Trunk Road Assessment and co-author of its three reports including the 1994 report on induced traffic. His other published research includes work on travel demand elasticity, road user charging, public transport fares, the value of time spent travelling, smarter travel planning, 'peak car' and young people's travel. He was Chair of the independent panel advising the Deputy Prime Minister on the 1998 White Paper on transport, and is currently a member of the DfT advisory panel on demand forecasting and appraisal.

David Gray is a Professor in the School of Creative and Cultural Business, at Robert Gordon University. His principal area of expertise is transport in remote, rural and island communities. He has worked on a number of rural transport research projects and has advised bodies such as the Scottish Government, the UK Commission for Integrated Transport and DEFRA's Rural Evidence Research Centre. David is a Board member of the Highlands and Islands Transport Partnership, was a special adviser to the Scottish Executive during the preparation of Scotland's (first) National Transport Strategy and advised the Scottish Government as it prepared its original Strategic Transport Projects Review. He was born and brought up in Shetland, which cartographically speaking may or may not be located in a box in the Moray Firth.

Robin Hickman is Reader in Transport and City Planning at the Bartlett School of Planning, UCL. He has research interests in transport and climate change, urban structure and travel, social equity, the affective dimensions of travel and project appraisal. He is Director of UCL's MSc in Transport and City Planning. His recent books include *Transport, Climate Change and the City* (Routledge 2014) and the *Handbook on Transport and Development* (Edward Elgar 2015).

Juliet Jain is a Senior Research Fellow at the Centre for Transport and Society, University of the West of England, Bristol. She is a social scientist who applies social theory and methodologies to transport and mobility related 'problems'. The focus of her research has been on the nexus of travel, technology and everyday life. Juliet has made significant contributions to research examining travel time use in the information age and the journey experience. She has a particular interest in passenger rail, from how rail futures are imagined through to the impact of free Wi-Fi on rail passengers. She has also researched the impact of work-related travel on family life in the digital age.

Glenn Lyons is the Mott MacDonald Professor of Future Mobility at the University of the West of England, Bristol. He is seconded for half his time to Mott MacDonald, creating a bridge between academia and practice. Throughout his career he has focused upon the role of new technologies in supporting and influencing travel behaviour, both directly and through shaping lifestyles and social practices. A former secondee to the UK Department for Transport and more recently to the New Zealand Ministry of Transport, Glenn has led major studies into traveller information systems, teleworking, virtual mobility, travel time use, user innovation, road pricing, public and business attitudes to transport and future mobility. He is now actively engaged in examining the future prospects for technological innovations including connected and autonomous vehicles and Mobility as a Service.

Greg Marsden is Professor of Transport Governance at the Institute for Transport Studies at the University of Leeds. He has researched issues surrounding the design and implementation of new policies for over 15 years. Current work examines how the smart mobility transition will change how we think about what, how and who governs the mobility system. Greg is Chair of the Commission on Travel Demand, looking at how to deal with alternative transport futures, Secretary General of the World Conference on Transport Research Society and the Co-Chair of its Special Interest Group on Governance and Decision-Making. He has served as a Specialist Adviser to the House of Commons' Transport Committee and regularly advises governments in the UK and abroad.

Jennie Middleton is a Senior Research Fellow in the Transport Studies Unit in the School of Geography and the Environment at Oxford University. With a background in urban, social and cultural geography, Jennie's research strongly relates to the field of transport and mobilities. Her work explores everyday urban mobility, particularly people's different mobile experiences, and the implications of these things for urban and transport policy. Jennie's research has been funded by the British Academy, the ESRC, the Wellcome Trust and the University of Oxford John Fell Fund. Her forthcoming book *The walkable city: the dimensions of walking and overlapping walks of life* will be published by Routledge.

Charles Musselwhite is Associate Professor in Gerontology at the Centre for Innovative Ageing at Swansea University. His research specialism is environmental gerontology, with a particular interest in mobility, transport and travel, examining road safety, health, wellbeing and modal choice for an ageing population. Current research is investigating how to make transport systems age-friendly and how far technology can support mobility in later life.

Graham Parkhurst is Professor of Sustainable Mobility and Director of the Centre for Transport and Society at the University of the West of England, Bristol. He has over 25 years' experience in transport and mobility studies. His current research interests are examining the wider implications of trends to greater automation, electrification, flexibility and use of digital technologies in the transport sector. He is currently leading work in five UK government funded research consortia examining connected and automated vehicles (*Venturer*, *Flourish*, *CAPRI* and *MultiCAV*) and flexible collective transport solutions (*Mobility on Demand Laboratory Environment*). Electric mobility, instead, is the focus of a European Commission-funded project (*Replicate*) which seeks to pilot and 'upscale' electric car and cycle sharing.

John Preston is Professor of Rail Transport and Head of the Transportation Research Group at the University of Southampton. He has over 35 years of experience in transport research and education and has taught transport options on economics, engineering, geography, management and planning courses. His research in transport covers demand and cost modelling, regulatory studies, land-use and environment interactions and the appraisal and evaluation of projects, programmes and policies. His initial work concentrated on rail but subsequent work has covered all the major modes of transport. He has held over 140 research grants and contracts worth almost £14 million, and has over 300 publications.

Andrew Seedhouse has been working in the sustainable transport sector for 28 years. Following a period at the Devon and Cornwall Rail Partnership, he went on to head the Transport Operations Directorate at Plymouth City Council. He joined FirstGroup in 2001, becoming a director of four companies, before returning to the public sector with the Department for Transport in 2005. He joined the University of Plymouth in 2010, and after completing his doctorate now leads on research and commercial consultancy between the private, public and academic sectors. In addition, he founded and is the chairman of Smart Applications Management, the UK's largest member-owned partnership for delivering smart ticketing solutions.

Justin Spinney is Lecturer in Human Geography in the School of Geography and Planning at Cardiff University. His research interests focus on the intersections between mobility, embodiment, governance and technology, with a particular interest in cycling. These interests are underpinned by a political-economic focus on the production and maintenance of power and inequality and the application of post-structuralist theories including Actor Network Theory, Governmentality and bio-politics.

Georgiana Varna is Lecturer in Planning and Urbanism at Newcastle University. She is a multi-disciplinary scholar, working in between the realms of geography, urban planning, urban design, architecture, sociology and urban policy. Her research focuses on issues related to the urban public realm, place-making and urban regeneration in post-industrial landscapes and urban policy. Between 2013 and 2017 she worked intensively with various urban stakeholders from the public and private sectors while at the Scottish Cities Knowledge Centre at the University of Glasgow, part of the Scottish Cities Alliance dedicated to improving the cities of Scotland through meaningful exchange and dialogue.

Geoff Vigar is Professor of Urban Planning at Newcastle University. His research focuses on spatial planning and transport questions. Recent work has been orientated towards evaluating online and offline methods for debating place futures using design thinking and deliberative, collaborative and participatory planning theory; citizen-led place-making; and ideas of professionalism with regard to the built environment using ethnographic methods to explore the significance of changing institutional settings for planning work.

David Waite is a Research Associate in Policy Scotland and in the Department of Urban Studies at the University of Glasgow. His research interests focus on the processes underpinning and the governance of second-tier, city-region economies. Prior to his appointment at Glasgow, David worked as a post-doctoral researcher at Cardiff University on city-regional issues with colleagues in the School of Geography and Planning. His doctoral research was undertaken at the University of St Andrews. David's interest in policy-focused work is derived from experience in New Zealand as well as in the UK.

Foreword

John McTernan

*Political strategist for Burson Cohn & Wolfe
and former Political Secretary to Tony Blair*

Why does transport matter?

I asked this question when running a leadership seminar in a government transport department. Everyone in the room was smart enough to know that transport is bigger than just services running smoothly, whether bus, tram, train or the roads themselves. They quickly got to 'the economy, stupid!', which is, one has to admit, a good point; but it is a means, not an end. After a rich conversation about purpose, which is as central to government as it is rare, the examples, the stories, were all about people. 'It's so an apprentice can get to work'. 'So a grandparent can babysit for his daughter, giving her and her partner their first night out since the baby was born.' In the end, it's agency: the ability to shape your choices to make the life that you want to live.

So, 'Transport Matters'. Though this book's title can be read as an exasperated assertion – 'No, it really does matter!' – the essays collected here give a deep and thoughtful response to the question. From a range of perspectives, the authors demonstrate that transport has, does and will always matter. The long view shows how path-dependent transport policy can be, how the missteps of the past literally drive the present and shape the future. The richly comparative take shows that it needn't be this way. The interrogation of trends shows the truth of William Gibson's adage: 'The future's here already, it's just unevenly distributed.'

This is a book that believes profoundly in the public sphere – the creation of shared value through shared values. I have long believed that public transport makes social democrats of most of us; it is the ultimate combination of personal choice and collective provision working together. My hunch was confirmed when I asked a US demographer to explain why the exurbs had trended Republican during the late 1980s but were becoming solidly Democrat under Obama. 'After enough densification', he remarked, 'top political concerns shift from the right to bear arms to the need for mass transit.'

The niggling question at the heart of this book is why transport sits so low down the political agenda. Partly, it's the lack of salience; the issue lies low down voters' priorities except during spikes when there are massive controversies, such as the level of fuel duty, or transport accidents and disasters. Partly, it's the long lead-in time for capital expenditure. I asked one Labour Secretary of State for Transport what the job was like. 'I spend all my time opening things that were agreed by a Tory minister and the rest of it agreeing things that will be opened by a future Tory minister,' he responded.

But it's not just the raw politics. There is a gap between the normal discourse of transport economics, academics and the public. That's understandable – all professions have their jargon. The gap is real but it is bridgeable. It's reminiscent of Molière's *bourgeois gentilhomme*, Monsieur Jourdain. As a character in a seventeenth-century French play, he thinks he should be speaking in Alexandrines. When he discovers he isn't he exclaims, 'Well, what do you know about that! These forty years now I've been speaking in prose without knowing it!' This shock of surprise would be shared by the general British public were they to read this book. They think they are walking, cycling, driving, commuting by train or bus. In reality, they are doing transport, and their options, their choices and their agency are shaped by transport policy. This book is at its best, most passionate and most persuasive in its core argument: that transport is about life and that it 'is best seen as an enabler of a bigger economy, a fairer and healthier society and a cleaner environment' (page 23).

That vision – and the hope of its fulfilment – is what makes this an essential book.

Preface and acknowledgements

This is the third of our edited books that has focused on transport, travel and mobility in Britain. The first, *A New Deal for Transport?*, was published in 2003 and took its title from the then Labour government's 1998 White Paper. After the work undertaken by a range of academics, politicians and other interested parties in the late 1980s and 1990s – culminating in Phil Goodwin and colleagues' *Transport: the New Realism* report in 1991 and the Labour Party's *Consensus for Change* document in 1996 – there was considerable optimism that the White Paper, the first for a generation on transport as a whole rather than individual modes, would kick-start a new approach to transport policy resulting in major improvements. Our aim in the book was straightforward enough: to assess the government's record on transport. We concluded that people's optimism might have been misplaced, and found ourselves wondering if the time had 'come to ask whether the heralded New Deal for Transport [was] a chimera.' The government was showing signs of reneging on the headline commitments of *A New Deal*, its cautiousness heightened by a swiftly developing sensitivity to the demands of the motoring lobby. Despite enormous majorities in the House of Commons (179 seats in 1997 and 167 in 2001), senior ministers were spooked by fuel tax protests that arose after an unlikely (and unholy) alliance of lorry drivers, farmers and countryside campaigners blocked fuel depots and threatened to bring the country to a standstill.

Five years later in *Traffic Jam* we confirmed our earlier fears. By this point it was obvious that Labour ministers had no real intention of pursuing the kind of 'sustainable transport' policies that had been trumpeted when basking in 1997's electoral glory. The jaunty cover of *Traffic Jam* – a brightly coloured collection of toy cars in staged gridlock – was deliberately chosen to convey our sense of frustration with senior government figures who seemed to be treating the electorate like children, at least in policy delivery terms.[1] No doubt they thought they were playing the politics splendidly, as evidenced by the 'more-than-occasional perception of conceited self-congratulation among ministers, their civil service and costly array of special advisers…,' even if this appeared at odds with 'the situation "on the ground" – outmoded and unsuitable infrastructure, an absurd project complexity fetish, resultant project cost inflation…, more congestion and so on.' In 2007, a decade after having first been elected, the government itself admitted the extent of its ineffectiveness when Ruth Kelly, the Transport Secretary of the day, wrote that her new 'discussion' document, published fully nine years after *A New Deal for Transport*, 'begins a process of debate about how we best ensure that our investment and policies result in real-world improvements that are both sustained and sustainable.' Phil Goodwin noted in his concluding chapter to *Traffic Jam* that his fellow authors 'would raise their eyebrows at that first word – "begins".' At the launch event at the Scotch Malt Whisky Society in London, we raised more than eyebrows, but only to the thought that as long as Labour was in power we'd never run out of material for future incarnations of our book.

Now, more than a decade after that gathering, much has happened in British transport policy and politics (in the context of much happening in British policy and politics more generally). We have seen the Labour Party replaced in government with a Conservative–Liberal Democrat Coalition and then, when Liberal Democrat voters essentially punished Nick Clegg for bringing university funding to the forefront of political debate, a short-lived Conservative majority government led by David Cameron that itself, after the Brexit vote, gave way to a Conservative minority government 'led' by Theresa May. Notwithstanding – or in part, because of – such political upheaval, transport seems to have gained a new lease of life at the UK government level, with several large-scale infrastructure projects being carried through to completion and others, most notably the High Speed 2 (HS2) railway line, being endorsed almost too enthusiastically, regardless of their cost.[2] Inter-urban road building has been prioritised, and although at least two major electrification schemes have been cancelled by the Department for Transport (DfT), the 'legacy' railway is still receiving levels of investment unseen for generations. Of course, there are still problems in British transport policy that remain resilient and unresolved – it is unlikely this book would have seen the light of day if there weren't – but at least in relation to the delivery of inter-urban infrastructure capacity, whatever one might think of this as a transport policy priority per se, there is a flicker of hope that transport has returned to some level of political attention.

It is in this context that we offer this third-in-a-series book. Unlike *Traffic Jam*, which was essentially an update of *A New Deal for Transport*, we have adopted a different approach this time. Rather than providing commentary on the progress the government has or has not made on delivering its transport policy by mode, we have sought to focus not only on key issues that are important in transport, but also how and why transport is itself important to broader policy imperatives. The real value of appreciating the extent to which transport enables and constrains these things has eluded many in government. High-quality, reliable and affordable transport systems can't themselves guarantee that ministers will accomplish their wider policy goals – well-crafted suites of complementary approaches are needed for that – but they do make promoting economic development (businesses can transact with other businesses, their workforces and their customers) and social inclusion (people can access goods and services regardless of whether they own a car) very much more attainable. They can also reduce environmental harm (making best use of modes and technologies that produce the fewest and least dangerous emissions) in pursuit of socio-economic benefit. Who knows, they may even have a political function if commuters notice their daily grind on the train becoming less hassle and more comfortable, or if the traffic jams en route to the coast on summer Sundays disappear. In this sense, the book is more internationally applicable than its predecessors: although the examples discussed are largely (but not exclusively) British, the analyses should be relevant to most developed economies.

What we also confirm from working with our fellow authors is that there is a variety of views among advocates of 'sustainable' transport (by this we mean broadly the collection of policy approaches to transport policy advocated in *Transport: The New Realism*). Our positions represent a spectrum from 'deep(ish) green' approaches that involve restricting travel at different spatial scales, to actively embracing the virtues of a modern transport system and the proposition that it's perfectly fine that some people need to have more mobility, not less. Such a variety of views is good for healthy debate and reminds us that there are many valid, sometimes contradictory, ways of achieving sustainable transport objectives. We all, for example, agree on the need for more infrastructure investment, but depending on our convictions are inclined to favour different interventions ranging from cycle paths and car-free streets, to the construction – subject to appropriate means of 'locking in' arising capacity benefits – of new inter-urban roads and additional runways. Or, indeed, all of the above. Collective viewpoints can become stronger when engaging with and learning from others' ideas, and we all accept the need for nuance when defining a coherent macro-level response to apparently intractable policy problems. This is particularly important when it comes to lobbying policy makers – see recent 'Professors' letters' on the strategic direction of British transport policy (led by Greg Marsden) and cycling in London (led by Rachel Aldred).

One of the great privileges of bringing together a project such as this is precisely that it allows us to engage with and learn from the ideas of a large number of our most excellent colleagues. We'd like to thank all of them for providing their chapters, not least as they have striven to do this against the backdrop of the increasingly demoralising, bureaucratic, managerialist, uninspiring, metric-obsessed and thus stifling system that is contemporary British academia, in which producing books like this is increasingly viewed as a curious indulgence. (Perhaps New Zealand is still different; we defer to Angela and David's judgement. If it is, we hope it remains so.)

Phil Goodwin, who has more than earned himself the right to engage in British academia in the manner that he chooses, once again provided invaluable insight – not to mention hot cross buns – all the way from before the first authors' meeting to manuscript submission. Glenn Lyons has likewise given sage counsel and the book is all the better for his across-the-board input. Rob Hickman very kindly arranged rooms and refreshments for the authors' meetings at UCL, and Patricia Brown tried hard to make an important introduction just down the road. Jamie Quinn, of the University of Plymouth's Geomapping Unit, has for the fifth time in one of our projects expertly drawn all of the maps and diagrams, and Stuart Cole, Richard Parsons and an anonymous referee cast their expert eyes over the text. We are also grateful to Policy Press, especially Emily Watt, Caroline Astley-Brown and Sarah Bird, for their administrative support and impressive reserves of patience. The only way this book could be described as punctual would be to categorise it as 'very, very long-distance' in the Public Performance Measure terms of Britain's railways. Finally, our families, friends and immediate colleagues are due our sincere thanks for all of their help and encouragement. Iain would especially like to thank Andrea for her unstinting support, and to apologise (again) to Ruaridh and Athol for not having come up with a book on something 'more interesting than trains'. Jon wants to make particular mention of Paul Simpson, Mark Anderson and the 'ferry friends' and crew of the Mount Batten Water Taxi. In relation to what we're saying in this book, it's difficult to imagine a better commute than crossing the Sound twice every weekday.

As always, we've tried to fashion the collection of essays that follow into a coherent story. Please let us know how we've got on. With luck, by the time this book's successor is published, you'll have more comfort and perhaps less time to read it in, although we're sure you'll still be much better off with regard to these things in France or Germany. If your blue passport will get you in, that is…

Iain Docherty and Jon Shaw
On an under-invested-in island, just off the coast of the EU
February 2019

Notes

1. To our dismay, the publisher of *A New Deal for Transport?*, Blackwell, had edited the cover image of traffic congestion on a motorway to obscure the banner unfurled across a lorry's radiator grille that read 'Tell Gordon Brown 2p off'. This reference to the then Chancellor of the Exchequer's proposed modest increase in fuel duty was apparently deemed too fruity for an academic book.

2. The devolved administrations in Scotland, Wales and London have been making their own progress with varying degrees of success, although matters in Northern Ireland have not been helped by suspensions of the province's Legislative Assembly. On HS2, we were spectacularly wrong – or, given that in 2019 a week is an *extraordinarily* long time in politics, we are at least still currently spectacularly wrong – in the preface to *Traffic Jam*, opining that High Speed 1 would remain 'HS1 and only for the foreseeable future.' Among others, our friend Jim Steer has played a blinder. Britain: you might not think it, but you owe him one.

PART I

Setting the scene

PART I

Setting the scene

1

Transport matters

Jon Shaw and Iain Docherty

Introduction

Perhaps some of those watching the gathering storm on a stretch of Britain's southern coastline on 4 February 2014 had the fleeting thought that local railway workers might be busy that night. On a good day, the views out to sea from the railway line that runs between the cliffs and the beach from Teignmouth to Dawlish Warren are truly magnificent; the English Channel's sparkling blue set against red sandstone cliffs and stacks that mark the train's arrival at the 'English Riviera'. Other than London and its surroundings, the South West attracts more inbound visitors than any other part of England (Visit Britain 2013), and the railway still identifies itself as emblematic of the region.[1] But by the following morning, when the storm that did indeed keep railway workers up had blown through, it was clear how much the whole of the region identified with its railway. As the tracks of the Great Western mainline just up from Dawlish station dangled in thin air (Figure 13.3), it was also clear how much local politicians and business owners were worried that people *outside of the region* were identifying with its railway. With the rail corridor through Devon into Cornwall severed for the foreseeable future, the potential for the counties to be perceived as 'closed for business' was headline news (BBC 2015). Although the predictable instant rash of doom-laden 'studies' appeared – our colleague Greg Marsden (2014: unpaginated) wrote an article for *The Conversation* pointing out that '[w]ithin hours of the news [of the line closure], calculations adorned the backs of hundreds of envelopes, producing seven, eight or even nine figure sums of economic turmoil' – the key point was that even if they weren't sure precisely what the impact would be, people very quickly realised that *transport matters* to themselves and their communities.

This may not seem especially surprising given that individuals' livelihoods and holiday plans were apparently under threat, but the sudden, panicked concern in fact highlights how *little* attention the public generally pays to transport, despite its importance to their daily lives or the functioning of the country as a whole. Back in 2010, while researching for a paper on the record of Tony Blair and Gordon Brown's Labour governments on transport (Docherty and Shaw 2011), we looked in detail at several sources of information on this issue. What we found depended on the context of the original research. From a *policy* perspective, there was evidence to suggest that people have some awareness of the negative externalities of the British transport system, with one study noting 30 per cent of the public identifying transport as a 'main problem facing Britain today' (Commission for Integrated Transport (CfIT) 2002: 10). But from the point of view of *political* attitudes research, especially that seeking to identify matters that sway voting intention, transport seemed less important to people. We have updated the findings, and Figure 1.1 tracks the results of Ipsos MORI's polling from 1997 to 2017, asking people "What do you think is the most/other important issues facing Britain today?" Generally, transport registers 2 to 4 per cent of responses, increasing only in reaction to extraordinary events such as the Dawlish line closure, a fatal rail crash or particularly acute or controversial policy 'moments' such as the suddenly escalating cost of petrol and diesel.

Writing in February 2019, it is hardly surprising that the most frequently cited answer in the latest iteration of Ipsos MORI's (2019)

Figure 1.1: Identification of 'transport as an important issue facing Britain today' over time

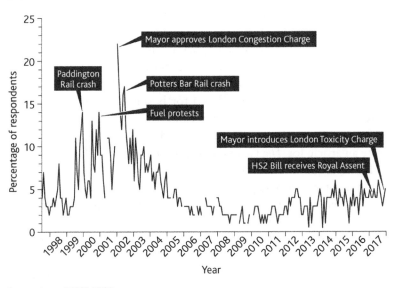

Source: Ipsos-MORI 2018

survey – by 63 per cent of respondents (with 54 per cent identifying it as *the* most important issue) – is Europe and the unfolding national calamity of Brexit. Second, with 44 (7) per cent of responses, is healthcare/the National Health Service (NHS), followed by education and schools (21/1 per cent), poverty/inequality (20/3 per cent), immigration (19/7 per cent), housing (19/2 per cent), crime/law and order (17/4 per cent), the economy (17/3 per cent) and pollution/ the environment (12/1 per cent). To some extent or another, public attitudes to most of the issues identified seem to peak in relation to a particular controversy or significant incident, but especially in the case of transport it seems that in the normal course of events people are just too concerned about other things to worry all that much about the fact that their train journey takes ten minutes longer than it used to, or that it takes half an hour to drive just a few miles on a Tuesday morning. In specific relation to congestion, Goodwin and Lyons (2010: 7) suggest that people have come to accept traffic jams as a fact of life, even if they sense that others think they have negative consequences: "well, I am not bothered myself," they say, "but it must be serious because everybody else says so."

What strikes us reading Ipsos MORI's data is the extent to which transport is fundamentally related to each of the issues identified as more important by the Great British Public. With Brexit, for instance, the biggest sticking point in negotiations between the UK government and the EU is movement across the Northern Irish border (*The Guardian* 2018). This vexed question of course comprises layers of history, politics and cultures, but underpinning all of these and the everyday experience of dealing with them is the need to maintain mobility. The public's second most important issue is healthcare/ the NHS, and we can be clear that the world's fifth-largest employer (Nuffield Trust 2017) would be unable to function without its medical supplies and patients being in the right place at the right time. From a rather different perspective, the NHS might receive fewer patient visits in the first place if a greater proportion of the British population was less car dependent and walked and cycled more (Chapter 8).

And so it goes on. If you've ever wondered why the roads in towns and cities tend to be at their busiest at around 8.45 am, or why at the same time in the summer holidays you can drive to work unhindered, look no further than the 'school run'. A combination of our increased reluctance to have children walk or cycle to school – in part because of fears about personal safety related to crime (and traffic!) – and education policies that encourage children to travel to schools of their (parents') choice rather than the local comprehensive, results in a particularly inefficient use of scarce road space in many places over concentrated periods of time, for little appreciable benefit to society as a whole. Poverty/inequality lead to all manner of transport-related exclusion problems for those who don't have cars to access jobs, essential services and the broader range of social opportunities that underpin wellbeing (Chapters 4 and 8), and the differential access to opportunity that the transport system offers between people and places reinforces this. Even those who are fortunate enough to be in well-paid work are increasingly likely to suffer stress from longer commutes (and Britain has one of the longest average commute times in Europe).[2] The issue of immigration is evidently linked to public interpretations of the impacts of population growth on health, housing, schools and other services. But the views of many Brexiteers about why the free movement of people coming *into* the UK must be stopped, while Britons should remain at liberty to travel *out of* the country to their holiday or retirement destination of choice unencumbered by European impositions such as visas, reveal contradictions in what people think about who can and should be mobile beyond their own borders, and in what conditions (see Cresswell 2010 and Nikolaeva et al 2019).[3]

Then there is congestion, which acts as a brake on the performance of the economy, arising from too much car dependence. There are, famously (at least among transport professionals), any number of estimates of how much congestion costs the British economy each year through loss of 'productive time'. These estimates vary wildly, by a factor of over four (*Local Transport Today* 2012), but they all run into the billions of pounds (one is as high as 30 billion). We will come to see that it's not necessarily helpful to set great store by time gained or lost through making journeys (Chapters 2 and 6), but still it's difficult to argue that traffic congestion is a beneficial use of anyone's day even if we are now able to use our travel time in more ways than ever before (Chapter 10; see Chapter 15 for a discussion of the potential impact of autonomous vehicles (AVs) in this regard). And all of this is to say nothing of the globally-significant issues of energy use and pollution. Transport quickly depletes natural resources and is responsible for a range of very serious impacts from the poor air quality that contributes to tens of thousands of premature deaths per year in the UK alone, all the way up to climate change (Chapter 3).

In short, transport really does matter, or, as Lyons (2004: 485) puts it, transport 'does not merely serve society: it shapes society, as in turn society shapes transport.' It is our aim in this book to undertake a detailed review not just of key issues that are important in transport, but also of how and why transport is itself important in addressing broader policy goals. The obvious (but ultimately rather unfulfilling) comment to make here is, 'of course transport is important to other things; we can't do much as a society if we can't move people and goods around.' This is an expression of the truism – albeit one that too many transport professionals seem to forget at the first opportunity – that transport is essentially a derived demand.[4] We live in one place and go to work in another; crops are grown in one place, processed in another and consumed somewhere else. Global production networks (GPNs) have sprung up to underpin the design, production and consumption of consumer goods all over the place (Coe and Yeung 2015). But it seems from the Ipsos MORI data that these things are so obvious, or routine, or perhaps plain invisible, that they are taken for granted, and thus not considered any further, by most of the population. In this context it's necessary to expand upon and clarify our aim, and in so doing we identify three main areas of focus in the remainder of the book:

- *How we 'do' transport, as a result of available technologies and how we use them.* What is the nature of the transport system, and what is our travel behaviour within that system? In Britain, for example, it is our contention that our transport infrastructure – all of it, from railways to roads, runways to cycle paths – is under-developed (see Shaw and Docherty 2014). Demand is nevertheless high, probably unnecessarily so, and much too focused on the private car (which helps explain the level of traffic congestion), often because of a lack of genuine or perceived alternatives. These things have come to pass over a long period of time, and are the result not just of individuals' transport (mode) choices but also the broader context of deep-rooted cultural norms that pervade and exert very significant influence over how we as a society think about and 'do' transport (Chapter 5).
- *How the ways in which we 'do' transport have certain consequences, across a range of policy areas.* Most of us are lucky enough to benefit enormously from the transport system, both in terms of how we use it ourselves and how others use it on our behalf. We access work and leisure opportunities and take advantage of GPNs to an extent never before possible in human history, but there are also negative consequences, which are unevenly distributed at both individual and societal levels, and across a range of spatial scales. We've already made mention of the inefficiencies of congestion, and the problems of social exclusion, compromised health and wellbeing and environmental degradation.
- *How we could do things differently, to bring about different consequences.* To what extent is change possible and, indeed, desirable, and

how might we go about securing it if we decide it's a good idea? Essentially this is about society shaping transport to (re)shape society, to change for the better the ways in which, and why, transport is important to other areas of public policy. For example, if we walked, cycled and used public transport more than we currently do, and we drove our cars less as a result, it is possible that there would be less congestion and pollution, and we would live in a fitter and less socially divided society. Bringing about such change would be an immense test of existing public policy, would depend on tackling decades of social, cultural and policy norms, and most difficult of all would involve saying something controversial to motorists and those who like to fly a lot. This is a tall order indeed, but one that, as Glenn Lyons suggests in his conclusion to the book (Chapter 16), is there to be grappled with and, we would add, one that we have a moral obligation to address properly.

It's not that any of our questions are especially new – these and questions like them have underpinned the interests of sustainable transport advocates for years – but we hope that this book's explicit focus, by such a wide range of authors, on their connections with a wide range of issues *other* than transport does amount to at least something of a novel contribution.

Before we move on to consider such complex connections, it remains important to understand the basic policy context that has evolved to determine the characteristics of our current transport system. Even the briefest of reviews suggests that had Ipsos MORI been polling ministers and civil servants about the 'most important/ other issues facing Britain today', the answers they received would not have been all that different from those of the population at large.

A short history of transport policy matters

It's not that UK governments haven't been heavily involved in transport policy, or even that they haven't recognised links between transport and other policy areas, it's just that they've been better at writing and commissioning policy documents than delivering things 'on the ground'. Highlights over the last few decades include the seminal *Traffic in Towns* report (Ministry of Transport (MoT) 1963), predicting how increasing traffic volumes would impact upon historic towns and cities (Chapter 9):[5] *Roads for Prosperity* (Department of Transport (DoT) 1989), that promised the 'biggest roadbuilding programme since the Romans' in response to official forecasts of the demand for road space significantly outstripping supply (Chapter 7); and *A New Deal for Transport* (Department of the Environment, Transport and the Regions (DETR) 1998), prompted by the recognition that, in fact, demand for road space could never feasibly be met by supply, and thus that policy efforts should be directed to matching demand to available supply rather than the other way around (see Goodwin et al 1991). Labour's *A New Deal* was the first genuinely transport White Paper for years – the previous, Conservative, government had dealt with each mode separately – and reflected 'the Government's commitment to giving transport the highest possible priority' (DETR 1998: Foreword). Its follow-up delivery plan mapped out how ministers would 'deliver radical improvements for passengers, motorists, business – all of us as citizens concerned about congestion, safety and a better environment' (DETR 2000: 2). Key to the plan was a marked shift in policy emphasis from a 'predict and provide' approach to road building, which had preoccupied the previous Conservative administrations for much of their time in office, to a more sustainable, or 'integrated' transport system with a proportionally bigger role for public transport and the active modes in the context of significantly enhanced levels of investment.

We were to learn over Labour's term of office that the 'highest possible priority' didn't actually amount to very much – Wolmar (2008: viii) understatedly argued that transport 'was the area in which the Blair governments least exerted themselves' – but then history should have taught us to expect a certain amount of path dependency at play. For years the big contradiction in British transport policy has been that despite a collection of commendably ambitious policy statements, the transport system falls some way short of those of other major European countries (Table 1.1). UK governments of whatever party have generally failed to turn policy rhetoric into action, apparently working within a policy tradition of scepticism towards large-scale infrastructure spending (Orr and Vince 2009, Docherty et al 2018). It is notable over recent decades that major policy *delivery* successes (that is, policies with a large-scale impact that have actually been rolled out to completion) have often revolved around revenue rather than capital expenditure, or required corporations and travelling individuals to spend their own money rather than that already appropriated by the state. Barbara Castle's Public Service Obligation for the railways – committing British Rail to operating loss-making but socially necessary services (Gourvish 2002) – and Gordon Brown's Concessionary Fares initiative – guaranteeing free bus travel for retirees and the disabled (Andrews et al 2012) – are two examples of policies with significant

Table 1.1: Key transport infrastructure statistics of selected European countries

	GDP per capita 2017, PPP (Int. $)	Population, 2017 (m)	Size (km²)	Roads (000 km, 2013)	Expressways (000 km / % of all roads, 2013)	Rail (000 km / % electrified, 2013)	HSR (km operational / km under construction / km long-term planning, 2017)	Tram/light rail (track km, 2015)
United Kingdom	43,269	66.2	243,000	394	3.5/0.89	16.2/34.1	113/0/531	308
France	42,850	65.0	552,000	102	11.8/1.2	29.0/54.2	2142/634/1786	692
Germany	50,639	82.1	357,000	644	12.9/2.0	37.8/59.4	1475/368/324	3,061
Italy	39,427	59.4	301,000	488	6.8/1.39	16.8/71.0	981/67/1269	307
Netherlands	52,503	17.0	37,000	141	2.8/1.99	3.0/76.1	120/0/0	271

Sources: World Bank 2017; United Nations 2017; Docherty et al 2018

revenue expenditure implications that spring to mind. The banning of leaded petrol (after research showing its harmful effects on human health) and the fuel tax escalator (above-inflation increases in the price of petrol and diesel – see Lyons and Chatterjee 2002) are examples where people and companies have had to dip into their own pockets. This is not to belittle the importance of such initiatives, not least since they underscore important relationships between transport and other policy areas such as social inclusion, health and wellbeing, and environmental protection. But it does help to explain why Britain's roads are so heavily congested, its railway network so intensively used and its two major airports so highly trafficked in relation to available runway capacity (CfIT 2001, *The Guardian* 2015, Rail Delivery Group 2018). Without slack in the system – what Goodwin (1992) calls a 'quality margin' – delays and disruption are all too commonplace.

Specific reasons for the failure of Tony Blair and Gordon Brown's Labour governments to roll out their integrated transport strategy have been examined elsewhere (see, for example, Bulkeley and Rayner 2003, Docherty and Shaw 2008, 2011, Headicar 2009), but with hindsight perhaps the early-to-mid 2000s weren't entirely wasted: despite a preoccupation with churning out successive statements of policy rather than delivering capital projects, the documents do reveal some grasp of transport's importance as a means of underpinning various social, economic and environmental policy objectives, even if this was only at a vague, conceptual level (Table 1.2). Eventually this led to government support for an increasing number of road building schemes, a major programme of railway electrification, two large rail schemes in London (Crossrail and the Thameslink upgrade) and a new high-speed railway line from London to the Midlands and the north of England (HS2) (Figure 11.1), but it was all too little, too late. Delivering its verdict on Labour's transport record more than a decade after the party had come to power, the House of Commons' Transport Committee (2010: 22) wrote that although the Department for Transport (DfT) had 'established a new direction in its longer-term strategy […] much remains to be done, including supporting economic growth, integrating local transport and tackling climate change.' Our analysis at the time went further, suggesting that in writing successive White Papers, 'the Department had achieved little more than displacement activity' (Docherty and Shaw 2011: 236).

The switch to a Conservative–Liberal Democrat Coalition government in 2010, although inherently interesting as a new direction in modern British politics, did not on the face of it suggest a radical departure from the status quo of non-delivery in transport policy.

Table 1.2: 'Headline' aims of government transport policy strategy documents, 1998–2008

A New Deal for Transport (DETR 1998)	Transport 2010 (DETR 2000)	The Future of Transport (DfT 2004)	Delivering a Sustainable Transport System (DfT 2008a)
We need a transport system which supports our policies for more jobs and a strong economy, which helps increase prosperity and tackles social exclusion. We also need a transport system which doesn't damage our health and provides a better quality of life now – for everyone – without passing onto future generations a poorer world. This is what we mean by sustainable transport and why we need a New Deal... [This means we need to] achieve transport that is safe, efficient, clean and fair... [and] create a transport system that meets the needs of people and business at an affordable cost and produces better places in which to live and work.	Our vision for transport in this country is for a modern, safe, high quality network that better meets people's needs and offers more choice to individuals, families, communities and businesses... [We want to] benchmark our performance against the best in Europe and, through greatly increased investment, to transform our transport infrastructure over the next ten years... [At the same time we want] to lessen the impact of transport on the environment at both global and local levels.	We need a transport network that can meet the challenges of a growing economy and the increasing demand for travel, but can also achieve our environmental objectives.	We want our transport system: • to support national economic competitiveness and growth, by delivering reliable and efficient transport networks; • to reduce transport's emissions of CO_2 and other greenhouse gases, with the desired outcome of tackling climate change; • to contribute to better safety, security and health and longer life expectancy by reducing the risk of death, injury or illness arising from transport, and by promoting travel modes that are beneficial to health; • to promote greater equality of opportunity for all citizens, with the desired outcome of achieving a fairer society; and • to improve quality of life for transport users and non-transport users, and to promote a healthy natural environment.

Source: Docherty and Shaw 2011

This was partly because long-standing differences in party attitudes to transport matters – the Liberal Democrats were starting from a much more pro-environmental standpoint, for example – could have led to something of a stalemate over what, if anything, to prioritise. But also it was because ministers were announcing a programme of austerity that looked to threaten expenditure in all but a very few areas of government activity (HM Government 2010). Certainly there was no hint that transport was regarded as 'the highest possible priority': as a policy area it merited only half a page of text in the Coalition agreement, and even then, the 12 bullet-point summaries addressed important policy challenges in loose terms ('we will make Network Rail more accountable to its customers;' 'We will stop central government funding for new fixed speed cameras') (HM Government 2010: 31). Yet over time, the Coalition revealed itself as taking a quite different approach to Labour. While the Blair and Brown administrations had established a new direction in their longer-term strategy, most notably by viewing transport as an integrated whole (their initial scepticism towards large-scale road building had melted away rather quickly – see Shaw and Walton 2001), ministers now seemed to favour a return to individual modal priorities, at least at the inter-urban level (a White Paper covering all local transport modes and emphasising lower carbon growth was published a year after the Coalition took office (DfT 2011)).

A key reason for this seems squarely related to a perceived need *actually to deliver things*, in particular to help stimulate economic growth (Docherty et al 2018). Within months of taking office, the new Chancellor of the Exchequer, George Osborne, had reversed initial cuts in the transport infrastructure budget and committed the Coalition to completing those large-scale interventions finally approved by Labour before it lost power (Table 1.3). Some of the projects – six roads schemes, the electrification of the Midland and Trans-Pennine main lines and the rebuilding of Bristol Temple Meads station – have been cancelled or postponed by the current minority Conservative administration, but progress *seems* to remain on track for the others, albeit subject to some delays and cost escalations (BBC 2018, Office of Rail and Road (ORR) 2018). Osborne would have been aware that for every government report emphasising the marginal returns of new large-scale infrastructure interventions in an already mature economy (for example, Eddington 2006) – such things had proved rather useful to Labour ministers not wanting to commit to building anything – there were others (for example, Canning and Bennathan 2007, Crafts 2009, Egert et al 2009) that continued to

Table 1.3: Headline transport scheme commitments, 2014

Strategic road	Rail
• Resurfacing 80% of the network • Starting over 100 major projects, including smart motorways, widening and dualling to bring key routes up to 'expressway' standard	• HS2 • Crossrail • Thameslink • Inter-city Express Project • Electrification of Great Western, Midland and Trans-Pennine mainlines, and strategic local lines in the North of England • Rebuilding Birmingham New Street, Bristol Temple meads and Manchester Victoria stations • Northern Hub capacity improvements • Further developing the strategic freight network • Implementing ERTMS (European Rail Traffic Management System)

Source: After DfT 2014

argue for transport infrastructure investment as one important part of any economic policy designed to pursue growth (Chapter 2). This strong focus on the role of transport in supporting economic growth was reflected in the individual transport policies pursued by the Coalition during its time in office (Docherty et al 2018), and is a preoccupation that remains unchanged for the current government (DfT 2018).

Although deviating quite sharply from the integrated approach championed by *A New Deal for Transport*, it would be wrong to accuse the Coalition and its successors of having no kind of transport strategy at all. Instead of repeating the mistake of having some kind of grand, deliberate strategy document but limited delivery, their approach seems to have been one of focusing on the delivery of particular transport schemes and letting the strategy – that is, a sustained effort to build inter-urban road and rail projects in pursuit of economic development – emerge later (Docherty et al 2018). Still, one very obvious weak link in this approach is its relative lack of investment in local transport, despite the publication of a dedicated White Paper. It is one thing being able to move efficiently between major cities, but transport's potential contribution to economic growth (not to mention social inclusion and health and wellbeing) is especially obvious in cities and city regions where the density of activity and trip making is highest. It is also in these places where transport's negative externalities are at their most severe, and thus where local and regional governance networks are keenest to develop detailed strategies to deal with these problems.

Devolved structures such as Transport for West Midlands (TfWM), Transport for the North (TfN) and the administrations of directly elected mayors throughout England are now emerging to take greater control over transport and related policy areas than 'traditional' local authorities, but they face tough challenges as they attempt to secure for their own jurisdictions the kind of benefits Transport for London (TfL) has delivered in the UK capital. Assuming wide-ranging powers over transport as part of a wider programme of devolution to Scotland, Wales, Northern Ireland and Greater London in 1999 and 2000, TfL has been remarkably successful – we almost can't emphasise enough how successful in British terms – in transforming its network, with investment totalling tens of billions of pounds in its rail, underground and bus operations, as well as supporting infrastructure for simplifying its ticketing and information systems. In setting up TfL, the first Mayor of London, Ken Livingstone, chose to pursue a complete break with the UK civil service traditions of caution and incrementalism by creating the organisation as a dedicated technocracy staffed with people used to successful project delivery. It has been strongly supported by successive mayors of both main political parties, and (until recently) enjoyed relatively generous funding settlements from central government alongside the ability to raise its own external finance (MacKinnon et al 2008).

Although there have been some positive developments in the regions (Chapter 2), until TfWM, TfN and their equivalents elsewhere find themselves in the same position as TfL has enjoyed they are unlikely to be able to achieve comparable levels of change across their own transport systems.[6] Happily things have been better than might have been expected north of the border given that the Scottish Government has been obliged to retain a civil service rooted within the broader UK system. Both the Labour–Lib Dem and SNP administrations have pursued concerted programmes of inter-urban road and rail improvements, justified both as a means to stimulate economic growth and to improve the quality and speed of journeys between major centres. Mirroring the London experience, the creation of a specialist government agency, Transport Scotland, deliberately designed as a technocratic 'centre of excellence', has paid dividends in terms of the successful delivery of several major capital projects. These include the 'completion' of the central belt motorway network, the Queensferry Crossing across the Forth and the reopening, upgrading and/or electrification of several railway lines that have also involved a significant programme of rolling stock replacement.

Transport commentary matters

Against this background, the authors of the following chapters pick up a wide range of themes. While each focuses specifically on one theme or another, collectively they show why and how, as a key part of a wider and connected approach to public policy, a better transport system will result not just in better journey experiences, but will also be better for the economic, environmental and social wellbeing of the country. To a greater or lesser extent, depending on the existing mix of transport system quality, cultural context and supporting public policy infrastructure, this will be true internationally as well. To aid the narrative, we have divided the chapters into three sections. The remainder of this first section is designed to set the scene, and concentrates on transport's relationship with the 'three pillars' of sustainability, namely economy, environment and society. Along with our colleague David Waite, we consider in Chapter 2 the political economy of transport and travel, focusing in particular on why we spend money on some things and not on others, and why this matters. Our point is that transport investment can create both winners and losers, and it is important to be open and honest about this, and fully aware of the consequences, before committing public resources. Failing to do so runs the risk of perpetuating existing inequalities in a policy environment where a) there is already plenty of inequality and b) public resources for investment are scarce.

In Chapter 3, Jillian Anable and Christian Brand focus on energy, pollution and climate change. They outline the nature and scale of the environmental problems associated with current transport activity – our understanding of these is consistent in dozens of national and international studies – and discuss the extent to which these are likely to be addressed by current policy approaches. Their stark message, uncomfortable reading for those who believe in the possibilities of a 'technological fix', is that transport's energy consumption and environmental degradation impacts will not be ameliorated without both technological *and* behavioural change. Writing about transport's relationship with inclusion and equality, Jennie Middleton and Justin Spinney outline in Chapter 4 the concept of transport-related social exclusion before developing the idea of accessibility to include what they term the 'emotional' and 'temporal' work demanded of travellers. Their argument is that while accessibility is undoubtedly a powerful device for tackling transport-related social exclusion, its effectiveness has been limited by a failure to recognise limitations in the way it is understood. They outline a more inclusive means of deploying the concept to address social inequalities between transport-dependent groups.

Section Two of the book focuses on what we term 'dealing with policy inheritance'. By this we mean issues that characterise the interaction between transport and other policy areas that have arisen from the prevailing attitude of successive governments to transport and mobility. Writing about behaviour change in Chapter 5, Stewart Barr and John Preston explain how the UK government has come to view its relationship with voters on transport issues, namely that ministers' role is generally to exhort 'good' behaviour through market mechanisms. While the idea of 'nudging' people towards a particular set of behaviours has become commonplace, ministers should be aware that they are unlikely ever to encourage significant behaviour change using techniques that are unambitious in scope and top-down in style. This is important in the context that a lot of change will be needed if the transformational potential of a better transport system is to be realised.

Chapters 6 and 7 discuss the relationship between transport appraisal and forecasting mechanisms and the policies they are meant to support. The authors of both chapters uncover the disturbing extent to which these mechanisms have the power to render strategic policy subservient to the assumptions and methodologies of appraisers and forecasters, rather than the other way around. In Chapter 6, Robin Hickman describes what he characterises as the 'gentle tyranny' of cost–benefit analysis in UK government transport appraisal. His argument is that ministers pursue a top-down approach that allows a limited range of economic costs and (supposed) benefits to dominate proceedings to the point that it skews the playing field against proper consideration of potentially highly effective sustainable interventions designed to address transport – and thus wider economic, environmental and social – problems. Phil Goodwin focuses in Chapter 7 on traffic forecasting and the significant role it plays in the development of transport policy. He notes 'an uncomfortable interweaving of feelings that road appraisal was either the jewel in the crown of formal strategic thinking, or a biased and distorted barrier to it,' and his chapter is an important reminder that the particular mix of infrastructure projects actually delivered on the ground is arguably the most potent expression of any government's strategic transport policy intent.

Angela Curl and Julie Clark's starting assertion in Chapter 8 is that the underlying purpose of *any* public policy is to improve the health and wellbeing of its citizens. Reviewing the place of health in transport policy and vice versa, they illustrate the importance of understanding the full range of impacts – both positive and negative – the two realms of policy can have on each other, if the potential for mobility to play a central role in improving the health and wellbeing of the population is to be fulfilled. Key to their thinking is a supportive planning environment to create liveable places, and this topic is picked up by Geoff Vigar and Georgiana Varna in Chapter 9. Reviewing the general literature and their experience of particular case studies, they highlight the linkages between transport planning and urban design and place-making strategies. The crux of their argument is that macro-level action, while clearly necessary, is insufficient to tackle resilient policy dilemmas in cities without supporting street- and neighbourhood-level interventions that involve the local communities they affect. They situate their discussion alongside the recent fashion towards 'smart' cities, which they regard as overlooking the need to harness the power of 'ordinary technologies' in creating more liveable urban areas.

Chapter 10 focuses on the experiences we have while we are making our journeys, and Juliet Jain and Billy Clayton draw upon a range of studies to show why policy makers and transport companies should pay close attention to such things. Their findings are significant because they challenge decades-old assumptions that value for money from transport investment is best achieved by increasing journey speed and/ or configuring individual buses and train carriages to maximise the number of people they can seat. Lots of productivity – in all senses of the word, not just economic – can take place on journeys, but the nature of people's experiences on the move reveals itself to be an important contributory factor in achieving this. In Chapter 11, Tom Cohen and Dan Durrant investigate the way in which public consultation took place for HS2, the new railway line between London and the Midlands/north of England that is set to provide the fastest train journeys ever undertaken in Britain. Especially in the context of decades of relatively meagre infrastructure spending it was always likely that the project would be controversial, but the nature of the public consultation – described here as 'Decide and Defend' – was insufficiently pluralistic in character. Pursuing what is something of a recurring theme in the book, they argue that in future more deliberative consultation processes would allow a greater range of views to be captured and thus provide a potentially richer source of ideas with regard to tackling some of Britain's most resilient (transport) problems.

Finally in Section Two, David Gray investigates in Chapter 12 issues that concern journey makers in remote, rural communities.

Unlike, as we have seen, for much of the public and the government, people in peripheral communities regard transport as *the* most salient local concern, and ministers have been slow to grasp that different policy responses than those suited to urban and inter-urban areas can have the greatest positive effect. He calls for a much more radical stance that would force policy makers to abandon their received wisdom of six decades.

Section Three is designed to look towards the future. The chapters cover a challenging set of issues that have recently increased in prominence and potential consequence. The first of these is disruption. In Chapter 13, David Dawson and Greg Marsden explain how threats to the smooth operation of the transport network have grown in number, both internally – its now routine over-use – and externally – from sources including terrorism and extreme weather events. The impacts of transport disruption are many and varied, but government policy seems to be one of managing deterioration and expecting people and companies to respond accordingly. For Kiron Chatterjee and Charles Musselwhite, the pressing policy concern is that of changing demographics. In Chapter 14 they explain how society is ageing, but also that large numbers of younger people seem to be adopting and then maintaining different travel behaviours than previous generations. In this context, the likelihood of a top-down, 'business as usual' approach to transport provision delivering the kind of transport system future society actually needs is diminishing, and policy makers will be well advised to adopt a more bottom-up approach that examines mobility more from the viewpoint of individuals' needs.

Regardless of the approach taken by governments to disruption or demographic change, it is inevitable that mobility in future years will become 'smarter'. In considering in Chapter 15 whether the 'smart mobility' revolution will matter, Graham Parkhurst and Andrew Seedhouse review the four key technological shifts currently underway, namely AVs, electric vehicles (EVs), digitally enabled mobility (DEM) and collaborative/shared mobility (CM). Their discussion critically examines familiar claims made by protagonists of 'smart' mobility, and while some (such as the impending large-scale arrival of AVs) are almost certainly overblown, the degree of change it is ultimately likely to bring about will need careful policy oversight if its benefits are to outweigh its disadvantages at the societal level. Finally, in Chapter 16, Glenn Lyons weaves together key threads from throughout the book to strike an optimistic note about the potential for policy makers – indeed, all of us – to shape the future, providing we grasp the challenges inherent in transport matters and are willing to act on them.

Uncertainties can be turned into an opportunity rather than a threat if we 'decide and provide', or 'decide what type of society we want and the forms of connectivity that might best support it.'

Transport dialogue matters

Reading through the book you should find the chapters following broadly comparable formats, although clearly each contains distinctive elements depending on the subject matter and the authors' particular experience and expertise. Some are 'traditional' works of review, bringing out key issues from published studies and discussing them in relation to the general aim of the book. Others give more of an insight into their authors' current research projects and illustrate broader points with arguments revealed for the first time in these pages. We were particularly keen that so far as possible the chapters were co-written, and to prompt debate we also arranged two open authors' meetings, promoted open email exchanges and, of course, encouraged authors to read and comment on each others' chapters. During the process of assembling and editing the book it became quite apparent that while we would all describe ourselves as advocates of sustainable transport – aligned, essentially, more with 'new realist' thinking than with that underpinning 'predict and provide' – we are placed at quite different points across the sustainability spectrum. It was both fun and hugely instructive discussing various aspects of transport policy and its implications with such a wide range of authors. You will encounter the significant variety of views the authors chose to raise throughout the book, but to conclude this chapter we thought it might be revealing to mention the issues about which there was particularly significant discussion – even if a lack of universal consensus – in the authors' meetings (these resurface to a greater or lesser extent in the final versions of the chapters that follow).

One, which might appear surprising in the context of our discussion of transport policy, is that *there is plenty of good practice going on already*, and thus plenty of opportunity to build further on this good practice. We discussed initiatives across the country that have brought much improved transport experiences to people across a range of spatial scales from neighbourhoods (for example, Chapter 9), to cities and regions (for example, Chapter 2) and beyond (for example, Chapter 8). At the same time, there are significant barriers to such good practice becoming as plentiful as we would like to see; policy makers are not yet, in other words, heeding Glenn Lyons' call to 'decide and provide'. Four points dominated our discussions in this regard.

The first was that there has been *a lack of investment* and, second, when ministers do decide to sanction particular schemes, *things cost far too much*. Aside from the obvious consequences of not spending enough on our transport system – too much pollution and congestion, not enough connectivity, social inclusion and wellbeing, and so on – the tendency towards the minimalist and stop/start investment programmes pursued for decades by UK governments has significantly reduced the value for money we realise on those occasions we do decide to build something. Even relatively straightforward projects like electrifying a railway line – or even, farcically, installing an accessible footbridge at a railway station – end up costing much more than they should and would be considerably cheaper in other countries (see HM Treasury 2010). This partly explains why successive governments have become so bad at actually delivering on their transport policies: too frequently ministers' response has been to panic and pull the plug on further investment on the grounds of ensuring 'savings for the taxpayer'. The irony is that they do precisely the opposite by reducing competition (fewer construction companies want to invest in training up their workforce to deliver something that won't get funded) and causing a loss of institutional memory and capacity in the sector. Repeat this cycle even once, and then throw in any number of further, peculiarly British complicating factors such as an unfavourable planning system and a fragmented transport sector, and over a relatively short period of time costs rise to the point where it would have been possible to electrify far more of the inter-city rail network, or build hundreds more miles of trunk roads, or put in place countless more small-scale 'everyday' walking or cycling schemes that when aggregated have enormous benefit, for the price of what we actually end up doing. For the sake of being able to secure better value for money in the future it is crucial the Secretary of State thinks long and hard before abandoning any more schemes approved by her or his predecessors on the basis that they have started to run over budget (Table 1.3).

Thirdly and relatedly, *the way we appraise transport investment is unfit for purpose* (Chapter 6). It is claimed that in Britain we have the most sophisticated transport appraisal system in the world (see Worsley and Mackie 2015), but to us its proponents seem to privilege complexity and spurious accuracy over efficacy and alignment with strategy, where and in what guise this exists (see Institute for Government 2017). Despite ostensibly taking into account any number of social and environmental concerns, British government transport appraisal is too often reduced to a crude estimation of things that may or may not happen in response to an artificially limited range of interventions in particular elements of the economy that (ministers think) can be quantified. This is certainly not to claim the economy should not be a significant factor in transport decision making, for a strong economy is the basis of the wealth generation needed for a high standard of living. But in another irony, this approach results in our squandering many of the economic advantages that would result from cleaning up the quality of our air, bringing more people into the labour market, improving public health or providing commuters with a pleasant and productive travelling environment.

There is also, finally, a sense in which *key decision makers are often too enthusiastic to take the path of least resistance*, despite what they may say about taking 'difficult decisions' in the best interests of the country. If government is supposed to be about leadership, ministers have been too reluctant to say 'no' to people who want more car travel but don't want to pay the real cost of having it. This leads to unfortunate outcomes. For example, from social, environmental and economic perspectives Britain's provincial urban transport systems are among the worst in the developed world because they rely far too heavily on the private car, which in densely configured cities is an especially inefficient form of moving people around (Chapters 2, 6 and 8). London's, by contrast, is comparable with many of the world's highest-quality transport systems, not least because of local political leadership that has championed controversial schemes like the Congestion Charge, and massive investment in public transport and (latterly) cycling networks. Those people in the UK government making decisions about transport policy elsewhere in the country would do well to pay more attention to why things function better in the city where they work than in other places whose capacity to invest they determine.

At the same time, the transport industry itself is far from blameless. Often paraded as the world-leading result of 1980s and 1990s government policies designed to harness the dynamism of privatisation, there are those in Britain's transport sector who have been more than happy to support a mediocre *status quo*. Consultants have comprehensively mapped out the habitat of the 'magic money tree' that thrives in the complex jungle of British transport, and too many operators have been unwilling or unable to provide even the most basic of improvements like reliable Wi-Fi or smart-ticketing in a passenger-friendly and inter-operator format. The bus industry in particular is notorious for having contested initiatives to provide a more stable, higher quality, area-wide network of services that would bring better transport options to many excluded communities

(Chapters 4 and 12) and, in a third irony, promote modal shift away from the car to the bus companies' own commercial advantage. Maybe passengers are themselves complicit in all of this, since both the government and the transport industry seem to know the old adage that 'no-one ever made any money over-estimating the taste of the Great British Public'. Still, whichever way we look at it, we can't escape the conclusion that significant transport behaviour change is going to be an inevitable part of any large-scale shift towards a more sustainable future (Chapter 5).

All of this brings us back to the reason we wanted to put this book together in the first place: that governments have all too often failed to act beyond a conception of transport as something that just deals with conveying people and goods between places. They have not done enough to address the real point of what transport policy is *for* and *why it matters*. A recent cover of *Rail Review* magazine more-or-less hit the nail on the head with its bracketed hint '(Clue: it's not transport)'. We say more-or-less because clearly it can't *not* be about moving people and goods from A to B. But what's also crucial is to remember *why* we want people and goods to be able to move efficiently, reliably and, between certain times and places, in great number. All of the authors in this book agree that we can't continue to shy away from developing and implementing a genuinely transformational transport strategy that will necessarily be bold in its ambition and have at its heart the recognition that its main focus isn't transport per se, but rather our quality of life: transport is best seen as an enabler of a bigger economy, a fairer and healthier society and a cleaner environment.

Notes

[1] Great Western Railway, the region's dominant train operating company, marketed the upcoming introduction of its new Inter-city Express Trains with a computer-generated image of an IET passing Dawlish Warren, and scenes from the south west peninsula feature strongly in its most recent 'Famous Five' styled advertisements.

[2] See Bissell (2018) for an impressively rich insight into people's lived experiences of commuting.

[3] We can't help wondering whether the EU referendum result would itself have been different if more politicians had felt able to engage in an open and mature debate about immigration that forced people to reflect on how far those seeking to live in Britain boarded planes originating from within or outside of the EU – see Office for National Statistics (ONS) (2018).

[4] There is obviously intrinsic value in some journeys – going for a walk or bike ride, the Sunday drive, and so on – that is not connected to

some other activity purpose in a different location (see Mokhtarian and Handy 2009).

5   See Gunn (2011), and Bianconi and Tewdwr-Jones (2013) for articles looking back to *Traffic in Towns* at around the time of the 50th anniversary of its publication.

6   TfL is now facing its own problems, with falling patronage (and thus farebox revenue) and the delayed opening of Crossrail (and thus more loss of revenue) compounding the reduced levels of central government financial support.

References

Andrews, G, Parkhurst, G, Susilo, Y and Shaw, J (2012) 'The grey escape: investigating older people's use of the free bus pass', *Transportation Planning and Technology*, 35(1): 3–15.

BBC (2015) 'Dawlish rail line: closure "costs economy up to £1.2bn"', www.bbc.co.uk/news/uk-england-devon-31140192 Accessed 1 October 2018.

BBC (2018) 'Crossrail delay: new London line will open in autumn 2019', www.bbc.co.uk/news/uk-england-london-45367990 Accessed 22 October 2018.

Bianconi, M and Tewdwr-Jones, M (2013) 'The form and organisation of urban areas: Colin Buchanan and *Traffic in Towns* 50 years on', *Town Planning Review*, 84(3): 313–6.

Bissell, D (2018) *Transit Life. How Commuting is Transforming Our Cities*, Cambridge, MA: MIT Press.

Bulkeley, H and Rayner, T (2003) 'New realism and local realities: local transport planning in Leicester and Cambridgeshire', *Urban Studies*, 40(1): 35–55.

Canning, D and Bennathan, E (2007) *The rate of return to transportation infrastructure*. www.oecd-ilibrary.org/transport/transport-infrastructure-investment-and-economic-productivity_9789282101254-en Accessed 7 June 2017.

Coe, N and Yeung, H (2015) *Global Production Networks: Theorizing Economic Development in an Interconnected World*, Oxford: Oxford University Press.

Commission for Integrated Transport (2001) *A study of European best practice in the delivery of integrated transport*. CfIT, London.

Commission for Integrated Transport (2002) *Public attitudes to transport in England*. CfIT, London. http://webarchive.nationalarchives.gov.uk/20110310110642/http://cfit.independent.gov.uk/pubs/2002/mori2002/mori2002/index.htm Accessed 10 October 2018.

Crafts, N (2009) 'Transport infrastructure investment: implications for growth and productivity', *Oxford Review of Economic Policy*, 25(3): 327–43.

Cresswell, T (2010) 'Towards a politics of mobility', *Environment and Planning D: Society and Space*, 28(1): 17–31.

Department of Transport (1989) *Roads for Prosperity*, Cm 693, London: HMSO.

Department of the Environment, Transport and the Regions (1998) *A New Deal for Transport: Better for Everyone*, Cm 3950, London: TSO.

Department of the Environment, Transport and the Regions (2000) *Transport 2010: The 10 Year Plan for Transport*, London: TSO.

Department for Transport (2011) *Creating growth, cutting carbon: making sustainable local transport happen.* https://assets.publishing.service. gov.uk/government/uploads/system/uploads/attachment_data/ file/3890/making-sustainable-local-transport-happen-whitepaper. pdf Accessed 11 October 2018.

Department for Transport (2014) *Road Investment Strategy: Investment Plan.* https://assets.publishing.service.gov.uk/government/uploads/ system/uploads/attachment_data/file/382813/dft-ris-road-investment-strategy.pdf Accessed 1 June 2019.

Department for Transport (2018) *About us.* www.gov.uk/government/ organisations/department-for-transport/about Accessed 22 October 2018.

Docherty, I and Shaw, J (eds) (2008) *Traffic Jam: Ten Years of 'Sustainable' Transport in the UK*, Bristol: Bristol Policy Press.

Docherty, I and Shaw, J (2011) 'The transformation of transport policy in Great Britain? "New Realism" and New Labour's decade of displacement activity', *Environment and Planning A: Economy and Space*, 43(1): 224–51.

Docherty, I, Shaw, J, Marsden, G and Anable, J (2018) 'The curious death – and life? – of British transport policy', *Environment and Planning C: Politics and Space*, 36(8): 1458–79.

Eddington, R (2006) *The Eddington transport study: the case for action. Sir Rod Eddington's advice to government.* HM Treasury, London.

Egert, B, Kozluk, T and Sutherland, D (2009) *Infrastructure and growth: empirical evidence.* www.oecd-ilibrary.org/economics/infrastructure-and-growth_225682848268 Accessed 7 June 2017.

Goodwin, P (1992) *A quality margin in transport.* Transport Studies Unit, University of Oxford, Oxford.

Goodwin, P and Lyons, G (2010) 'Public attitudes to transport: interpreting the evidence', *Transportation Planning and Technology*, 33(1): 3–17.

Goodwin, P, Hallett, S, Kenny, F and Stokes, G (1991) *Transport: the new realism*. Transport Studies Unit, University of Oxford, Oxford.

Gourvish, T (2002) *British Rail 1974–97*, Oxford: Oxford University Press.

The Guardian (2015) 'Heathrow's two runways – how do other airports compare?' www.theguardian.com/world/datablog/2015/jul/02/heathrow-two-runways-other-airports-europe-compare Accessed 22 October 2018.

The Guardian (2018) 'Brexit and the Irish border question explained', www.theguardian.com/uk-news/2018/sep/19/brexit-and-the-irish-border-question-explained Accessed 10 October 2018.

Gunn, S (2011) 'The Buchanan Report, environment and the problem of traffic in 1960s Britain', *Twentieth Century British History*, 22(4): 521–42.

Headicar, P (2009) *Transport Policy and Planning in Great Britain*, London: Routledge.

HM Government (2010) *The Coalition: our programme for government*. www.gov.uk/government/uploads/system/uploads/attachment_data/file/78977/coalition_programme_for_government.pdf Accessed 11 October 2018.

HM Treasury (2010) *National Infrastructure Plan 2010*. www.gov.uk/government/uploads/system/uploads/attachment_data/file/188329/nip_2010.pdf Accessed 7 June 2017.

House of Commons (2010) Session 2009–10, HC76, 4 March.

Institute for Government (2017) *What's wrong with infrastructure decision making?* www.instituteforgovernment.org.uk/publications/whats-wrong-infrastructure-decision-making-June-2017 Accessed 1 October 2018.

Ipsos MORI (2018) *Issues index archive*. www.ipsos.com/ipsos-mori/en-uk/issues-index-archive Accessed 28 September 2018.

Ipsos-MORI (2019) *Ipsos-MORI Issues Index January 2019: Worry about Brexit and EU Has Fallen However Remains Britain's Number One Worry*. www.ipsos.com/ipsos-mori/en-uk/ipsos-mori-issues-index-january-2019-worry-about-brexit-and-eu-has-fallen-however-remains-britains Accessed 1 June 2019.

Local Transport Today (2012) 'In passing: just how much does congestion cost the economy?' www.transportxtra.com/magazines/local_transport_today/news/?id=30150 Accessed 9 January 2013.

Lyons, G (2004) 'Transport and society', *Transport Reviews*, 24(4): 485–509.

Lyons, G and Chatterjee, K (eds) (2002) *Transport Lessons from the Fuel Tax Protests of 2000*, Abingdon: Routledge.

MacKinnon, D, Shaw, J and Docherty, I (2008) *Diverging Mobilities? Devolution, Transport and Policy Innovation*, Oxford: Elsevier.

Marsden, G (2014) 'Will it be "all change" on the railways after Dawlish? More likely just the usual service'. *The Conversation*, 26 February. https://theconversation.com/will-it-be-all-change-on-the-railways-after-dawlish-more-likely-just-the-usual-service-23701 Accessed 1 June 2019.

Ministry of Transport (1963) *Traffic in Towns*, London: HMSO.

Mokhtarian, P and Handy, S (2009) 'No particular place to go: an empirical analysis of travel for the sake of travel', *Environment and Behavior*, 41(2): 233–57.

Nikolaeva, A, Adey, P, Cresswell, T, Yeonjae Lee, J, Nóvoa, A and Temenos, C (2019) 'Commoning mobility: towards a new politics of mobility transitions', *Transactions of the Institute of British Geographers*, 44: 346–60.

Nuffield Trust (2017) *The NHS workforce in numbers.* www.nuffieldtrust.org.uk/resource/the-nhs-workforce-in-numbers Accessed 11 October 2018.

Office for National Statistics (2018) *Migration statistics quarterly report: August 2018.* www.ons.gov.uk/peoplepopulationandcommunity/populationandmigration/internationalmigration/bulletins/migrationstatisticsquarterlyreport/august2018#trends-in-international-migration Accessed 22 October 2018.

Office of Rail and Road (2018) *Review of Highways England's capital delivery plan.* http://orr.gov.uk/__data/assets/pdf_file/0020/28172/review-of-highways-england-capital-delivery-plan-july-2018.pdf Accessed 22 October 2018.

Orr, K and Vince, R (2009) 'Traditions of local government', *Public Administration*, 87(3): 655–77.

Rail Delivery Group (2018) *UK rail industry.* https://www.raildeliverygroup.com/uk-rail-industry.html Accessed 22 October 2018.

Shaw, J and Walton, W (2001) 'Labour's new trunk-roads policy for England: an emerging *pragmatic multimodalism?*', *Environment and Planning A: Economy and Space*, 33(6): 1031–56.

Shaw, J and Docherty, I (2014) *The Transport Debate*, Bristol: Policy Press.

United Nations (2017) *World population 2017.* https://population.un.org/wpp/Publications/Files/WPP2017_Wallchart.pdf Accessed 22 October 2018.

Visit Britain (2013) *Inbound tourism to Britain's nations and regions. Profile and activities of international holiday visitors.* www.visitbritain.org/sites/default/files/vb-corporate/Documents-Library/documents/Regional_Activities_report_FINAL_COMPRESSED.pdf Accessed 1 June 2019.

Wolmar, C (2008) Foreword, in I Docherty and J Shaw (eds) *Traffic Jam: Ten Years of 'Sustainable' Transport in the UK*, Bristol: Policy Press. pp viii–x.

World Bank (2017) *GDP per capita, PPP (current international $).* https://data.worldbank.org/indicator/NY.GDP.PCAP.PP.CD Accessed 22 October 2018.

Worsley, T and Mackie, P (2015) *Transport policy, appraisal and decision-making*, RAC Foundation, London. www.racfoundation.org/wp-content/uploads/2017/11/Transport_policy_appraisal_decision_making_worsley_mackie_May_2015_final_report.pdf Accessed 23 October 2018.

2

The political economy of transport and travel

Iain Docherty, Jon Shaw and David Waite

Why think in terms of a 'political economy' of transport and travel?

> Multi-million pound road improvements will
> create hundreds of jobs. (*Sussex Express* 2018)

> £16m Doncaster link road plan will create
> 7000 new jobs. (*Doncaster Free Press* 2017)

> Ambitious plan for Cambridge-Oxford (road and rail)
> link to create a million new jobs. (*ITV News* 2018)

Any casual observer of the ways in which transport investment is portrayed in the media would be forgiven for asking why we spend public money on almost anything else given the economic miracles that seem to result from the mere act of pouring asphalt. For many years now, transport projects from the smallest access road to multi-billion-pound high-speed railway lines have been promoted on the basis of the numbers of jobs that they will create, or in the case of the very largest schemes, the almost magical 'economic rebalancing' that they will induce. Start with an economic development orthodoxy that consistently boils down the highly complex problem of stimulating growth to one of spending money on skills and infrastructure, mix with consistent demands from business leaders to address the 'urgent need' for investment in whatever transport projects are deemed 'shovel ready' at the time, and add a sprinkling of politicians keen to find a ribbon to cut and you have the recipe for the consistent, almost unquestioning belief that spending money on transport leads to economic growth per se.

The snag is that the evidence base on the links between transport investment and the economy is more inconclusive than we would perhaps like it to be, and it is often far from clear how spending money on infrastructure in particular actually improves economic performance in the real world. While macroeconomic reviews claim links between the overall level of investment with growth at the country level, finding evidence in the real economy, in real places and in real firms about the causal links that explain how such investment promotes better economic performance is usually much more difficult. Even well-cited papers claiming a link between improved infrastructure, the larger markets that result and therefore improved economic performance do so at the level of the economy as an abstract whole, acknowledging substantial caveats in their analysis. For example, Nick Crafts (2009: 332) notes that 'in practice, it may be thought that these arguments… are most likely to matter when there is a step change in the quality of the transport system and could generally be more relevant for developing countries with a major infrastructure deficit than for mature economies.' Indeed, the last significant independent review carried out for the UK government on the impacts of transport infrastructure on economic performance, by the former Chief Executive of British Airways Sir Rod Eddington (Eddington 2006), set out quite unambiguously that in advanced industrialised countries with mature infrastructure systems, the potential for subsequent investment to deliver large economic stimulus is much less than is commonly assumed (Box 2.1).

Box 2.1: The diminishing impact of transport infrastructure improvement on regional development

In highly developed countries new transport infrastructure tends to have a diminishing impact on regional development as the economy matures. Reasons for this tendency are:

1. Regional accessibility is already high
In general, industrialised nations already have a well-developed transport network, meaning that the level of accessibility is high. Therefore further improvements of the transport infrastructure will result in only minor reductions in travel time and will not open up new areas or markets.

2. Transport costs become less important
Due to economic changes such as the shift towards services, the relative importance of transport-intensive sectors is decreasing. In contrast to traditional activities such as manufacturing or mining, the growing service sector or the

so-called 'new economy' does not rely as much on effective transport systems. Thus, transport costs become less important as a location factor, although the quality and efficiency of transport networks may become more important in line with shift to just-in-time production systems, for instance.

3. Proximity is better than speed
Geographical proximity to major economic centres and clusters as a precondition of economic growth cannot be fully substituted by new transport facilities – thus peripheral regions tend to remain remote and do not substantially gain from improved accessibility. Indeed, in some cases, further transport improvements may result in externally-located firms penetrating local markets more effectively and in local residents spending more of their income externally.

4. Disparities may be deepened
Finally, an improvement in the connection of peripheral regions with central regions always works in both directions. According to the New Economic Geography, due to agglomeration effects – the advantages derived from the spatial concentration of large numbers of firms, suppliers, workers and consumers – central regions benefit most from such an improvement whereas peripheral regions are likely to be drained with regard to purchasing power or skilled labour. In particular, transport improvements may facilitate increased migration from peripheral to core regions.

Source: Docherty and Mackinnon 2013

How, then, should we go about investing in transport so that we have the best chance of that investment making a real difference to economic performance? Perhaps the best summary of the transport and economy conundrum remains David Banister and Yossi Berechman's (2001) simple yet important assertion that locations with poor quality transport are likely to be at a competitive disadvantage when compared with those with higher quality transport infrastructure, and thus that there remains a strong case for transport investment targeted at boosting the economy *so long as the complexities of the task are properly understood.* They go on to identify a series of three necessary conditions that must be in place for transport investment to stimulate regional economic development in developed country contexts. These are (a) positive economic externalities, basically meaning an already well-functioning local economy, particularly in terms of the links between firms and suppliers and the operation of the labour market; (b) investment factors referring to the availability of funds, the quality of the overall network and the timing of the investment; and (c) a favourable political environment, in terms of other supporting policies and a generally enabling policy framework. All three factors must be in place for transport investment to have a positive impact on the regional economy. If only one or two of these factors are present at the time of investment, certain effects such as an improvement of accessibility may occur – but not additional economic growth. As Linneker (1997: 60) concludes, 'whether further development towards higher or lower levels of economic development potential are realised … is determined by a large number of other factors outside the transport sector.'

A large part of the reason for the disconnect between the impacts often claimed for new transport schemes by those promoting them and what actually seems to happen in the real economy once projects come to fruition, is that on its own transport investment is much better at moving economic activity around rather than growing the size of the economy overall (see Venables et al 2014). The point that transport infrastructure is – sometimes literally – a two-way street, and that economic activity can move in both directions as relative accessibility changes, is rather obvious yet often wilfully ignored in the UK. In some countries, most obviously France with its long-standing notion of *aménagement du territoire* (literally 'territorial layout'), but also in Denmark, Ireland and the Netherlands where there are strong national planning traditions, the idea that the distribution of socio-economic opportunity can (and indeed *should*) be shaped by state investment in transport and other key policy domains is explicitly understood, and so investment decisions are made after having had a debate about which activities and places should be prioritised, and why. But in Britain the policy mantra for decades, at least in relation to transport investment, has been that regions are not in competition with each other for economic growth and development, and that such investment should therefore be directed to wherever it benefits 'the economy' overall the most, using appraisal mechanisms that are argued to be the most sophisticated in the world given their precision and neutrality (Worsley and Mackie 2015, Docherty et al 2018; Chapter 6).

The same issues appear at more local levels, too. If we assume that well-targeted transport investment can indeed improve the level of accessibility and therefore economic potential (and quality of life) of the places in which it occurs, then such investment not only raises the absolute number and quality of journey opportunities in these places, but also alters their relative accessibility and thus the economic potential and quality of life of other places. Sometimes transport investment can actually make things worse rather than better for some people and places. In the same way that a headline trumpeting 'new supermarket creates hundreds of jobs' conveniently ignores the myriad small independent shops that will shut their doors as a result, similar proclamations about new roads or railways creating new employment and economic growth also fail to mention the (re-distributive) effects of these transport improvements as, for example, jobs get moved around within a city, or a branch office closes altogether when transport improvements make it just as quick for a firm to get to its clients from HQ. Despite the win-win narratives, there are almost always both winners and losers from transport investment decisions, and coming to a democratic decision about who the winners and losers will be, and managing the differential impacts of winning and losing, is precisely what politics is about.

I'm a government economist and I'm here to help...

The traditional approach to conceptualising the *economics* of transport – as opposed to the *political economy* of transport – is to use quantitative modelling techniques that give some kind of summary output of the 'Transport Economic Efficiency' (TEE) of various proposed projects (see Graham 2007). As Robin Hickman explains in detail in Chapter 6, the underlying assumption of this kind of econometric modelling is that can we deduce the likely economic benefit of a transport improvement in terms of the reductions in travel time it creates for people and goods moving around, and how these time savings are translated into better economic performance through mechanisms such as improved productivity arising from faster supply chains, and so on. These estimates are then monetised using further assumptions to give an indication of the notional return on investment, or, to use the hideous contemporary phraseology, a 'business case' for the project concerned. Even very large investments, such as motorway widening or major rail capacity enhancements, still largely rely for their justification on the assumed economic benefits derived from making it possible for more people to travel more quickly (sometimes not that much more quickly), despite the fact that small changes in the assumptions fed into such models can completely change the outcomes they generate.

Quantitative modelling techniques in transport have been criticised on a number of levels for several decades, yet they remain resilient, in large part because they spit out numbers that give superficial credibility to the ongoing narrative that transport investment is good for the economy whatever the circumstances.[1] It is not our purpose in this chapter to explore the debate about whether the technical approaches of such models are fit for purpose: a significant literature has grown up over time exploring the extent to which modelling has come to be regarded as increasingly narrow in its representation of how the economy really works, and therefore whether it is possible to adequately and accurately reconcile complex factors such as the importance to firms of journey time reliability rather than average journey times themselves, and the changing behaviours of passengers during the journey given the ubiquity of smart phones and the potential to remain connected to work while travelling (Laird and Venables 2017; Chapters 6 and 10). Instead, what is important to note here is the extent to which a supposedly 'neutral' approach to transport investment decision making has grown up, which is anything but neutral in practice, and which privileges some people, places and activities more than others. In short, whenever we address the cases made for the economic growth to be had from transport expenditure, we need also to think about the *distributional* effects of such investment. Why we spend money on some things, and by definition not on others, is just as important an issue for transport as it is for health or education.

The irony here is that despite clinging to them in order to justify investment decisions, even government itself knows that its modelling techniques for the economic impact of transport investment are at best incomplete, and at worst potentially misleading (see Docherty et al 2018). The most recent *Value for Money Framework* (Department for Transport (DfT) 2015; Table 2.1) demonstrates that the DfT regards estimates of the actual economic uplift made possible by transport investment – including fundamentals such as improved productivity and additional overall gross value added (GVA) – to be at best 'evolving', and often 'indicative'. This is not only because of the fundamental uncertainties about the causal mechanisms through which transport investment can stimulate the economy, but also because the actual numbers generated in models can vary significantly with relatively minor adjustments to the assumptions used, such as the cost of fuel or average vehicle occupancy. Indeed, as Mullen and Marsden (2015) suggest in their review of the growth-focused cases made for transport investment across England, it is very difficult indeed to find empirical data supporting the GVA uplift assumptions usually made in such investment cases.

If, then, we admit that we are unable to fully quantify and model the real impacts of transport investment in practice, it quickly becomes evident that any apparently 'rational' and/or 'economic' decisions

Table 2.1: DfT transport investment 'impact types'

Established monetised impacts	Evolving monetised impacts	Indicative monetised impacts	Non-monetised impacts
Included in initial and adjusted metrics	*Included in adjusted metric*	*Considered after metric using switching values approach*	
• Journey time savings • Vehicle operating costs • Accidents • Physical activity • Journey quality • Noise • Air quality • Greenhouse gases • Indirect tax	• Reliability • Static clustering • Output in imperfectly competitive markets • Labour supply	• Moves to more/less productive jobs • Dynamic clustering Induced investment • Supplementary Economy Modelling*	• Security • Severance • Accessibility • Townscape • Historic environment Landscape** • Biodiversity • Water environment • Affordability Access to services • Option and non-use values

*These are a class of models rather than a specific economic impact.

** A widely-used methodology for monetisation exists, but this is not included in WebTAG guidance because of concerns about its robustness. Detailed guidance is found in the Supplementary Guidance on Landscape.

Source: DfT 2015

on where to spend the transport pound are in fact highly complex political-economic ones, in which a variety of different evidence, of varying veracity, intersects with any number of other considerations, most obviously those concerning the (perceived) fairness and equity of resource distribution. The crucial questions raised by taking an explicitly political economy approach to analysing transport investment decision making are therefore: 1) Why do we spend money on some projects, and not on others? 2) Who are the winners and losers from these choices? and 3) How should we take decisions openly and honestly if we know that the numbers we use only paint a partial picture of reality?

To illuminate these questions, we are drawn to a statement made to us[2] by a senior policy maker several years ago, but which nonetheless remains painfully relevant: "There are two definitions of policy. Policy is either what you put in your policy documents, or it's what you spend your money on." There is now a large literature analysing the stated objectives of UK transport policy over several decades, and how well these objectives have been turned into policy delivery in practice (Chapter 1). Government policy documents contain recurring warm words about promoting economic growth, making significant headway into reducing the environmental impact of transport (Chapter 3) and promoting better social inclusion, cohesion and wellbeing (Chapters 4 and 8). But even the most cursory analysis of the patterns of transport expenditure across the UK reveals the kind of extraordinary mismatches between the rhetoric of these policy statements and the cold, hard reality of where the money goes, that our interview respondent pithily identified.

North of Watford

The long-standing UK government position that regions are not in competition with each other for economic activity, and that engaging is any sort of *aménagement* of the national territory is therefore a zero-sum game for the public purse, is often disconcertingly yet, we would argue, rather accurately, caricatured as the belief that the economy operates over a mythical 'flat, featureless plain'. It is also completely at odds with much of the 'New Economic Geography' (NEG), most closely associated with the work of Paul Krugman (1996, 2011), which has focused on trying to understand the nature of contemporary regional economic inequality, and how policy interventions such as transport investment might change things. A key conclusion of the NEG is that reducing costs (in terms of both money and travel time) by improving transport networks often favours the concentration of economic activity in a small number of places, rather than a more even dispersal across space. It also notes that the 'two-way street' effect is real and important: contrary to many conventional assumptions, improving transport links to 'peripheral' regions can just as easily suck economic activity out of them as it can help redistribute activity to them.

In the UK context, this means that better inter-city transport may well promote the further concentration of economic activity in already favoured locations, primarily London and the south east of England. The realities of the UK's long-standing head-in-the-sand policy posture on the spatial impacts of transport investment are immediately obvious to anyone trying to travel around the north of England. The slow, sardine can-like experience[3] of taking the train between any two major cities in the region immediately illustrates the double whammy the North has experienced. This is both in missing out on the stimulus to transport policy that has been apparent in, most notably, Scotland under devolution (Chapter 1), and in remaining dependent on the Treasury's unerringly confident implementation of its 'neutral', macro economy-focused distribution of transport investment that sees three times as much spent per person in London than in the North East (Table 2.2; Raikes 2018, although see Overman 2014 for an alternative view).

Table 2.2: Transport spending by region/country, 2012/13–2016/17

	2012/13 (£bn)	2013/14 (£bn)	2014/15 (£bn)	2015/16 (£bn)	2016/17 (£bn)	2012/13 to 2016/17 per capita (£)
England						349.06
North East	0.57	0.58	0.64	0.75	0.77	250.28
North West	1.86	1.83	1.93	2.8	2.68	305.58
Yorkshire and the Humber	1.51	1.58	1.54	2.04	1.82	311.50
East Midlands	0.84	0.96	1.06	1.22	1.04	214.89
West Midlands	1.29	1.26	1.48	1.93	1.82	265.55
East	1.43	1.48	1.58	2.07	2.04	278.96
London	5.75	5.73	5.95	7.62	8.30	755.26
South East	2.01	2.29	2.33	3.01	3.34	286.22
South West	1.05	1.0	1.13	1.47	1.68	227.99
Scotland	3.13	3.02	2.87	3.16	3.35	573.25
Wales	1.15	1.07	1.05	1.23	1.17	362.49
Northern Ireland	0.60	0.55	0.54	0.44	0.57	288.69

Source: Rutherford 2018

This is, of course, a massive ongoing issue for those policy makers in regions such as the north of England dealing with the long-term implications of de-industrialisation and trying to continue the multi-generational task of re-orientating their economies to the realities of the 21st-century service-led, globalised world. The distribution of expenditure by transport mode tells a similar (and not unrelated) story. For example, while *Transport Statistics Great Britain* (TSGB) (DfT 2017a) shows that total expenditure on roads across the UK in 2016/17 amounted to some £9.7 billion, expenditure on the railways totalled fully £15.7 billion, despite accounting for around only *2 per cent* of trips. Spending on 'other transport', which includes the bus, by far the most commonly used mode of public transport with nearly 4.5 billion passenger journeys per year (DfT 2017b), was much lower at £1.4 billion. Not only is support for rail an order of magnitude higher than bus in absolute terms, but the distributional implications of this expenditure profile are also significant. Given that rail trips tend to be longer than bus trips, that 64 per cent of all rail trips start or end in London, and that 'rail travel becomes increasingly common as income increases, and those with the highest income level in England made almost four times as many rail trips per year than those with the lowest income level on average in 2016' (DfT 2017c: 3), it is clear that whatever the policy documents might say, UK (or at least English) transport policy has become increasingly focused on enabling more and more better off people to travel to London more easily.

Perhaps it is not surprising therefore that the economy of London and the South East continues to outpace almost everywhere else given its relative accessibility continues to increase: Chen and Hall (2011: 689) found that the impact of the last 30 years' improvement in inter-city rail connections in the UK were neither 'automatic nor universal', but that those locations brought within two hours' journey time of London tended to do better, sometimes at the expense of those further away. And of course we might be on the threshold of spending tens of billions of pounds to make this problem even worse: unless the entire government machine gets its act together properly and embeds the HS2 high-speed rail project in a much wider set of regional economic policies consistent with Banister and Berechman's (2001) rubric, there remains the risk that rather than 'Rebalancing Britain' as HS2 Ltd (2014) boldly claims, the new railway will suck even more activity into London (Tomaney and Marques 2013).[4]

Then there is the issue of aviation. As Philip McCann (2016) has highlighted, the debate about expansion of London airspace capacity has been notable for its scant consideration of UK-wide effects given the impact new runways in the capital might have on the viability of direct flights to and from regional airports. Just as for surface transport, for which the Treasury's apparently 'neutral' appraisal methodologies have created a self-sustaining cycle justifying an ever-higher share of surface transport investment for the South East, so expanding Heathrow has become at best a shibboleth, at worst a kind of multi-billion-pound virility test about whether the transport sector is fully prepared to support the economic ambitions of UK plc. As is evident from the narratives used to support the new runway, for some policy decisions, especially the largest ones most likely to benefit the elite decision makers themselves, some outcomes are simply too highly prized for competing regional claims to get a look in. Heathrow equals Britain, and Britain equals Heathrow, it would seem.

At this point, it is worth reminding ourselves that the *absolute* level of transport spending in London is not somehow 'wrong'; indeed given London's scale, its role as a top-tier world city competing for investment with places with (even) better transport provision, and that like the UK as a whole, its infrastructure suffered from decades of underinvestment, it should be expected that transport in the capital receives as much funding as possible. (In any case, on some measures, most notably spend per unit GVA generated, it is argued that London is not necessarily out of line with the other devolved administrations of Scotland and Wales; see Wingham 2017). Instead, it is the *relative* level of expenditure on transport in and to/from London and the wider South East compared with other parts of England that helps to continually reinforce the region's dominant economic position – one so dominant as to make the UK overall the most spatially unequal European economy by some distance (Office for National Statistics (ONS) 2014, McCann 2018; see Dorling 2018 for a detailed and illuminating analysis of social polarisation in Britain).

Further, there is an extremely large opportunity cost to this pattern of expenditure. One of the several inconvenient truths contained in the Eddington Review (which was largely ignored by the government) was the scale of the highly evident and increasing gap in standards of transport provision between most UK cities and their peers across much of Europe. In his discussion about why we should be concerned about this state of affairs, Eddington made two further important points consistent with Banister and Berechman's (2001) analysis: first, the cumulative impact of several relatively small improvements to the transport system – such as better bus priority on urban radial roads, or improving busy junctions – can often be at least as big as that of the large 'megaprojects' that steal the limelight. Second was that even if the links between better transport and improved economic performance are hard to measure precisely, it remains the case that the most compelling empirical evidence for the existence of these links is often to be found in those places where poor transport acts as a significant and evident *constraint* to growth, especially where there are obvious bottlenecks or missing forms of transport provision altogether.[5]

Looking across Britain, it is once again not hard to see where these conditions are most apparent. Within and between almost all of the major cities in the North and Midlands of England, the transport system is clearly – and in some cases profoundly – underdeveloped, to the extent that they obviously qualify as the kind of places Eddington identified where the existing level of infrastructure provision is poor enough to generate clear constraints on the functioning of key markets, such as the housing market or commercial property market, due to congestion or unreliable journey times. For example, before the construction of its first, originally rather isolated, tram line, Birmingham was regularly touted as the largest city in Europe not to have some kind of light rail or metro system. In comparison to its European peers, it remains highly dependent on the bus as the key means of public transport, rather than on trams and metros as in similar places such as its twin cities of Frankfurt, Lyon and Milan. This matters because bus journey times are massively affected by traffic congestion, especially in the peak periods when most people are trying to get to or from work. Using analysis of real time bus journey data in Birmingham, Forth (2019) has demonstrated how the city is in fact economically much 'smaller' than might be assumed, simply because of the underdevelopment of its fixed public transport network. The 'effective' size of the city, measured by the number of people who can access the city centre within 30 minutes, is only 1.3m, compared to the city's population of 1.9m. During peak hours, when bus journeys are slowed by congestion, the 'effective' size of the city is even smaller, at 0.9m. Having a more extensive tram network (which Birmingham is in the process of developing) would enlarge the size of the 30-minute work catchment area to 1.7m, close to the city's actual population.

The unwelcome accolade of largest city in Europe without a tram or metro now belongs to Leeds, a city which has had both its tram and then subsequently rather less ambitious trolleybus proposals dashed by central government. Sixteen billion pounds for Crossrail in London is achievable, whereas a light rail scheme in England's second-largest local authority area at one twentieth of the cost is not (see also Chapter 6 for a discussion of the lack of light rail in Liverpool, another northern city to have its plans rejected by central government). More work on effective city size might be the means to generating better empirical evidence about the importance of transport investment and economic performance, in cities at least.

Cities are doin' it for themselves

Perhaps we should not be surprised that, fed up with their cities and regions being consistently presented as sites of decline and disadvantage over several decades, policy makers in the regions have for some years now attempted to challenge the centralised nature of the UK's political economy of transport. Much of the most sophisticated contemporary analysis of the potential for transport investment to unlock economic growth can therefore be found in the major provincial city regions, not least because the conditions for success identified in Banister and Berechman's model of transport policy making for economic growth – especially the existence of cross-functional structures of policy formulation and governance, with real local knowledge – are theoretically in place. It is here too that the political *cojones* required to actually do something about the transport problem have been most apparent, with Greater Manchester's consistent push to develop the Metrolink light rail network, and Nottingham's introduction of a workplace parking levy being the most celebrated examples (see, respectively, Knowles and Ferbrache 2016, Dale et al 2014).

Indeed, the major cities are also the places in which the kinds of opportunities identified by another keynote study commissioned by the UK government, the 1999 *Transport and the Economy* report by the Standing Advisory Committee on Trunk Road Assessment (SACTRA), are arguably most likely to be present. Docherty and Waite (2019) noted that the SACTRA report set out a series of six specific positive outcomes from transport investment that the available empirical evidence deemed the most likely to generate genuine economic uplift:

- reorganisation or rationalisation of production, distribution and land use;
- extension of labour market catchments;
- increases in output resulting from lower costs of production;
- stimulation of inward investment;
- unlocking previously inaccessible sites for development;
- a 'catalytic' effect whereby triggering growth through the elimination of a significant transport constraint unlocks further growth.

The extent to which this 'catalytic' effect, or what are now commonly described as the 'Wider Economic Benefits' (WEBs) of transport investment, is real has been one of the most vibrant areas of research into the links between transport and the economy ever since SACTRA highlighted its potential. In particular, the extent to which increasing what is known as economic agglomeration, in simple terms the density of economic activity in space, might stimulate additional economic growth in cities, has become a key focus of attention (see, for example, Venables et al 2014; Melo et al 2017). The key underpinning idea is simple enough: that significant changes in the level of accessibility of key locations might lead to equally significant shifts in the locations and operations of firms and their workers: Dan Graham's (2007) term 'effective density' reflects one version of this, underpinned by a notion of accessibility to a significant economic mass of the scale only found in larger cities. But the reason agglomeration arguments are so intuitively attractive to urban policy makers is because they suggest that raising productivity by increasing job density beyond critical thresholds so that people in different firms and sectors are more likely to interact with each other, is only possible in (larger) cities. And so the argument goes on to claim that it must surely be the case that investment in urban transport is more likely to realise economic benefit than investment elsewhere...

Despite their recent popularity with many policy makers – the 'additional' economic benefit of transport investment ascribed to agglomeration effects has been claimed to be as much as 40 per cent – the key problem with agglomeration analyses, as for many of the purported links between transport and economic growth more generally, is once again that the chain of causality is far from obvious (see for example, Venables 2016, Puga 2010). In particular, there are significant challenges regarding the potential for double counting of economic gains, and there is little, if any, clarity as to whether density drives productivity or whether productivity drives density. The upshot of all of this is another version of the story running throughout this chapter: while we can paint a broad brush picture about density being beneficial for productivity, despite what some officers and politicians lobbying for their longed-for transport scheme might wish, we can't be sure that investing in improved transport on its own will generate a clear and unambiguous economic improvement in a specific location (Laird and Venables 2017). Indeed, in their 'meta-analysis of the relationship between infrastructure and economic growth', Johan Holmgren and Axel Merkel (2017) found that as the modelled estimations of productivity enhancements due to infrastructure investments become more precise, the closer they tend to zero. Hence Roger Vickerman's (2017: 5) elegantly euphemistic counsel that, given the difficulty in accurately quantifying benefits, 'the desire of policy makers for precise estimates may have to be modified.'

City Dealing

Another recent (non-transport) policy initiative has also improved the *potential* for urban transport interventions to be planned and implemented in a more cohesive manner, reflecting what we know from SACTRA, Eddington and others about those approaches that have the best opportunity of genuinely stimulating economic growth. The idea of 'City Deals', essentially multi-year agreed packages of central government funding for city regions which are incentivised to spend the money on investments that increase local growth (and therefore future tax revenues), emerged from a 2011 UK Government White Paper (HM Government 2011) that viewed the decentralisation of powers and responsibilities to local leaders as essential for driving sub-national growth. Many of the first wave of City Deals have comprised a relatively standard toolkit of policy interventions, from transport infrastructure investment to skills and labour market initiatives, and innovation programmes. But what is different about City Deals is that, by their very nature, they aim to be bespoke to local conditions in that they seek to promote those policies and investments most required to spur development and growth in the particular local context concerned (albeit that they retain a strong element of central government oversight; see O'Brien and Pike 2018). Thus, assuming they can be put into practice effectively, City Deals have the potential to create the kind of ideal conditions described by Banister and Berechman as essential if transport investment is actually to lead to regional economic growth.

Given the increasingly rare opportunity for cities to secure the large injections of cash they represent, it is no surprise that many City Deals have some kind of major transport infrastructure at their heart. One such example is the proposal for a 'metro' rail/light rail network across the Cardiff city region, which forms the centrepiece of the Cardiff Capital Region City Deal. The metro typifies *la mode du jour* in terms of the political economy of transport at the regional level: it seeks to enhance the agglomeration potential of the region by increasing the accessibility of its urban core, and does so in large part by better connecting the valleys of south east Wales – whose economic challenges are well documented – to the regional centres of Cardiff and

Newport, thus promoting 'inclusive growth' (Cardiff Capital Region City Deal: undated). But there remain divergent views on who and where will capture the benefits of the investment. For some, the metro is an obvious step to support investment and economic development in a region where sustained growth has proven elusive. For others, concerns remain about which parts of the region will gain most from the project and, making one of the recurring points of this chapter, that simply parachuting in better transport is in itself no guarantee of improving economic performance, particularly in places of multiple deprivation where there exist many layers of complex problems from poor health and skills to substandard, unattractive housing. The trick, of course, will be to ensure the metro is developed as one part of a coherent suite of policy measures and support packages designed to promote growth in the places that most need it (Institute of Welsh Affairs (IWA) 2018).

I look up to him because he is in a BMW, but I look down on her because she is on the bus

In addition to the unequal allocation of resources at the inter-regional level, our current political economy of transport is also skewed towards particular localities, communities... and men. Given that we know there is 'little evidence that would allow us to draw conclusions on whether large-scale projects (for example, high-speed rail or motorway construction) have larger economic growth impacts than spending similar amounts on a collection of small-scale projects,' (What Works Centre for Local Economic Growth, 2015: 3) it is surely incumbent on observers of transport policy to ask why we continue to spend (relatively) so much money on larger schemes designed to enable the already better off to travel further, as opposed to those people for whom even modest improvements to their local transport offering, such as better bus services, safer cycle routes or even better pavements, would open up many more economic and social opportunities.

Perhaps the best example of this is to consider the typical pattern of investment within a typical British city region. The idea of the rent/ distance curve is well understood: that the value of land, measurable in terms of its economic rent per unit area, decreases as distance from the centre of the city increases. There are different curves for commercial, industrial and residential land uses, representing the typical land use structures of urban areas. For our analysis, the residential curve is the most important, as it is peak commuting flows that have dominated infrastructure development, and thus transport investment priorities, for decades. Now consider the (cultural) morphology of the typical British city region, in which the better off have for those same decades tended to move to the suburbs or ex-urban commuter belt in order to take advantage of larger (better) housing per unit cost. The rent/distance curve suggests that the price payable for this choice is a longer commute back to the central business district (CBD) in order to take advantage of the concentration of employment there.

Yet the focus of transport policy for a very long period – as evidenced by successive waves of large investment in the roads network and latterly the railways – has been on *deliberately disrupting* the rent/distance curve so that it is faster to travel further to the CBD from favoured commuter nodes than it is from much of the inner core. Again, Birmingham is an instructive example. The middle-class suburb 8 miles from the city centre in which one of the authors grew up is 20 minutes from the city by train; the same amount of time on the bus in the same direction in the evening peak would barely get you a couple of miles across the inner-city. Thus, given that we spend pretty much the same time travelling around now as we did years ago (Metz 2008), not only do long, unreliable bus journey times impact on the effective size of the city economy as a whole, but they also have a profoundly polarising effect: the typical middle-class, relatively wealthy suburban rail commuter potentially has access to many times more jobs, educational, social, cultural and leisure opportunities than the person – more likely to be young, poor and/or a lone parent – living in the inner city where buses remain the most common form of public transport and where the number 74 actually turning up really *matters* in the context of their immediate struggles. Add to this that men are still more likely to drive a car, have preferential use of the car in one-car households, and be less likely to undertake caring responsibilities that require complex trip chaining in a typical day, and the scale of the gender as well as social class implications of differential travel opportunities and the investment choices that underpin them becomes all too readily apparent (Chapters 4 and 14).

The huge discrepancies in relative access to socio-economic opportunity locked in by the transport system are therefore a good example of why the role of public policy should perhaps more often be to *stop* people getting what they want, rather than giving it to them. For the majority of middle-class, car-owning people, the political economy of transport has for too long been one of cakeism, in which their commute is improved by new trains, their leisure activities subsidised by successive Chancellors keen to 'help the long suffering motorist', government financial support for car purchase schemes and the glaring omission of proper road pricing, and their retail opportunities made more fun by the huge out-of-town shopping complexes with free parking that killed the traditional town centre down the road. But for millions of others, especially those without access to a car and/or reliant on the bus, the quality of transport services available to them is both poor in itself, and an allegory for the wider malaise of the communities in which they live.

There is nothing new in the world except the history you do not know

We know the arguments we make in this chapter may make some people uneasy. People intrinsically like the idea of better transport provision – although as we noted in the preface and Chapter 1, we each have different ideas about which forms of transport should be prioritised – and it is hard not to want to believe the claims for the economic benefits, such as the creation of new jobs, that are made to justify our expenditure on transport. As our many personal conversations with policy makers over the years have demonstrated, it can be a disconcerting experience to explain how the evidence base for the links between transport investment and economic progress is much more tenuous than we might automatically assume, want to believe, or need to say that it is in order to secure a pet project.

But our own collective hint of unease in writing this chapter is not because its analysis is problematic; rather it is because almost nothing it contains would come as much of a surprise to those familiar with what is probably the best transport book ever written, albeit one that is not normally regarded a transport book per se. Jane Jacobs' (1961) seminal *Death and Life of Great American Cities* was published at the time when advances in computing power made possible the assent to dominance of econometric modelling in transport policy that continues to this day. Transport economists, engineers and planners used the new modelling capabilities available to them to demonstrate why it was imperative to completely alter the fabric of the built environments in which millions of people lived so that the calculated TEE gains of the maximum possible use of the maximum possible numbers of cars running at the maximum possible speed could be captured. That transport investment supported economic growth became axiomatic because the models said it was so.

Jacobs' critique of the dash to build freeways is now of course well known: that the environmental and social implications of the rise of the private car and the infrastructure required to provide for it were not recognised by models focusing on abstract notions of economic efficiency, and therefore that negative externalities ranging from local air pollution, through noise and declining personal safety, to the complete destruction of established communities and their histories and cultures, were somehow not deemed important enough to outweigh notional economic gains (Chapter 9). But more fundamentally, what she was doing was pointing out that, far from the exact 'science' its proponents made it out to be (Docherty et al 2018), properly understanding the impacts of transport investment requires a much broader, qualitative and frankly more sophisticated outlook than that of the quantitative hard core that believes real life can be whittled down to five or six statistically well-behaved variables. In other words, as for any area of public policy, decisions about where to allocate resources in transport represent a qualitatively complex political economy of action.

If there is nothing new to this, why are we still making the same mistakes? The answer perhaps lies in one of the other key issues that Jacobs' crusade in defence of cities and their neighbourhoods helped eventually reveal, and which remains important today: how the politics of who wins and who loses from transport investment decisions is *framed*. The policy narrative *before* the decision to go ahead with a particular transport project is nearly always solely about the 'winners' that the scheme will create: how many jobs will be created, how much quicker the commute will be, and so on. Evaluation of who actually 'won' to the extent claimed is rarely undertaken with any substantial rigour, and analyses of who actually lost out, for example through the changing relative accessibility of different sites leading to a relocation of employment away from disadvantaged areas, even less so (see Gärling and Steg 2007, Haywood and Hebbert 2008, Shaftoe 2008). In other words, there is no shortage of claims made for the economic benefits and merits of transport investment, backed up by often inaccurate but seemingly extraordinarily clever 'science', but there is a dearth of genuine evaluation evidence that can be used to either understand the real changes to people's lives that transport investment brings, or to challenge whether the processes that underpin decisions are robust in the sense that they deliver what they say they will. Worse still is that this lack of robust critique of investment decisions after the event means that the policy narrative inevitably moves on to evangelise about the winners of the next scheme for which there is the inevitable urgent need. And so the show goes on.

Thus despite important research work such as the What Works Centre for Local Economic Growth's (2015: 3) recent meta-review on the empirical evidence on transport and the economy, which found that most road and rail projects had no or mixed effects on employment, and (astonishingly) that there were no 'high-quality evaluations of the impacts of trams, buses, cycling and walking schemes on any economic outcomes' to be found, spending large sums of money on transport is still largely justified on the basis of gains to the economy. Our argument in this chapter is therefore two-fold: first, that these promised gains are often likely to be illusory given what we actually know about the causal links between transport and the economy, but second, that because we are still spending hugely disproportionate amounts of money on road and rail schemes in particular, we are privileging the needs or, perhaps more accurately, the wish lists, of a small set of interests.

The answer, of course, as to why some particular interests – the business lobby, supermarkets, rail users, car drivers – are the winners from our current transport investment choices while others – such as pedestrians, young people and perhaps most obviously bus passengers – are the losers, lies in the fact that it is the former groups that are *politically powerful*. For the avoidance of doubt, we are not arguing against spending significant (or indeed, more) public money on transport; we have said that we regard our transport system as underdeveloped, and better transport has the potential to improve our quality of life in all sorts of ways (Chapter 1). But it is imperative to recognise that how we do this, which aspects of life we prioritise, and where and to whom we allocate these resources are intensely political choices that need debating thoroughly and robustly if we are to make the best possible decisions. In order to understand fully the political economy of transport as it currently plays out, it is necessary not only to interrogate the mismatch between policy rhetoric and where the money actually ends up, but also to shine a light on who has privileged access to the corridors of power, or lives in the kind of marginal constituency that actually makes a difference in elections.

Notes

[1] The importance of modelling to ensuring that transport was not seen in government (especially the Treasury) as being 'analytically lagging' was once memorably communicated to our colleague Greg Marsden in an interview. See Docherty et al 2018.

[2] Iain and Jon.

[3] In 2019 the north of England is finally receiving investment in new trains with more capacity in the Northern and Transpennine Express franchises, but journeys will remain slow until a large package of (as yet undecided) infrastructure improvements is completed.

4 It is instructive to note that while the HS2 debate in the north of England focuses on the notion of economic 'rebalancing' from south to north, there is an equal and opposite debate in the South East about why the £30 billion 'Crossrail 2' project will be necessary to cope with the additional people flooding into London from the north as a result.

5 Dublin is often argued to be the classic example of a city that grew quickly – and to a high level of prosperity – with poor transport provision, but then had to invest significantly in improved infrastructure to ensure the continuation of its growth trajectory. See also the *What Works Centre for Local Economic Growth* (2015) report.

References

Banister, D and Berechman, Y (2001) 'Transport investment and the promotion of economic growth', *Journal of Transport Geography*, 9(3): 209–18.

Cardiff Capital Region City Deal (undated) *Cardiff Capital Region City Deal* www.cardiffcapitalregioncitydeal.wales Accessed 24 October 2018.

Chen, C-L and Hall, P (2011) 'The impacts of high-speed trains on British economic geography: a study of the UK's InterCity 125/225 and its effects', *Journal of Transport Geography*, 19(4): 689–704.

Crafts, N (2009) 'Transport infrastructure investment: implications for growth and productivity', *Oxford Review of Economic Policy*, 25(3): 327–43.

Dale, S, Frost, M, Gooding, J, Ison, S and Warren, P (2014) 'A case study of the introduction of a Workplace Parking Levy in Nottingham', in S Ison and C Mulley (eds) *Parking Issues and Policies*, Bingley: Emerald, pp 335–60.

Department for Transport (2015) *Value for money framework. Moving Britain ahead*. https://assets.publishing.service.gov.uk/government/uploads/system/uploads/attachment_data/file/630704/value-for-money-framework.pdf Accessed 23 October 2018.

Department for Transport (2017a) *Transport statistics Great Britain: 2017*. www.gov.uk/government/statistics/transport-statistics-great-britain-2017 Accessed 23 October 2018.

Department for Transport (2017b) *Annual bus statistics: England 2016/17*. https://assets.publishing.service.gov.uk/government/uploads/system/uploads/attachment_data/file/666759/annual-bus-statistics-year-ending-march-2017.pdf Accessed 25 October 2018.

Department for Transport (2017c) *Rail factsheet November 2017*. https://assets.publishing.service.gov.uk/government/uploads/system/uploads/attachment_data/file/663116/rail-factsheet-2017.pdf Accessed 23 October 2018.

Docherty, I and Mackinnon D (2013) 'Transport and economic development', in J-P Rodrigue, T Notteboom and J Shaw (eds) *The Sage handbook of transport studies*, London: Sage, pp 226–40.

Docherty, I and Waite, D (2019) *Evidence review: infrastructure*. https://productivityinsightsnetwork.co.uk/app/uploads/2018/07/Evidence-Review_Infrastructure-1.pdf Accessed 1 June 2019.

Docherty, I, Shaw, J, Marsden, G and Anable, J (2018) 'The curious death – and life? – of British transport policy', *Environment and Planning C: Politics and Space*, 36(8): 1458–79.

Dorling, D (2018) *Peak Inequality: Britain's Ticking Time Bomb*, Bristol: Policy Press.

Eddington, R (2006) *The Eddington transport study. The case for action: Sir Rod Eddington's advice to government*. HM Treasury, London. http://webarchive.nationalarchives.gov.uk/20090115123503/http://www.dft.gov.uk/162259/187604/206711/executivesummary.pdf Accessed 23 October 2018.

Forth, T (2019) *Real Journey Time, Real City Size, and the disappearing productivity puzzle*. https://productivityinsightsnetwork.co.uk/2019/01/real-journey-time-real-city-size-and-the-disappearing-productivity-puzzle/ Accessed 26 February 2019.

Gärling, T and Steg, L (2007) *Threats from Car Traffic to the Quality of Urban Life: Problems, Causes, and Solutions*, Oxford: Elsevier.

Graham, D (2007) 'Agglomeration, productivity and transport investment', *Journal of Transport Economics and Policy*, 41(3): 317–43.

Haywood, R and Hebbert, M (2008) 'Integrating rail and land use development', *Planning Practice and Research*, 23(3): 281–4.

Holmgren, J and Merkel, A (2017) 'Much ado about nothing? A meta-analysis of the relationship between infrastructure and economic growth', *Research in Transportation Economics*, 63(C): 13–26.

HM Government (2011) *Unlocking growth in cities*. https://assets.publishing.service.gov.uk/government/uploads/system/uploads/attachment_data/file/7523/CO_Unlocking_20GrowthCities_acc.pdf Accessed 23 October 2018.

HS2 Ltd (2014) *Rebalancing Britain: from HS2 towards a national transport strategy*. Department for Transport, London. https://assets.publishing.service.gov.uk/government/uploads/system/uploads/attachment_data/file/374709/Rebalancing_Britain_-_From_HS2_towards_a_national_transport_strategy.pdf Accessed 26 February 2019.

Institute of Welsh Affairs (2018) *Metro & me: making spaces and going places*. Available at: www.iwa.wales/wp-content/uploads/2018/10/MetroAndMeDigiFinal.pdf Accessed 23 October 2018.

Jacobs, J (1961) *The Death and Life of Great American Cities*, London: Penguin.

Knowles, R and Ferbrache, F (2016) 'Evaluation of wider economic impacts of light rail investment on cities', *Journal of Transport Geography*, 54: 430–9.

Krugman, P (1996) 'Urban concentration: the role of increasing returns and transport costs', *International Regional Science Review*, 19(1-2): 5–30.

Krugman, P (2011) 'The New Economic Geography, now middle-aged', *Regional Studies*, 45(1): 1–7.

Laird, J and Venables, A (2017) 'Transport investment and economic performance: a framework for project appraisal', *Transport Policy*, 56(C): 1–11.

Linneker, B (1997) *Transport Infrastructure and Regional Economic Development in Europe: A Review of Theoretical and Methodological Approaches*. Sheffield: University of Sheffield.

McCann, P (2016) *The UK Regional-National Economic Problem: Geography, Globalisation and Governance*, Abingdon: Routledge.

McCann, P (2018) *Perceptions of regional inequality and the geography of productivity*. University of Sheffield. https://productivityinsightsnetwork. co.uk/app/uploads/2018/12/Discussion-Paper_Perceptions-of-Regional-Inequality-and-the-Geography-of-Discontent-updated-19.12.18.pdf Accessed 26 February 2019.

Melo, P, Graham, D, Levinson, D and Aarabi, S (2017) 'Agglomeration, accessibility and productivity: Evidence for large metropolitan areas in the US', *Urban Studies*, 54(1): 179–95.

Metz, D (2008) 'The myth of travel time saving', *Transport Reviews*, 28:3, 321–336.

Mullen, C and Marsden, G (2015) 'Transport, economic competitiveness and competition: a city perspective', *Journal of Transport Geography*, 49: 1–8.

O'Brien, P and Pike, A (2018) '"Deal or no deal?" Governing urban infrastructure funding and financing in the UK City Deals', *Urban Studies*, 56(7): 1448–76.

Office for National Statistics (2014) *Regional and subregional productivity comparisons, UK and selected EU countries: 2014*. https://www.ons.gov. uk/economy/nationalaccounts/uksectoraccounts/compendium/ economicreview/april2018/regionalandsubregionalproductivity comparisonsukandselectedeucountries2014 Accessed 26 February 2019.

Overman, H (2014) *How unbalanced is infrastructure spending?* http://eprints.lse.ac.uk/82597/1/SERC_%20Spatial%20Economics%20Research%20Centre_%20How%20Unbalanced%20is%20Infrastructure%20Spending_.pdf Accessed 23 October 2018.

Puga, D (2010) 'The magnitude and causes of agglomeration economies', *Journal of Regional Science*, 50(1): 203–19.

Raikes, L (2018) *Future transport investment in the north: a briefing on the government's new regional analysis of the national infrastructure and construction pipeline.* IPPR North, Manchester and Newcastle. www.ippr.org/publications/future-transport-investment-in-the-north-briefing Accessed 26 February 2019.

Rutherford, T (2018) *Transport spending by region.* House of Commons Library, Briefing Paper 8130, 12 February 2018. https://researchbriefings.parliament.uk/ResearchBriefing/Summary/CBP-8130 Accessed 26 February 2019.

Shaftoe, H (2008) *Convivial Urban Spaces: Creating Effective Public Places*, London: Earthscan.

Standing Advisory Committee on Trunk Road Assessment (1999) *Transport and the economy.* https://webarchive.nationalarchives.gov.uk/20050304041634/http://www.dft.gov.uk/stellent/groups/dft_econappr/documents/pdf/dft_econappr_pdf_022512.pdf Accessed 1 June 2019.

Tomaney, J and Marques, P (2013) 'Evidence, policy and the politics of regional development: the case of high-speed rail in the United Kingdom', *Environment and Planning C: Politics and Space*, 31(3): 414–27.

Venables, A (2016) *Incorporating wider economic impacts within cost–benefit appraisal.* OECD ITF Discussion Paper 2016–05.

Venables, A, Laird, J and Overman, H (2014) *Transport investment and economic performance: Implications for project appraisal.* Department for Transport, London. www.gov.uk/government/publications/transport-investment-and-economic-performance-tiep-report Accessed 23 October 2018

Vickerman, R (2017) 'Beyond cost–benefit analysis: the search for a comprehensive evaluation of transport investment', *Research in Transportation Economics*, 63: 5–12.

What Works Centre for Local Economic Growth (2015) *Evidence review 7: transport.* July 2015. www.whatworksgrowth.org/public/files/Policy_Reviews/15-07-01-Transport-Summary.pdf Accessed 23 October 2018.

Wingham, M (2017) *Transport expenditure in London*. GLA Economics, London. www.london.gov.uk/sites/default/files/transportexpenditure_final_cin54.pdf Accessed 23 October 2018.

Worsley, T and Mackie, P (2015) *Transport policy, appraisal and decision-making*. RAC Foundation, London. https://www.racfoundation.org/wp-content/uploads/2017/11/Transport_policy_appraisal_decision_making_worsley_mackie_May_2015_final_report.pdf Accessed 23 October 2018.

3

Energy, pollution and climate change

Jillian Anable and Christian Brand

Introduction

> There is little in common between 'e' when a physicist writes it and 'energy' when the word is used by an economist, politician, or windmill fan. 'E' is an algorithm, 'energy' is a loaded word. 'E' is meaningful only within a formula, 'energy' is charged with hidden implications: it refers to a subtle something that has the ability to make nature do work. Even the engineer who routinely handles megawatts talks of 'energy' when he [*sic*] speaks to his client. Energy now, as work formerly, has become something that individuals and societies need. It is a symbol that fits our age, the symbol of that which is both abundant and scarce. (Illich 2010: 13)[1]

Mobility is a service that demands energy. Energy, in turn, is fraught with complexity in terms of its forms, availability, infrastructure, ownership, extraction, conversion and combustion, and the socio-political implications of all of these factors. It is also complex in that the fundamental laws of thermodynamics render it simultaneously extremely productive and profligately wasteful. This has led to a science and policy of energy conservation which is a testing mix of calls to use energy resources more sparingly while applying an engineering focus on maximising work and minimising waste.

Turnbull (2017: 26) traces the history of energy resource conservation using the example of steam engines, which he explains led to 'industrialists and engineers becoming preoccupied with using fuels with utmost efficiency, and maximizing the work that could be derived from irreversibly consumed and geologically distributed resources such as coal.' Turnbull is by no means the first author choosing to adopt transport cases to illustrate the consequences of the homage paid to energy. In *Energy & Equity*, Illich (1974) described how cars and aeroplanes force people to devote more and more time, money and effort to getting themselves from here to there each day. He claims there would be no 'crisis' in energy if society chose to adopt speed limits that favoured walking and cycling. In his later essay, *Energy as a Social Construction*, from which the quote at the top of this chapter is taken, he evolved his arguments to stress how energy had been equated with doing the work of natural systems, with the implication that 'the universe itself is placed under the regime of scarcity' so that humans are 'no longer born under the stars but under the axioms of economics' (Illich 1974: 13). In other words, the energy-economy, or sub-systems within it such as transport, are engineered and operated with the goal of distributing limited supplies to the population. The consequent fear of irreversible shortage then frames efforts to use fuel more efficiently to 'save energy' so that 'politicians could win by the mere promise of more watts and jobs' (Illich 2010: 17). More recently, the approach to energy saving has shifted the emphasis on energy resource governance by placing the onus on consumers of energy rather than producers (Turnbull 2017), thereby adding to the complexity.

The transport sector remains at the centre of debates around energy conservation, exaggerated by the stubborn and overwhelming reliance on fossil fuels by its motorised forms, whether passenger and freight, road, rail, sea and air. The very slow transition to alternative fuel sources to date has resulted in this sector being increasingly and convincingly held responsible for the likely failure of individual countries, including the UK, to meet their obligations under consecutive international climate change agreements (Anable and Boardman 2005, Committee on Climate Change (CCC) 2018a, Intergovernmental Panel on Climate Change (IPCC) 2014). In this chapter we examine the allegation that the transport sector may be ultimately responsible for a climate crisis, alongside other serious environmental consequences attributed to the combustion of fossil fuels for transport. Detailed accounts of these impacts, along with analyses of scenarios and technical solutions focused on vehicles and fuels, are well rehearsed elsewhere. Therefore, our main purpose here is to take a step back from the prognoses themselves and ask what a focus on energy has ever done for the formation of sustainable transport policy. The received view is that if current (fossil fuel based) energy systems are problematic, they need to be replaced by sustainable alternatives in order to allow people to continue their consumption practices. In this way, the energy transition is seen as a mostly technical endeavour requiring society to innovate around technologies that can reliably harvest and distribute energy from a sustainable source like the sun, preferably in a form that fits current practices, that is, electricity and liquid fuels. We attempt to take stock at this pivotal point among a constellation of so-called transport 'revolutions' (Chapter 16), and ponder the need to reframe the core concept of 'energy efficiency' if it is to be a useful focal point around which to continue to galvanise sustainable action in this sector.

Our chapter has a core purpose: to propose an alternative framework with which to define, target and deliver a clean and efficient transport sector with explicit adherence to environmental, affordability, security and equity goals. In so doing, we organise our discussion into four substantive sections. The first of these briefly elaborates upon the energy-related environmental challenges referred to earlier, with particular focus on forward projections based on recent UK policy announcements. This allows us to discuss the progress achieved, or expected to be achieved, towards addressing these challenges by the dominant solutions proposed, before we offer a dissection of the main flaws in the energy efficiency approach. We present a new interpretation of efficiency before offering our brief conclusions.

The environmental consequences of mobility as an energy service

Not accounting for the energy involved in extracting and refining fuels, transport accounts for 32 per cent of total final energy consumed globally, with the figure increasing to 38 per cent for OECD countries and 34 per cent for the UK (International Energy Agency (IEA) 2018a). The IEA (2018b) estimates that the transport sector is responsible for 25 per cent of global energy-related emissions of carbon dioxide (CO_2), and transport-related emissions are increasing faster than emissions from any other sector (International Transport Forum (ITF) 2017). The expectation is that the share of transport energy demand and associated emissions will grow in developed as well as developing economies.

The transport sector has a significant dependence on oil, with a share of 95 per cent of all global transport energy use in 2015, and this has not changed since the 1970s (IEA 2018b). Despite well-established pockets of electrification (light and heavy rail) and rapidly evolving ones (light-duty vehicles and motorised two-wheelers), scenario exercises by fuel companies, international energy agencies, environmental NGOs and utility companies all come to uncannily similar conclusions about the transport sector – a lot of fossil fuel will still be being burnt globally within the sector in 2050 and beyond. This is despite the fact that these modelling exercises all start with many different framings and use a multitude of modelling approaches and assumptions to explore societal or economic trajectories for world energy production and consumption (Creutzig 2015). When combined with the inertia in the system infrastructure, vehicle fleet turnover and consumer behaviour, the transport systems in developed economies are likely to look very similar in most respects in 2050 as they do today.

In the UK, energy use from transport has increased by 16.1 per cent since 1990 against an economy-wide *decrease* of 4.1 per cent (Department for Business, Energy and Industrial Strategy (BEIS) 2018, CCC 2018a). Transport is also the largest carbon-emitting sector of the UK economy with 28 per cent of greenhouse gas emissions in 2017. As emissions in other sectors have reduced, transport has grown as a share of overall emissions with no net reduction since 1990 vis-à-vis a 43 per cent reduction for all sectors combined (Figure 3.1a and 3.1b). Cars, vans and heavy goods vehicles (HGVs) remain the three most significant (and rising) sources of emissions, together accounting for 87 per cent of domestic transport emissions (CCC 2018a). Demand for travel continues to grow for cars and particularly vans, whereas efficiency improvements have slowed (see next section).

Recent years have witnessed three decisive events that have brought about a fundamental shift in the international community's framing of climate change. First, the IPCC's (2014) Fifth Assessment report proposed the concept of carbon budgets as a scientifically credible foundation for developing mitigation policy. Second, the Paris Agreement established a near universal covenant among world leaders to take action to hold 'the increase in... temperature to well below 2°C... and to pursue efforts to limit the temperature increase to 1.5°C' (United Nations Framework Convention on Climate Change (UNFCCC) 2015). Combining the Paris commitments with the IPCC's carbon budgets demonstrates a profoundly more challenging post-Paris mitigation agenda than has thus far been countenanced in the UK, either by its independent CCC, or by most of its academic community. As it stands, the IPCC Synthesis report's headline budget range for a low and medium probability of 1.5°C will have been exceeded within three to 14 years of current annual emissions levels (Anderson 2015). While the timeframe is longer for avoiding a two-degree Celsius rise, the equity dimension of the Paris Agreement still brings the mitigation challenge into much closer focus. Whether it's 'pursuing ... 1.5°C' or staying 'well below 2°C', unprecedented rates of mitigation are required across all sectors between now and 2030.

Figure 3.1: Emissions reductions from each sector of the UK economy, 1990–2017 and changes in emissions per sector, 2012–17

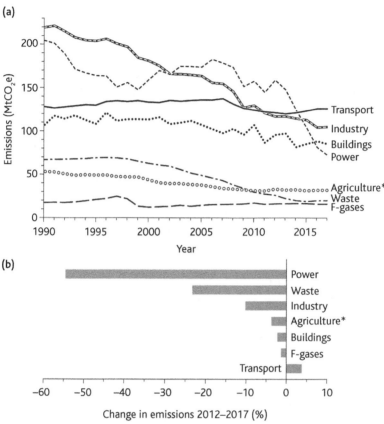

*Agriculture includes land use, land-use change and forestry (LULUCF)

Source: CCC 2018

Third, the most recent IPCC (2018) Special Report on global warming of 1.5°C stressed that such near-term mitigation cannot wait for wholesale infrastructure change, but must begin to deliver within the existing socio-technical system while at the same time fostering the need for a wider system-level transformation. Early quantitative analysis of the IPCC budgets and Paris Agreement suggests mitigation rates for wealthier industrialised nations of at least 10 per cent a year; higher still if the 1.5°C commitment is to seriously inform UK policies (Anderson 2015). For transport, this means that lifestyle changes will be critical, alongside energy efficiency and fuel-switching measures (IPCC 2018). Given that within the sector there are sub-segments (HGVs, aviation) that are very difficult to wean off fossil fuels, and these happen to be the same segments that are increasing most rapidly, the blame for any failure to meet agreed international targets is being placed firmly at this sector's door.

Yet climate change is only one clear environmental imperative for which the transport sector needs to shoulder disproportionate blame. The other is local air pollution. Air pollution is the largest environmental cause of disease and death in the world today, responsible for an estimated nine million premature deaths in 2015 (Landrigan et al 2018). 92 per cent of all air pollution-related mortality is seen in low- and middle-income countries, mainly in Asia and Africa, followed by low- and middle-income countries of the eastern Mediterranean region, Europe and the Americas. In the UK, current regulatory breaches relate to nitrogen dioxide (NO_2), generated from emissions of nitrogen oxides (NO_x), and particulate matter, the latter both in its coarser PM_{10} form (particles with an average diameter of 10 micrometres or less) and the fine $PM_{2.5}$ form (2.5 micrometres or less). NO_x is mainly a by-product of fuel combustion, while PM results from fuel combustion as well as road, brake and tyre wear (Grigoratos and Martini 2015).

Though domestic and background emissions also contribute to the problem, road transport is the principal reason why many urban areas are in breach of air pollution regulatory limits (Hitchcock et al 2014). While heavy-duty vehicles (buses and lorries) are still a key source of NOx and $PM_{2.5}$ emissions, the contribution from diesel cars and vans has increased rapidly over the last decade because of the gradual 'dieselisation' of the car and van fleets, which is a consequence of the government and industry focus in Europe on climate change and better fuel economy of diesels since the late 1990s (Hitchcock et al 2014). Conventional diesel cars emit nearly ten times more nitrogen oxide (NO_x) and three times more particulate matter ($PM_{2.5}$) per car and year than their petrol equivalent. Battery electric cars are the cleanest overall as they produce zero tailpipe emissions but are liable to non-tailpipe emissions from tyre, brake and road wear, just like conventional fossil fuel vehicles.

Human health damage from air pollution caused by road traffic is significant, particularly in urban areas where most people live and/or work (House of Commons 2018). The total annual health costs for cars and vans in the UK alone correspond to more than 10,000 premature deaths each year with associated annual health costs estimated at between £22.6 billion and £71.3 billion. When attributed to a typical UK car over its 14-year lifetime or a van over its shorter nine-year lifetime, these costs are about £1,640 and £5,107 respectively (Brand

and Hunt 2018). Such societal costs are comparable to the road tax (or Vehicle Excise Duty in the UK) paid for by the vehicle's owner. The lifetime costs per car or van greatly depend on whether they run on petrol, diesel or electricity. They also depend greatly on *where* they are driven, being most acute in urban environments, particularly in densely populated cities. In inner London, for instance, the lifetime health costs rise to £7,714 and £24,004 for fossil fuel cars and vans respectively. The health costs of battery electric cars and vans are respectively nine (£827) and 17 (£1,443) times lower than for their fossil fuel equivalents, on average.

Direct environmental implications from the sector are not just from the burning of fuel, but also from land take and other resource implications from fuel extraction, vehicle production and the direct impacts of building and maintaining transport infrastructure. Nevertheless, the overwhelming focus in addressing transport's environmental impacts has been on burning less fuel through efficiency and moving towards cleaner fuels. We now go on to briefly outline the dominant proposed solutions and mitigation of local and global pollutants expected from them.

Dominant solutions and projections

Decoupling travel activity and its associated energy use from CO_2 and local pollutants is an essential policy priority at all scales. Changes in energy demand in the transport sector and its associated CO_2 and local pollutants is a combination of three broad targets of action:

- *vehicle* efficiency through (a) regulating/target setting for vehicle efficiency, and (b) operating vehicles more efficiently (for example, through logistics planning or eco-driving);
- *vehicle* demand through influencing (a) the types of vehicles on the road, and (b) the number of vehicles in use;
- *travel* demand through the utilisation of vehicles (including mode switch, distances and frequencies of travel, vehicle passenger/ load occupancy).

In addition, the fuels and the technology involved in combusting or converting those fuels to power are also a main target for the achievement of 'cleaner' mobility. The main focus of the UK's (and other developed economies') transport and decarbonisation efforts has been, by far, on the first of our list, in the form of mandatory regulations on the average CO_2 intensity (or fuel consumption in the case of the US) of new cars. This has been in place in Europe since 2009 for cars and 2011 for vans. This regulation, complemented by instruments designed to influence vehicle demand in the form of some alignment of fiscal instruments relating to the purchase and use of vehicles and fuels, has been generally hailed as a success in that since 2010, emissions of the average new passenger car have decreased by 16 per cent per kilometre (International Council on Clean Transportation (ICCT) 2018). But recent developments have exposed serious issues.

Stalling progress in emissions reduction

The first is the stalling of recent progress in reducing emissions from cars. Test-cycle new car CO_2 emitted per mile increased in 2017 for the first time since records began (in 2000), and it is now unlikely that the sector will meet the EU 2020/21 target of 95 gCO_2/km for cars unless it can achieve a 5.9 per cent decrease year on year between now and then, against an average of only 3 per cent in previous years. The recent increase is mainly due to people buying larger cars: sports utility vehicles (SUVs) now represent 18.1 per cent of new car sales, compared to 7.7 per cent in 2010. If car sales of each size had remained as in 2016, then average test-cycle CO_2 intensity would have fallen by 0.8 per cent in 2017 rather than risen (CCC 2018). Another factor, though smaller, arises because of a switch away from diesel cars since the 'Dieselgate' story broke in September 2015. Not only did manipulation of the test cycle by motor manufacturers seriously enter public awareness, but governments have since had little choice other than to face the air quality implications and signal more stringent fiscal and other restrictions to the use of diesels. These developments have unsurprisingly suppressed consumer preference for diesel vehicles with sales in the UK falling to 32 per cent of the new car market in September 2018, from a high of 50 per cent in 2014 (Society of Motor Manufacturers and Traders (SMMT) 2018). Nevertheless, because the gap between new petrol and diesel car efficiency has reduced over time, particularly as the average intensity of upper-medium sized diesel cars has actually increased, this switch contributes a relatively small proportion of the recent CO_2 intensity increase.

Recent sales-weighted average CO_2 targets, and future ones, are reliant to a large extent on enough conventional hybrid (HEV) and plug-in electric vehicles (EVs) (including plug-in hybrids (PHEVs)) being sold to offset the now increasing proportion of petrol and larger vehicles. In the UK, sales of EVs increased in 2017, and early 2018 stood at around 2 per cent of all sales, but are lagging behind the CCC's projections of what is required by this stage (CCC 2018a). Moreover, one in every four EVs sold in 2017 was a PHEV, with the most popular vehicle, a Mitsubishi Outlander – an SUV that runs for a maximum of 28 miles on its battery, according to the new test-cycle figures – accounting for the majority of PHEV sales.

Internationally, several governments have now committed to phasing out conventional vehicles between 2025 (Norway) and 2040 (UK), and many manufacturers have also announced targets. There is much literature on various governments' ambitions, measures and progress towards accelerating the uptake of EVs (see IEA 2018c, CCC 2018a, SMMT 2018), but here we focus on a recent and long-awaited report by the UK Department for Transport (DfT) as a good illustration of current policy rhetoric and wider tensions with respect to the continued focus on tailpipe 'performance' of new vehicles (DfT 2018). The *Road to Zero* strategy, as it was eventually called, had initially been expected to address the decarbonisation of the transport sector as a whole given the lack of such a dedicated strategy by the DfT. In the end, it turned out to be focused on roads only, with the major emphasis on passenger cars. The strategy sets an interim ambition for ultra-low emission vehicle sales (ULEVs) of 50–70 per cent by 2030 (increased from 30–70 per cent), and 40 per cent for vans, ahead of a ban on diesel and petrol cars and vans by 2040.

The criticism of this strategy was immediate and widespread. Firstly, there is ambiguity over the definition of ULEVs. They are defined in the report as cars having 'significant zero emission capability', leaving the door open for hybrid vehicles, even conventionally fuelled ones, to be sold after 2040. It is especially interesting to note that these apparently more ambitious targets are certainly no greater, and possibly less stringent, than those proposed in the 2011 *Carbon Plan* in which all new cars *and vans* were proposed to be near zero emission at the tailpipe by 2040 (HM Government 2011). Secondly, the 2040 target is already weak by international standards, with many calling for the target date to be a decade earlier to represent a clear signal to the car industry and speed up emissions reduction. Thirdly, the policies identified to achieve this are deemed by many to be inadequate. These include committed improvements to the charging infrastructure, maintenance of grants for purchase of some ULEVs, potential reforms to vehicle tax. Supporting legislation in the form of the Automated and Electric Vehicles Bill is currently passing through Parliament, and will give the government powers to require motorway services and large fuel retailers to install charging points and to ensure that all chargers are 'smart', providing grid flexibility by adjusting the rate of charge when necessary and practical for the consumer. The government will also gain powers to mandate the method of payment for EV charging points. The CCC sums up the critique of most as follows:

> Leaving open the possibility of sales of conventional hybrids and very short-range plug-in hybrids in 2040 and following years is inconsistent with the UK's climate change commitments. To meet the Government's stated goal of every car and van being zero emission in 2050, only pure battery electric vehicles and long range plug-in hybrids can be sold after 2035, enabling the majority of journeys to be completed in electric mode. (CCC 2018b: 1)

Test cycles and the real world

The second issue relates to the discrepancy between the official test-cycle figures and the achieved fuel economy and emissions (not just CO_2) achieved in real-world driving. Data collected on approximately 1.1 million vehicles from 14 data sources and eight EU countries indicate that the divergence, or gap, between official and real-world CO_2 emission values of new passenger cars increased from approximately 9 per cent in 2001 to 42 per cent in 2016 (Tietge et al 2017). Also, the average level has been virtually unchanged from 2015. This gap has effectively entirely negated any reported savings from car energy efficiency improvements over the past decade. Figure 3.2 shows that while type-approval figures declined 30 per cent between 2001 and 2016, the real-world estimate decreased by less than 10 per cent and has stagnated since 2010.

Despite the now acknowledged reality that such a regulatory failure has essentially wiped out any benefit that the new car regulations achieved over the past decade, it was not mentioned in the most recent UK government's strategy for 'Clean Growth' (HM Government 2017). The EU is phasing in a new test-cycle, the Worldwide Harmonised Light Vehicle Test Procedure (WLTP), from September 2017 which reduces opportunities to cheat the test. Vehicles have to be driven for longer and use a wider variety of speeds and acceleration, and some practices that manufacturers have used to artificially lower test results (which include over-inflating tyres and choosing to test the lightest possible version of the vehicle) have been eliminated. While this is a step in the right direction, the WLTP is not a silver bullet and will not close the gap on its own. There are of course also uncertainties as to

Figure 3.2: Real-world versus type-approval CO_2 emission values of new EU passenger cars based on Spritmonitor.de estimates and type-approval data

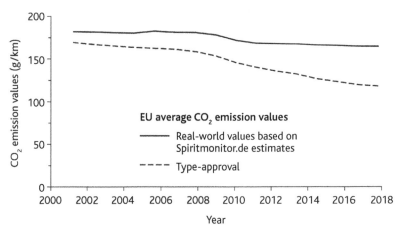

Source: Tietge et al 2017

how the UK will interface with these EU regulations once it has left the Union. The new test still allows flexibilities that manufacturers can exploit, including using different tyres for testing than those available for sale, using special test drive modes and installing technologies that do not reduce emissions as effectively on the road. Use of such flexibilities further damages public trust in the testing regime. Indeed, scandals such as Dieselgate and increasing awareness and disquiet about real-world emissions has dented public confidence and works against attempts to encourage a process of deliberative and informed vehicle choice as consumers lose faith in the information and believe all cars are as bad or as good as each other (Hafner et al 2017).

The gap between the test-cycle and real-world driving performance is also an issue for plug-in vehicles. The energy and emissions performance of PHEVs is heavily dependent on the proportion of their distance driven on the battery charge. Unfortunately, we do not know much at all about the usage profiles of these vehicles. Indeed, another 'real world' phenomenon that will ultimately determine energy demand will be the amount that all of these cars are used. The term 'rebound effect' has been applied to where at least some efficiency cost benefits are taken in the form of more service (that is, more or longer journeys, or larger cars – see Sorrell 2007, Walnum et al 2014). But the dynamic responses between technological and societal changes and behaviour are more complex than such a linear concept suggests. Suffice to say that it is misleading to assume that new vehicle technologies will simply enter into a household or business vehicle fleet and be used to undertake the same journey patterns as any car it may have replaced. New charging regimes, materials, habits, meanings and assessments of costs and benefits (monetary or otherwise) will alter the decision-making context and the utilisation patterns of these vehicles.

Limited ambitions

The third, and most important, issue is that the ambition set for vehicle efficiency and fuel decarbonisation falls far short of the scientific evidence on what is required to meet carbon targets, even if the two failures cited earlier were not causing slower than expected real progress. The risks of under-delivery by the transport sector as a whole were presented by the CCC in their 2018 report, and their analysis is reproduced in Figure 3.3.

The top of the grey area in the chart represents baseline emissions projections, followed by lower risk policies which the CCC regards as having sufficient funding and delivery certainty. The medium and dark grey segments represent policies that are judged to have significant delivery risks because of lack of funding or intention clarity or both. The striped segment represents additional cost effective policies that the CCC has identified and believe should be funded (including clarifying the regulatory approach, stretching the CO_2 targets for vehicles, accelerating the uptake of EVs, restricting the uptake of

Figure 3.3: Risks around the delivery of transport sector policies to meet the cost-effective path

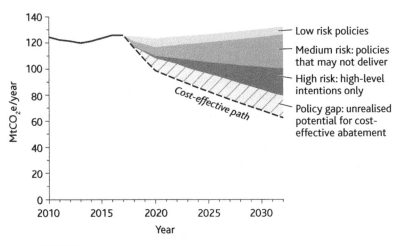

Source: CCC 2018

short-range PHEVs, agreeing on HGV emissions targets, increasing walking and cycling, incentivising public transport, eco-driving training in the freight sector, enforcement of speed limits and update plans for rail electrification).

Yet this CCC assessment has not caught up with the implications of the carbon budgets implied by the Paris Agreement targets. The Paris Agreement rewrites the scale of the international mitigation challenge, and the implications for UK mitigation rates and timeframes are profound. With 60 per cent of UK surface transport's carbon emitted by the car fleet, the sector is pivotal to any post-Paris programme of action. Notwithstanding the most optimistic predictions of carbon intensity based on the new test-cycle figures, and the most optimistic view of what the current EU negotiations will settle on for cuts in CO_2 from new cars by 2030, the mix of cars sold for the next decade or two will lock in fossil fuels for some time to come. Contradictory policies such as the abandonment of the fuel duty escalator (price increases set above inflation) after the fuel protests in 2000 and no increases even in line with inflation since 2010 have left pump prices 13 per cent lower than they would have been since 2010 alone, not to mention recent road building announcements (Begg and Haigh 2018), add further brakes on progress. There is no available measure of new HGV gCO_2/km, as this is not currently regulated and until the *Road to Zero* strategy introduced a voluntary emissions target, there had been no policy to reduce emissions from this sector. Vans, the fastest growing segment of road traffic with their distance travelled increasing by almost 5 per cent in 2016 and 3 per cent in 2017, have also seen a deterioration in CO_2 intensity of late due to reduced operational efficiency. Aviation, particularly international aviation, is still growing faster than economic growth with a 7 per cent increase in the number of passengers flying, a 6 per cent increase in the number of kilometres flown and a 4 per cent increase in the number of flights in 2016. Better load factors and some improvements in fuel efficiency meant that the increase in emissions was kept at only 1 per cent (CCC 2018a).

For all transport modes, fuel diversification needs to happen more quickly. Yet the full lifecycle impact of any transition is another serious consideration. The environmental benefits of EVs are clearly dependent on the carbon intensity of the electricity grid. It is true to say that decarbonisation of the power sector is happening faster than predicted, though some of the easier wins have been secured and the policy towards renewable energy of the current government in 2018 appears less favourable than in recent years. Also, electrification has whole system consequences in that many other parts of the economy, such as heating, are also striving to electrify, and this has implications for the level of grid infrastructure investment required in various parts of the network. Likewise, competition for biofuels, between different transport modes and between transport and other uses such as heat and food, presents a problem given wider sustainability and thus availability issues. Early biofuels policies in the UK (and around the world) had good intent, but were often ill-thought-out in terms of consequences. For the main part, the initial targets were way too ambitious and because this forced the pace of change before the industry was able to comply, numerous ethical and environmental own goals were scored (Royal Academy of Engineering (RAE) 2017). Nevertheless, biofuels may be the only realistic option for aircraft and perhaps shipping. For all transport modes, the uptake of biofuels has reduced or remained flat in recent years at 2.3 per cent by energy in 2017.

Energy efficiency achieved largely through low emission vehicles is not the only approach taken to mitigate carbon and other pollutants from the transport sector. Indeed, especially at the local level, measures attempting to increase walking and cycling, improve public transport services and in some cases, reduce journey lengths and trips do feature in transport plans. Critical breaches of safe air pollution levels have led to the designation of clean air zones or low emission zones in the UK, whereby plans are being made to restrict or charge certain classes of vehicles in different areas at different times. Nevertheless, in most plans, including the CCC recommendations, such measures, including improvements in logistics planning and eco-driving for freight movements, account for a maximum of approximately 5 per cent of potential emissions reductions by 2030. For air quality, the tendency to devolve responsibility to the local level (beyond the economy-wide transition to the car market through regulation and fiscal measures) has received criticism due to the lack of local authority control and political resistance to measures such as low emission zones which have the possibility to ban access to the most polluting vehicles (Brand 2016, see also Bache et al 2015). Given the scale of the challenge of cleaning the air in our cities and towns, many jurisdictions acknowledge that existing strategies, plans and measures may at best deliver the pollutant emissions reductions needed in the medium term to meet local, national or the tougher World Health Organization (WHO) recommended air quality standards, particularly for NO_x (WHO 2016).

This section has focused on the most recent UK government announcements about how it plans to reduce carbon and other pollutants from the transport sector. Had there been broader transport policy documents to draw from which situated the energy and environmental objectives among others related to economic growth (Chapter 2), accessibility (Chapter 4), congestion (Chapter 7), public health (Chapter 8) or place making (Chapter 9), we would have done so, but they do not exist as a holistic strategy (Docherty et al 2018). That in itself summarises the issue at the core of this chapter and to be addressed directly in the next section – that such myopia in policy making has created a form of self-deception which is based on unquestioned faith in efficiency as a route to energy and emissions reductions and broader sustainability objectives.

The failure of energy efficiency

Unpalatable as it is to admit, the level of attention paid to energy efficiency is strongly implicated in the wider failures of transport policy. On the face of it, there can be no good reason to suggest that we should not strive to reduce the amount of energy required to operate a given transport mode or service. Yet the debate is a far more fundamental one. The question is whether this goal has become so embedded in the discourses attached to low carbon transport that it has crowded out discussion of any unintended consequences or, most importantly, where we want the taken-for-granted efficiency pathways to ultimately lead. Even when unintended consequences become impossible to ignore, such as with consumer rebound to larger vehicles or failures of regulation that render efficiency standards meaningless in the 'real world', the deep-rootedness of the energy efficiency paradigm means the 'go to' solution is just *even more* energy efficiency. Even acknowledged failures rarely lead us to 'challenge the conceptual foundations of "efficiency" as a topic in its own right' (Shove 2018a: 779).

Where efficiency measures have reduced energy demand 'in its own terms' (Shove 2018b), the focus on it cannot be equated with any appreciation of the underlying assumptions about the level, trajectory, composition or measure of what is being 'demanded'. For example, the focus on energy efficiency has been successful if judged by the official goals and tests set for the fuel consumed and emissions produced per kilometre by an average new car sold. But where efficiency improvements fail to outpace the increased demand for the number of kilometres driven, they do not lead to absolute reductions in energy used. This has been the situation in the past two years in the UK with respect to energy demands from cars, and much longer with respect to HGVs and aircraft. Unfortunately, the consequences for overall energy use or efficiency gains lagging behind demand are, as with the 'rebound' and regulatory failures cited earlier, themselves taken for granted as essentially part of the efficiency 'formula'. The core issue, therefore, is the embedded belief that energy efficiency improvements are 'a given', like part of a natural evolutionary cycle that, by definition, are inevitably taking us in the right direction. This faith serves to stifle debate around whether those levels of demand are themselves unsustainable and 'in so doing helps perpetuate unsustainable ways of life' (Shove 2018a: 787).

In their rebuttal to Shove, Fawcett and Rosenow (2018: unpaginated) take on her forceful suggestion that energy efficiency perpetuates 'unsustainable concepts of service,' by pointing out that 'by contrast, many detailed studies and scenarios show it is possible to have lower carbon futures through varied mixtures of energy efficiency, fuel switching, better control, demand response and renewable energy, while maintaining current service standards' (they cite studies from the CCC, the IEA and the National Grid). This may indeed be the case in the area of energy efficiency in the home, especially studies which predated the recent 'crisis' report from the IPPC (2018). Increasingly, however, authoritative assessments strongly dispute the suggestion that economy-wide carbon targets can be met without absolute levels of demand reduction, particularly in the transport sector (Brand et al 2019, IPCC 2018). For the first time, the IPCC will include an entire chapter dedicated to demand-side climate solutions in its next (Sixth) assessment report.

Fawcett and Rosenow (2018: unpaginated) settle on the idea that 'good' efficiency is the way forward; that is, to only design energy efficiency measures 'with the aim of reducing total consumption levels rather than focusing on relative efficiency improvements.' Yet, this definition shies away from suggesting that the underlying levels of demand could benefit from some critical discussion, or that targeting demand itself might be a more effective and potentially equitable route to lower energy demands (Mullen and Marsden 2016). Such logic also pervades government thinking: with the exception of some local authority congestion hotspots, any discussion of purposefully reducing the total consumption of energy from transport by reducing the associated mobility demands is absent from UK policy discourse. And this is particularly evident so long as the associated energy sources are assumed to be on their way to being decarbonised. Phil Goodwin explains in Chapter 7 how this has not always been the case: the 1989 traffic forecasts had the effect of sparking the realisation that traffic demands could not be provided for, and demand management, partially supported by the rhetoric of 'reducing the need to travel', entered subsequent policy pronouncements (Department of the Environment (DoE) and Department of Transport (DoT) 1994). This is akin to the debate about 'sufficiency' outside of transport but within core energy demand circles (Darby 2007, Crivits et al 2010). Sufficiency strategies make the levels of energy service itself a target for examination and possible reduction.

A discussion about sufficiency is of course not new and marks the core of the environmental movement in the 1960s and 1970s. But neither the 'need to travel' rhetoric, nor the more fundamental 'small is beautiful' ethos, has impacted the ultimate implementation of sufficiency strategies. Instead these are plagued by negative assumptions around behaviour change and social engineering and accusations of ideological, anti-liberal thinking. Up until around 2010 it was not hard to find references to 'reducing the need to travel' in strategic policy documents, being essentially put forward as a sensible way to make efficient use of the existing network. What could be more efficient than not needing to use energy in the first place? Yet this intention was never actually accompanied by detailed and costed analysis of the measures that could be used to achieve it, and certainly not with the commitment applied to the equivalent assessments undertaken for technical efficiency measures (for example, Kampman et al 2006, Department of Trade and Industry (DTI) 2007).

The 'marginal abatement cost curve' exercises that pervaded carbon mitigation policy during the decade straddling the UK Climate Change Act in 2008 are particularly revealing of the 'commitments and assumptions' (Shove 2018b: unpaginated) involved in the energy efficiency discourse. In summary, results of these exercises are skewed by 'the assumptions about future costs and level of travel demand, the methods applied to compare policies for cost-effectiveness and the evidence base used in relation to different types or combinations of policy instrument' (Anable 2008: 4). Indeed, there were specific biases against demand management policies that stacked the odds very highly against them. Firstly, it was unquestionably assumed that baseline travel demand growth would be a continuation of historical high rates of demand, representing a failure to consider alternative futures and assess needs against a responsive and dynamic trajectory of traffic growth into the future. Indeed, travel demands (that is, vehicle kilometres/tonne kms) are most often an input into energy system models – that is, taken as a given level of mobility to be 'serviced' by more and more efficient vehicles and less carbon intensive fuels. Most of these models cannot adjust a given trajectory of demand increase within the modelling framework, and technologies and fuels are 'optimised' to meet these demands. This serves to reinforce (conceptually and quantitatively) the need for technological solutions: the higher the travel demand assumed, the greater and costlier the task of reducing it.

Secondly, the underlying models assumed any technical measures would be applied *before* any demand management measures. This meant any motorised demand would use less energy mile for mile, thus reducing the net cost-effectiveness of reducing those miles. Such (biased) assumptions about the ordering of impacts requires careful consideration in cost–benefit assessments to date. Thirdly, the evidence on the potential for behavioural measures was put through a much harsher assessment than technical measures. For instance, 'smarter choices', involving packages of tailored behavioural interventions to influence the rate, length and travel mode of local journeys, were subject to harsh judgements about welfare costs, effectiveness and decay rates (Cairns et al 2008). These assumptions were clearly disproportionate considering that the equivalent recognised failures on the technical side, such as rebound effects and the typically slower than expected rates of technology diffusion, were not factored in to modelled assessments in the same way.

Consequently, there have not been meaningful efforts to ensure that any demand management measures are consistently and comprehensively applied. This is especially evident in the disappearance of local facilities and the permissions granted for large traffic generating developments including new 'energy efficient' housing stock (Buchan et al 2018). The phrase 'reducing the need to travel' has all but disappeared from policy discourse, in favour of what might be understood as policy 'pragmatism' representing, at best, aspirations of 'good energy efficiency'. This fluid and somewhat enigmatic role of the energy service demands which form the basis of all energy use is clearly related to the rhetoric of policy making and politics and 'symptom[atic] of much bigger and deeper political battles' (Shove 2018b). But whereas Shove's arguments are undoubtedly situated in the performativity of discourses, ideas and practices, Goodwin (2008: 235) comments more explicitly on the ebbs and flows of communications and actions around travel demand management by suggesting they have 'not, in my view, been a series of U-turns, but instead a series of what might be called "J-turns", or incomplete U-turns – a series of statements, each of which pleases or displeases now one group of stakeholders, and now another, but there is no feeling that there is an overarching vision.' It is to this failure of vision that we now turn.

A new formula for efficiency

Nothing said so far in this chapter suggests that energy efficiency should not be part of the whole energy or transport systems policy mix, alongside the development of renewable and low carbon energy sources and vehicle and travel demand management. Also, it has not been the intention to suggest energy efficiency measures are straightforward and without their challenges financially, behaviourally or politically. Instead, the emphasis here is on the need for a fundamental reconceptualisation and positioning of energy efficiency in the sustainable transport policy agenda. The contention is that we need to stop energy efficiency from being used to reproduce false beliefs that we can change little of what we do but still achieve energy reductions and sustainability (see Chapter 5). To do this, we need to revisit basic notions of the 'work' that we believe energy should be used to perform in the transport system. This takes the pure physics-based notion of energy efficiency as the 'ratio of useful outputs to energy inputs' for a specified system (for example, a motor in a vehicle) (Sorrell 2015) and centres the debate around those useful outputs.

First, then, we must identify the useful outputs from the transport system. For transport, the useful output is typically conceived of in terms of the physical work produced – that is, mobility in the form of vehicle kilometres or, at the very least, a more meaningful measure of the number of passenger or tonne kilometres achieved. Yet such measures disguise and do not engage with the ways in which present and future demands are made, or that efficiency measures will themselves be part of this 'making' process. An approach based on vehicle or even passenger kilometres renders the 'what people do' core element of behaviour to something that is either inevitable (that is, it is in the baseline and ruled by responses to economic conditions that cannot be changed) or what happens once other largely technical solutions have been exhausted. But 'societal needs and demands are not given: they are negotiable, dynamic, and in part constituted by technologies and policies, *including those of efficiency*' (Shove 2018a). This means we do not have to, and should not, take the needed mobility (and therefore energy) services for granted.

Given the plethora of societal objectives for which mobility can be a positive or negative factor, the useful outputs could instead be framed in terms of alternative levels of service in the form of those objectives: accessibility, job security, wellbeing, obesity reduction. But even once they are defined, how is 'enough' determined and who determines it? Darby's (2007) review of some of the sufficiency literature shows how it is both a quantitative and qualitative concept. Where energy services are concerned, it involves setting minimum standards for services as well as for the technology that provides them, as well as maximum permissible environmental impacts. Still, defining what energy or energy services people 'need' (as opposed to want) is problematic. Concrete values for sufficient use levels can hardly ever be achieved with rational arguments. There is no clear agreement that energy or energy service needs can be distinguished from energy wants, with an immense literature on the subject (Dobson 1995, Faiers et al 2007, Walker et al 2016). There is a long history of debate over meanings of sufficiency, excess and luxury versus necessary consumption, which continues (Fawcett 2016). But, as difficult as this may be, without tackling the question of need, we are still in danger of using more and more energy to satisfy any given outcome.

Many of the challenges to rapid and early decarbonisation of the car sector stem from a perception of public hostility towards coercive demand reduction policies (hence an aversion to stringent interventions) and the inability of voluntary demand management to deliver deep reductions in car use. Consequently, policies have favoured incremental technological approaches focusing primarily on reducing the carbon intensity of fuels and, to a lesser extent, vehicles, thus sustaining politically convenient interpretations about levels of service and need. Even stated policy intentions to 'reduce the need to travel' meant reducing the number or length of journeys or both, not reducing the freedom to travel. Any effort to avoid questions of need is arguably related to the narrow conceptualisation of routes to energy demand or emissions reduction in this sector (and others). A reconceptualisation requires attention to be refocused onto what mobility/energy, and so on is for. A pragmatic approach in transport would be to at least think about what comes together to influence different journey purposes and how these might develop over time. A social practice perspective would provide an even more radically different framing which takes thinking far away from discrete moments and individuals to looking at bundles of activities which bring together the means by which certain end projects (for example, eating, working, caring) are performed (Shove and Walker 2014). The way in which these projects or practices come to be, grow and change is the key to understanding technology adoption and use and final energy demands. A social practice approach also moves the focus away from individual behaviour and looks at the potential for change at the level of institutions, cultures and societies (Chapter 5).

To apply a social practice lens to reformulate interventions for energy and emission reductions would be a significant undertaking but could lead to a longer-term systems perspective that brings innovative cross-cutting projections and measures to the fore. Indeed, this perspective leads quickly to the realisation that the transport or energy 'system' is far more than infrastructure and technology, patterns of travel are not as they are due to transport policy and energy demands are relatively untouched by energy policies. Instead, the impact of 'non-energy policy on energy demand' needs to be acknowledged (Royston et al 2018). While we spend a lot of effort debating the abatement potential of individual measures, the scale of this potential is likely to be dwarfed in some cases by wider trends or events such as changes to the pensionable age, to the type of work in the economy, to the education system, to the way we communicate, to the move back to urban living. In many ways, society is changing in ways which makes flexibility an increasing feature or possibility. *Do we want to shape all of this change or are we going to be shaped by it?* In this context, where *behaviour is already changing*, this presents an opportunity to explore how this lower traffic growth trajectory could be *deliberately* locked in (Chapter 16). Instead, the overwhelming message from the framing of current policy assumptions and attention is that 'you can continue to live your lives as you do now' when this is not going to happen anyway (that is, things are always changing) and is not necessarily what people want. This may mean relaxing the emphasis on voluntary paths to progress. Mandatory action in a liberal democracy may be seen as viable only in extreme circumstances. When is the number of attributable deaths to transport activity extreme enough?

Conclusions

In our chapter we have illustrated how trying to address climate change and dangerously poor air quality with a focus on the fuel burnt within the transport system has essentially failed: primary energy used is on the rise and global and local pollution is at critical levels. Other societal objectives, to which the transport system is a key contributor, are also not being met. Yet, even while in the midst of this storm and increasing evidence that there will be a misalignment between the techno-optimistic solutions and the deadlines for action, the solution space is narrowing. It would appear that any focus and urgency placed on carbon emissions and local air pollutants serves to funnel even more attention to the fuel that is burnt in the vehicles. In other words, the attention paid to technological solutions is arguably increasing, not diminishing. The goals of current policy for sustainable transport systems are to develop strategies assuring constant or increasing levels of mobility with decreasing energy input, while at the same time decarbonising those sources of energy. Even if full decarbonisation were achieved, the goal of maximum energy efficiency would still be desired in order to allow more and more growth (the 'work' of energy) to happen. Thus, it is the premise and definition of growth that explains the taken for granted central position of energy efficiency in transport policy.

The focus on energy efficiency as a route to reduction and sustainability has crowded out alternative visions of the energy service levels themselves and, by so doing, has facilitated increasingly unsustainable demands for those energy services, especially mobility. While there are situations where this is beneficial – for example, by delivering mobility to people who would not otherwise be able to access it – we have contended that if emissions, local or global, are to be reduced on any significant scale, then it is essential to consider the meanings and levels of service and the types of consumption and demand that efficiency policies support and perpetuate. The implication is that it is not only new measures to reach current goals of emissions reductions that will be required; it will also be necessary to re-examine those goals with a focus on the level of mobility and what it is for. This may require moving not so much towards an energy transition as towards a political transition that better recognises plural forms of energy, efficiency and sustainability.

Note

[1] Ivan Illich's *The Social Construction of Energy* was written in 1983 but only published in 2010 by *New Geographies*, a journal out of Harvard University's Graduate School of Design. This paper serves as a follow-up to and rethinking of his provocative and widely quoted essay *Energy & Equity* published in 1974.

References

Anable, J (2008) *The cost-effectiveness of carbon abatement in the transport sector*. Report for the Campaign for Better Transport. https:// bettertransport.org.uk/sites/default/files/research-files/Carbon_ abatement_research.pdf Accessed 20 October 2018.

Anable, J and Boardman, B (2005) *Transport and CO$_2$*. UKERC Working Paper. www.ukerc.ac.uk/publications/transport-and-CO$_2$. html Accessed 20 October 2018.

Anderson, K (2015) 'Duality in climate science', *Nature Geoscience*, 8: 898–900.

Bache, I, Bartle, I, Flinders, M and Marsden, G (2015) 'Blame games and climate change: accountability, multi-level governance and carbon management', *The British Journal of Politics and International Relations*, 17(1): 64–88.

Begg, D and Haigh, C (2018) *The unintended consequences of freezing fuel duty*. Report for Greener Journeys. https://greenerjourneys.com/publication/the-unintended-consequences-of-freezing-fuel-duty/ Accessed 20 October 2018.

Brand, C (2016) 'Beyond "Dieselgate": Implications of unaccounted and future air pollutant emissions and energy use for cars in the United Kingdom', *Energy Policy*, 97: 1–12.

Brand, C and Hunt, A (2018) *The health costs of air pollution from cars and vans. Report for Clean Air Day 2018*. Global Action Plan, London. www.cleanairday.org.uk/News/the-health-costs-of-air-pollution-from-cars-and-vans Accessed 20 October 2018.

Brand, C, Anable, J and Morton, C (2019) 'Lifestyle, efficiency and limits: modelling transport energy and emissions using a sociotechnical approach', *Energy Efficiency*, 12(1): 187–207.

Buchan, S, Billinger, J and Petts, J (2018) *Transport for new homes: Project summary and recommendations*. www.transportfornewhomes.org.uk/wp-content/uploads/2018/07/transport-for-new-homes-summary-web.pdf Accessed 20 October 2018.

Cairns, S, Sloman, L, Newson, C, Anable, J, Kirkbride, A and Goodwin, P (2008) 'Smarter choices: assessing the potential to achieve traffic reduction using "soft measures"', *Transport Reviews*, 28(5): 593–618.

Committee on Climate Change (2018a) *Reducing UK emissions – 2018 progress report to parliament*. /www.theccc.org.uk/publication/reducing-uk-emissions-2018-progress-report-to-parliament/ Accessed 31 October 2018.

Committee on Climate Change (2018b) *Government's road to zero strategy falls short, CCC says*. CCC Press Release, 10 July 2018. www.theccc.org.uk/2018/07/10/governments-road-to-zero-strategy-falls-short-ccc-says/ Accessed 20 October 2018.

Creutzig, F (2015) 'Evolving narratives of low-carbon futures in transportation', *Transport Reviews*, 36(3): 341–60.

Crivits, M, Paredis, E, Boulanger, P, Mutombo, E, Bauler, T and Lefin, A (2010) Scenarios based on sustainability discourses: constructing alternative consumption and consumer perspectives, *Futures*, 42(10): 1187–99.

Darby, S (2007) Enough is as good as a feast – sufficiency as policy. In *Proceedings, European Council for an Energy-Efficient Economy*. La Colle sur Loup, June.

Department for Business, Energy and Industrial Strategy (2018) *Final UK greenhouse gas emissions national statistics 1990–2016*. www.gov.uk/government/statistics/final-uk-greenhouse-gas-emissions-national-statistics-1990-2016 Accessed 31 October 2018.

Department for Transport (2018) *The road to zero*. https://assets.publishing.service.gov.uk/government/uploads/system/uploads/attachment_data/file/739460/road-to-zero.pdf Accessed 31 October 2018.

Department of the Environment and Department of Transport (1994) *Department of the Environment and Department of Transport planning policy guidance: Transport PPG 13 (revised)*. London: HMSO.

Department of Trade and Industry (2007) *Synthesis of the analysis of the energy white paper*. URN 07/971. DTI, London.

Dobson, A (1995) *Green Political Thought*, London: Routledge.

Docherty, I, Shaw, J, Marsden, G and Anable, J (2018) 'The curious death – and life? – of British transport policy', *Environment and Planning C: Politics and Space*, 36(8): 1458–79.

Faiers, A, Cook, M and Neame, C (2007) 'Towards a contemporary approach for understanding consumer behaviour in the context of domestic energy use', *Energy Policy*, 35: 4381–90.

Fawcett, T (2016) *Policy and extreme energy consumption*. Paper presented for DEMAND Centre Conference, Lancaster, 13–15 April 2016.

Fawcett, T and Rosenow, J (2018) 'Writing the wrongs of energy efficiency', *Bricommunity.net* https://bricommunity.net/2018/01/04/commentary-writing-the-wrongs-of-energy-efficiency/ Accessed 20 October 2018.

Goodwin, P (2008) 'Traffic jam? Policy debates after 10 years of "sustainable" transport', in I Docherty and J Shaw (eds) *Traffic Jam: Ten Years of 'Sustainable' Transport in the UK*, Bristol: Policy Press, pp 231–39.

Grigoratos, T and Martini, G (2015) 'Brake wear particle emissions: a review', *Environmental Science and Pollution Research*, 22(4): 2491–504.

Hafner, R, Walker, I and Verplanken, B (2017) 'Image, not environmentalism: a qualitative exploration of factors influencing vehicle purchasing decisions', *Transportation Research Part A: Policy and Practice*, 97: 89–105.

Hitchcock, G, Conlan, B, Kay, D, Brannigan, C and Newman, D (2014) *Air quality and road transport: impacts and solutions*. RAC Foundation. www.racfoundation.org/wp-content/uploads/2017/11/racf_ricardo_aea_air_quality_report_hitchcock_et_al_june_2014.pdf Accessed 31 October 2018.

HM Government (2011) *The carbon plan. Delivering our low carbon future*. https://assets.publishing.service.gov.uk/government/uploads/system/uploads/attachment_data/file/47613/3702-the-carbon-plan-delivering-our-low-carbon-future.pdf Accessed 31 October 2018.

HM Government (2017) *The clean growth strategy. Leading the way to a low carbon future*. https://assets.publishing.service.gov.uk/government/uploads/system/uploads/attachment_data/file/700496/clean-growth-strategy-correction-april-2018.pdf Accessed 31 October 2018.

House of Commons (2018) *Improving air quality*. Environment, Food and Rural Affairs, Environmental Audit, Health and Social Care, and Transport Committees, London. Accessed 18 April 2018 at: https://publications.parliament.uk/pa/cm201719/cmselect/cmenvfru/433/43305.htm Accessed 26 February 2019.

Illich, I (1974) *Energy and Equity*, London: Marion Boyars.

Illich, I (2010) 'The social construction of energy', *New Geographies*, 2: 11–19.

Intergovernmental Panel on Climate Change (2014) *Fifth assessment report*, Cambridge: Cambridge University Press.

Intergovernmental Panel on Climate Change (2018) *Global warming of 1.5°C, Special Report*. www.ipcc.ch/report/sr15/ Accessed 5 October 2018

International Council on Clean Transportation (2018) *The role of standards in reducing CO_2 emissions of passenger cars in the EU*. www.theicct.org/sites/default/files/publications/Role_of_EU-CO2_Standard_20180212.pdf Accessed 31 October 2018.

International Energy Agency (2018a) *Key world energy statistics 2018*. International Energy Agency. www.iea.org/statistics/kwes/consumption/ Accessed 16 October 2018.

International Energy Agency (2018b) *CO_2 emissions from fuel combustion overview*. International Energy Agency, Paris. https://webstore.iea.org/co2-emissions-from-fuel-combustion-2018-overview Accessed 26 February 2019.

International Energy Agency (2018c) *Global EV Outlook 2018*. https://webstore.iea.org/global-ev-outlook-2018 Accessed 16 October 2018.

International Transport Forum (2017) *ITF transport outlook 2017*, Paris: OECD Publishing. http://dx.doi.org/10.1787/9789282108000-en Accessed 31 October 2018.

Kampman, B, de Bruyn, S and den Boer, E (2006) *Cost-effectiveness of CO_2 mitigation in transport*. Report to the European Conference of Ministers of Transport, Delft.

Landrigan, P et al (2018) 'The Lancet commission on pollution and health', *The Lancet*, 391: 462–512.

Mullen, C and Marsden, G (2016) 'Mobility justice in low carbon transitions', *Energy Research and Social Science*, 18: 109–17.

Royal Academy of Engineering (2017) *Sustainability of liquid biofuels*. www.raeng.org.uk/publications/reports/biofuels Accessed 31 October 2018.

Royston, S, Selby, J and Shove, E (2018) 'Invisible energy policies: a new agenda for energy demand reduction', *Energy Policy*, 123: 127–35.

Shove, E (2018a) 'What is wrong with energy efficiency?', *Building Research & Information*, 46(7): 779–89.

Shove, E (2018b) 'Response: writing the wrongs of energy efficiency', *Bricommunity.net* https://bricommunity.net/2018/01/04/commentary-writing-the-wrongs-of-energy-efficiency/ Accessed 20 October 2018.

Shove, E and Walker, G (2014) 'What is energy for? Social practice and energy demand', *Theory Culture and Society*, 31(5): 41–58.

Society of Motor Manufacturers and Traders (2018) *New car CO_2 report. The 17th Report*. www.smmt.co.uk/wp-content/uploads/sites/2/SMMT-New-Car-Co2-Report-2018-artwork.pdf Accessed 31 October 2018.

Sorrell, S (2007) *The rebound effect: an assessment of the evidence for economy-wide energy savings from improved energy efficiency*. UKERC report. www.ukerc.ac.uk/programmes/technology-and-policy-assessment/the-rebound-effect-report.html Accessed 31 October 2018.

Sorrell, S (2015) 'Reducing energy demand: A review of issues, challenges and approaches', *Renewable and Sustainable Energy Reviews*, 47: 74–82.

Tietge, U, Mock, P, German, J, Bandivadekar, A and Ligterink, N (2017) *From laboratory to road. A 2017 update of official and 'real world' consumption and CO_2 values for passenger cars in Europe*. International Council on Clean Transportation Europe. www.theicct.org/publications/laboratory-road-2017-update Accessed 31 October 2018.

Turnbull, T (2017) *From paradox to policy: the problem of energy resource conservation in Britain and America, 1865–1981.* Thesis submitted for the Degree of Doctor of Philosophy, School of Geography and the Environment, University of Oxford.

United Nations Framework Convention on Climate Change (2015) *Adoption of the Paris Agreement.* Report No. FCCC/CP/2015/L.9/ Rev.1, http://unfccc.int/resource/docs/2015/cop21/eng/l09r01. pdf Accessed 31 October 2018.

Walker, G, Simcock, N and Day, R (2016) 'Necessary energy uses and a minimum standard of living in the United Kingdom: energy justice or escalating expectations?', *Energy Research & Social Science*, 18: 129–38.

Walnum, H, Alle, C and Løkke, S (2014) 'Can rebound effects explain why sustainable mobility has not been achieved?', *Sustainability*, 6(12): 9510–37.

World Health Organization (2016) *Burden of disease from ambient and household air pollution*, WHO, Copenhagen. www.who.int/phe/ health_topics/outdoorair/databases/en/ Accessed 21 January 2016.

4

Social inclusion, accessibility and emotional work

Jennie Middleton and Justin Spinney

Introduction

This chapter is about issues of inclusion, equality and accessibility in relation to everyday mobility. Along with others (for example, Bhat et al 2000, Curtis 2011, Simoes 2013, Ganning 2014, Martens 2017) we argue that accessibility to transport is essentially an issue of social justice and social mobility; accessibility is crucial for all groups in society to facilitate opportunities in order to accrue social, economic and cultural capital. Yet despite much progress in recent years, there remains a great deal to do in tackling transport-related social exclusion. Indeed, as stated in a Commission for Architecture and the Built Environment (CABE) (2008: 3) report, 'social, cultural and economic inequalities are still being literally built into new places, and planners and designers need to examine more closely the impact of their decisions.' There is already a sizeable literature on equality and accessibility (Martens 2017, Martínez et al 2017, Ricci et al 2016), but our argument here is that studies to date have been overly concerned with the *'objective' causes* of (in)accessibility, such as the proximity of a transport interchange, and the *outcomes* of (in)accessibility, such as the inability to get a job. Much less attention has been focused on 'making', 'gaining' or 'doing' access – in other words, the *experience* of actually being mobile, of taking a journey, in the context of how it relates to accessibility more generally. In particular, there is little on what we term the 'emotional work' involved in gaining accessibility, and how this is unequally distributed between social groups.

Accessibility can be defined as 'a measure of the ease of an individual to pursue an activity of a desired type, at a desired location, by a desired mode, and at a desired time' (Bhat et al 2000, in Ganning 2014: 5). Definitions such as Bhat et al's might imply an emotional component, with its reference to 'ease', but important elements of accessibility such as affective, embodied and emotional exertion remain marginalised concerns in the literature. Indeed, most current measures of accessibility – a good example is Transport for London's (TfL's) (2015) tool for assessing transport connectivity, Public Transport Accessibility Level (PTAL) – assume journeys are being taken by non-disabled, male commuters and fail to take into account different bodies, temporal requirements or social safety concerns of different users, and how these can affect ease of accessibility. Such factors are unevenly distributed among the population in the same way as cost (affordability of transport) and distance (proximity of services) as sources of inequality.

The notion of emotional work is not new, and can be deployed in different ways. For example, the concept of emotional labour emerged in relation to the work required of employees, in a range of different employment settings, to maintain the quality of interactions with their clients (Hochschild 1979, 1983). In discursive psychology, emotional work can be considered in relation to the 'work' that people do with talk of emotions, in terms of '"avowing" their own or "ascribing" them to other people' (Edwards, 1997: 170). Here we employ a slightly different understanding of emotional work, defining it as *the extra emotional work and impact on the individual of having to adapt to, and perform within, a mobility system that does not accommodate their needs.* As such, emotional work encompasses the additional frustration, anxiety, stress, vulnerability and so on that some users experience as a result of having to use and adapt to a system not necessarily designed with them in mind. Our reading of the concept shares with Hochschild's the idea that the greater the emotional work, the higher the chance of emotional exhaustion and/or aversion behaviours.

We foreground this lack of sustained attention on the emotional work of accessibility to help refine conceptions of inequality and equity in relation to accessibility. By identifying and explaining emotional work and how it varies between different people, we are contributing to an enhanced understanding of inequality of access, not just as it relates to 'objective' causes and outcomes of (in)accessibility, but also how it is related to the very act of being on the move. A truly just mobility system would place the same or a minimal burden of emotional work on all users, regardless of their differing needs. We will show how in our current mobility systems there is an unequal distribution of work across different user groups, with the result that some people must work significantly harder to achieve the same levels of access as others. A key point about emotional work is that it is internalised, rarely visible and hard to quantify, unlike traditional measures of access (in)equality such as journey cost, proximity to and availability of services. It is well known that the focus of much transport research and policy has been on 'objective' and 'tangible' qualities rather than on 'softer' social qualities that are far more difficult to measure (Vella-Brodrick and Stanley 2013).

Lucas (2012) points out that a more nuanced understanding of journey time – another traditionally easily quantified measure – as a factor of (in)accessibility has emerged in recent years, through accounts of how the demands of tight scheduling, multi-tasking and multiple responsibilities are experienced differently by different populations. Structural changes in society and the economy have created new inequalities in the opportunities that are available to different people within given timeframes, causing time-poverty based exclusion for certain social groups, particularly working women with children (Uteng 2009) and those living in rural areas and on peripheral urban estates (Lucas 2004). This new focus on time-poverty is undoubtedly helpful and illuminating, although it still tends to rely on linear conceptualisations of time, or 'clock-time passing'. We would suggest that understanding time simply as a resource that people have more or less access to runs the risk of overlooking the significance of how people actually *experience* time on the move (see, for example, Watts 2008) and how this experience is significant in terms of transport-related (in)accessibility. An important part of our focus on the emotional work of accessibility considers the multiple temporalities which collide, and the associated 'temporal work' that arises, as different groups attempt to gain access through mobility.

To set the scene, we continue our chapter with a review of the broader literature on social exclusion and accessibility to transport. In particular, we reflect upon the different ways in which accessibility has been conceptualised and the inequalities that are associated with/ produced by differing levels of (in)accessibility. This leads us to highlight the importance of focusing on the *process* of (in)accessibility rather than just its 'objective' causes and outcomes, a point we then develop with reference to our own research on both the everyday experiences of new mothers and visually impaired young people as they negotiate the transport system in London.

Inclusion, equality and accessibility

Issues of inclusion, equality and accessibility in transport research have grown substantially in prominence over the last two decades, especially in relation to how transport systems play a role in shaping social exclusion (see, for example, Farrington 2007, Hine and Mitchell

2001, Lucas and Musso 2014, Rajé, 2007). Consistent with other areas of public policy (for example, urban regeneration, public health), the factors that make a transport system more or less accessible are numerous. One such factor is cost (see Brennan et al 2014). Preston and Rajé (2007) argue that where the price of transport exceeds its affordability, social exclusion occurs. The policy recommendations emerging from such research include reducing the price of transport, increasing social contact through virtual mobility, reducing distance of facilities/contacts through land-use planning, and/or increasing incomes. Another key determinant is the mode of transport available to access locations and services. Kawabata and Shen (2007) demonstrate the difference between those with access to a car and those relying on public transport in their ability to access jobs in the San Francisco Bay area. Their analysis shows that when using a car, most areas within 60 km can be considered accessible in terms of time and cost, but when using public transport the accessible area shrinks to only a small part of the immediate metropolitan area within 7 kilometres of the centre. The design of the built environment is also important in determining accessibility. Using a GIS-based mapping tool of the local walking environment and data collected through footfall surveys, Mackett et al (2008) demonstrate the importance of micro-level infrastructure for some disadvantaged groups. Similarly, Imrie (2000a, 2000b, 2000c) argues for an understanding of the inaccessibility of different environments for wheelchair users as premised upon (mis)alignments of perceived and actual bodily needs. Experiences of disability – and to some extent associated emotional work – have been explored in relation to material infrastructure, vehicle design and informational mobility (Edwards and Imrie 2003, Lavery et al 1996, Pyer and Tucker 2014, Rosenkvist et al 2010).

Since the publication of the Social Exclusion Unit's (SEU) (2003) report *Making Connections*, numerous academic studies have explored the various issues of mobility, accessibility and transport disadvantages in different geographical contexts in the UK. A key contribution of these studies has been to identify the highly complex and person-specific nature of transport-related exclusion: the experiences of low-income rural and urban residents are clearly different and these differences are further cross-cut by other social factors (for example, Rajé 2007, Preston and Rajé 2007). According to Rajé (2007: 43), five social groups are likely to experience problems accessing transport: disabled people, the elderly, women, those on low incomes and minority ethnic groups. As Cahill (2010) notes, if driving licences were given out based on need, then those unable to walk would be first in the queue, although in reality some 60 per cent of disabled people do not have access to a car and are a fifth more likely than non-disabled people to use the bus (Chapter 14). Those with a physical, sensory or learning disability are also less likely to use 'active' modes such as walking and cycling. Consequently, disabled people are less mobile overall: according to Rajé (2007) they make roughly half as many journeys as non-disabled people, and those journeys that are made tend to be shorter. The implications of this are stark: the SEU (2003) found that half of all disabled people had turned down a job interview because of the absence of accessible transport. As a direct result, while 80 per cent of working age, non-disabled people are in employment, only half of those with a physical, sensory or learning disability have a job. Poor accessibility for disabled people is also characterised by a negatively reinforcing combination of low income and inaccessible environments.

Older people also have greater problems with mobility than the general population. In the UK, 18 per cent of adults aged 60–69 have a mobility difficulty compared to 12 per cent of everyone aged 16 and over (Department for Transport (DfT) 2012; see also Chapter 14). Jones et al (2016) have emphasised the link between social capital and spatial mobility, stating the importance of access to transport, for maintaining networks and enhancing wellbeing. This is particularly important in later life when these networks tend to diminish, and access to a car has been correlated with greater participation in social activities and improved perceptions of quality of life for the elderly (Banister and Bowling 2004, Gray et al 2006, Johnson et al 2017). Social capital has been shown to have a significant relationship with accessibility across all groups, not just the elderly. In the context of people's need to be able to participate in civil society (Preston and Rajé 2007), Frei et al (2009) note the importance of social networks, as these are generally seen to be the main way in which individuals and communities maintain their social capital. The stronger the social network, the greater the level of social capital, and thereby access to life opportunities and resources. Frei et al (2009) identified that car ownership and its associated mobility had a positive effect on the size and strength of their respondents' social networks, while those who faced mobility constraints were less likely to be able to build and maintain social capital (Chapter 14). Viry et al (2009) found much the same thing in their study locations of Zurich, Genoa and Basel, with disadvantaged groups such as migrants, those with little or no education, disabled people and women with children particularly affected.

Indeed, women as a group consistently experience mobility constraints. This is for several reasons. Firstly, they tend to shoulder multiple responsibilities as carers, workers and for domestic work. As a result, women not only make shorter journeys than men – who tend to travel much further – but their journeys are also more complex and require more planning (Rajé 2007). Women are more reliant on walking and public transport, something that means that those females in rural areas without access to a car experience greater exclusion because of the paucity of public transport. It is also the case that women are much more likely to avoid making journeys in certain places and at night due to fears over personal safety, and are less likely to use public transport for this reason (Markovich and Lucas 2011). Those travelling with young children also tend to experience public transport very differently, experiencing many of the same issues as wheelchair users such as longer waiting times and lack of independence, and it is not unknown for women with pushchairs to come into conflict with wheelchair users on public transport with limited wheelchair/buggy space (Rajé 2007, BBC 2017). As a result, while transport systems may on the face of it appear equally accessible to men and women, in reality they are anything but, due to the gendered nature of caring and personal safety (see also Uteng and Cresswell 2008, Lucas and Musso 2014).

According to the DfT (2011) only half of the poorest in society, those in the bottom income quintile, have access to a car compared with 90 per cent in the top quintile. Those on low incomes make fewer journeys overall, but twice as many on foot and three times as many by bus, as those in the highest income deciles (Hine and Mitchell 2001). Minority ethnic groups in the UK often experience similar accessibility issues as those on low incomes because of the relationship between the two factors. This is further cut across by specific cultural issues. Begum (2014) found in the case of cycling in London that Muslim women effectively felt excluded from cycling, because of its cultural status as an immodest activity and existing 'honour codes' held by first generation community members regarding how Muslim women should comport themselves. In a Norwegian study, Uteng (2009) researched the mobility patterns and transport-related exclusion of non-Western female immigrants, identified as particularly isolated from mainstream economic and social participation in Norwegian society. Like Begum (2014), she found that transport becomes a highly internalised personal confine acting against accessibility and integration.

Accessibility as process

Despite these significant social inequalities and the ways in which they shape individuals' access to transport and services, measures of accessibility exhibit gendered, ableist, racialised, classed and aged assumptions. In most instances studies of accessibility have involved detailed local accessibility mapping of local travel survey data in combination with the transport system, using enhanced GIS-based tools. Crucially, though, Preston and Rajé (2007) and Martens (2017) argue that this emphasis on aggregate measures of accessibility is counter-productive and ignores differing levels of individual accessibility within any given area. TfL's PTAL (2015), for example, assumes a walking speed of 4.8km/h, that journeys end at a station entrance, that all users have the same perceptions of social safety (and thus can walk any route at any time), that terrain will be flat, and that all users travel at times of peak demand (and thus most frequent services). Accordingly, the accessibility values it produces are arguably only applicable to non-disabled, commuting men travelling in daylight in areas with no hills.

In a review of transport disadvantage, Lucas (2012) picks up on this point, arguing that social exclusion in relation to transport policy should force a focus not only on the economic and social outcomes of exclusion, but also, crucially, the experience of disadvantage. Preston and Rajé (2007: 151) agree, suggesting that exclusion should be conceptualised as 'more of a process than an end-state.' What then, of this *process*, this experience of actually securing access through mobility? Or, put more simply, this experience of being on the move? Undeniably, the process of journey making is easier for some people than it is for others, even where a transport system exists and is relatively affordable and extensive. Those working in the Access/ Design for All area have long understood such concerns (see Design for All Foundation 2018), but have concentrated more on system attributes than the issue of emotional work of interest to us here. Bringing such issues centre-stage requires us to follow Lucas (2012) and Preston and Rajé's (2007) calls to think of accessibility in terms of process, although we also make explicit the related concepts of quality and choice. In essence, in order for something to be equally accessible, all users of a mobility system should expend a comparable amount of work – including emotional work – in the process of gaining their access; everyone should be able to attain the same journey quality, and have a choice in how they make a given journey in order to give priority to those journey qualities they value most highly.

A key component of this conception of accessibility is *adaptation*, considered here as a process of change. Adaptation, we would suggest, imposes a cost on the user, and those who have to adapt very little experience the least cost while those who must adapt more experience a greater cost. Any design of built environments and objects (and specifically the interaction between the two) that fails to accommodate a diversity of bodily, familial and practical circumstances requires greater adaptation of some users to achieve the same goal. The extra cost of any adaptation is experienced by the user as work. For example, an 'ideal' mobility system, accessible to all, would be one constituted by 'good' inclusive design[1] of objects and environments. A system compliant with the principles of inclusive design requires little adaptation from passengers and is therefore easier for the greatest number of people, regardless of their circumstances, to use. An inclusive bus service would demand little of young and old, disabled and non-disabled men and women, at all times of day; it would require a minimal and equal amount of adaptation and as such a minimal amount of additional *work*, by all types of passenger. As we have explained, it is the emotional work and associated temporal work of adaptation that we wish to address for the remainder of the chapter.

Studies in organisational contexts demonstrate the presence of emotional exhaustion and corresponding reduction in satisfaction for those employed in roles where emotional work is most prevalent (Hochschild, 1983). In a similar vein, we argue here that in transport studies instances where journeys are avoided altogether because of the additional perceived or actual work of making the journey are not only due to additional financial, temporal and physical costs, but should in part be seen as the result of additional emotional costs. Pyer and Tucker's (2014) research on the experiences of becoming mobile for a group of young wheelchair users is one of the few studies that engages with issues around the impacts of accessibility as actually experienced. Reporting on the experiences of becoming mobile for this group, Pyer and Tucker (2014: 8) use the term 'transport anxiety' to conceptualise the emotional work of becoming mobile and accessing places and services. They argue that: 'rather than representing mobility as a means of accessing leisure spaces, public transport was often viewed in a negative way by the teenagers, (re)presenting instead their bodies as dependent and frustrated. In this research, both parents and young people could be identified as experiencing transport anxiety.'

Through such accounts we begin to see accessibility as not only something that is attained (or not) as an end state, but as something practised and always in process (access as a verb, in the sense of *doing*).

When we see accessibility as a process, we are sensitised to the work that it requires as an ongoing accomplishment. In the next sections we build upon Pyer and Tucker's work by showing how transport anxiety is not confined to those with physical impairments, such as wheelchair users. We begin by focusing on the outcomes of one of our research projects (Justin's) with new mothers in London, to highlight how the concept can also arise at different life stages due to the ways in which these (temporarily) reshape our capabilities.

Anticipating emotional work

The *Making Mobile Mothers* project involved 20 households in three inner-city East London neighbourhoods (Hackney, Islington and Newham) in 2011 and 2012 (see also Boyer and Spinney 2016). Parents in these households were contacted through antenatal classes and asked to complete a mapping exercise, travel diary and in-depth interview approximately three months prior to the due date of their first child, and six to eight months afterwards. During the course of the project Justin almost exclusively researched the experiences of new mothers. While we acknowledge that men also have roles as carers, in contemporary Britain the burden of caring and associated inequalities still fall disproportionately on women. As such it was their experiences that were of interest in the first instance.

The first thing evident in accounts of journeys is the way in which anxieties were generated through anticipating what it would be like to travel in public transport with a young child:

> 'I can see in the bus, sometimes the driver don't stop because the buggy is open, the woman is waiting with the buggy open, and plus inside the bus is full, there's already two buggies there, so they don't stop and they start arguing and, oh, so I can see myself in a few months (laughs)… I look and say, "Oh, my gosh. It's going to be me in the future" (laughs). But it's true, it's true. Most of them, they say, "Oh, you need to close the buggy," but the baby's sleeping. How's she going to carry the baby and the buggy closed and then, no, it's hard? I think, if you have a car, it's easier to travel.' (Carla)

In this first quote from Carla, when she was six months pregnant, we see a form of adaptation required by the mother – closing the buggy – because of the way she and baby are hybridised with the buggy, and its incompatibility with the design and usage of the bus. We also get a sense of how, through watching other mums, this adaptation is perceived to require additional emotional work, in particular the anxiety caused by not knowing if you can get on the bus, the stress of arguing with the driver and other passengers and the upset and frustration at having to close the buggy and wake the sleeping baby. Indeed, as Carla says, even though she has very little money she would rather try and save for a car because she thinks travel will be much easier. What Carla is referring to here is that she believes the journey by car would produce less anxiety, stress and frustration.

The diary data from the study demonstrated how such anticipation translated into real stress, as in this example from Laura when taking her baby on the Tube:

> Monday 3pm: Went from Dalston to Walthamstow to view a flat by train with Milla in the pram. Journey took 35 minutes, I had to carry the pram up the steps at the train station, no one offered to help.

> Monday 4.30pm: Went to view another flat. Journey took ten minutes. I was feeling tired and it was cold, I wished I could get in a car.

> Friday 1.30pm: Home from Walthamstow having viewed another flat. Journey took 30 minutes. Tiring, was very tired from all the viewings and was dreading the stairs at the end of the journey. I was really struggling getting the pram and everything down them and near the bottom a man helped me, was very grateful. Was relieved to get home. (Laura, second diary)

These excerpts from Laura's diary were written when her baby was around five months old. Laura points to the additional physical work required when moving with her baby/buggy – feeling tired, cold, carrying and struggling with the buggy up steps at train stations – and also the additional emotional work compared to if she were making the journey alone, that is, without buggy and baby. This is illustrated in the language she uses: the fact she was "dreading" the journey home, feeling "alone" when no one offered help, and the "relief" when someone offered to help. What we want to highlight here is that despite the ubiquity of the hybridised figure of the mother (woman plus buggy plus baby), it is not a type of user that public transport has necessarily been scripted to accommodate, nor one that social norms take account of. As a result, in trying to negotiate the system, the mother is required to do much more physical *and* emotional work than other users whose capabilities align more closely with those anticipated by the system's designers.

In addition to expressing a preference for using private cars to avoid excessive emotional work, other new mothers such as Tamana related how they began to avoid some journeys altogether because they did not want to endure the additional emotional work:

> Saturday 12pm: Went clothes shopping to Ilford with my baby on the bus. Journey took 30 minutes. It was the first time I got on the bus with a pushchair. I didn't like it – too squashy and packed. Nowhere to sit.

> Sunday 3pm: Planned to go the city shopping by tube with my baby but changed my mind as I didn't want to go in the train with a pushchair – was too scared! (Tamanna, second diary)

Here the extra emotional work of adapting to the public transport system is seen to contribute to 'aversion behaviours' (Geurs et al 2009), as Tamana's experience of using the bus one day puts her off enduring the train on the next day. Whether due to a temporary or more permanent misalignment between user capabilities and mobility system, what we highlight here is the additional emotional work this misalignment produces and the implications of this for understanding inequalities in accessibility. Accordingly, emotional work needs to be viewed as an impact and cost in its own right.

Temporal work

Associated with emotional work is the notion of temporal work, which forms the basis of discussion in this second empirical section. We report upon research conducted by Jennie between 2014 and 2016 for a small-scale, exploratory study developed in collaboration with the Royal Society for Blind Children (RSBC), to investigate concerns about independent mobility and the everyday mobility practices and experiences of visually impaired young people. Eight respondents were recruited through the charity to take part in the pilot study that involved recording some of their everyday journeys using a 'Go-Pro' camera and follow-up interviews to discuss some of the footage and the broader issues it raised. One of the participants, Ali, was 27 years old and has a small degree of peripheral vision. He is able to see some very close up images but his sight is still very limited. In an interview about his everyday mobility experiences, he discusses the importance of being on time for things:

> 'Because of our vision it makes things more time-consuming and more difficult, being reliable and on time is a hundred-percent possible for us. Now what I was saying was people don't think about, about stress and anxiety. A person, a visually impaired blind person can't work in an, in an environment that is all to do with being pressured, being under pressure. A lot of stress and anxiety, which will create for the blind person, will disorientate them and, you know, will lose their focus and concentration and will, will mess up other things because of other people around them pressing them. So, you know, anxiety and stress isn't good, because we need peace and ease and time to ourselves to do things in a very easy slow manner, in our own way. Because we've got our own method and system of organising and orientating ourselves, you know, our own method.' (Ali)

Ali starts his account by explaining how reduced vision makes many everyday tasks more "time-consuming and more difficult". He moves on to qualify this statement in making the claim that despite these difficulties it is still possible for visually impaired people ("us") to be "reliable" and on time. What follows, though, is an account providing further details of the difficulties Ali first identified. He frames his account around notions of "anxiety and stress" (mentioned on three separate occasions) and, in so doing, the discursive context is orientated to, and framed around, what it is to *feel*. Ali explains his everyday navigation experiences and how they relate to concerns with time by using a range of emotional and affective resources constructed around notions of "stress and anxiety" and "being under pressure". Yet what Ali alludes to, and what also emerged in other participants' accounts, is that the temporal work of mobility begins well before leaving the house, in terms of extra planning required to check accessibility and journey links, and extra time being set aside to gather things together before setting off. Here we see clear links between temporalities, capacities and emotional work and the importance of understanding transport not in isolation but in relation to the broader complexities of everyday life. Furthermore, this perspective makes clear the ongoing accomplishment of accessibility and the significance of considering the concept as a process.

Cresswell (2014: 714) uses the notion of 'friction' as a means of thinking about how movements are hindered and enabled; he highlights how friction slows things down but also enables movement and is a 'social phenomenon with its own politics.' In the context of Jennie's research on visually impaired people, it is possible to identify the temporal and material frictions (see also Cook 2017), and associated emotional and temporal work, that emerge when everyday mobility is hindered. During the course of the project, Jennie had arranged to meet another respondent, Katerina, at Victoria Station in order to conduct a follow-up interview. Katerina is in her mid-twenties and lives independently in South London. On the day of their meeting Jennie arrived 15 minutes early at a pre-arranged meeting spot and waited for Katerina to arrive at 11am. After 40 minutes Katerina sent a text explaining that she would be there in "10 minutes or so". A further 30 minutes passed and Katerina texted again to explain that the trains were running late making it "a bit of a thing to get there". At this point Jennie began to get anxious as she knew that if Katerina arrived much later there would not be time to do the interview before she had to get a return train to do the nursery pick-up. Katerina eventually arrived very distressed at 12.45pm following further complications with her gaining access to travel assistance at the station.

While research participants cited examples of good practice in terms of public transport travel assistance, they also drew attention to several instances where travel assistance was either slow to turn up or did not turn up at all when help had been requested. In this example, the temporal frictions emerging from Katerina being late brought to the fore transport anxieties of both the participant/visually impaired young person and the researcher/mother. Different actors' temporalities (the station staff, station environment, the participants, the researchers) are interrelated and interconnected in complex ways, which reveal some of the barriers to access and the difficulties faced by visually impaired people when trying to negotiate different modes of transport and their associated temporal constraints, frameworks and limits. Overall, the point we wish to emphasise is the need for assistance from others, combined with the misalignment between the amount of time the system designers consider something will take and the actual experiences of some users to complete a task, is generative of additional anxieties (see Freund 2001, Emanuel 2017).

Conclusions

Making clear her view that social exclusion and accessibility constraints are exacerbated by neo-liberal policies, Lucas (2012: 112) highlights that: 'wholly new, radical and transformative research programmes are needed in order to overthrow the redundant social development paradigms of a bygone era. To meet this challenge,' she continues:

> ...we need to develop new interdisciplinary theories and innovative methodological approaches so that policy makers can move beyond the ineffective "trickle-down" models they are currently applying and towards the development of "just cities" for all. Transport and access has [*sic*] a fundamental role to play in this transition and so understanding the processes, actions and decisions which lead to transport-related exclusion should be one of the key foci of our future transport policy research. (Lucas 2012)

Our focus in this chapter on accessibility as a process, and in particular on emotional and temporal work, responds to Lucas' challenge in four key ways. Firstly, we have reasserted the need to ensure that attempts to assess transport-related (in)accessibility and the resultant social inclusion/exclusion cannot assume a homogeneous type of mobile person, and certainly not, as was the effectively case with TfL's TPAL, a non-disabled man. Future accessibility studies seeking to address issues as they pertain to society as a whole need to be undertaken with a wide range of people to ensure representativeness and thus a more credible picture of conditions 'on the ground' (Martens 2017). We have also highlighted the importance of approaching accessibility as a process rather than focusing solely on its 'objective' causes and its outcomes. Uncovering a wider range of factors such as emotional work that impact significantly on people's experiences while on the move will render the findings of studies more relevant and, we would hope, increase the potency of policy responses. Relatedly, the important distinction between 'clock-time passing' and time as it is experienced by different people on the move, on journeys that are genuinely door-to-door and not doorstep to station entrance, will further enhance the credibility and purchase of accessibility studies by bringing into focus the travails of people dealing with a heavy burden of temporal work.

Secondly, in making the case for the importance of emotional and temporal work in conceptions of accessibility, we highlight again their 'invisible' nature and emphasise the methodological challenge in bringing them into the mainstream. We noted in the introduction that 'tangible' and 'objective' qualities are easier to measure than subjective and context-driven factors and as such have tended to obscure 'softer', social aspects of transport systems in the analyses of both academics and policy makers (see Vella-Brodrick and Stanley 2013). The UK government, heavily influenced as it has been by economistic and utilitarian approaches to policy issues, would benefit from a more open engagement with qualitative-based approaches that reveal the depth and complexity of accessibility (although, as the editors remarked when we were drafting this chapter, there is also the argument that this requires more effective ways of communicating such things on the part of some who reveal them). Nevertheless, some experimentation with more 'objective' and quantifiable ways of measuring factors such as journey stress is taking place. For example, research on older people's everyday experiences of urban cycling have used sensor-based Galvanic Skin Response, Heart Rate monitors and adaptations of the Positive and Negative Affect Scale[2] as a way of trying to gather data on stress and relaxation (Jones et al 2016). These approaches are exciting but remain in their infancy and will require more development before they are reliable enough to be considered as evidence.

Thirdly, and relatedly, because of their 'invisibility', emotional and temporal work become externalities in current market-based frameworks – a cost incurred by travellers even though they have no choice in whether or not they want to foot the bill. In economic terms, because the costs of the externalities (the emotional and temporal work) do not have to be paid by the operator(s) of the mobility system, it is easy for the operator (TfL, National Rail companies, the government or whoever) to turn a blind eye and in so doing allow more of them to occur than if they had to bear the cost themselves. The most common example of externalities in the transport sector is environmental costs, which almost certainly lead to the production of more pollution and carbon emissions than would be the case were the costs of these things internalised (Goodwin 1993, Musso and Rothengatter 2013; see also Chapter 3). As such, the (inflated) costs of dealing with the mess are passed on to society as a whole, including those people who had nothing or little to do with creating it in the first place (Jackson 2009). The same can be argued in conjunction with emotional and temporal work, with the Chartered Institute of Highways and Transportation (CIHT, 2016: unpaginated) questioning whether '…health and wellbeing outcomes should be considered in scheme development, taken into account in the design process, and embedded in the economic assessment and justification for transport projects.' While we share Lucas' (2012) view that neo-liberal, market-based mechanisms are not equipped to address transport inequalities, we do propose that rendering emotional and temporal work more visible as factors in accessibility assessments would at least mark some progress towards ensuring a more equitable distribution of the costs of making difficult adaptations between transport operators and travellers.

Finally, we wish to emphasise the extended implication of the equalisation of emotional and temporal work across society. As the editors also noted when we were still in draft stage, just removing the steps from UK train stations and replacing them with something more accessible would extend to billions of pounds; applying principles of Inclusive Design universally would cost tens of billions. It therefore has great opportunity cost and in any event is unlikely to happen anytime soon, and certain groups will continue to be excluded from full societal membership as a result. In the political climate of the day we are forced, sadly, to agree. If, however, we apply a Liberal Egalitarian[3] perspective rather than a market-based utility perspective, this situation becomes untenable because we would not choose to subject ourselves to such conditions of inaccessibility and corollary aversion behaviours, and would instead, as a society, seek to eradicate the circumstances that produce them. It is worth remembering that the crucial point about inclusive design is that it is exactly that – it promotes access for all, not just for specific groups. Investing in enhanced accessibility will help remove a cost to society in the form of under-utilised labour, and provide additional economic stimulus to regional economies in the form of wages and manufacturing as travel environments are reshaped to be more inclusive. The cost of action will be high but will produce a multitude of positives, and although the costs of inaction are uncertain and evolving (Currie and Delbosc 2010), we can all agree that there is a cost to doing nothing and that it is disproportionately borne by some groups and individuals. In this context, one might well argue, cost be damned: the principles of social justice and equal citizenship place a duty on government and society to minimise and ultimately eradicate transport and associated inequalities (Martens 2006, 2017) for all citizens.

Notes

[1] According to the British Standards Institute, Inclusive Design is defined as 'The design of mainstream products and/or services that are accessible to, and usable by, as many people as reasonably possible… without the need for special adaptation or specialised design.'

[2] The PANAS is a scale commonly used in psychological studies to measure, through self-response, the range and intensity of feelings experience by participants in relation to a particular phenomenon.

[3] Informed by John Rawls' (1971) landmark work *A Theory of Justice*, a liberal egalitarian perspective foregrounds distributive economic justice requiring equality of opportunity through reduction in 'natural' inequalities. In particular Rawls argued that institutions (including those overseeing transportation) should be founded on ideals of 'justice maximisation' rather than the utilitarianism underpinning forms of assessment such as cost–benefit analysis. For an interesting attempt to apply these principles, see Martens 2017.

References

Banister, D and Bowling, A (2004) 'Quality of life for the elderly: the transport dimension', *Transport Policy*, 11(2): 105–15.

BBC (2017) '"Wheelchair v buggy": disabled man wins supreme court case', www.bbc.co.uk/news/uk-38663322 Accessed 10 July 2018.

Begum, S (2014) *British Bangladeshi women and cycling.* Unpublished undergraduate dissertation. QMUL, London.

Bhat, C, Handy, S, Kockelman, K, Mahmassani, H, Qinglin, C and Weston, L (2000) *Development of an Urban Accessibility Index.* University of Texas, Austin. http://ctr.utexas.edu/wp-content/uploads/pubs/4938_1.pdf Accessed 2 June 2019.

Boyer, K and Spinney, J (2016) 'Motherhood, mobility and materiality: material entanglements, journey-making and the process of becoming mother', *Environment and Planning D: Society and Space*, 34(6): 1113–31.

Brennan, M, Olaru, D and Smith, B (2014) 'Are exclusion factors capitalised in housing prices?', *Case Studies on Transport Policy*, 2(2): 50–60.

Cahill, M (2010) *Transport, Environment and Society*, Maidenhead: Open University Press.

Chartered Institute of Highways and Transportation (2016) *Transport mobility and wellbeing.* www.ciht.org.uk/knowledge-resource-centre/resources/transport-mobility-and-wellbeing/ Accessed 10 July 2018.

Commission for Architecture and the Built Environment (2008) *Inclusion by Design: Equality, diversity and the built environment.* London: CABE.

Cook, S (2017) 'Rushing, dashing, scrambling: the role of the train station in producing the reluctant runner', in J Spinney, S Reimer and P Pinch (eds) *Mobilising Design*, Abingdon: Routledge, pp 62–75.

Cresswell, T (2014) 'Mobilities III: moving on', *Progress in Human Geography*, 38(5): 712–21.

Currie, G and Delbosc, A (2010) 'Modelling the social and psychological impacts of transport disadvantage', *Transportation*, 18: 31–41.

Curtis, C (2011) 'Integrating land use with public transport: the use of a discursive accessibility tool to inform metropolitan spatial planning in Perth', *Transport Reviews*, 31(2): 179–97.

Department for Transport (2011) *National Travel Survey 2010 Statistical Release*. https://assets.publishing.service.gov.uk/government/uploads/system/uploads/attachment_data/file/8932/nts2010-01.pdf Accessed 2 June 2017.

Department for Transport (2012) *Evaluation of the cycling city and towns programme*. www.cycling-embassy.org.uk/sites/cycling-embassy.org.uk/files/documents/cct-qualitative-research.pdf Accessed 4 October 2011.

Design for All Foundation (2018) http://designforall.org Accessed 10 July 2018.

Edwards, C and Imrie, R (2003) 'Disability and bodies as bearers of value', *Sociology*, 37(2): 239–52.

Edwards, D (1997) *Discourse and Cognition*. London: Sage.

Emanuel, M (2017) 'Designing signals, mediating mobility: traffic management and mobility practices in interwar Stockholm', in J Spinney, S Reimer and P Pinch (eds) *Mobilising Design*, Abingdon: Routledge, pp 103–16.

Farrington, J (2007) 'The new narrative of accessibility: its potential contribution to discourses in (transport) geography', *Journal of Transport Geography*, 15(5): 319–30.

Frei, A, Axhausen, K and Ohnmacht, T (2009) 'Mobilities and Social Network Geography: Size and Spatial Dispersion – the Zurich Case Study', in T Ohnmacht, H Maksim and M Bergman (eds) *Mobilities and Inequalities*, London: Routledge, pp 99–120.

Freund, P (2001) 'Bodies, disability and space: the social model and disabling spatial organisations', *Disability and Society*, 16(5): 689–706.

Ganning, J (2014) *Accessibility-Based Transportation Planning: Literature and Applications for Shrinking Cities*. NITC-SS-736. Transportation Research and Education Center, Portland, Oregon.

Geurs, K, Boon, Wouter, W and Van Wee, B (2009) 'Social impacts of transport: literature review and the state of the practice of transport appraisal in the Netherlands and the United Kingdom', *Transport Reviews*, 29(1): 69–90.

Goodwin, P (1993) 'Efficiency and the environment: possibilities of a green-gold coalition', in D Banister and K Button (eds) *Transport, the Environment and Sustainable Development*, London: Spon Press, pp 257–69.

Gray, D, Shaw, J and Farrington, J (2006) 'Community transport, social capital and social exclusion in rural areas', *Area*, 38(1): 89–98.

Hine, J and Mitchell, F (2001) 'Better for everyone? Travel experiences and transport exclusion', *Urban Studies*, 38(2): 319–32.

Hochschild, A (1979) 'Emotion work, feeling rules, and social structure', *The American Journal of Sociology*, 85: 551–75.

Hochschild, A (1983) *The Managed Heart: Commercialisation of Human Feeling*, Berkeley, CA: University of California Press.

Imrie, R (2000a) 'Disability and discourses of mobility and movement', *Environment and Planning A: Economy and Space*, 32(9): 1641–56.

Imrie, R (2000b) 'Disabling environments and the geography of access policies and practices', *Disability and Society*, 15(1): 5–24.

Imrie, R (2000c) 'Responding to the design needs of disabled people', *Journal of Urban Design*, 5(2): 199–220.

Jackson, T (2009) *Prosperity without Growth*, Oxford: Earthscan.

Johnson, R, Shaw, J, Berding, J, Gather, M and Rebstock, M (2017) 'European national government approaches to older people's transport system needs', *Transport Policy*, 59: 17–27.

Jones, T, Chatterjee, K, Jones, H, Leyland, L, Spencer, B, Spinney, J, Street, E and Van Reekum, K (2016) *Cycle Boom Final Report*, Oxford Brookes University, Oxford.

Kawabata, M and Shen, Q (2007) 'Commuting inequality between cars and public transit: the case of the San Francisco Bay Area, 1990–2000', *Urban Studies*, 44(9): 1759–80.

Lavery, I, Davey, S, Woodside, A and Ewart, K (1996) 'The vital role of street design and management in reducing barriers to older people's mobility', *Landscape and Urban Planning*, 35(2–3): 181–92.

Lucas, K (ed) (2004) *Running on Empty: Transport, Social Exclusion and Environmental Justice*, Bristol: Policy Press.

Lucas, K (2012) 'Transport and social exclusion: where are we now?', *Transport Policy*, 20: 105–13.

Lucas, K and Musso, A (2014) 'Policies for social inclusion in transportation: an introduction to the special issue', *Case studies on Transport Policy*, 2(2): 37–40.

Mackett, R, Achuthan, K and Titheridge, H (2008) 'AMELIA: a tool to make transport policies more socially inclusive', *Transport Policy*, 15(6): 372–78.

Markovich, J and Lucas, M (2011) *The Social and Distributional Impacts of Transport: A Literature Review.* Transport Studies Unit, Oxford.

Martens, K (2006) 'Basing transport planning on principles of social justice', *Berkeley Planning Journal*, 19(1): 1–17.

Martens, K (2017) *Transport Justice*, New York: Routledge.

Martínez, F, Hodgson, F, Mullen, C and Timms, T (2017) 'Creating inequality in accessibility: the relationships between public transport and social housing policy in deprived areas of Santiago de Chile', *Journal of Transport Geography*, 67(C): 102–9.

Musso, A and Rothengatter, W (2013) 'Internalisation of external costs of transport – a target driven approach with a focus on climate change', *Transport Policy*, 29: 303–14.

Preston, J and Rajé, F (2007) 'Accessibility, mobility and transport-related social exclusion', *Journal of Transport Geography*, 15: 151–60.

Pyer, M and Tucker, F (2014) '"With us, we like physically can't": transport Mobility and the leisure experiences of teenage wheelchair users', *Mobilities*, 12(1): 36–52.

Rajé, F (2007) *Negotiating the Transport System: User Contexts, Experiences and Needs*, Farnham: Ashgate.

Rawls, J (1971) *A Theory of Justice*, Cambridge, MA: Harvard University Press.

Ricci, M, Parkhurst, G and Jain, J (2016) 'Transport policy and social inclusion', *Cogitatio*, 4(3): 1–6.

Rosen, R and Guenther, E (2015) 'The economics of mitigating climate change: what can we know?', *Technological Forecasting and Social Change*, 91(C): 93–106.

Rosenkvist, J, Risser, R, Iwarsson, S and Stähl, A (2010) 'Exploring mobility in public environments among people with cognitive functional limitations: challenges and implications for planning', *Mobilities*, 5(1): 131–45.

Simoes, A (2013) 'Mobility-impaired travellers and public transport: a framework to assess quality of service', *Theoretical Issues in Ergonomics Science*, 14(3): 247–57.

Social Exclusion Unit (2003) *Making the connections: final report on transport and social exclusion.* Office of the Deputy Prime Minister, London.

Transport for London (2015) *Assessing transport connectivity in London.* TfL, London.

Uteng, T (2009) 'Gender, ethnicity and constrained mobility: insights into the resultant social exclusion', *Environment and Planning A: Economy and Space*, 41(5): 1055–71.

Uteng, T and Cresswell, T (eds) (2008) *Gendered Mobilities*, Farnham: Ashgate.

Vella-Brodrick, D and Stanley, J (2013) 'The significance of transport mobility in predicting well-being', *Transport Policy*, 29: 236–42.

Viry, G, Kaufmann, V and Widner, E (2009) 'Social integration faced with commuting: More widespread and less dense support networks', in T Ohnmacht, H Maksim and M Bergman (eds) *Mobilities and Inequalities*, London: Routledge, pp 121–44.

Watts, L (2008) 'The art and craft of train travel', *Social & Cultural Geography*, 9(6): 711–26.

PART II

Dealing with policy inheritance

5

Influencing travel behaviour

Stewart Barr and John Preston

Introduction

It's only necessary to take a short trip in an urban area to see how encouraging certain types of travel behaviour has become highly prevalent. Advertising boards exhort us to use 'park and ride', roadside signs encourage car sharing, bus advertisements promote the latest public transport app, while local and national government campaigns promote the health and wellbeing benefits of more walking and cycling. All of these interventions in our travel experience are now quite routine. Yet this has not always been the case, and the promotion of behavioural change as a viable strategy to meet particular policy goals (for example, reducing carbon emissions, cutting local air pollution, reducing congestion and promoting healthy lifestyles) is a relatively new entrant into the policy toolkits of central and local government. In this chapter, we explore why and how influencing behaviour is regarded as so critical for managing transport flows and spaces. In particular, we highlight the ways in which the rise of behavioural change as a policy tool can be linked to broader and underpinning shifts in the development of a neo-liberal political economy. We also highlight how behavioural change neatly fits with the progressive upholding of individual choice as the marker of a free market, consumer-based society – a political philosophy that necessitates exhortation and persuasion as devices of government, rather than public ownership and tight regulation.

Our chapter is divided into three main sections. First, we examine the ways in which transport researchers and other social scientists have researched travel behaviour and the underpinning theories and methods they have adopted. As with other areas of transport and travel research, different theoretical frameworks have led to distinct and often contrasting understandings of behaviour and we explore the ways in which both psychological and sociological framings of travel behaviour can lead to important, but very different, insights into what influences travel decision making. Second, we place these intellectual trajectories into a policy context by examining the ways in which the social science of (travel) behaviour has been mobilised to meet a range of policy goals. In particular, we stress the ways in which certain kinds of insights from behavioural research have led to particular strategies, such as social marketing and the use of Nudge Theory (Thaler and Sunstein 2008) to guide policy on influencing behaviour. Finally, we use two case studies to explore the ways in which theoretical and policy insights have been used to investigate and promote behavioural change in practice, using everyday and tourism travel as research contexts.

Behavioural underpinnings

Conventional approaches to transport planning, in their reliance on a close relationship between economics and engineering, have very much worked within a particular paradigm of mobility, which has focused on the notion of derived demand (Rodrigue et al 2016) and more broadly has been implicated in prioritising economic growth as the major rationale for movement (Banister 2008). The classic four-stage Land Use and Transport Model, with its focus on trip generation, distribution, mode split and assignment, was linked to the post-war development of the road networks of Chicago and Detroit before being enthusiastically adopted in the UK and elsewhere (Boyce and Williams 2015, Oi and Shuldiner 1962, Lane et al 1971). In essence, the drivers of behaviour were rising incomes and car ownership, with transport decisions dictated by travel times and costs and analogies with hydrology and physics used to determine equilibria. Economics provided the theoretical rationale, ultimately in the form of the random utility model (Domencich and McFadden 1975; Chapters 2, 6 and 7). Over recent decades, however, the assumptions of conventional approaches to transport planning have been progressively challenged, in part because the environmental impacts of transport policy have been called into sharp focus, making it imperative to change the way we travel (Chapman 2007, Knowles et al 2008; Chapter 3). There are also critiques of the underpinning behavioural rationale, namely the atomistic rational utility maximiser concerned only with time and costs and the equilibrium states that emerge from the resultant aggregate behaviour (Goodwin 1998). This in turn has led to questioning of the underlying philosophy of traditional approaches (Timms 2008). This up-ending of many of the assumptions made by economists and engineers about why we travel and the impacts of mobility has been the starting point for what we can characterise as two broad intellectual trajectories in the social sciences, both of which are concerned with understanding why we move in the ways that we do (see also Department for Transport (DfT) 2011a). This has led many scholars to critically analyse mobility in and of itself, and to question how deeply we have engaged as researchers in understanding mobility practices in daily life (Freudendal-Pedersen 2009).

First, one of the most enduring intellectual traditions in the social science of transport is drawn from psychological understandings of individual decision making (Barr 2014). Developed over the last four decades, psychological models of individual behaviour such as the Theory of Reasoned Action (Fishbein and Ajzen 1977) and Theory of Planned Behavior (Ajzen 1991) have been utilised by transport researchers to explore the influences of decision making, examining constructs such as attitudes, intentions, norms and perceived behavioural control (Anable 2005, Bamberg et al 2011, De Groot and Steg 2007). Indeed, Anable's (2005) research has demonstrated how such influences can be explored within the context of different traveller segments. Her work on visitors to National Trust sites in the UK identified, for example, four different car driving segments, each with a distinct set of behavioural influences: Die-Hard Drivers, Car Complacents, Malcontented Motorists and Aspiring Environmentalists.

The fundamental assumptions underpinning this research tradition are that travel mode choices are a function of the individual and that universal psychological models can be applied to provide frameworks for understanding decision-making processes. As such, the psychological approach is drawn very much from the traditional scientific paradigm, basing its empirical research on quantitative methods and the formation of modelling techniques to underpin the development of policies for changing travel behaviours (Barr and Prillwitz 2014). Its practical manifestation can be found in the application of human factors approaches to transport behaviour (for example, Stanton et al 2013). In the last two decades, the reliance of transport social scientists on individual decision making as the major unit of analysis has been developed in several ways. For example, Verplanken and Aarts (1999) have argued that many daily travel behaviours can be characterised as habits, in which routinised behaviours become unquestioned and rapidly adopted into daily life, often moulded by particular contexts (Kenyon and Lyons 2003). As such, habits become deeply embedded and hard to shift, requiring recognition of the wider lifestyle, work and consumption contexts in which people operate.

The second intellectual trajectory we aim to highlight is the growing interest of social scientists in what has become known as the new mobilities paradigm (Cresswell 2010, Cresswell and Merriman 2011, Urry 2002, 2007), drawing on sociological interpretations of travel and society. In this radical alternative to psychological approaches, mobilities researchers stress the contingent meanings of travel and recognise that movement is imbued with significance for the individual, while also being part of a rapidly and dynamically evolving set of social practices. Crucially, mobilities research emphasises the value of travel beyond getting from A to B; travel holds significance in and of itself. Here then the mobilities paradigm connects with other research in sociology to emphasise the links that contemporary individual travel behaviours have to what Reckwitz (2002) and latterly Shove (2003, 2010) have described as social practices. Such practices represent the ways in which people share common ways of being that are deeply connected to their economic and social environment and which have a clear lineage over time.

Perhaps the most effective example in travel research would be to use the illustration of travelling to work by car. For those adopting a psychological approach, car use may be the result of a set of individually based decisions based on information, attitudes towards car use, social expectations and the ability to conform or deviate from the behaviour. Yet for mobilities researchers, this is representative of the social practice of car-based commuting, which is grounded in 100 years or so of land-use planning decisions, the promotion of motor vehicles as the mode of choice, the marketing and social status associated with car ownership, and so on. In other words, to understand why people travel by car for work, we need to think about more than individual decisions, but about how we support and promote the car as a valued means of transport.

Policy developments: behaviour change to the rescue?

The dominant policy paradigm of the traditional approach to understanding travel behaviour has been characterised as 'predict and provide' (Owens 1995; Chapter 7). The four-stage Land Use and Transport Model was used to predict future demand, and infrastructure was provided to supply that demand. The growing realisation that the predicted demands could not be met without large environmental, social and economic costs led to a re-focus on travel demand management and 'predict and prevent' approaches. This inevitably led to an interest in behaviour change. But talking about behaviour change and how it should be done is not value-free; it is representative of a particular way of governing that has resulted in what we will argue is a narrow set of policies for nudging people this way and that, but it does not substantively tackle the bigger issues of shifting social practices.

Behaviour change has attained particular prominence because it is perhaps the policy approach with which central governments feel most at ease. We ought to ask why this is so. As Whitehead et al (2011) have argued, current conceptions of behaviour change policy are particular interpretations of science and policy that represent a relationship between state and citizen that can be traced back to the 1980s. This was a time of widespread neo-liberalisation of government and the so-called Washington Consensus, which emphasised the importance of a small state, deregulation and the role of individual consumers in driving economic growth (Williamson 2009). In the UK, the Thatcher administrations of 1979–90 and subsequent Labour and Conservative led governments pursued what many argue is a fundamentally neo-liberal project (Giddens 1991) by reducing the role of the state in both owning and managing infrastructure and regulating consumption. Nevertheless, as Clarke et al (2007) have argued, nation states still have the need to achieve their policy goals and so in the UK at least, a form of governing at a distance (Jessop 2002) has emerged, whereby the state encourages 'good' citizenship through exhortation, exercised by the choices afforded in the market economy. The state does not regulate or reduce choice, but instead tries to influence it. Accordingly, this tightrope of citizen-consumption (Johnston 2008) necessitates a delicate balance of consumer choice, mediated by 'right' decision making.

This tightrope has been managed in the UK by the emergence of behaviour change as an agenda for 'nudging' people to make different choices in their daily lives (Department for Environment, Food & Rural Affairs (DEFRA) 2005, Thaler and Sunstein 2008), and in the field of travel behaviour has been the subject of focus for both DEFRA (2008) and the DfT (2004) in the form of their *Smarter Choices* programme. Similar to many central government messages on changing behaviours, *Smarter Choices* placed emphasis on incremental behaviour change through changes in daily travel behaviours, in particular reducing personal car use, the uptake of public transport options and, connected to the health and wellbeing agenda, increases in walking and cycling (Chapter 8). This approach was further refined in the local sustainable transport White Paper (DfT 2011b) with the emergence of the ladder of interventions (Figure 5.1), with an implicit preference for interventions at the lower rungs that provide more information and promote individual choice.

Figure 5.1: The ladder of interventions

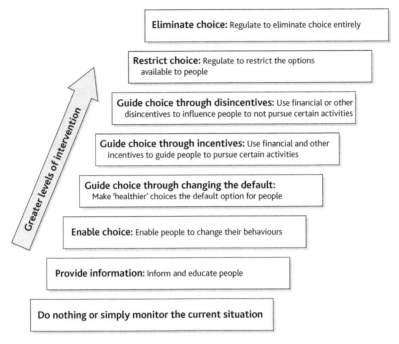

Source: DfT 2011b

What has governed these campaigns is a range of insights from research by psychologists, behavioural economists, and latterly social marketers and Nudge theorists (French et al 2009, Thaler and Sunstein 2008) which has taken theoretical insights from frameworks like the Theory of Planned Behavior (Ajzen 1991) and applied them to particular behavioural questions. Both DEFRA (2008) and the DfT (2011c) have applied social marketing techniques, in which key behavioural goals are identified, audiences segmented and marketing messages delivered. As an approach, social marketing emphasises the use of conventional marketing techniques to promote a social or environmental goal and highlights the positive aspects of participating in a behaviour (French et al 2009). Moreover, the recent interest in Nudge Theory (Thaler and Sunstein 2008) has amplified the perceived potential for positively adjusting what the authors refer to as 'choice architecture' for promoting shifts in behaviours.

Yet we want to stress that despite the huge investment in social marketing strategies and nudges to promote shifts in travel behaviour, the potential for such approaches to deliver major changes in travel habits is limited. As such, we provide an important note of caution when using the term 'behaviour change'; as it is currently conceived, it is a particular manifestation of behaviour and its potential to be changed. Accordingly, we need to exercise caution in three ways. First, we must be mindful of the fact that behaviour change policy has largely been driven by research and evidence underpinned by assumptions from the psychological tradition and as such privileges quantitatively verifiable data about individual decision making. As Jones et al (2011) and Whitehead et al (2011) have highlighted, this leads to new forms of governing at a distance that perpetuate a sense that decision making can be manipulated to achieve particular policy outcomes whereby: '…using the new sciences of choice from psychology, economics and the neurosciences – as well as appealing to an improved understanding of decision making and behaviour change – a libertarian paternalist mode of governing is being promoted in the UK' (Jones et al 2011: 15).

This distancing of the state from citizens and the sense that people are disempowered from collaboratively identifying approaches for travel behaviour change leads to a second note of caution focused on the apparent contradictions in policy for promoting shifts in travel practices (Barr and Prillwitz 2014). For example, on the one hand citizens may be exhorted to reduce personal car use, use public transport and cycle or walk more frequently. Yet in the UK recent changes to the planning system (Department for Communities and Local Government (DCLG) 2015) have promoted the use of so-called green field sites for retail and housing developments, all of which are based ultimately on private car use. This contradiction is inscribed, in other words, in the built environment around us and it is little wonder that people who do opt to use public transport or to walk or cycle are largely swimming against the prevailing tide of cultural and infrastructural symbols that promote and sustain car use.

Finally, our current interpretation of behaviour change is simply likely to fail in tackling the issues of the day on the grounds that the challenges posed by climate change and the need to rapidly de-carbonise the economy are of such a scale that incremental shifts in behaviours are unlikely to be effective (Crompton and Thøgersen 2009, Peattie and Peattie 2009; Chapter 3). This leads us to think of new ways of wrestling the behaviour change agenda away from those who would see it as a fundamentally conservative instrument of neo-liberal governance, towards a conception of change that is deliberative, co-creative and ambitious. This means considering the important connections travel has to working practices, economic development (Chapter 2), the built environment (Chapter 9) and quality of life

(Chapter 8). In other words, we ought to view behaviour change as something which leads us to radically re-consider our mobility practices, so that they are driven more by our need for wellbeing rather than an apparent need for narrow economic growth.

Case studies

To illustrate our arguments we highlight two contrasting case studies. The first, led by the University of Exeter, examines medium range inter-urban leisure travel and the competition between air and rail services. The second, led by the University of Southampton, examines attempts to make local transport more sustainable.

Co-creating change: from plane to train

What arises from the discussion of both the theories that underlie our understanding of behavioural change and its current manifestation in policy is that there is a need to engage far more with citizens to both understand and promote change. In the spirit of breaking out from traditional and expert-led agendas of policy making (Owens 2000; Chapter 11), we here outline an attempt to break down hierarchies of knowledge in the process of attempting to deal with a well-known but 'wicked' policy problem: trying to reduce short-haul flying for leisure trips. As Graham and Shaw (2008) have highlighted, the deregulation and liberalisation of the European air travel market has led to a major expansion in so-called low cost airlines, which have highly responsive and dynamic pricing structures, offering frequent, cheap and regionally accessible air travel to hundreds of European destinations. Accordingly, access to air travel has been significantly increased, leading to a major diversification in travel patterns and the evolution of weekend European city breaks, Stag and Hen weekends, short-term skiing trips and even the possibility for long-distance weekly commutes.

The research challenge of the emergence of these new forms of travel practice is closely connected to evidence that those most likely to engage in short-haul leisure flying are also those who demonstrate higher than average concern for the environment and who are environmentally conscious in and around the domestic sphere (Barr et al 2011). Indeed, evidence from the social sciences highlights that when it comes to climate change and tourism in general, individuals are able to disaggregate their pro-environmental practices in and around the home from those which are seen as non-negotiable on holiday (Becken 2007, Gössling and Peeters 2007). Accordingly, the question arises: how can a carbon intensive practice like flying be replaced by rail travel as a viable option for short-haul breaks?

This was a question that was grappled with when attempting to demonstrate the value of developing collaborative behaviour change programmes that went beyond a simple manipulation of choice architectures. Rather, the concern was to explore how knowledge co-production and campaign co-creation with consumers in our target audience could generate more innovative and potentially meaningful ways to promote change. Working with four social change companies (Uscreates, Strategic Social Marketing, Hyder Consulting and CAG Consultants), researchers at the University of Exeter used previous academic research and insights from commercial industry reports (such as those published by Mintel) to identify both a specific behavioural goal and specific target audiences, which were summarised as:

- Can we get 'aspiring green travellers' to switch from plane to train for half of their short-haul journeys?

- 'Aspiring green travellers' were defined as those individuals who expressed above-average positive attitudes towards being environmentally conscious in their everyday practices, but also took above-average numbers of leisure flights annually, often for short breaks in continental Europe. Specifically, the two socio-demographic groups of interest were:
  - 'Generation Y': young professionals, with relatively high incomes and a high propensity to travel in small groups for a range of short breaks, such as city or skiing holidays;
  - 'Empty nesters': retired couples, with high levels of disposable income, whose children have moved away from home. This group had a high propensity to take frequent short-haul city breaks and more luxurious holidays.

For the purposes of the research, we worked with consumers representative of these two demographic groups in London, given the proximity to both international airports and international rail connections via the Eurostar service. In brief, the approach adopted comprised five stages, each designed to connect the aspirations and needs of consumers to the travel experience they wanted to have, working with industry partners to achieve a meaningful outcome (Table 5.1).

Table 5.1: Stages adopted for knowledge co-production for a sustainable mobility behaviour change campaign

Stage 1 Partner collaboration	Problem identification and developing relationships between researchers and social change practitioners
Stage 2 Market-based research	Identifying the key characteristics of the target audience and its mobility practices with social change partners
Stage 3 Consumer co-production workshop	Working with consumers to explore understandings of current practices and the barriers and motivations for future changes. Identifying ideas for behavioural change campaigns
Stage 4 Industry co-production workshop	Working with industry representatives to shortlist ideas for a behavioural change campaign
Stage 5 Development and launch	Working with industry and social change partners to develop an app for promoting sustainable mobility

Source: Authors

Having completed Stages 1 and 2 and successfully identified our behavioural goal and target audiences, in Stage 3 a series of consumer co-creation workshops was run in which a range of data was produced on current travel experiences and some of the challenges consumers might face in taking holidays by rail rather than air. Tables 5.2 and 5.3 provide an overview of these data and were the basis for identifying some key themes that consumers suggested, notably:

- the value of travel as part of the holiday experience;
- the accepted but nonetheless serious deficiencies of flying as a travel experience;
- the need for much simpler, faster and integrated booking systems for rail travel for holidays;
- the importance of service levels to be enhanced for holidays by rail;
- the need for key perceptual barriers to be overcome (for example, that air travel is always faster and cheaper).

These findings were then used to hold a half-day, industry-focused workshop with key sector organisations (Table 5.4). At this interactive workshop, a series of potential intervention scenarios were identified (Table 5.5) that covered the range of potential strategies to increase rail use for holidays. Some of these, such as service changes, are clearly longer-term and require an integrated effort from industry partners. But in the spirit of attempting to explore the potential for using behavioural change as a tool for shifting practices, the research team focused on the role mobile technologies and re-imagining the holiday experience could play in shifting behaviours. Accordingly, in Stage 5,

Table 5.2: Positives and negatives identified by participants for air and rail travel for holidays

	Positives	Negatives
Air travel	• Cost • Speed • Choice of departure points • Convenience • Peace of mind • Familiarity • 'Starting the holiday at the airport'	• Delays • Poor food offering • Waiting at airports • Cramped conditions • Luggage costs and constraints • Greater carbon emissions
Rail travel	• Higher quality of travel experience • Greater level of comfort • The train as part of the holiday experience • Pleasant stations and facilities • Better food • More sociable • Less waiting time	• Cost • Extra time involved in travelling to destination • Perceived lack of personal safety and security • Changing trains in unfamiliar cities • Carrying luggage long distances • Travel to London to get the Eurostar train

Source: Authors

Table 5.3: Key changes required for each segment to shift behaviours

	Empty nesters	Young professionals
Service changes	• High-speed rail links to more destinations (for example, Madrid) • No changes/seamless connections/baggage transfers/transfer assistance • Train 'packages' from specialist providers – everything organised door-to-door • Train miles/reward scheme • Information about public transport at destination	• Easy online booking • A connection service such as a shuttle bus to the next train station • A budget/'slumming it' train option that is really an option worth considering
Booking changes	• Easy online booking • Cost/time comparisons	• Transparency – true costs and benefits of using train (door-to-door)
Fringe benefits/ package benefits	• Comfort extras such as a bottle of wine • Better station facilities • Comfortable seating • Commentary on surroundings	• Package stop off options for round the world flights (for example, Paris-Venice-Rome) • Inspiring and customised routes

Source: Authors

the research team and Uscreates in particular worked with Loco2, a rail holiday booking agency, to develop a travel app specifically designed to promote destination-based travel through marketing at particular audiences. Available from app stores, consumers can

Table 5.4: Organisations and participants invited to the co-creation workshop in London, July 2012

Organisation/participant	Description
Seat 61	European rail travel advice website
Loco2	European rail travel booking site
Snowcarbon	Ski holidays by train
Travel Foundation	Independent UK charity promoting social and environmental benefits of tourism to host communities
Forum for the Future	Environmental lobbying organisation
Virgin Trains	UK rail operator
Green Traveller	UK promoter of sustainable travel
PricewaterhouseCoopers (PwC) Sustainability Unit	Professional services and major UK auditing company
DEFRA	UK Government Department for Environment, Food & Rural Affairs
Sustainable tourism consultant	
Travel consultant and fast rail lobbyist	
Inn Travel	Specialist in walking and cycling holidays

Source: Authors

Table 5.5: Potential social marketing interventions for changing holiday travel behaviours

Intervention type	Examples
Service changes	• Providing more services direct from London to destinations in continental Europe, to avoid the need to change trains in large urban centres, such as Paris • Simpler booking systems to allow booking rail and holiday packages in one place • Integration of European rail booking systems
Social advertising	• Promoting destinations as part of rail holiday advertising • Promoting the travel to and from a destination as part of the holiday experience • Invoking romantic images/memories of rail travel as luxurious
Viral campaigns	• Snowcarbon's approach to promoting ski holidays by train using video
Incentives	• Railcards or other frequent traveller discounts • Integrated incentives for travelling on a range of rail companies to a holiday destination

Source: Authors

view destinations, hotel options and other information, linked to an integrated rail booking service.

This process raises many questions about the potential of behavioural change to deliver a significant shift of consumers from one mode of travel to another. Certainly the research with consumers and providers highlighted the need for major service improvements and the integration of booking systems. Yet it also demonstrated the potential of uncovering and working with existing perceptions of air and rail travel, which need to be challenged through forms of social marketing. Indeed, this example of campaign co-creation illustrated the ways in which consumers can become part of the process of developing interventions to promote changes in 'hard to shift' practices. Most importantly, it stresses the importance of working with, rather than above or without, the very consumers who hold the key to successful behavioural change strategies. As such, although the success of such an intervention on a wider scale cannot yet be evaluated, it is certainly the case that the process itself raises a number of crucial points about the role of consumer knowledge and the ways in which people can be integrated into a research framework for collaboratively developing behavioural interventions.

Local sustainable transport: doing a little to change a lot?

The change in policy emphasis towards behaviour change in relation to local transport has been accompanied by two related developments. Firstly, funding is tightly rationed and increasingly awarded on a competitive basis, rather than in long-term settlements. While this has always been the case for major projects, it is now increasingly common for more routine expenditure. Secondly, funding is targeted towards 'softer' measures that build on the perceived success of measures such as workplace travel plans (Enoch, 2016; Roby, 2010) – information provision, ticket integration and marketing – rather than 'harder' measures such as infrastructure provision. Where infrastructure is to be provided the emphasis is on improvements for public transport, walking and cycling. Our case study city of Southampton has been relatively successful in recent funding competitions, although this in part may be seen as compensation for past failures to secure major project funding, particularly related to light rail, in contrast to some other cities such as Edinburgh and Nottingham. It was awarded £3.96 million from the Local Sustainable Transport Fund (LSTF) for the years 2012/13 to 2014/15, with a subsequent £1.0 million awarded for 2015/16, for the Southampton Sustainable Travel City project. As part of Transport for South Hampshire,[1] it was awarded £5.75 million for the Better Connected South Hampshire project for the period 2012/13 to 2014/15. Again as part of Transport for South Hampshire, it also shared in an award of £4.5 million from the Better Bus Area Fund (BBAF) for the period 2012/13 to 2013/14. The University of Southampton was commissioned by Southampton City Council to undertake a monitoring and evaluation study of the impact of these funding streams (Preston et al 2015).

With respect to process evaluation, we found that the funding programmes broadly did what they intended to do, albeit sometimes slightly later than intended. At the same time, in-depth interviews indicated that the dominant motivation was to ensure continuation of funding of local authority activities (and staff) rather than the achievement of policy objectives per se (Champion 2015). Moreover, the strong influence of social marketing was also apparent, with Southampton City Council adapting the Five Levers for Change Model as used by Unilever (Figure 5.2) which is strongly related to the psychology-based trans-theoretical stages of change model of Prochaska and DiClemente (1983). Drawing on the experience of public health campaigns (for example, to help people stop smoking), advertising and other promotional activities were undertaken to raise awareness. Direct marketing was then used to increase contemplation, while trials were undertaken to encourage participation and, if those trials were successful, behaviour change. Key components of the funding programmes were the development of the MyJourney website[2] and roadshows to improve information provision on modal choice and Personalised Journey Plans (PJPs) and Workplace Travel Plans to encourage trials of alternative modes, although the PJPs were relatively light touch compared to other variants of this approach such as individualised travel planning (Brög et al 2009), Travel Smart

Figure 5.2: Approach adopted by Southampton City Council

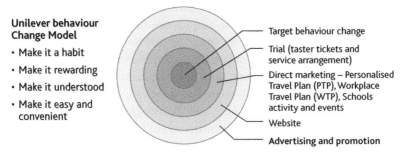

Unilever behaviour Change Model

• Make it a habit
• Make it rewarding
• Make it understood
• Make it easy and convenient

Target behaviour change

Trial (taster tickets and service arrangement)

Direct marketing – Personalised Travel Plan (PTP), Workplace Travel Plan (WTP), Schools activity and events

Website

Advertising and promotion

Source: Southampton City Council

(Taniguchi and Fujii 2007) or Travel Blending (Rose and Ampt 2001). The focus was on six corridors radiating from the city centre (Figure 5.3).

In order to undertake an impact evaluation, a mixed methods approach was adopted, based on a combination of primary data

Figure 5.3: Local Sustainable Transport Fund interventions in and around Southampton

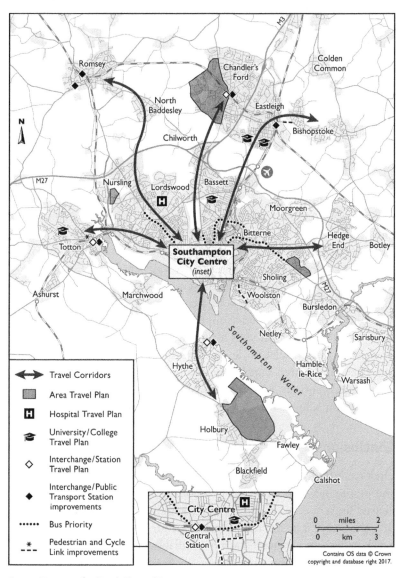

Source: Transport for South Hampshire

collection (involving online, postal and telephone surveys) and secondary data collection (primarily manual and automated traffic counts) (Wong et al 2015). Some of the headline findings were as follows. Detailed before and after surveys indicated that there were reductions in car driving for a treatment group (who had attended MyJourney Roadshows) compared to a control group (who had not and who lived in an area of the city little impacted the interventions) by 12 per cent, although this was largely due to different patterns of trip suppression rather than mode switching and, due to modest sample sizes, these changes were not statistically significant. It was estimated that around a quarter of the adult population was directly affected by the interventions over the four years of the funding programmes and this would suggest a 3 per cent reduction in car driving citywide (Preston et al 2015).

Secondary data indicated that between 2010 and 2014, road traffic within the city was down by around 9 per cent if factors such as changes in income levels and fuel prices are taken into account. By contrast, bus use was constant, rail use was up a tenth, walking to school likewise and cycling was up by over 20 per cent. This suggests that around one third of the traffic reduction within the city was associated with the interventions, but that the majority was related to the spatial transfer of economic activity (and traffic) from the city to the outer suburbs beyond the city boundary, with traffic continuing to grow strongly on the surrounding motorway network. Tellingly, mode share for travel into the city centre remained broadly constant, when the ambition had been for a 12 percentage-point reduction in car use. This broadly quantitative approach thus has mixed findings, but suggests the relatively modest set of interventions led only to modest changes at the population level. These findings are consistent with other recent research that has questioned the value of some smarter choice interventions, particularly in contexts where 'quick wins' have already been achieved (Behavioural Insights Team 2017).

Conclusions

Understanding and influencing travel behaviour is both theoretically and pragmatically complex. Theoretically, travel behaviour has been viewed from both psychological and sociological perspectives, meaning that the very basis for defining behaviour is debated. On the one hand, behaviour is regarded as a quantifiable, measurable and universal construct that can be understood with reference to linear models of decision making, tested using the traditional scientific method.

Contrastingly, sociologists and researchers from other social science disciplines have advocated an interpretivist approach that views mobility as a form of social practice, imbued with meaning and linked to socio-economic processes and infrastructures, as well as individual attributes. As such, the modus operandi of mobilities research are qualitative, highly contextual and fluid.

These theoretical considerations lead us to engage with some fundamental issues of policy and pragmatism. In essence, the question is 'how much can behavioural change deliver?' We might add to this 'how much can *current prescriptions* of behavioural change deliver?' The argument we have put forward in this chapter is that central government interpretations of the behavioural change agenda have been both narrow and defined by the political dogma of individual choice. This does not fully represent what might be possible through engaging with citizens about the kind of mobility they want; it is one interpretation only. We argue here that it is a fundamentally unambitious approach, which does not enable behavioural change to be seen in the wider context of how citizens might collectively and democratically consent to changes in infrastructures, the built environment and transport services that promote reduced mobility. And we know that a more collective approach can work, as the evidence from both continental Europe (for example, Freiburg, Germany) and North America (for example, Portland, Oregon) shows (Buehler and Pucher 2011, City of Portland 2016, Melia 2015). In both of these cases, transport and land use planning have been used by local government to guide development and provide spatially based approaches to reducing mobility and improving places, and through which major influence on travel behaviour has been achieved.

In this context, we are reminded of the quote by David MacKay (2009: 114): 'Don't be distracted by the myth "every little helps". If everyone does a little, we'll achieve only a little. We must do a lot.' The evidence to date is that in the transport sector the Nudge hypothesis only seems to have modest effects at a population level. Contrary to the assertion of Gladwell (2000), in this context little things do not make a big difference, although this could be because the transport system remains some way from a critical threshold or tipping point. It could also be that our Southampton case study is atypical, but as far as we can tell the LSTF has led to similar results elsewhere (Sloman et al 2017). We would argue that the underlying social practices to encourage widespread behavioural change are largely absent. Changes in planning policy (through the National Planning Policy Framework) and in local transport governance (through the powers given to Local Enterprise Partnerships) seem to be giving a boost to car dependent economic development. The fragmented and commercialised public transport industry finds it difficult to deliver innovations such as network-wide smartcards, while the continued hollowing-out of the state is reducing the capabilities of governmental bodies to deliver even small interventions. This reflects the trends of the distancing of government, the contradictory nature of policies and the over-emphasis of marginal gains highlighted earlier in this chapter.

Notes

[1] Now Solent Transport.

[2] See http://myjourneysouthampton.com/. A video highlighting the main programmes and activities of the Solent Transport LSTF may be found at www.youtube.com/watch?v=z3e_E9eeYXM

References

Ajzen, I (1991) 'The theory of planned behavior', *Organizational Behavior and Human Decision Processes*, 50(2): 179–211.

Anable, J (2005) '"Complacent Car Addicts" or "Aspiring Environmentalists"? Identifying Travel Behaviour Segments Using Attitude Theory', *Transport Policy*, 12(1): 65–78.

Bamberg, S and Möser, G (2007) 'Twenty years after Hines, Hungerford, and Tomera: a new meta-analysis of psycho-social determinants of pro-environmental behaviour', *Journal of environmental psychology*, 27(1): 14–25.

Bamberg, S, Fujii, S, Friman, M and Gärling, T (2011) 'Behaviour theory and soft transport policy measures', *Transport Policy*, 18: 228–35.

Banister, D (2008) 'The sustainable mobility paradigm', *Transport Policy*, 15(2): 73–80.

Barr, S (2014) 'Practicing the cultural green economy: where now for environmental social science?', *Geografiska Annaler: Series B, Human Geography*, 96(3): 231–43.

Barr, S and Prillwitz, J (2014) 'A smarter choice? Exploring the behaviour change agenda for environmentally sustainable mobility', *Environment and Planning C: Politics and Space*, 32(1): 1–19.

Barr, S Gilg, A and Shaw, G (2011) 'Citizens, consumers and sustainability: (re)framing environmental practice in an age of climate change', *Global Environmental Change*, 21: 1224–33.

Becken, S (2007) 'Tourists' perception of international air travel's impact on the global climate and potential climate change policies', *Journal of Sustainable Tourism*, 15(4): 351–68.

Behavioural Insights Team (2017) *An Evaluation of Low Cost Workplace-Based Interventions to Encourage Use of Sustainable Transport*. www.gov.uk/government/uploads/system/uploads/attachment_data/file/586376/sustainable-travel-evaluation-of-low-cost-workplace-interventions.pdf Accessed 7 March 2016.

Boyce, D and Williams, H (2015) *Forecasting Urban Travel: Past, Present and Future*, Cheltenham: Edward Elgar.

Brög, W, Erl, E, Ker, I, Ryle, J and Wall, R (2008) 'Evaluation of voluntary travel behaviour change: experiences from three continents', *Transport Policy*, 16(6): 281–92.

Buehler, R and Pucher, J (2011) 'Sustainable transport in Freiburg: lessons from Germany's environmental capital', *International Journal of Sustainable Transportation*, 5: 43–70.

Champion, S (2015) *How successful was the Local Sustainable Transport Fund in Hampshire?* MSc Dissertation, University of Southampton.

Chapman, L (2007) 'Transport and climate change: a review', *Journal of Transport Geography*, 15(5): 354–67.

City of Portland (2016) *CC2035 Proposed Draft*. City of Portland, Portland, OR.

Clarke, J, Newman, J, Smith, N, Vidler, E and Westmarland, L (2007) *Creating Citizen-Consumers; Changing Publics and Changing Public Services*, London: Sage.

Cresswell, T (2010) 'Towards a politics of mobility', *Environment and Planning D: Society and Space*, 28(1): 17–31.

Cresswell, T and Merriman, P (eds) (2011) *Geographies of Mobilities: Practices, Spaces, Subjects*, Aldershot: Ashgate.

Crompton, T and Thøgersen, J (2009) *Simple and Painless? The limitations of spillover in environmental campaigning*. WWF UK, London.

De Groot, J and Steg, L (2007) 'General beliefs and the theory of planned behavior: the role of environmental concerns in the TPB', *Journal of Applied Social Psychology*, 37, 1817–36.

Department for Communities and Local Government (2015) *2010 to 2015 government policy: planning reform*. DCLG, London.

Department for Environment, Food & Rural Affairs (2005) *Securing the Future*, Cm 6467, London: TSO.

Department for Environment, Food & Rural Affairs (2008) *A Framework for Pro-Environmental Behaviours*. DEFRA, London.

Department for Transport (2004) *Smarter Choices: changing the way we travel. Final report of the research project: the influence of 'soft' factor interventions on travel demand.* DfT, London.

Department for Transport (2011a) *Behavioural Insights Toolkit.* Available at: www.gov.uk/government/publications/behavioural-insights-toolkit Accessed 24 August 2016.

Department for Transport (2011b) *Creating Growth, Cutting Carbon. Making Sustainable Local Transport Happen.* DfT, London.

Department for Transport (2011c) *Climate Change and Transport Choices. Segmentation Model: A framework for reducing CO_2 emissions from personal travel.* DfT, London.

Domencich, T and McFadden, D (1975) *Urban Travel Demand,* Amsterdam: North Holland.

Enoch, M (2016) *Sustainable Transport, Mobility Management and Travel Plans,* Abingdon: Routledge.

Fishbein, M and Ajzen, I (1977) *Belief, Attitude, Intention, and Behavior: An Introduction to Theory and Research.* Reading MA: Addison-Wesley.

French, J, Blair-Stevens, C, McVey, D and Merritt, R (2009) *Social Marketing and Public Health: Theory and Practice,* Oxford: Oxford University Press.

Freudendal-Pedersen, M (2009) *Mobility in Daily Life,* Aldershot: Ashgate.

Funtowitz, S and Ravetz, J (1993) 'Science for the post-normal age', *Futures,* 25(7): 739–55.

Giddens, A (1991) *Modernity and Self-Identity,* Cambridge: Polity Press.

Gladwell, M (2000) *The Tipping Point: How Little Things Can Make a Difference,* New York: Little Brown.

Goodwin, P (1998) 'The end of equilibrium', in T Garling, T Laitila and K Westin (eds) *Theoretical Foundations of Travel Choice: Modelling,* Amsterdam: Elsevier Science.

Gössling, S and Peeters, P (2007) '"It does not harm the environment!" An analysis of industry discourses on tourism, air travel and the environment', *Journal of Sustainable Tourism,* 15(4): 402–17.

Graham, B and Shaw, J (2008) 'Low-cost airlines in Europe: reconciling liberalization and sustainability', *Geoforum,* 39(3): 1439–51.

Heath, Y and Gifford, R (2002) 'Extending the theory of planned behavior: predicting the use of public transportation', *Journal of Applied Social Psychology,* 32(10): 2154–89.

Huddart, E, Cohen, M and Krogman, N (eds) (2015) *Putting Sustainability into Practice: Applications and Advances in Research on Sustainable Consumption,* Cheltenham: Edward Elgar.

Jessop, B (2002) 'Liberalism, neoliberalism, and urban governance: a state–theoretical perspective', *Antipode*, 34(3): 452–72.

Johnston, J (2008) 'The citizen-consumer hybrid: ideological tensions and the case of Whole Foods Market', *Theory and Society*, 37, 229–70.

Jones, R, Pykett, J and Whitehead, M (2011) 'Governing temptation: changing behaviour in an age of libertarian paternalism', *Progress in Human Geography*, 35(4): 483–501.

Kenyon, S and Lyons, G (2003) 'The value of integrated multimodal traveller information and its potential contribution to modal change', *Transportation Research Part F: Traffic Psychology and Behaviour*, 6(1): 1–21.

Knowles, R, Shaw, J and Docherty, I (eds) (2008) *Transport Geographies: Mobilities, Flows and Spaces*, Oxford: Blackwell.

Lane, R, Powell, T and Prestwood-Smith, P (1971) *Analytic Transport Planning*, London: Gerald Duckworth.

MacKay, D (2009) *Sustainable Energy without the Hot Air*, Cambridge: UIT Cambridge.

Melia, S (2015) *Urban Transport Without the Hot Air: Sustainable Solutions for UK Cities*, Cambridge: UIT Cambridge.

Oi, W and Shuldiner, P (1962) *An Analysis of Urban Travel Demands*, Evanston, IL: Northwestern University Press.

Owens, S (1995) 'From "predict and provide" to "predict and prevent"?: Pricing and planning in transport policy', *Transport Policy*, 2(1): 43–9.

Owens, S (2000) 'Engaging the public: information and deliberation in environmental policy', *Environment and Planning A: Economy and Space*, 32(7): 1141–8.

Peattie, K and Peattie, S (2009) 'Social marketing: a pathway to consumption reduction?' *Journal of Business Research*, 62(2): 260–8.

Preston, J, Wong, A and Hickford, A (2015) The impact of smarter choices on the use of active travel and public transport. *Presented to the 14th International Conference on Competition and Ownership in Land Passenger Transport*. Santiago, Chile.

Prochaska, J and DiClemente, C (1983) 'Stages and processes of self-change of smoking: toward an integrative model of change', *Journal of Consulting and Clinical Psychology*, 51(3): 390–5.

Reckwitz, A (2002) 'Toward a theory of social practices a development in culturalist theorizing', *European Journal of Social Theory*, 5(2): 243–63.

Roby, H (2010) 'Workplace travel plans: past, present and future', *Journal of Transport Geography*, 18(1): 23–30.

Rodrigue, J, Comtois, C and Slack, B (2016) *The Geography of Transport Systems* (4th edn), Milton Park: Routledge.

Rose, G and Ampt, E (2001) 'Travel blending: an Australian travel awareness initiative', *Transportation Research Part D: Transport and Environment*, 6(2): 95–110.

Shove, E (2003) *Comfort Cleanliness and Convenience: The Social Organization of Normality*, Oxford: Berg.

Shove, E (2010) 'Beyond the ABC: climate change policy and theories of social change', *Environment and Planning A: Economy and Space*, 42(6): 1273–85.

Sloman, L, Cairns, S, Goodman, A, Hopkin, J, Taylor, I, Hopkinson, L, Ricketts, O, Hiblin, B and Dillon, M (2017) *Meta-analysis of Outcomes of Investment in the 12 Local Sustainable Transport Fund Large Projects. Final Report.* DfT, London.

Stanton, N, McIlroy, R, Harvey, C, Blainey, S, Hickford, A, Preston, J and Ryan, B (2013) 'Following the cognitive work analysis train of thought: exploring the constraints of modal shift to rail transport', *Ergonomics*, 56(3): 522–40.

Steg, L and Gifford, R (2005) 'Sustainable transport and quality of life', *Journal of Transport Geography*, 13: 59–69.

Steg, L and Vlek, C (2009) 'Encouraging pro-environmental behaviour: an integrative review and research agenda', *Journal of Environmental Psychology*, 29(3): 309–17.

Taniguchi, A and Fujii, S (2007) 'Process model of voluntary behaviour modification and effects of travel feedback programs', *Transportation Research Record: Journal of the Transportation Research Board*, 2010(1): 45–52.

Thaler, R and Sunstein, C (2008) *Nudge: Improving Decisions about Health, Wealth and Happiness*, New Haven, CT: Yale University Press.

Timms, P (2008) 'Transport models, philosophy and language', *Transportation*, 35(3): 395–410.

Urry, J (2002) *The Tourist Gaze*, London: Sage.

Urry, J (2007) *Mobilities*, Cambridge: Polity Press.

Verbeek, D and Mommaas, H (2008) 'Transitions to sustainable tourism mobility: the social practices approach', *Journal of Sustainable Tourism*, 16(6): 629–44.

Verplanken, B and Aarts, H (1999) 'Habit, attitude, and planned behavior: is habit an empty construct or an interesting case of goal-directed automaticity?', *European Review of Social Psychology*, 10(1): 101–34.

Whitehead, M, Jones, R and Pykett, A (2011) 'Governing irrationality, or a more than rational government? Reflections on the rescientisation of decision making in British public policy', *Environment and Planning A: Economy and Space*, 43(12): 2819–37.

Williamson, J (2009) 'A short history of the Washington Consensus', *Law and Business Review of the Americas*, 15(1): 7–23.

Wong, A, Preston, J and Hickford, A (2015) Big Data, Small Changes: Evaluating the Impact of the Local Sustainable Transport Fund on Travel Behaviour and Awareness. Paper presented to the *International Association of Travel Behaviour Research* conference, Windsor, July 2015.

6

The gentle tyranny of cost–benefit analysis in transport appraisal

Robin Hickman

Introduction

Jonathan Swift's *Modest Proposal* warned us as early as 1729 of the dangers of relying on narrow economic criteria to make seemingly informed decisions, and as Adams (1974) pointed out over four decades ago, similar problems are evident in the application of simplistic cost–benefit analysis (CBA) approaches in the appraisal of public transport projects.

Since the 1950s onwards, transport appraisal in the UK has been gradually developed and refined, initially to support the building of the highway network and later to include public transport projects and even other modes such as cycling. The current appraisal system in England (broadly comparable approaches are used elsewhere in the UK) is documented in the Web-based Transport Appraisal Guidance (WebTAG) (Department for Transport (DfT) 2017). WebTAG uses CBA within a broader multi-criteria analysis (MCA) framework. The process is described by its proponents as the leading appraisal process in the world (Mackie et al 2014) and certainly it is the most 'well developed' in terms of number of pages of guidance. But, beyond this, there is much debate: the practice on the ground, and the state of public transport, pedestrian and cycling networks in the UK suggest that the decision-making process has not led to the delivery of a balanced range of transport infrastructure projects across the modes.

CBA holds an uneasy place in transport planning, sometimes used as a 'political football' to suit different ends at different times. Projects with seemingly obvious benefits, which are potentially popular with the public, can be refused by project promoters due to perceived low benefit–cost ratios (BCRs); other projects with low BCRs can be supported by project promoters, perhaps with the BCRs manipulated to give higher results. Equally, projects with high BCRs may be very controversial with the public, but supported through the appraisal process. The MCA process itself can be viewed as weakly applied due to its checklist nature, and because the quantified impacts are often given priority over the qualitative ones. The views of different actors are also given little influence in the final decision. It seems an appraisal process has developed to allow ease of centralised funding prioritisation and allocation, rather than one to respond to the plurality of transport problems and opportunities found in different contexts.

The question I ask in this chapter is whether a transport appraisal system largely developed decades ago, conceptually at least, remains useful to respond to contemporary problems faced by society. My starting point is that greater progress is required towards more sustainability in travel, where multiple policy objectives need to be debated and weighted, perhaps with limits applied to certain impacts, and in this context we need to more carefully consider whether the dominance of CBA in British transport appraisal practice helps deliver the 'right' projects in the transport sector. A (failed) proposal from the early 2000s – Merseytram, a light rapid transit (LRT) project in Liverpool and surrounds, in the north west of England – is examined as a case in point. Though the CBA was not the only reason the LRT project was cancelled, it was an important contributory factor, and its wider contributions to policy objectives, including environmental, social and economic dimensions, were given much less weight in the decision. My conclusion is that using narrow economic criteria is too weak a basis for transport appraisal, and that the use of a participatory, multi-actor MCA would strengthen the appraisal process (Leleur 2012, Macharis et al 2012), lead to a wider public policy debate on project prioritisation (Chapter 11) and provide better clarity over why we invest in transport in the first place (Chapter 2).

The framing of transport appraisal and CBA

Transport appraisal, in practice and also in much of academia, is broadly uncritical as a discipline. This means that the discipline is usually applied from the perspective of the natural sciences, attempting to develop and reflect general relationships between, say, transport investment and associated impacts. It has a tendency to become rule-based and struggles to reflect contextual difference. Transport appraisal, and indeed transport planning as a wider practice, is often seen as a technical exercise, value-free and almost apolitical in developing an optimal solution, such as in improving traffic flow. Applying 'traditional' transport appraisal logic, a transport planner would view traffic flow as equivalent to a liquid, with a fixed volume, that is capable of more effective distribution through additions or modifications to the road system (Newman and Kenworthy 2015). In reality, the evidence suggests that far from having a fixed volume, traffic expands and contracts to fit the available space, responding to policy interventions including the management of space and demand (Cairns et al 2002; Chapter 7). On the other hand, those viewing transport from the perspective of the *social* sciences and humanities have increasingly understood this not only in terms of observation, description and prediction (perhaps few 'general truths' can be found in human behaviour), but also in relation to human factors such as how and why individuals travel and participate in activities, and how they respond to new infrastructure. From this standpoint, the focus is on understanding the complexity of travel behaviours, their political context, the social norms and subjectivity that underpin them, and how individuals and societies interrelate relative to different interventions and contexts (Chapter 5).

Despite recent attempts by the DfT to broaden its approach to transport appraisal by including criteria such as accessibility and integration in the decision-making process, WebTAG remains heavily influenced by 'traditional' approaches. Project options designed to address a particular transport problem are examined against five cases: Strategic, Economic, Commercial, Financial and Management. Projects are assessed against a range of likely costs and benefits – appraisal summary tables (ASTs) summarising the analysis for each project against multiple criteria – and the best performing options are subject to a more detailed appraisal, with a final option(s) usually taken forward for implementation. The five cases for a given project are considered together as a Business Case, upon which ministers base their decisions (Hickman and Dean 2017). All of the process leading to the point of a minister's decision is developed by the analyst, usually a consultant specialising in transport appraisal, and there is very little wider discussion including different actors, such as debate over the policy objectives to use, the project options to test, or the estimation of impacts.

Critically, CBA is often a very significant part of the process, featuring particularly in the Economic Case but potentially retaining strong influence over any final decision. CBA has been heavily critiqued in wider public policy (Ackerman and Heinzerling 2004), including for attempting to 'quantify the unquantifiable', and despite long-standing debate (Self 1970, Adams 1994, Næss 2006, 2016, Hickman and Dean 2017) is still used in the planning of almost all transport projects in the UK. In the highly centralised government regime of Whitehall (and, in their own way, the devolved administrations – see Docherty et al 2018), one of its attractions to politicians is that it permits the prioritisation of funding between many competing projects. But a major downside is that this takes place with little understanding of local context. Projects are rarely approved unless they receive at least a BCR of 2:1 (high value for money) although more preferable is 4:1 (very high value for money). Because of the difficulty in quantifying and monetising many of the costs and benefits arising from transport projects, BCRs in the transport sector remain overly reliant on impacts that are both easily counted and can be assumed to be a reasonable proxy for issues that are perceived to be good (for example, journey time saved) and bad (for example, cost of environmental remediation). As such they are often a very partial calculation of costs and benefits (Hickman and Dean 2017), and certainly historically have led to a heavy bias towards highway investment; it is easy to show huge aggregate benefits from journey time savings if lots of motorists, whose time is valued as relatively precious depending on the purpose of their journey, each save even a small amount of time. There can also be an element of 'game playing', with much scope for project promoters to add in 'benefits' to the BCR to ensure that projects are presented in a favourable manner (Figure 6.1).

Figure 6.1: Applying cost–benefit analysis in transport projects?

Source: Rob Cowan

Transport appraisal, CBA and sustainability

In the broader context of this book, a key question of interest is the extent to which the use of CBA helps us achieve sustainability objectives. If we consider the components of a CBA relative to the UK's Sustainable Development Indicators (SDIs), the answer is broadly no. The criteria from the WebTAG AST (DfT 2014a) represent quite an odd collection, which have been developed iteratively over time, and have a poor relation to the SDIs (Department for Environment, Food & Rural Affairs (DEFRA) 2013). Figure 6.2 presents the indicators used within WebTAG alongside the UK's SDIs, and it is immediately evident that there is a mismatch across each of the three objectives, with often poor proxies used. Generally speaking, in a process where only items that can easily be quantified are incorporated into the

Figure 6.2: Cost–benefit analysis in relation to the UK's Sustainable Development Indicators

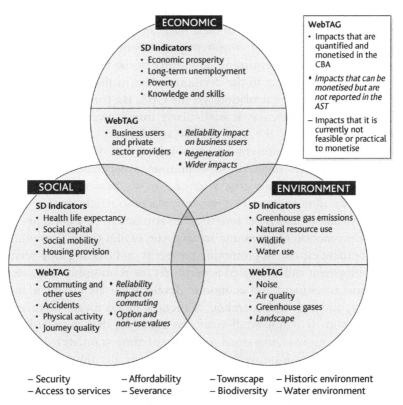

Sources: Department for Food and Rural Affairs 2013; Department for Transport 2014a

assessment of costs and benefits, many issues – townscape, biodiversity, severance and others – are left outside the CBA completely.

In social terms, the SDIs are interested in impacts on life expectancy, social capital, social mobility and housing provision, whereas CBA is focused on accidents, physical activity and journey quality. Clearly there is overlap between, say, the prevention of accidents and healthy life expectancy, but such is the influence of CBA (and its reliance on journey time savings) in the Business Case that it is difficult to see how, for example, promoting physical activity increases the chance of many transport project options being funded (Chapter 8). We might also expect a much greater focus in WebTAG on estimating accessibility changes, including people's abilities to reach their required activities following a given project investment (Chapter 4). Environmentally, many important impacts such as carbon dioxide (CO_2) emissions are poorly estimated in WebTAG and usually undervalued (for example, to not include lifecycle analysis), or discounted to 'present day' values (Chapter 3). There is almost no attempt to assess the integration of schemes with urban planning objectives, such as the impact on the quality of urban design (Chapter 9). Although some of these issues are picked up in the multi-criteria analysis, they are consistently undervalued in the resulting ASTs because of the remaining dominance of the CBA. Critically, it is often not made clear to the decision makers or the public that the economic efficiency calculation, via the CBA, is a partial calculation.

This lack of awareness is particularly ironic given the obvious mismatch between the way BCRs are derived and what they are supposed to represent in economic terms. Economic SDIs are interested in impacts on economic prosperity, long-term unemployment and poverty, whereas, as we have seen, CBA is focused on time savings. The reason it places so much emphasis on journey time savings is because they are assumed to be a good proxy for the promotion of economic activity – or, in SDI terms, economic development capable of promoting prosperity and tackling long-term unemployment and associated poverty. Yet the relationships between transport investment and economic development are complex and indirect, and our understanding of them is by no means complete (Chapter 2). It is not at all clear, for example, that thousands of individuals each saving small amounts of time translates directly into productivity improvements. This is especially the case where networks are already well developed, or where time savings are barely noticeable (one or two minutes in a much longer journey), or if they are unevenly distributed to favour leisure rather than business travel, or if they do not materialise at all, perhaps due to traffic 'induced' by drivers taking advantage of better road conditions to the point that its newly expanded capacity is soon exceeded (Banister and Berechman 2000, Metz 2008; Chapter 7). The reliance on time savings breaks down further when applied to non-highway schemes, such as public transport, walking or cycling investments, where elements of the journey can be productive or enjoyable (Jain and Lyons 2007, Hickman et al 2013). In these cases, travel time might be seen as at least partially 'positive', rather than something that it is desirable to reduce (Chapter 10).

Some policy areas, such as regeneration – which is included in WebTAG as an 'economic' indicator, but also has large social implications – are very poorly understood in terms of the likely impact transport investment will have. An immediate shortcoming of the reliance on estimated time savings is that funding tends to favour successful, busy urban areas, where the assumed 'benefits' are greatest and most easily quantified. Investment in non-highway projects and in more deprived areas is much more difficult to justify, resulting in too many missed opportunities for transport projects to contribute to important social policy objectives, as well as a reinforcement of spatial inequity. A set of projects is selected that helps with perceived time savings, but not with objectives for regeneration, social inclusion, the economy, the environment or the development of attractive cities.

This situation is compounded because the WebTAG guidance on regeneration is weak, attempting to quantify likely impacts relative to known developments (DfT 2014b) on the assumption that transport will somehow stimulate development and that this can be easily estimated. The problem, as with productivity improvements, is that there are only indirect relationships between transport investment and developmental impacts, particularly in areas with severe social deprivation issues. Any developmental impact is likely to be a combination of transport investment as well as planning and economic policies, prevailing economic characteristics, the local skills/jobs match and any number of other factors (Banister and Berechman 2000). In other words, there are multiple contributory factors, with multi-directional relationships, all of which are prone to differ, relative to the local context.

Asking the question solely from the transport planning perspective – that is, what impact will the transport project have? – and expecting a definitive answer, is only likely to lead to a simplistic understanding because of the many contributory factors at play. What is planned in terms of surrounding development is critical to the 'impact', but often an urban strategy that would need to be integrated with the infrastructure investment is missing. There are unlikely to be general elasticities to be derived and synergistic impacts are also likely to be underestimated. But ignoring the developmental impacts in the CBA also means that transport projects with potentially important regeneration and social elements are undervalued. Although there are examples of projects being built for regeneration or development objectives despite low BCRs – such as the Jubilee Line Extension from Westminster to Stratford (with a BCR of 0.95:1) – these are exceptions. Crossrail, now renamed as the Elizabeth Line, led to a change in the appraisal methodology so that the process could more fully incorporate development change or 'agglomeration factors' – the BCR increased from 1.8:1 to 2.6:1 once estimated wider economic benefits were included. But, usually, it is only well-resourced, large-city authorities that can develop the evidence base to justify projects beyond a poor BCR. To stand a chance of being funded, most projects usually need a good 'transport only' BCR.

Although WebTAG is difficult to reconcile with the UK's SDIs, it does nevertheless recognise the concept of sustainability, drawing its understanding from the conventional 'three pillars' concept. This assumes there is equal weight given to all of the pillars in the process and, also, that a solution can be found that contributes well against each of the economic, social and environmental objectives identified (Figure 6.3(a)). Yet in the messy reality of the world to which policies are applied, there is no guarantee that this is the case and, in any event, the economic pillar is given much greater weight in the decision-making process through the CBA. Perhaps there is not a solution to be found that contributes to all objectives (Figure 6.3(b)). But what if we were to adopt a different interpretation and application of the sustainability concept itself; might this lead us to a different framing of transport appraisal? An alternative to the three pillars is the 'nested' concept of sustainability (Giddings et al 2002, Hickman 2017), where all three objectives need to be met for a project to go ahead (Figure 6.3(c)). The idea is that economic objectives are closely linked to and dependent on social and environmental objectives. Indeed, proponents argue that economic objectives cannot be met, certainly in the long term, if social and environmental objectives are breached. A solution is to set thresholds for achievement against particular objectives, beyond which a project would not gain approval. If this interpretation of the sustainability concept were incorporated into the MCA process, with thresholds or targets for certain criteria, it might lead to very different projects being developed.

Figure 6.3: Interpreting sustainability in transport

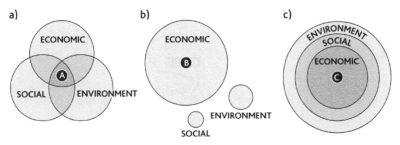

Source: Author

Case study: Merseytram

I use the Merseytram LRT project to illustrate the problems experienced in using CBA and the WebTAG ASTs to appraise transport projects. It is a project that in my view should have been developed but central government funding was ultimately withdrawn by the DfT despite much pro-active work from Merseytravel, project consultants Steer Davies Gleave (SDG) and others. The city of Liverpool has a history of trams, with a very extensive network developed from 1898 onwards. The original tram system was abandoned by the City Council in 1957, but the wide streets remained, and these are still suitable for modern-day LRT systems. The Merseytram proposal, from the early 2000s, was for three tram lines to serve Liverpool and the wider Merseyside area. Line 1 was initially planned in detail, with a loop around Liverpool city centre, connecting to Liverpool Lime Street station and suburban parts of the city, including the Royal Liverpool University Hospital, West Derby and Croxteth. The line was to terminate at Kirkby, in the Borough of Knowsley, a route distance of 18 km (Figure 6.4). More than 100,000 residents lived within 800 metres of the proposed Line 1, 60 per cent of whom without access to a car, so there was a strong social dimension to the project (SDG 2008).

Until quite a late stage in the development of the project it appeared that funding approval would be given. In 2002, the DfT gave provisional approval for £170 million towards the total of £225 million needed for Line 1, with the gap in funding to be met by local sources, mostly Liverpool City Council. The planned opening date was 2007, to precede Liverpool's 'City of Culture' status in 2008. The tram project successfully passed through a Public Inquiry in 2004, but with the DfT's share of the costs rising to £238 million for the DfT (with a project total of £350 million), the local authority was

Figure 6.4: The proposed Merseytram network

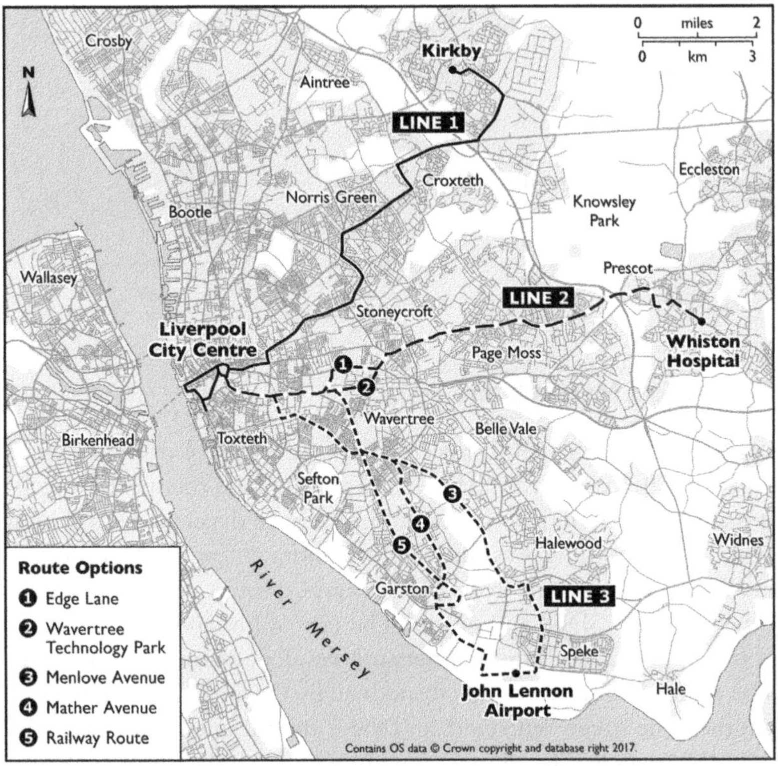

Source: Author

asked to underwrite any cost escalation, which it felt unable to do. DfT funding was subsequently withdrawn in 2005 and the project was cancelled. Some planning work continued on the project subsequent to 2005 with the objective of a revised bid for funding, and an updated CBA from 2008 (Steer Davies Gleave 2008) is given in Table 6.1. This assumed that a revised opening date would be in 2012, with the project assessed for a period of 60 years after the trams started running. All costs and benefits were discounted to 2002 prices. The BCR was given at 1.82:1 – with benefits of £503 million, costs of £277 million and a Net Present Value (NPV) of £226 million – still below the critical DfT 2:1 threshold of 'good' value for money.

Of course, the supposedly technical and objective CBA is based on a range of assumptions that can be disputed and estimated in different ways. The first thing to say is that there was only a small number of factors that went into the CBA, with consumer users (commuting, shopping) and business users (travel during work) accounting for

Table 6.1: Cost–benefit analysis for the proposed Merseytram Line 1

	Monetary value (£000s)*
User benefits (consumer)[1]	523
User benefits (business)[2]	148
Private sector provider impacts (Merseytravel operating costs/revenue)	−182
Accident benefits	10
Greenhouse gas benefits	0.9
Local air quality	2.2
Noise	0.7
Present value of project benefits	503
Present value of scheme costs	277
Net present value (NPV)	226
Benefit–cost ratio (BCR)	1.82**

*Monetary values in 2002 prices.

[1] Consumer user benefits refer to users who are not on business trips, for example commuting and shopping.

[2] Business user benefits refer to users travelling on business trips or travelling between workplaces on working time.

**Adding estimations of wider economic benefits (£32 million) and Kirkby retail and office development brings the BCR to 1.99:1.

Source: Steer Davies Gleave 2008

almost all of the estimated benefits. Other issues were marginal and made very little difference to the BCR. For example, estimated reductions in accidents, greenhouse gases (GHGs), local air quality and noise represented only 2.4 per cent of the benefits. Other costs and benefits remained unquantified and many were unquantifiable. All of this means that the CBA calculation was very partial and, in practice, only *really* represents time savings relative to cost (Hickman and Dean 2017). The BCR is thus quite an arbitrary figure, simply representing the issues that have been quantified and the manner in which this has been done. A second point is that the scale of some of the calculations seems very difficult to justify, such as the order of significance given to time savings relative to reductions in greenhouse gases. Can the impact on GHGs really only be 0.1 per cent of the scale of benefit of time savings? The tradeability principle used in CBA is also difficult to defend, particularly when there is a final aggregated ratio where large estimated impacts can offset others; for example, should a project with large estimated time savings be able to offset a slightly smaller set of adverse social and/or environmental impacts?

The proposed Merseytram scheme demonstrates how the process of CBA is just too simplistic for complex transport projects, where many important impacts are indirect, difficult to quantify and remain outside of the calculation.

Clearly there was a wider multi-criteria analysis, set against the DfT's WebTAG objectives, which was used alongside the CBA to inform the final decision on whether or not to proceed with the project. Table 6.2 gives a summarised version of the AST. Again there is much debate to be had as it seems the MCA process, like the narrower CBA, also greatly underestimates the positive impacts of the LRT system. A further issue is that the AST was constructed relative to an estimated 'do-nothing' projection. Again this is subject to assumptions: had a different projection in usage of the private car been assumed, then Merseytram may have demonstrated more positive environmental and social impacts. The estimation of the reference case in appraisal is critical to the calculated impacts, but rarely discussed in detail and often inaccurate if subsequently evaluated (Nicolaisen and Næss 2015). Here, the AST as framed did not allow other sustainability issues to be considered, including some which are very important in Merseyside, such as economic prosperity, long-term unemployment, poverty, healthy life expectancy, social capital, social mobility, housing provision and natural resource usage. None of these issues was included in the appraisal process.

Another way forward: participatory, multi-actor MCA?

The Merseytram example shows how the transport appraisal process, as applied, fails to provide a useful consideration of the likely impacts of a project against sustainability criteria. While MCA as a concept has strengths, its deployment through the AST criteria was very weak, neither representing local policy priorities nor, for that matter, incorporating the views of different actors. There was no reflection, for example, of whether the project was popular locally or whether there was much controversy – in this case the residents of Merseyside showed great support for LRT, with local opinion polls showing 90 per cent in favour. Other schemes, typically highway projects but also mega-projects such as HS2 (Chapter 11), may attract great opposition yet none of this is reflected in the project appraisal. We should ask whether the system used to appraise the Merseytram proposal could be improved, perhaps by attempting a more intricate assessment and quantification of likely impacts. Could more factors have been added into the CBA? There may well have been some uplift in the range

Table 6.2: Appraisal summary table for the proposed Merseytram Line 1

Objective	Sub-Objective	Impacts	Assessment
Environment	Noise	Some noise from tram operation; some reductions from reduced road traffic	Slight adverse
	Local air quality	No significant impact from trams; mode shift from car results in lower emissions; £2.2m PV	Slight beneficial
	Greenhouse gases	Mode shift from car outweighs increased electricity usage from trams; overall negligible impact; £0.9m PV	Neutral
	Landscape	No significant impact	Neutral
	Townscape	Passes through or adjacent to Conservation Areas and urban green space and open space; loss of trees	Slight adverse
	Heritage	Potential archaeological impacts	Slight adverse
	Biodiversity	Passes through conservation designations	Neutral
	Water environment	No significant impact	Neutral
	Physical fitness	Enhanced provision for pedestrians and cyclists	Slight beneficial
	Journey ambience	High quality in vehicle and interchange	Strong beneficial
Safety	Accidents	Reduction in accidents due to mode shift from car; £10m PV	Slight beneficial
	Security	High visibility at stops and park and ride due to lighting and CCTV	Beneficial
	Transport efficiency	Operating BCR of 1.46:1; Full economic BCR of 1.82:1; Cost to government (central and local) of £277 PV; Benefit PV of £503m	Good Value
	Reliability	Fast, reliable service with off vehicle ticket sales and vehicle priority	Strong beneficial
	Wider economic benefits	Support to regeneration objectives, agglomeration and labour supply impacts; £32m PV WEBs	Strong beneficial

(continued)

Table 6.2: Appraisal summary table for the proposed Merseytram Line 1 (continued)

Objective	Sub-Objective	Impacts	Assessment
Accessibility	Option values	Population of 103,687 within 800m catchment of route	Beneficial
	Severance	Some severance on segregated sections, but better pedestrian crossings provided	Neutral
	Access to transport system	Route serves area of high deprivation and low car ownership; all vehicles and stops fully accessible	Strong beneficial
Integration	Transport interchange	Improved interchange with bus, rail (city centre), park and ride and cycle; integrated ticketing	Strong beneficial
	Land use policy	Consistent with land use and transport strategy for Merseyside; national policies	Beneficial
	Other government policies	Consistent with Government initiatives – access to work, education, social inclusion	Beneficial

Source: Based on Steer Davies Gleave 2008

of analysis, but equally there could have been an increased likelihood of spurious accuracy, especially if analysts had attempted to 'quantify the unquantifiable'.

An alternative – for Merseytram, and more generally – might be a more rigorous use of MCA to assess the scheme against the existing policy objectives of the City Council, with multi-actor views incorporated as part of the process (see Macharis et al 2012). Transport projects might then be more effectively prioritised against what it is that councils are trying to achieve, and policy interventions would have the potential to be more locally rather than nationally derived. A more rigorous ex-post appraisal could also be used to evaluate the success of projects in delivering against policy objectives over time. Such a process could be applied using the five stages outlined in Figure 6.5. In this way, the process of transport planning is carried out in coordination with the urban strategy for the area, on the basis that transport projects have no strategic rationale without the master planning stage. This could draw on the current devolution trend taking place in England – the creation of Transport for the North, for example – where policy priorities are decided more locally, but critically would need greater levels of funding to pass down to decision makers based outside of London. Local policy objectives are then examined and, specifically to move beyond the problems of the partial CBA, wide-ranging quantitative *and qualitative* MCA criteria are developed that enable projects to be assessed against local policy concerns.

Stages 2–4 are carried out in a participatory manner, incorporating multi-actor views on the weighting of criteria and the assessment of impacts. Consistent with the framework of 'nested' sustainability, limits or targets can also be applied to particular criteria, so that a threshold of progress has to be made in some areas – CO_2 reduction or social equity, perhaps – and without this a project would not be given approval. A workshop or decision conference(s) can be used to discuss the different actor views and to debate the issues. In the UK, public inquiries are sometimes used to help discuss transport projects, but the decision conference can be a less formal version that allows a much more open discussion of issues, albeit structured by the participatory MCA process. Emerging work in this area (Leleur 2012, Macharis et al 2012, Dean et al 2019) is helping to define better working processes which could be much more thoroughly tested in the UK. Again building on England's devolution trend, the use of MCA could be part of a process of strengthened regionalism, where local planning strategies and transport projects are decided against a funding stream managed beyond centralised DfT control. The final stage is

Figure 6.5: A participatory, multi-actor, multi-criteria analysis process

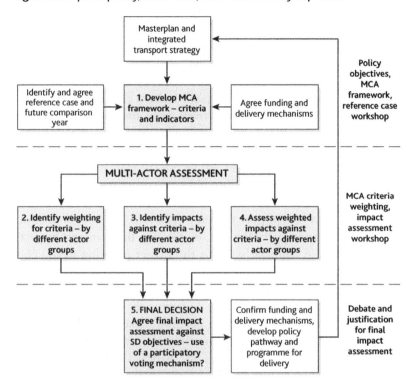

Sources: Dean et al 2019; Hickman et al 2017

to debate the weighted impact analysis, to develop some consensus across the multi-actor viewpoints and to reach the final funding decision. Hence there is a form of deliberative and positional analysis, including different perceptions of issues, alternatives and mediation between common interests and conflicts of interest (see Söderbaum 2005). The level of participation could differ according to context – either it is carried out in the workshop setting or perhaps there could be a more formal voting process, similar to the referendums held on major projects in Switzerland.

None of this is to claim that MCA is immune to problems already discussed in relation to CBA – quantification, the trading of criteria and the potential for manipulation of the process. But a strengthened process of participatory, multi-actor MCA would help in raising the level of debate among the public on major transport projects (Chapter 11). It would also be much more transparent, and as such a much-strengthened process relative to that carried out under WebTAG, with a greater potential to avoid accusations of manipulation. A judicious appraisal process would help prioritise the appropriate projects and facilitate the development of high-quality public transport systems, and high-quality towns and cities.

The history of Merseytram, and indeed many other attempts to fund local public transport in the UK, is not positive when viewed relative to practice in mainland Europe. There is an unrelenting struggle to fund effective urban public transport systems, yet funding once again appears for a series of highway projects (especially in England since the introduction of the Road Investment Strategy; see Chapters 1 and 7) and there is ongoing – if poor value-for-money – support for some national rail schemes. Much better practice can be seen in countries in North West Europe, such as Germany, France and the Netherlands. In Germany, for example, 44 cities have modern LRT systems, most of them upgrades to old networks developed from the late 1890s and early 1900s. In France, 27 cities have built LRT projects. Nantes led the way with the development of its modern tram system from 1985, and others have followed with high-quality projects, including Strasbourg, Bordeaux, Montpellier and Tours. Many of the LRT systems have supported the redevelopment of attractive historic city centres, with some later examples supporting the regeneration of deprived smaller urban areas, such as in Valenciennes.

The contrast with UK practice is stark – Oxford, Cambridge, Bath, Bristol, Leeds, Liverpool, Glasgow, Cardiff, much of central and suburban London and many other cities and urban areas still have no LRT lines. There are just nine cities in the UK with LRT systems, and network coverage and the quality in streetscape design is extremely limited. John Prescott's vision for 25 new LRT lines (Department of Transport, Local Government and the Regions (DTLR) 2000), the high point of aspiration for modern LRT investment in the UK, failed to be implemented due to a lack of political support, funding and subsequent less-supportive administrations (Docherty and Shaw 2008). The projects that have been built also compare poorly to the practice in continental Europe, with too little attention given to the integration of the systems with urban planning and public realm improvements.

This is a sorry story, which does not seem to register on the political, or indeed public, consciousness. In part, this is due to the lack of deliberation in the transport planning process – projects are developed with little thought given to participation and education. The appraisal system in the UK is significantly to blame in this regard, with the effect of moving investment away from high-quality urban public transport projects that include a level of public realm design capable of enhancing cities' attractiveness. Think of many revitalised cities in Germany or

France, and it is the tram systems, imaginative and inclusive streetscape design, and an associated investment in walking and cycling that help to facilitate a high quality of urban life. Perhaps critically, it is progress against transport and planning policy objectives, rather than an over-reliance on central government's determination of 'good value for money' BCRs, that seems to be important in French and German decision-making processes (Hickman and Osborne 2017). The current transport appraisal process in the UK is severely outdated – it is not addressing contemporary policy objectives and it incorporates only very weak participation, and the results in our cities are disastrous.

Conclusions

The reliance of UK transport appraisal on a partial CBA, alongside a weak application of MCA, means that the prioritisation of transport projects is made mostly against economic efficiency criteria. By definition, the analysis poorly quantifies variables or leaves out unquantifiable variables – such as the impact of LRT projects on reduced CO_2 emissions, levels of deprivation, social equity, urban quality, quality of life, and the opportunity for social mobility – which, from a city planning perspective, are by far the most important. In addition, the practice of appraisal is wrapped up in economic jargon, which few non-specialists can understand and engage with. This 'black boxing' makes the process non-transparent, difficult to debate and open to manipulation, far from the objective, value-free and systematic process that CBA is proffered as. From a social science perspective, transport projects and their impacts are complex, involving people and difficult to model behaviours that render partial quantitative analyses unable to take us beyond a limited understanding of likely impacts, costs and benefits of different interventions. It is unwise to prioritise transport projects according to a simplistic calculation of time savings versus cost.

An LRT scheme, serving a city such as Liverpool and its surrounds, is not built just for reasons of saving its passengers' time, but also to deliver large numbers of people into a vibrant city centre and other successful urban districts. Transport projects can be developed in support of urban planning strategies to help regenerate development sites, improve access to services and jobs for city populations and enhance the public realm. A narrow focus on 'economic efficiency' is a very partial calculation and excludes all of these important issues, and in this context a cost overrun for Merseytram from £225 million to £350 million, and a relatively low BCR, are largely irrelevant.

Perhaps the initial costing had been too low; perhaps a higher quality specification should cost more money? Perhaps improving social equity in the city, so that everyone and especially non-car drivers can access jobs and other activities, is worth a higher price? Many of these benefits (and costs) are not included in the CBA, and cannot be, as they represent indirect impacts that may/may not follow the transport investment and cannot effectively be quantified.

For some, CBA is viewed as 'promoting a deregulatory agenda under the cover of scientific objectivity' (Ackerman and Heinzerling 2004: 9). It certainly seems this is the case within UK transport appraisal, where public transport, walking, public realm and cycling projects prove difficult to justify, but highway projects, supporting the use of private vehicles, are much easier to develop. The CBA process was devised to support investment in highway networks and to this day it seems particularly ill-suited to prioritising investment in other modes. Its use in transport appraisal characterises it as a kind of 'technology of power' (Foucault 1997), used to maintain and enhance the current system of mainly car-based travel. It is a form of gentle tyranny, providing the illusion of objectivity, transparency and choice, but instead restricting the flow of funding to particular projects, areas and regions.

In the end, the current process leads to too little progress against important local and national policy goals, such as the social and environmental dimensions of sustainability, and too few LRT projects are being developed in the UK. Transport is not being utilised effectively as a tool in city development and regeneration, in the way that it is in Germany and France. Returning to the language of Jonathan Swift with which the chapter began, a modest proposal is that we more critically discuss our approaches to transport appraisal and test different processes according to projects and contexts. At the least we require such discussion to bring about an overhaul of our transport appraisal criteria, to better map them onto sustainability objectives and align them with contemporary policy objectives. That Merseytram has not already been running for over ten years is a serious indictment of UK transport planning: the project was critical to achieving more environmentally sustainable travel behaviours, social equity goals and an improved city centre. If we cannot deliver a tram system in Merseyside, then there is something wrong with the transport planning process in the UK. If we wish to develop attractive cities with environmentally, socially *and economically* sustainable transport systems (Chapter 2), then there needs to be some rethinking of the transport planning decision-making process. We have discussed the planning of an LRT system on Merseyside but, of course, the implications are much wider.

Acknowledgements

Thanks to Alan Jones from Steer Davies Gleave for providing the updated economic case for Merseytram and his views on the project, and to Rob Cowan for the CBA cartoon.

References

Ackerman, F and Heinzerling, L (2004) *Priceless: On Knowing the Price of Everything and the Value of Nothing*, New York: New Press.

Adams, J (1974) '... and how much for your grandmother?, *Environment and Planning A*, 6(6): 619–26.

Adams, J (1994) The role of cost–benefit analysis in environmental debates. http://john-adams.co.uk/wp-content/uploads/2006/The role of cost–benefit analysis in environmental debates.pdf Accessed February 2014.

Banister, D and Berechman, J (2000) *Transport Investment and Economic Development*, London: UCL Press.

Cairns, S, Atkins, S and Goodwin, P (2002) 'Disappearing traffic? The story so far', *Municipal Engineer*, 151(1): 13–22.

Dean, M, Hickman, R and Chen, C-L (2019) 'Testing the application of participatory MCA: the case of the South Fylde Line', *Transport Policy*, 73: 62–70.

Department for Environment, Food & Rural Affairs (2013) *Sustainable Development Indicators*. DEFRA, London.

Department for Transport (2014a) *Transport Analysis Guidance (WebTAG), TAG Unit A1.1, Cost–Benefit Analysis*. DfT, London.

Department for Transport (2014b) *Transport Analysis Guidance (WebTAG), TAG Unit A2.2, Regeneration Impacts*. DfT, London.

Department for Transport (2017) *Transport Analysis Guidance (WebTAG)*. DfT, London.

Department of Transport, Local Government and the Regions (2000). *Transport: The 10 Year Plan*, London: TSO.

Docherty, I and Shaw, J (2008) *Traffic Jam: Ten Years of 'Sustainable' Transport in the UK*, Bristol: Policy Press.

Docherty, I, Shaw, J, Marsden, G and Anable, J (2018) 'The curious death – and life? – of British transport policy', *Environment and Planning C: Politics and Space*, 36(8): 1458–79.

Foucault, M (1997) *Society Must Be Defended: Lectures at the Collège de France, 1975–1976*, New York, St. Martin's Press.

Giddings, B, Hopwood, B and O'Brien, G (2002) 'Environment, economy and society: fitting them together into sustainable development', *Sustainable Development*, 10(4): 187–96.

Hickman, R (2017) 'Sustainable travel or sustaining growth?', in J Cowie and S Ison (eds) *The Routledge Handbook of Transport Economics*, Abingdon: Routledge, pp 311–22.

Hickman, R and Dean, M (2017) 'Incomplete cost – incomplete benefit analysis in transport appraisal', *Transport Reviews*, 38(6): 689–709.

Hickman, R and Osborne, C (2017) *Sintropher Executive Summary*. Interreg IVB. UCL, London.

Hickman, R, Hamiduddin, I, Hosea, B, Roberts, S, Hall, P, Jones, P and Osborne, C (2013) 'Animating the future seamless public transport journey', *Built Environment*, 39(3): 369–84.

Jain, J and Lyons, G (2007) 'The gift of travel time', *Journal of Transport Geography*, 16(2): 81–9.

Leleur, S (2012) *Complex Strategic Choices: Applying Systemic Planning for Strategic Decision Making*, London: Springer Verlag.

Macharis, C, Turcksin, L and Lebeau, K (2012) 'Multi actor multi criteria analysis (MAMCA) as a tool to support sustainable decisions: State of use', *Decision Support Systems*, 54(1): 610–20.

Mackie, P, Worsley, T and Eliasson, J (2014) 'Transport appraisal revisited', *Research in Transportation Economics*, 47: 3–18.

Metz, D (2008) 'The myth of travel time saving', *Transport Reviews*, 28(3): 321–36.

Næss, P (2006) 'Cost–benefit analyses of transportation investments: neither critical nor realistic', *Journal of Critical Realism*, 5(1): 32–60.

Næss, P (2016) 'Inaccurate and biased: cost–benefit analyses of transport infrastructure projects', in P Næss and L Price (eds) *Crisis System: A Critical Realist and Environmental Critique of Economics and the Economy*, Abingdon: Routledge.

Newman, P and Kenworthy, J (2015) *The End of Automobile Dependence. How Cities are Moving Beyond Car-based Planning*, Washington DC: Island Press.

Nicolaisen, M and Næss, P (2015) 'Roads to nowhere: the accuracy of travel demand forecasts for do-nothing alternatives', *Transport Policy*, 37(C): 57–63.

Self, P (1970) 'Nonsense on stilts: cost–benefit analysis and the Roskill Commission', *The Political Quarterly*, 41(3): 249–60.

Söderbaum, P (2005) 'Democracy and sustainable development – what is the alternative to cost–benefit analysis?', *Integrated Environmental Assessment and Management*, 2(2): 182–90.

Steer Davies Gleave (2008) *Merseytram Line 1 Business Case. Final Report.* SDG and Merseytravel, Liverpool.

Swift, J (1729) *A modest proposal for preventing the children of poor people in Ireland, from being a burden on their parents or country, and for making them beneficial to the publick.* www.gutenberg.org/ebooks/1080?msg=welcome_stranger Accessed 30 May 2019.

7

Forecasting road traffic and its significance for transport policy

Phil Goodwin

Introduction

The context of transport policy development after the initial recovery and reconstruction period at the end of the Second World War was dominated by two main issues. The first was the ownership, regulation and service delivery of the transport industries, and the second was coping with rising road traffic by the development of what was seen as a modern road system. It was how the second of these tasks evolved and transformed over the next three quarters of a century which is the main topic of this chapter, and especially how this interacted with the technical methods of forecasting how much traffic there would be, the gradual death of 'predict and provide' as an intellectually respectable planning theory, its long after-life as planning practice, tensions in its policy consequences, the growth of alternatives grounded in an acceptance of uncertainty, and a recognition of fundamental changes to social life.

The interaction of technical appraisal and policy development affected everything in the sector, in ways which were an uncomfortable interweaving of feelings that road appraisal was either the jewel in the crown of formal strategic thinking, or a biased and distorted barrier to it. It is also a story reflecting my whole professional career, having worked as a young researcher with the people who had themselves previously started traffic forecasting in the UK, and then met, and sometimes worked with, the authors of nearly all of the reports acknowledged in the reference list. I should state that I have often been a protagonist in arguments I comment on in this text, which may colour my account.

Road Research Laboratory traffic forecasts 1958–75 and the ACTRA Review 1976–7

Technical work by Glanville and Smeed (1958) of the government's Road Research Laboratory (RRL) calculating likely future traffic levels can be regarded as the beginnings of modern traffic forecasting in the UK. The phrase 'predict and provide', whose origin is unknown, had not yet been used in a transport context, but essentially it was taken as given that the role of such forecasts was to guide how much road space would be needed, notably in the construction of what became the motorway network. RRL set about developing mathematical methodologies for traffic forecasting, led by the statistician John Tanner, who was treated with respect touching on awe in his time. He gave an overview in Tanner (1965).

A key part of the methodology was that its functional form was a long S-shaped growth curve. It was founded on the proposition that at some point in the future the number of cars and the volume of traffic they would generate had an upper limit, known as the saturation level. In general this was taken as deriving from social and economic factors (sometimes described in terms such as 'when everybody who wanted and needed a car would have one', *not* from the idea of a road network which would be 'full up'). The estimation of the upper limit was derived from observation of the behaviour of the richest people and the richest areas, and the speed at which car ownership and traffic approached this limit was thought to be influenced by incomes and (less so, at that stage) by prices. Empirical research suggested that the quality and price of public transport would have an influence on the eventual saturation level, as would demographic and planning trends, which in principle would have opened the door to considering the feedback effects of wider policy on traffic, but this work failed to get traction in official forecasts, being subsumed in rather generic 'external trends'. The absence of such factors in forecasting continued for decades, generally narrowing the consideration of what policy on land use or public transport would contribute to traffic problems. There was little or no consideration at all that the limit might be influenced as an act of deliberate policy or chosen as a strategic objective, for example to achieve environmental aims as appeared later. Thus the forecasts drove the policy rather than vice versa.

The high point of this form of forecasting was in the 1970s, a key example being published by Tulpule (1973), with a forecasting period of nearly 40 years, from 1972 to 2010. This period gave us the only work we have for which the complete period of a long-term forecast can be compared against the observed outcome. This is shown, for car ownership and traffic, in Figures 7.1 and 7.2.

An S-shaped curve with an upper bound, when saturation is deemed to be far away, can be quite sensitive to the effects of other factors such as prices and incomes, but over the longer term the saturation level will have an increasingly strong effect on constraining and limiting any errors due to other factors. This was its strength and its weakness. Its

Figure 7.1: Transport and Road Research Laboratory forecasts for car ownership, 1972 base

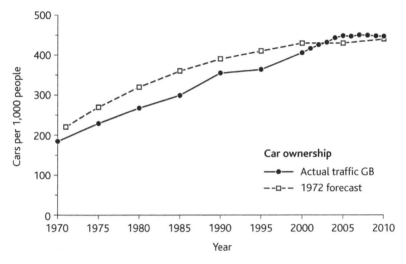

Source: Tulpule 1973

Figure 7.2: Transport and Road Research Laboratory forecasts for traffic, 1972 base

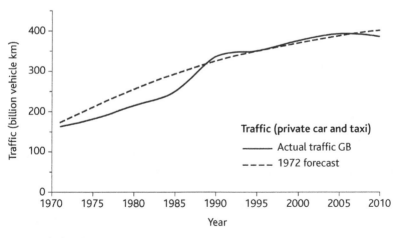

Source: Tulpule 1973

strength was only shown in the long term, when by 2010 the figures were quite extraordinarily close to reality, allowing the possibility of speculating that the ultimate saturation level was well-judged, enabling it to get forecasts right in the end in spite of the crudeness of other aspects of the model. There can be very few examples indeed where forecasts of major social trends, made 40 years ahead, are so spot-on accurate not only in broad direction but in the numbers as well.

By 2010, however, there was no hint of celebration of the achievement, no 'I told you so'; nobody even noticed. The key authors and their teams had all moved on, retired or died. The model itself had been completely lost from the collective memory of transport planners. Its concepts were off any technical or political agenda, though oddly they were on the brink of being revived, as discussed later. This deletion from history arose because of the shorter term weaknesses, which had already killed the method off in the early years, when it consistently underestimated traffic growth, and therefore was seen as providing insufficient justification for expanding an inadequate road system.

There was swift and decisive action. The policy needs demanded a new form of forecasting. Already by September 1976 the Department of Transport (DoT) established a committee of inquiry, the Advisory Committee on Trunk Road Assessment (ACTRA), independent and non-departmental in form. It had its own chair, Sir George Leitch, and reported in 1977, in the context of a wider assessment of the use of cost–benefit analysis, concluding that the process used for forecasting was flawed, and should be replaced by a new method based on what were described as 'causal' relationships (DoT 1977). This was almost immediately agreed. Though some in RRL were unconvinced, and an account of the internal civil service discussions is not available, it seems that its recommendations had been agreed in discussion with the DoT well before publication. A new model had to be produced which would not underestimate traffic growth.

This process took place in parallel (but hardly interacting) with the development of mass campaigns and political action protesting against large-scale road building, notably in the 'Homes before Roads' movement in London and spreading into other areas. The plans had been developed on the basis of other modelling methods, local and regional in character, which had indeed produced high traffic growth forecasts. Thus at the same time as decisions were being taken to encourage such methods, there were political signs that their use might be controversial, which indeed proved to be the case, as shown in 1989, discussed later.[1]

RHTM and ACTRA's Second Review, 1977–80

Meanwhile, the task at a national level proved to be less easy to do than expected. There was a very substantial effort to build a new regional highway traffic model, RHTM, under the leadership of Ron Bridle, the DoT's Chief Engineer (at that time a very senior post of great importance within the DoT). He was closely involved with the technical detail of the work, carried out partly under commission by external consultants. The work programme involved a large proportion of the academic and consultancy expertise of the country, with teams in the leading university transport institutes as well as the consultants and in-house scientific civil service, though not all those involved were convinced it was on the right track. By 1980, apparently from a leak, *New Scientist* described it as a failure, suggesting this had already been recognised internally by 1979.[2] It was abandoned.

Thus within one decade a new model had been adopted, assessed, found wanting, abandoned, a new procedure planned, developed, found wanting and abandoned. By later standards this would be considered as breakneck speed, and unusual openness about the deficiencies of current methods. All this was at a time of high and increasing rates of growth in traffic, and indeed many incremental road projects: the lack of a satisfactory method of forecasting did not stand in the way of plans and designs for many national and local road schemes, favoured projects of road engineers and some planners, which were either implemented, or abandoned following much controversy and political opposition (though often reverting to a semi-underground library of 'top drawer' schemes in local authorities, to be raised again every decade or so).

Traffic forecasts and policy development: the paradox of 1989

An alternative track was initiated based on a rather pragmatic and less ambitious methodology, which became known as the National Transport Model (NTM) and has been incrementally revised ever since. Its first tests found it capable of forecasting the high rates of traffic growth that were observed. It was evident that there had been a solution to the problem of underestimating traffic growth, though there appeared to be little link with rising opposition to the proposition that high forecast traffic growth necessarily would validate more road building. A provisional version of the new method was used for forecasts in 1987–8, revised for 1989, and then successively revised ever since. The turning point was provided by the 1989 Road Traffic Forecasts, which projected the high actual growth of the 1980s into the entire forecasting period, and were published alongside, and as a justification for, the *Roads for Prosperity* (DoT 1989) construction plans, described at the time as the 'largest road programme since the Romans'.

There followed a period dealt with in some detail in the two previous books in this series (Docherty and Shaw 2003, 2008; see also Chapter 1). 1989 turned out to have an effect on policy exactly opposite to what was expected and planned, an effect of profound significance to all subsequent policy argument. The forecast traffic growth was so high that the proposed extra road capacity was not enough to cope with it. The British Road Federation (the main lobbyists of the time) published an ill-fated report showing that even twice as much road building as planned would not keep pace with traffic, and the intended improvements in congestion would be, at best, slowing down the pace at which congestion got worse. Local authorities, especially some Conservative councils in the south east of England, concluded that the high forecasts required a new generic transport policy tool, 'demand management' (which included road user charging), to reduce traffic growth, instead of the declared approach of road building to provide for it. This duly became, for a time, the Conservative declared policy by about 1994, a period which later seemed to have been forgotten, a puzzle currently the topic of research by Steve Melia at the Centre for Transport & Society, and was extended in the Labour government's strategy from 1998, converted into policy in the White Paper *A New Deal for Transport* (Department of the Environment, Transport and the Regions (DETR) 1998) though subsequently shifted in direction in the *10 Year Plan for Transport* (DETR 2000).

But the key development was that high road traffic forecasts led to less road building. There were still unresolved arguments about the forecasting method and reliability, including challenges to the validity of the high forecasts. There were also unresolved policy arguments about the most appropriate transport policies that should be followed. But, crucially, the two sets of arguments did not map on to each other, leaving a fault line in the relationship between forecasting and policy which is only now starting to be resolved. Then, it suited both those who wanted more road building and those who wanted less, to construct their arguments around the same high forecasts, one side using the argument that they were 'so high that extra roads were necessary' and the other side that they were 'so high that extra roads would not be useful'. The uneasy synthesis 'necessary but useless' did not make for a long-lasting or comfortable consensus in policy formation, and the flaw kept re-emerging.

Between the 1989 traffic forecasts and *A New Deal for Transport*, Owens (1995) coined the phrase 'predict and prevent' to replace 'predict and provide' in an influential paper which broke the previous axiom that high traffic forecasts must justify high road building politically. But this did not change the link in the formal appraisal system for new road construction projects, where in general the social cost–benefit analyses based on high forecasts continued to show high benefits from extra capacity, by comparison with a counter-factual 'without' case, often being examples of benefits from things getting worse more slowly. There entered a strange and surprisingly long-lasting period where the forecasts were manifestly wrong and the appraisal results, to that extent, misleading.

What if the traffic forecasts are overestimated? 1989–2014

From the point of view of accuracy, the key point is that the new forecasting methods, initially triggered to avoid underestimation, developed a consistent record, for over 25 years, of substantially overestimating traffic growth, primarily due to overestimating car traffic growth, this overestimate increasing the longer the time period concerned. The forecasts needed to be revised downwards every few years, either by changing the relationships or rebasing the data. This is shown in Figure 7.3, originally from a very short article in 2012,

Figure 7.3: Traffic forecast overestimates from 1989 to 2011

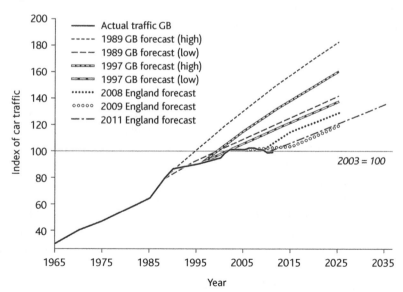

Source: Goodwin 2012

which became a key meme in the technical discussion about forecasts, and the consequential policy debates.

There is no challenge about the validity or relevance of this graph, and it has been the subject of discussion among most stakeholders concerned about the forecasts, including the Department for Transport (DfT), who produced their own (substantially similar) version of the figure, with annotations suggesting how it should be interpreted. The fact of overestimation and scale of overestimation are not in dispute. It must be purely a coincidence that Tulpule's (1973) long-abandoned forecasts started to map closely on to the actual figures in about 1989, as may be seen by comparing Figure 7.1 and Figure 7.3.

Explanations for the errors

DfT argued that the primary source for the errors was faulty input assumptions about economic growth and future population (and to a lesser extent, fuel prices). This argument is based on retrospectively rerunning elements of the model for the recent period, with correct input data, and producing an estimate of what the forecasts would have been if there had been accurate prior estimates of the future progress of national income, population and fuel price. It was argued that the forecasts would then have been acceptably close to the observed traffic. The model is very complicated and cumbersome, and not available for open access by other users, so the detailed calculations underpinning this conclusion have not been replicated or verified outside the DfT. In all models, inherently, there are other weaknesses, and alternative explanations have been offered, including structural weaknesses in the form and parameters of the model. (My own criticism would mainly be that its reliance on the economic concept of 'equilibrium' makes it biased when considering long periods of unstable trends, but that has not been a very widely shared professional judgement, and is outside the scope of this chapter.) In any case, the explanation meant that it was deemed not necessary formally to abandon the model and replace it with a new one, as had happened in the 1970s and 1980s.[3]

The conclusions that follow from that are different according to whether the DfT explanation is accepted or not. If it is accepted, it implies that the DfT model is broadly accurate, and the main problem is a long-term failure by other departments of government to forecast national income and population to sufficient accuracy to produce reliable road traffic forecasts, with a systematic bias in one direction. Remedial action might be sought by increasing emphasis on scenarios less dependent on the forecasts by other government departments. It is not considered acceptable (or practical) that one department should produce its own forecasts in conflict with others, but there are ways around this, for example to use past trend rates for national income or population. Another approach would be to change the functional form of the relationships with income and population to include damping factors – such as the concept of saturation – which reduce the build-up of errors over time. The model is still in use, and current work by DfT to develop a new model somewhat similar in scope to RHTM, is being done on the premise that there is nothing fundamentally wrong with the current one.

But the question of how the forecasts were to be used is in some ways more important than the question of how precisely accurate it is judged to be. During this period, such forecasts typically had a central (or 'base' or 'reference') forecast, and a narrow fan of alternative possibilities, comprised of sensitivity tests for other assumptions on income, population, and so on. In practice, most users treated the central case as being the official judgement on the most likely future, and alternatives as less likely, with the published upper and lower bounds representing the official view as being the outer bounds of possibility. As a result, forecasts on a single traffic trajectory, or a narrow range, dominated the appraisal of policies and, using more detailed local models, of specific projects. This narrow (and mostly retrospectively wrong) view of the future forecasts set a tone for national strategic discussion, and was very influential as the starting point for local project appraisal. In government, the pre-1989 intuitive judgement was followed that high forecasts merit an expanded road programme, though as the 1989–94 experience showed, the opposite can be true.

New issues for forecasting after 1989

Over the whole 25-year period from 1989 to 2014, the forecasts were for indefinitely continuing traffic growth – always overestimated, with a continuing argument about why, and an unceasing debate about the policy implications. I would say that this period was bounded by the forecasts in 1989, for the reasons discussed earlier, and 2015 which provided a key break-point in the presentation. By 2018 the whole logic of how forecasts could feed through into policy shows an important change. I will argue later that this is a key breakthrough, but first it is useful to track three specific changes in understanding and methodology which laid the basis for the recent change. These relate to induced traffic, 'peak car' and the re-emergence of the concept of saturation, and empirical research on shifts in behaviour, especially that of young people.

Induced traffic

Quite early in the 'overestimate' period there were important changes which came from the Standing Advisory Committee on Trunk Road Assessment (SACTRA), an independent advisory committee appointed by and reporting to ministers. Among a series of reports, one, SACTRA (1994), reported that the significant extra road capacity, in the context or presence of forecast future congestion, generated additional road traffic, hence reducing the period of relief of congestion, and the benefits available from reducing it, compared with assuming that there was no such extra induced traffic. (This had been a recurrent theme of road planning since the 1930s, with successive waves accepting or denying its importance.) The 1994 report, and a subsequent review by Cairns et al (1998) of the opposite effect, when reducing road capacity reduces the volume of traffic, together represent the most substantial evidence-based review, before or since.

Initially there was a lot of resistance to the emerging line of argument for the 1994 report, with the impression that the DfT had rather expected there would be little evidence available to draw clear conclusions, but by the time of publication officials were persuaded that it was right, and implementable, amending its guidelines subsequently. When it was published it received much media attention along the lines of 'devastating critique of government methods', and technical criticism including a set-piece formal debate at the Institution of Civil Engineers about whether the SACTRA report was a 'Millstone or Milestone',[4] but it was happily absorbed into subsequent orthodoxy without great difficulty. There is, however, some repeated experience that the promoters of road schemes have a tendency to underestimate the scale of induced traffic (and hence overestimate the benefit of schemes) requiring refreshment of the now entirely robust evidence of its importance.

A more recent example of this is a difference of judgement between Highways England (2016) and the Campaign to Protect Rural England (CPRE) (Sloman et al 2017) about the retrospective evaluation of major road schemes in England. A key point of difference was the significance of Highways England's claim that there was no obvious systematic overestimate or underestimate of the traffic forecast for major road building projects (that is, their errors were more or less evenly spread on both sides). On the other hand there was a systematic tendency to overestimate general background traffic growth, on the network as a whole.

In these circumstances the simplest reconciliation of the two findings is that benefits have been overestimated by two different calculations even if the forecast traffic on the improved sections is accurate. The first is that all benefits are calculated by the difference between what happens with the scheme and what would have happened without: it is never possible to observe both cases, so the difference cannot be verified by scientific measurement, but traffic growth on the rest of the network is likely to be the best approximation. If traffic on the implied 'without' case is overestimated, then so will be the congestion levels, the estimated 'without' case will be worse than really would have happened, and the benefit of having the scheme will be overestimated not by errors in the observed case but by errors in the unobserved counter-factual case. The second calculation is that it implies that the forecast 'with' case has been correct partly or fully as a result of induced traffic being higher than had been assumed, which would again reduce the calculated benefit even if the forecast post-construction traffic flows are correct.[5]

Peak car and the re-emergence of saturation

Although Tulpule's (1973) forecasts had been long forgotten, other approaches had reappeared from time to time with suggestions which supported the idea of a saturation or upper bound on car traffic. These gained little traction but took off in a flurry of interest in many countries from 2010, mostly using the label of 'Peak Car',[6] based on observation of very low growth in car ownership and use, and downturns in some places. The literature is very extensive and controversial in several respects, and widely reviewed, including work by Metz (2010, 2013), Goodwin (2011, 2012), Millard-Ball and Schipper (2011) and Newman and Kenworthy (2011). There was also an International Transport Forum (ITF) Paris Round Table conference on the subject in 2012, followed by a special issue of the journal *Transport Reviews* in 2013. Goodwin and Van Dender (2013) drew specific attention to the common feature in many countries of a tendency for young people to be less car-oriented than previous generations. A suggestion that the appearance of peak car could have been explained and predicted without changes to established national forecasting methods was made by Bastian et al (2016), and a criticism made of that criticism by Wadud and Baierl (2017).

There were different views among researchers in the field about what it implied for the future. There were three main possibilities:

that it was a temporary feature arising from economic difficulties, allowing for previous high growth to reassert itself when economies recovered; that it showed precisely those features of a more or less stable saturation level that had previously been abandoned; or that it represented the type of a temporary levelling-off typical when an increasing trend slows, stabilises, and then turns down. Each successive year's traffic statistics will be expected to continue this discussion, though reinterpretations of long-term trends should take at least five years and sometimes take decades. It is easy to specify a mathematical equation, fitting historic data well, which projects into each of these three courses, and a full proof cannot be seen in advance.

New trends in travel demand

Alongside the critical work related to induced traffic and peak car, a third factor which was changing the relationship was research work by academics, especially the Demand Commission led by Marsden et al (2018), and work on the changing trends of young people travel by Chatterjee et al (2018), as well as the underpinning in-house research by the DfT itself used for the forecasts. Chatterjee et al's study pursued the widespread observations that rising generations of young people, candidates for learning to drive and seeking car ownership in the early 2010s, did not seem to be doing so as much as earlier generations. In fact there had been a reversal of trend direction as long ago as the early 1990s, not noticed at the time. The two findings most relevant to long-term forecasting were that:

- With some variation from year to year, the general trend has been for each cohort of young people since the early 1990s to own and use cars less than the preceding cohort, this continuing to be seen now, when that cohort is in its 40s.
- The reasons for this were not primarily to be seen in the national average trends in economic growth, population and fuel price (the main drivers of national forecasting), but economic, social and technical factors specific to the new generations.

These causal factors were identified as increased higher education participation, rise of lower paid, less secure jobs and decline in disposable income, decline in home ownership and increases in urban living, and changes in when people start a family, their social interactions (including mobile communication and social media) and costs including learning to drive and insurance. As a result the traditional 'normal' progression from education or training to a job, starting a family, moving to a house in the suburbs and adopting a car-oriented lifestyle has been delayed for some and broken down for others. Reductions in driving and increases in public transport use had occurred to the greatest extent in London and other areas with high population density, where alternatives to driving are more readily available and there are greater constraints on driving. Many of these social changes are not likely to be reversed, and the logic suggests that taken together, they could have a cumulative effect, building up at the speed of generations and lifetimes, with a long-term downward effect on car use, as younger generations replace older ones.

One important implication of the work for national traffic forecasting is that it highlights how the national figures are composed of trends running in opposite directions for different segments of the population (for example, age) or different conditions (for example, urban and rural), and therefore makes it less likely that the same national average statistics for the underlying inputs can explain the underlying process. It also puts the policy discussion firmly within much wider issues of economic and demographic structure, employment conditions, education, planning, and the distribution of income between generations. The connection with 'peak car' was that it focused attention not on explaining the 'average' behaviour of a whole population, but the strengths and longevity of different trends in opposite directions (Chapter 14).

A new forecasting regime: 2015 and 2018

Road Traffic Forecasts 2015 (DfT 2015) was a landmark document, though not widely recognised as such at the time. For nearly half a century there had been some recognition of a form of uncertainty about the future, expressed in forecasts based on slightly higher or slightly lower versions of the same underlying relationships. Mostly a central or core forecast had been considered adequate to cope with planning and investing. The 2015 forecasts used scenarios, with a quite different function. They allowed for the idea that the future is not a set of variants of a single, understood, trajectory, but may be produced by different choices and relationships, so futures are contested, subject to human agency and decisions, in some respects inherently unknowable. The problem is not variants of a common trajectory, or statistical error bands, but different paths in different directions. The scenario approach typically does not produce a simple error band around a central future, but a much wider set of alternatives that may differ in kind (Chapter 16).

The second landmark feature was that in applying this approach to the largest, but most contested, element of traffic growth, namely car traffic, the tone in relation to 'peak car' was not dismissive, but thoughtful and serious. The problem in discussion had been that there was essentially no overlap between the DfT's views and those of its critics. Each side repeated its assertions, but gave little ground. In 2015 a version of the 'peak car' view was included as one of the scenarios, called 'Scenario 3'. In the report, the DfT (2015) wrote that:

- 'We concluded that the factors we typically highlight as being key drivers of road demand – income, costs and population – have been important drivers of recent trends but that they may not tell the whole story' (para 7), and;
- 'We believe our forecasts provide a reasonable range of outcomes for future traffic levels, and we remain confident that they are suitable for the uses to which they are put' (para 18).

As a result, the new set of scenarios established for the first time a slim area of overlap between the forecasts discussed by the DfT and the forecasts discussed by those involved in the concept of peak car. That did not imply that all would – or should – converge on this overlapping area as the territory for negotiating a compromise. But it meant that there could be a serious professional engagement between two approaches that had hardly spoken to each other. The 2015 forecasts did not make much difference in practice, however, as their implications about actually changing the appraisal process were muted. The different scenarios stayed in the report, rather than being used for influencing the choice of policies and projects.

The 2018 forecasts

Road Traffic Forecasts 2018 (DfT 2018) carried on the conversion to a new way of looking at the future. The forecasts needed to accommodate a large unexplained reduction in the base year trip rates simply to recalibrate all the scenarios to a lower level – this problem had not gone away. Having done so, the scenarios adopted were based on two different forecasting assumptions, that reductions in trip rates had now run their course and would stay stable indefinitely into the future, or would continue to decline. There was in addition a scenario (though this was an assumption, not a forecast) of the effects of take-up of electric cars (termed zero emission vehicles), and a further discussion, without quantified projections, of future development of autonomous vehicles (AVs). It became clearer that even (or especially) when the reasons for changes in the trends were not clear, a quite different mode of use in practice would be required, as I argued in a short paper in *Local Transport Today* after they were published (Goodwin 2018). The argument is shown in Figure 7.4, taken from the DfT forecasts, and Figure 7.5, re-imaged by extending the logic, its range inferred from the similar calculation for Scenario 1.

The point of traffic forecasting is to appraise transport policies and projects, and as usual the new DfT forecasts intended to describe the future before allowing for the feedback effects of the new policies and schemes. The theory and implantation of such 'policy neutrality' is difficult, and there are many continuing controversies and unresolved arguments. But whatever the outcome of those discussions, there is a much simpler question, with profound implications. Taking the forecasts as they are, how should transport professionals use them in practice? My proposition is that a simple application could herald the most important step forward in transport policy discussion and project appraisal since the beginning of the era of modelled traffic forecasts, some 50 years ago.

Figure 7.4: DfT road traffic forecast scenarios, 2018

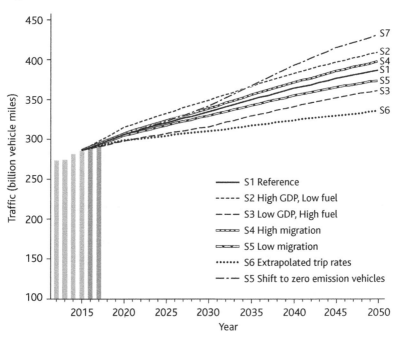

Source: DfT 2018

Figure 7.5: DfT scenarios re-presented as Reference Cases 1 and 6 with their variants

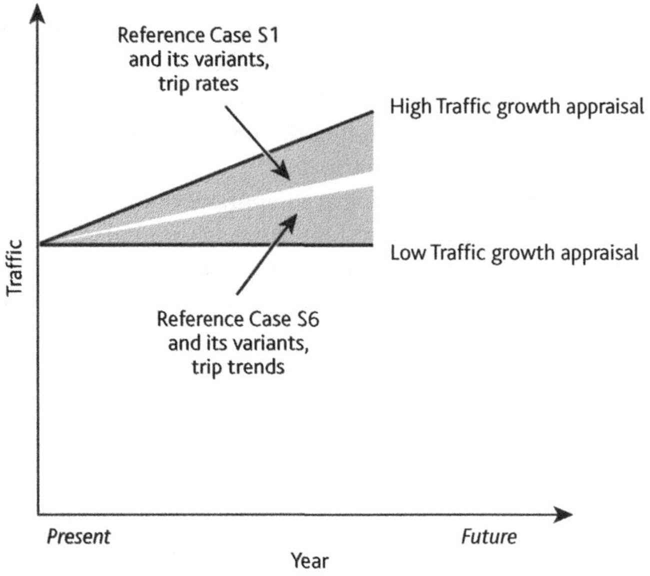

Source: Goodwin 2018

On first sight, the key diagram summarising the forecasts looks much like previous forecasts, with a 'reference case' (S1) generated from current government thinking on economic growth, population and fuel prices, surrounded by variants of these values, based on different assumptions. Until 2015 (and sometimes still), such pictures were usually interpreted, in practice, as describing a single, most probable, 'official' future, called the baseline or central or reference case. The variants, being thought less likely, did not get much attention, either in national discussion or in local forecasts based on local models with a similar logic. In the new forecasts, DfT explicitly explained that no single projection is to be treated as the 'most likely' case. Each of the main forecasting scenarios is intended to be an internally consistent, possible, viable future of what could happen, to be taken seriously in discussion of new projects, policies or interventions that will then affect the forecasts. For example, one scenario (S7, an assumption rather than a forecast) considers the future uptake of electric vehicles (EVs), and shows that in the absence of any new tax to replace petrol and diesel, the Treasury takes an intolerable hit on revenue, and traffic growth causes excessive congestion. Therefore the scenario indicates that discussion of some form of road pricing, or equivalent measures, is inevitable.

The remaining six scenarios show a reference case, S1, with four variants for different assumptions on economic growth, population and fuel price. There is also a different reference case, S6, which by the same logic has similar variants, embedded in the model but not actually listed. The variants are easy to calculate, approximately, and Figure 7.5 shows the S1 reference and the S6 reference, each with its comparable band of variants. All of these should be considered consistent future possibilities. At the same time the traffic forecasts were accompanied by estimated trajectories of the implications for future levels of congestion and energy use. (It would be simple to extend this to include tax revenue, which will become more important.) This presentation has the great advantage that it is not based on the change from an assumed reference level, but the forecast change from an actual starting point, enabling distinction between 'things getting better' and 'things getting worse more slowly than might otherwise have happened', which is rarely clearly stated in project appraisals.

So we now have a viable wide spread of futures, all possible, but the actual outcome undetermined and uncertain. How can that be handled in appraisal of road schemes, policy on charging, or local sustainable initiatives? It is impractical to carry out or explain formal appraisal on ten different assumptions. But it would be easy and practical to give the same detailed attention to two substantially different future traffic levels, ideally one towards the top of the S1 variants and one towards the bottom of the S6 variants.[7] These correspond to an increase in total traffic of about 8 per cent and about 40 per cent, from 2015 to 2050. These should be the two cases given detailed appraisal attention. Such twin appraisals, for a high and low traffic growth case, if done seriously, systematically, professionally and in open-minded mood, would transform the policy discussion about what to do, which projects are robust and which dependent on very specific futures. In summary, my suggestions are:

- treat the scenarios with respect over their whole range, steering deliberately away from the practice that a 'central' case is a 'most probable' case;
- include the same range of variants around S6 as around S1;
- use two substantially different traffic scenarios for full policy and project appraisal, preferably near the top and the bottom of the range identified;
- apply those in national discussions, and on the same principles for regional and local appraisals;

- present forecast effects in absolute units enabling comparison to be made with current conditions, not only with other forecasts.

For each policy or project tested, after considering its effects on the forecasts themselves, there would be appraisal of its performance under the low and low-growth case. Some would perform well under both scenarios, and are prima facie robust to a wide range of futures. Others would be robustly bad, in the same way. Others, however, would perform well only under one or the other scenario, or would need active policy support before they could be made good. The knowledge that this would be the case would itself encourage consideration of a wider range of alternative policies or projects. This would transform discussion about the range and desirability of different policies and projects, open discussion of different types of future, and allow alternative policy scenarios to be assessed as well as alternative traffic scenarios. It would help prepare ourselves for discussion on what sort of future we actually want.

My suggestions are entirely consistent with the principles and numbers in the DfT's new traffic forecasts. It would be helpful for WebTAG (Chapter 6) to confirm explicitly that this sort of approach would be required (or encouraged, or at least allowed). It will take some time for transport professionals to free ourselves from the outdated concept of a single most probable future, and recognise the very wide range of uncertainty that we are now faced with. Using at least two substantially different trajectories of traffic would recognise – even embrace – uncertainty, and improve appraisal.

Wider implications of the new forecasting regime

If forecasts of future mobility are as reliable as the forecasts of future economic variables which determine them, there will be an envelope of uncertainty of travel forecasts, but it is quite likely to be a rather narrow envelope. However, the situation now seems rather different, as the relationships themselves are contested and it cannot be assumed that there is only one viable forecast of travel corresponding with any particular assumption of, say, economic growth or fuel prices. In that case, it is logically necessary to consider the robustness of future policies and projects in terms of *scenarios* about the future, not *forecasts* of it (Chapter 16). This will remain true until the big research issues about future mobility are resolved to the point of a reasonable degree of consensus, which does not yet exist (and may never do so). The policy issue is of appraisal under conditions of *contested* futures, not just statistical uncertainty.

This raises another as yet hardly discussed issue. It means that there is a missing logical element in the intuitive jump to conclusions. I think that missing link is the view that is taken of the effects of policy and infrastructure on behaviour. If behaviour is fixed and hardly affected by policy intervention, the only thing to do is to ameliorate or provide for it. If, however, behaviour is fluid and changeable and responds, in the short or long run, to intervention, then it is more credible to provide transport services which encourage choices which are more benign. In practical terms, how much are the prevailing trends actually the result of earlier policies, and how much are the 'neutral' forecasts actually based on implicit future policies, on transport, housing, pensions, social care, tax and everything else? The empirical evidence, in my view, supports the idea that a wide range of policies influence fluid and changeable choices, especially in the medium and longer run that is relevant to appraisal of infrastructure. Philosophically, people make their own future, albeit not always in circumstances of their own choosing. Policy discussion now is simply not serious unless it entertains possibilities of forecasts of low or declining traffic, and the interventions that influence that outcome.

The whole mood of treating forecasts as reliable depictions of the future, uncertainty being captured in a rather narrow band of sensitivity testing, is no longer tenable. Many extrapolations previously asserted with confidence are no longer definite, especially (a) the presumption of indefinitely continued traffic growth; (b) the reliability of the established tools for explaining and forecasting it; (c) major technical, economic and social change, which is structural; and (d) behavioural responses to all these, which are already changing trends. In this context, it is logical that there should be ideas to reverse the whole planning process, working backwards from future desired, contested or speculative end-states, discussing which are preferable, and then working out viable trajectories to get there. Lyons et al (2014) termed this process as 'decide and provide', as part of a wider process termed 'regime testing'. Marsden et al (2018) discussed it in their report of the Demand Commission, *Time for a Change*. Jones et al (2018) used the term 'vision and validate' in the summary report from a European project, *Create*. (My own current proposal, cited earlier, is not as radical as these, still running from forecast to policy (with feedback), but applied to at least two substantially different traffic forecasts. It might turn out to be a transitional process. In tribute to the terminology of 'predict and provide' and its successors, I'll call this 'predict and appraise'.)

During the period of the dominance of a narrow band of exaggerated traffic forecasts, there was an additional factor of uncertainty, namely uncertainty about what confidence should be put on the future level of uncertainty. Politicians may want clear, uncaveated policy advice based on a reasonably well-defined assessment of the future. But encouraging over-confidence is as dangerous as explaining complexity. If political parties have different policies or views of behaviour, I can foresee them needing different traffic forecasts (accompanied by policies necessary to give effect to the desired traffic). This might require changes in the roles of government departments and/or politically independent advisers, and open access to tools and models. If we do not know (or do not agree) what future we want, or what levers will give effect to it, then we need flexible, adaptable and low-risk policies. When there are unresolved issues about the evidence and trends, and incomplete consensus on objectives, then perception of excessive confidence in the forecasts and almost complete certainty about policies and strategies is a most unwise combination. It is now almost a truism to say that we should focus less on forecasting the future and more on deciding what sort of future we *choose* – and the key point of all this is that there may be a rather wider choice than we have thought.

Notes

[1]   The political dimension of protests and campaigns and public opinion, whose influence was often important and sometimes decisive, mostly did not interact at all with the methodologies of traffic forecasting, but did come together when objectors at public enquiries appointed expert witnesses to challenge the traffic forecasts. Inspectors were rarely moved by such arguments, and sometimes ruled them out of order, but there were cases where the criticisms were sufficiently powerful to change the outcome of the enquiry. The history of this process is little recorded, and an important study remains to be written.

[2]   *New Scientist* 15 March 1980: 'The latest, unpublished, report from the Advisory Committee on Trunk Road Assessment (the Leitch Committee) is believed to condemn the model as useless.' *New Scientist* 12 June 1980 quoted Roads Minister Kenneth Clarke as saying in Parliament that the RHTM project had been 'concluded' in 1979 because of difficulties. A report on RHTM by the Leitch Committee, it said, was now 'being printed', but I have not found trace of it.

[3]   Rather, work on a new model, now approaching completion, proceeded on the argument that it would be more detailed, rather than more correct.

4   'Millstone' being stated by Sir Christopher Foster, and 'Milestone' by myself. 'Milestone' won the vote by a substantial majority, but with a minority strongly of the view that consideration of induced traffic was hindering necessary infrastructure development.

5   This has the disturbing significance that all schemes planned and appraised during the period of systematic overestimates of long-term traffic growth will have been approved on the basis of overestimated benefit, since although the traffic forecasts are rebased to reality every few years, the estimated benefits are not rebased. Sloman et al (2017) also report case studies of specific schemes which have not delivered the benefits claimed for them in advance, which tends to underpin this conclusion.

6   The phrase itself, copied from the widespread use of 'peak oil', seems to have been coined separately in 2010 by Millard-Ball and Schipper in pre-prints of their 2011 paper, and by Goodwin in a series of articles in the journal *Local Transport Today*, preludes to his 2011 paper. The concept was of course much older.

7   I acknowledge that this does not give the outer bounds of possibility. For example, S6 is given virtually the same level of car ownership forecast for 2050 as S1, which does not make sense, since the same factors affecting the trip rates are also affecting car ownership, at least for under-50-year-olds. Thus future development might consider trends in car ownership, not only trip rates, which could give lower traffic levels, and also help to resolve the unlikely proposition that the low traffic growth in scenario 6 would produce an increase in traffic speed. Alternatively, there are some speculations that AVs could imply very much higher rates of traffic growth, though not without policy support, for example, re-erection of pedestrian barriers in towns, which might sensibly be rejected.

References

Bastian, A, Börjesson, M and Eliasson, J (2016) 'Explaining "peak car" with economic variables', *Transportation Research Part A: Policy and Practice*, 88(C): 236–50.

Cairns, S, Hass-Klau, C and Goodwin, P (1998) *Traffic impact of highway capacity reductions*. Landor Publications https://issuu.com/landorlinks/docs/cairns-hass-klau-goodwin-1998 Accessed 17 October 2018.

Chatterjee, K, Goodwin, P, Schwanen, T, Clark, B, Jain, J, Melia, S, Middleton, J, Plyushteva, A, Ricci, M, Santos, G and Stokes, G (2018) *Young people's travel – what's changed and why? Review and Analysis*. Department for Transport. www.gov.uk/government/publications/young-peoples-travel-whats-changed-and-why Accessed 17 October 2018.

Department of the Environment, Transport and the Regions (1998) *A New Deal for Transport: Better for Everyone*, Cm 3950, London: TSO.

Department of the Environment, Transport and the Regions (2000) *Transport 2010: The 10 Year Plan for Transport*, London: TSO.

Department for Transport (2015) *Road traffic forecasts 2015.* https:// assets.publishing.service.gov.uk/government/uploads/system/ uploads/attachment_data/file/411471/road-traffic-forecasts-2015. pdf Accessed 17 October 2018.

Department for Transport (2018) *Road traffic forecasts 2018.* www.gov. uk/government/publications/road-traffic-forecasts-2018 Accessed 17 October 2018.

Department of Transport (1977) *Report of the Advisory Committee on Trunk Road Assessment / chairman Sir George Leitch.* DoT, London.

Department of Transport (1989) *National Road Traffic Forecasts (Great Britain) 1989*, London: HMSO.

Docherty, I and Shaw, J (eds) (2003) *A New Deal for Transport? The UK's Struggle with the Sustainable Transport Agenda*, Oxford: Blackwell.

Docherty, I and Shaw, J (eds) (2008) *Traffic Jam: Ten Years of 'Sustainable' Transport in the UK*, Bristol: Policy Press.

Glanville, W and Smeed, R (1958) *The basic requirements for the roads of Great Britain.* Institution of Civil Engineers, London.

Goodwin, P (2011) 'Three views on "peak car"', *World Transport Policy & Practice*, 17(4): 8–17.

Goodwin, P (2012) 'Due diligence, traffic forecasts and pensions', *Local Transport Today*, 13 April 2012.

Goodwin, P (2018) 'How should we use the road traffic forecasts in practice?' *Local Transport Today*, 12 October 2018.

Goodwin, P and Van Dender, K (2013) 'Peak car – themes and issues', *Transport Reviews*, 33(3): 243–54.

Highways England (2016) *Post Opening Project Evaluation (POPE) of major schemes. Main Report: meta-analysis.* www.gov.uk/government/ collections/post-opening-project-evaluation-pope-of-major-schemes Accessed 17 October 2018.

ITF (2012) *Long-Run Trends in Travel Demand.* ITF/OECD, Paris.

Jones, P, Anciaes, P, Buckingham, C, Cavoli, C, Cohen, T, Cristea, L, Gerike, R, Halpern, C and Pickup, L (2018) *CREATE project summary and recommendations to cities.* www.create-mobility.eu/ create/resources/general/download/Urban-Mobility-Preparing-for-the-Future-Learning-from-the-Past-WSWE-B42DAM Accessed 17 October 2018.

Lyons, G, Davidson, C, Forster, T, Sage, I, McSaveney, J, MacDonald, E, Morgan, A and Kole, A (2014) *Future demand: how could or should our transport system evolve in order to support mobility in the future? Final report*. Ministry of Transport, Wellington. www.transport.govt.nz/ multi-modal/keystrategiesandplans/strategic-policy-programme/ future-demand/ Accessed 17 October 2018.

Marsden, G, Dales, J, Jones, P, Seagriff, E and Spurling, N (2018) *All Change? The future of travel demand and the implications for policy and planning. The first report of the Commission on Travel Demand*. www. demand.ac.uk/wp-content/uploads/2018/04/FutureTravel_report_ final.pdf Accessed 16 October 2018.

Metz, D (2010) 'Saturation of demand for daily travel', *Transport Reviews*, 30(5): 659–74.

Metz, D (2013) 'Peak car and beyond: the fourth era of travel', *Transport Reviews*, 33(3): 255–70.

Millard-Ball, A and Schipper, L (2011) 'Are we reaching peak travel? Trends in passenger transport in eight industrialized countries', *Transport Reviews*, 31(3): 1–22.

Newman, P and Kenworthy, J (2011) '"Peak car use": understanding the demise of automobile dependence', *World Transport Policy & Practice*, 17(2): 31–42.

Owens, S (1995) 'From "predict and provide" to "predict and prevent"?' *Transport Policy*, 2(1): 43–9.

Sloman, L, Hopkinson, L and Taylor, I (2017) *The impact of road projects in England*. Report for CPRE. www.transportforqualityoflife.com/u/ files/170320%20The%20Impact%20of%20Road%20Projects%20 in%20England%20FINAL1.pdf Accessed 17 October 2018.

Standing Advisory Committee on Trunk Road Assessment (1994) *Trunk Roads and the Generation of Traffic*, London: HMSO.

Tanner, J (1965) 'Forecasts of future numbers of vehicles', in Road Research Laboratory (ed) *Research on Road Traffic*, London: HMSO, pp 63–84.

Tulpule, A (1973) *Forecasts of vehicles and traffic in Great Britain, 1972 revision*. Report LR543. Transport and Road Research Laboratory, Crowthorne.

Wadud, Z and Baierl, M (2017) 'Explaining "peak car" with economic variables: a comment', *Transportation Research Part A: Policy and Practice*, 95: 381–5.

Health, wellbeing and quality of life

Angela Curl and Julie Clark

Introduction

Following years of disconnect in UK public policy (Royal Town Planning Institute (RTPI) 2013), there is growing recognition of the importance of transport for health and wellbeing. Indeed, the explosion of interest in the health potential of active travel among health and transport researchers, policy makers and advocacy groups makes this an exciting time to study interactions between transport and health. To a large extent, the focus on active travel and the health benefits associated with physical activity is related to the convergence of transport and health research around obesity (Schwanen 2016), although as we shall see physical (in)activity is only one of many complex and subtle interconnections and relationships between transport, health and wellbeing.

If we think about what really matters in transport policy, we would argue that its underlying purpose is to improve the health or wellbeing of citizens, both by extending the length and improving quality of life. Wellbeing refers to a person's subjective evaluation of how their life is going, while quality of life generally involves an objective measure of an individual's position, relative to their environment (Duarte et al 2010, World Health Organization (WHO) 1997). Why else would transport policy makers strive to promote economic growth, or reduce congestion, journey times and accidents, or bring about environmental improvements, if not to somehow make things better for citizens? In many ways, as we see throughout this book, existing transport systems already do much to make things better for health and wellbeing in society: at the population level, people have unparalleled access to employment, leisure and social opportunities. At the same time, transport systems can make things worse. In Great Britain in 2017, for example, 1,676 people died in road traffic accidents and 128,306 were injured (Department for Transport (DfT) 2018). We also see in England that over-reliance on the private car contributes to over a quarter of adults being classed as physically inactive and almost a third as obese, both conditions that are associated with increased risk of disease and early death (Health and Social Care Information Centre 2017). Furthermore, in 2015, domestic and international transport was responsible for 160 million tonnes of greenhouse gas emissions (DfT 2017a), 14 per cent of PM10 and 13 per cent of PM2.5 emissions, and was the third largest contributor to nitrogen oxide emissions (Department for Environment, Food & Rural Affairs (DEFRA) 2016). Such things have clear health impacts through local air quality degradation (for example, respiratory conditions) and global climate change (for example, increased likelihood of severe weather events; Chapter 3).

For those who are already less well served by the existing transport system – perhaps due to low incomes or geographical isolation (Chapters 4 and 12) – there is the double whammy of reduced access to 'normal' opportunities such as employment and health care, and an increased likelihood of suffering from its adverse consequences, including exposure to road traffic incidents, pollution, noise and the social segregation of communities (Sustrans 2012). With a higher probability that their activity spaces are more restricted to their local area, those with lower incomes also tend to have poorer access than higher wage earners to health-promoting environments such as green space, while 'unhealthy' facilities like betting shops and fast-food outlets are often, conversely, more generously available.

Clearly transport policy does not exist in isolation from other policy fields, and it is the way in which it integrates (or not) with land use, housing, social, health, educational and employment policies that results in the scope for positive and negative outcomes (Figure 8.1). Conceptually, mobility is associated with health and wellbeing in a number of ways (Schwanen and Ziegler 2011, Gatrell 2013), and three important relationships can be emphasised at the individual level (Nordbakke and Schwanen 2013). First, it functions as a facilitator, enabling access to destinations and social connections intrinsically important for health and wellbeing. This means access not just to healthcare services but also to amenities that provide the opportunity for employment, education, food, cultural and leisure activities and other social activities (Urry 2007; Chapter 4). Second, being mobile can have physical health benefits, reducing risk of cardiovascular diseases, diabetes, obesity, fractures, colon and breast cancers (WHO 2018). Active travel, involving walking or cycling, is one of the types of physical activity most strongly correlated with positive physical and mental health outcomes (Mason et al 2016). Third, motility –

Figure 8.1: Direct and indirect pathways through which urban and transport planning design decisions influence health and wellbeing

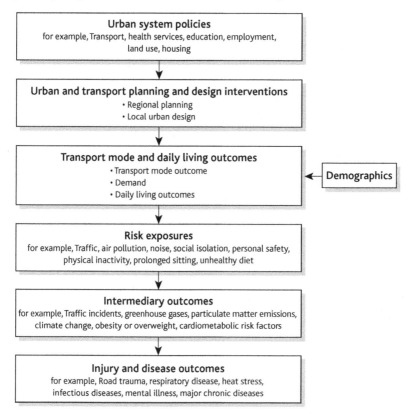

Source: Giles-Corti et al 2016

having the means to access – can be as important as the actual travel itself. For example, many people value having a good quality public transport system, even if they rarely use it, and car ownership is often associated with feelings of control and empowerment (Ellaway et al 2016). Relatedly, high-quality infrastructure is important in facilitating the efficient movement of people and goods (Delbosc 2012).

When considering relationships between transport and health, the private car as a mode of transport is paradoxical. Indeed, while recent moves to promote walking and cycling (Department for Infrastructure 2018, Public Health England 2016, Transport Scotland 2018, Welsh Government 2016) are to be applauded – active travel benefits individual health and addresses many population-level health issues related to an over-reliance on private vehicles – we do need to guard against approaches that brand car travel as 'bad' in opposition to the 'good' inherent in the active modes. As an aspirational good, the car is associated with quality of life and a higher standard of living (Banister 1997), to the extent that owning one is a widely accepted proxy for income and socio-economic status. Car ownership is also associated with better health because of psychosocial benefits including control, self-esteem, protection and prestige (Macintyre et al 1998, 2001, Ellaway et al 2016), and automobiles provide easy access to social, employment, leisure and healthcare facilities, especially for those of restricted physical mobility. It's important also not to overlook the potential for physical and mental strain arising from walking and cycling, especially where it is not undertaken as a lifestyle choice (safety concerns are frequently cited as one of the biggest reasons for not cycling). When exhorting people to leave their cars at home it is important to consider contextual factors, including journey purpose and quality of environment, rather than simply expecting them to change their travel behaviour almost regardless of circumstance. Still, in the context of its risks to public health, there has been mounting opposition to the dominance of the private car in modern societies, with Douglas et al (2011) even being moved to describe the car as 'the new tobacco'. While there is undoubtedly an element of hyperbole to such a characterisation (it is difficult to divine any health benefits from smoking), what is clear is that addressing the extent to which societies rely/depend on the private car is of increasing concern to policy makers in both the transport and health sectors (Goodwin 1995, Lucas and Jones 2009).

Our starting point in this chapter is that, despite adverse impacts on society at differing spatial and temporal scales, the accessibility and mobility afforded by transport systems are fundamental to positive health and wellbeing. In exploring how health is considered within transport policy, and vice versa, we identify where policies can better realise the benefits of transport for health and wellbeing, how they can mitigate its negative impacts, and what evidence is needed to support such policies. Before continuing with our discussion, we should be clear that our primary focus is on personal land transport, rather than freight and passenger air/sea travel. There are ways in which both contribute positively to health through, say, their roles in efficient supply chains for food, clothing and medicines, and their capacities to promote leisure opportunities and bring people closer together (we note in particular the phenomenon of 'health tourism'), although familiar stories of associated health hazards also arise, for example as a result of noise, pollutants and community disruption (Kjellstrom et al 2003). Air travel is in addition linked with specific issues such as deep-vein thrombosis (Byard 2018) and the global spread of communicable diseases (for example, the SARS epidemic in 2003 (Gatrell 2011)).

Health policy and (healthy) transport policy

For all the potential synergy between health policy and transport policy, health is often not a primary consideration in transport planning and vice versa. Historically, a nation's GDP, as an 'objective' measure of growth, has been the common rubric against which societies measure and compare progress, and externalities such as traffic congestion have even been seen as signs of 'prosperity and economic success' (Downs 2004: 27). But a naïve focus on economic growth can mean that transport appraisal methods prioritise projects which have detrimental environmental, health and indeed economic externalities (Chapter 6); research in US metropolitan regions, for example, has shown that higher congestion is associated with decreasing employment growth rates, to the point that prioritising alternative modes and peak-time pricing were seen as better policy interventions than the road building often associated with traditional appraisal methods that privilege time savings for individual motorists (Sweet 2014). The trend to more holistic thinking that promotes health and wellbeing as the ultimate aims of public policy has become more pronounced of late (Delbosc 2012, Dunlop and Swales 2012, Tomaney 2017), and since 2012 the Office for National Statistics (ONS) has measured wellbeing nationally. Initiatives like these (ONS 2012) provide the opportunity to consider subjective measures of wellbeing alongside economic indicators in policy evaluation, although we do not yet know of any examples where they have been used in transport project appraisal. Nevertheless, there is now tangible evidence of increasing integration and collaboration across health and transport policy agendas (Davis and Adrian Davis Associates 2015, DfT 2017c).

A transport perspective on health

Given that road injuries remain one of the top ten causes of death worldwide (WHO 2015), it is unsurprising that the primary arena in which the health impacts of transport are considered is safety. Transport policy interventions have brought about almost universal legislative requirements for seatbelts, road speed limits and child seat standards designed to reduce injury and deaths. While few would take issue with this kind of safety initiative, there remains the potential for unintended consequences, especially where the goal of reducing accident risk is shared with that of reducing car use. Take, for example, the ongoing debate around making cycle helmets compulsory (Goldacre and Spiegelhalter 2013). There is some evidence to suggest that campaigns promoting cycle safety may actually discourage cycling by raising awareness of risk (Gamble et al 2015), thereby reducing the scope for 'safety in numbers' which is key to the high levels of cyclist safety that is found in countries like the Netherlands and Denmark. Similarly with regard to foot traffic, although guard railing may reduce accidents by separating pedestrians from traffic, any reduction in pedestrian casualties occurring only because the reduced 'walkability' associated with such railing results in fewer pedestrians would be something of a perverse outcome. Mindful of this potential, Transport for London (TfL) provides detailed guidance on when guard railing is and is not appropriate, working on an assumption of no new provision of railing and being supportive of removal or partial removal (TfL 2012).

Reducing the risk of accidents is also of concern in the appraisal and regulation of road, rail, sea and air transport infrastructure interventions. In each of the devolved nations of the UK, transport appraisal guidance monetises accidents, and the expected accident reduction benefits of a proposed transport scheme contribute to a cost–benefit calculation. Yet the extent to which the value of accident reduction is prioritised relative to the aggregated time savings that are estimated to arise from any given infrastructure intervention remains controversial. In the UK, rather more than in many other countries, transport project appraisal has developed around the notion that time spent travelling is time wasted, the assumption being that people would rather use that time to be doing something more productive (Chapters 6 and 7). Evidence suggesting that lots of people each saving small amounts of time translates into noticeably enhanced economic productivity is rather hard to come by, and the whole premise overlooks the rather obvious point that travel time can be economically productive when people work on the move. It can also be of benefit to people's health if they use it to relax (Chapter 10). It is true that reducing travel time can mean lower stress (Martin et al 2014, ONS 2014) and, in theory at least, more time for other, healthier activities (see Royal Society for Public Health (RSPH) 2016, Chatterjee et al 2017), but the problem is that there's no guarantee people will use the time they gain for the benefit of their health. On average the amount of time people spend travelling has stayed remarkably constant for decades (Metz 2008), suggesting that time saved on certain journeys is just recycled into others. Alongside increasing travel speeds, this constant travel time allows greater distances to be covered, meaning individuals can access a wider range of destinations, and might result in low-density urban sprawl and the emergence of a new set of transport-related health problems associated with an over-reliance on the private car (Frumkin 2002, Newman and Kenworthy 1999).

Key to avoiding such outcomes is for the planning system to pay closer attention to where activities are located in relation to people's homes (so-called accessibility planning). The situation of key facilities has important consequences not just for the amount we travel, but also for mode choice, transport requirements and accessibility. Something of a vicious circle has arisen in many parts of the UK: the growth of private car ownership and a distancing of spatial planning from public health undermined public transport provision, and new retail, hospital, housing and other developments increasingly came into being under the assumption that people would travel to and from them by car. This leaves those in peripheral urban areas particularly vulnerable to a loss of access – to jobs, services and leisure opportunities alike – if they are unable to maintain a car or there is a reduction in public transport coverage and frequency, something not uncommon in the UK's privatised bus industry (Chapter 4). Numerous authors have highlighted the potential impacts on physical and mental health of being unable to access economic and social opportunities (Sinclair and Sinclair 2001, Social Exclusion Unit (SEU) 2003, Umberson and Montez 2010, Schmitz 2011).

Although the health impacts of transport are increasingly recognised within the UK government machine, they are still given relatively little attention in budget and prioritisation terms by the DfT. While health and wellbeing were in some way related to all four of the Department's Strategic Objectives reported in its Annual Report and Accounts of 2017, there was explicit mention of 'health' and 'safety' only in sub-objectives under the umbrella of number 4, 'Safe, secure and sustainable transport' (DfT 2017b).[1] Progress towards this was measured by the number of trip stages made per person by bicycle each year, a measure that is quite specific and certainly does not appear to capture the breadth of associations between transport, health and wellbeing. At a local transport planning level the Local Sustainable Transport Fund (LSTF), a DfT-led competitive funding mechanism for local authorities in England, included two high-level objectives ('supporting the local economy and improving access to jobs', and 'reducing carbon emissions') and four secondary objectives ('delivering social and economic benefits to communities', 'safety', 'air quality' and 'increased levels of physical activity') with some links to health. The Department's report into the impacts of the LSTF (DfT 2017c) seems to focus on individual health benefits from travel behaviour, particularly in terms of active travel and physical activity, without consideration, as at the national level, of broader relationships.

Since 2013, social and distributional impacts have been included in the DfT's (2013) Transport Appraisal Guidance. The social impacts have strong parallels with health impacts of transport, including journey quality, physical activity, security, severance and active modes. The focus on distributional impacts means that some consideration is given to who is impacted by transport investments rather than simply an aggregate appraisal that might benefit those least in need and have adverse health impacts for those who will not benefit from the investment (Chapter 6). Neither the social nor the distributional impacts are monetised, though, so it is unclear what importance they command in transport scheme appraisal. More recently, Tainio et al (2017) have presented detailed guidelines for monetising the physical activity impacts of walking and cycling interventions. While this is a positive move in the sense that it signals some willingness on the part of the DfT to take better account of health benefits in its appraisal mechanisms, those wider associations between transport and health beyond encouraging people to walk and cycle remain unaddressed. What is more, it seems these guidelines are to be applied only to proposed walking and cycling interventions, rather than the physical activity implications of all transport schemes.

Elsewhere, authorities are working more cross-sectorally to consider health impacts of transport policies. TfL, for example, has a health action plan (the Mayor's transport strategy includes an overarching focus on a 'Healthy Streets' approach), and health improvement was part of the rationale underpinning the Smarter Choices, Smarter Places programme in Scotland, which ran from 2008–2012 (DHC et al 2013). Seven pilot areas, including the relatively impoverished East End of Glasgow, received funding to implement local programmes of behaviour change. These were devoted to the provision of infrastructure and services (cycleways and cycle facilities, footpaths and pedestrianisation) and the promotion of transport and access options (active travel along with personal travel planning), and linked transport with wider policy goals including health improvement. The interventions generated both attitudinal and behavioural changes. Improved perceptions of walking and cycling were reflected in a higher proportion of trips made on foot in all areas, with modal share for walking increasing by over 20 percentage points in one area, while cycling modal share rose in five of the seven areas (DHC et al 2013). The programme has been followed up by intensive investment in active travel and cycling infrastructure in Glasgow, in an effort to secure an 'active' legacy from the Commonwealth Games which the city hosted in 2014. The period preceding the Games saw the development of new and upgraded cycle paths, the introduction of a mass cycle share scheme and, more controversially given the expense and its situation in a disadvantaged area, a velodrome. The cycle share scheme is thriving and the city has secured access for Glasgow school pupils to undertake 'taster' sessions at the velodrome, but challenges remain in bringing about a large-scale cultural shift towards the active modes, even for a city in which half of all households do not have access to a vehicle (Clark and Kearns 2015, Muirie 2017).

A health perspective on transport

Having reviewed examples of how health is accounted for in transport planning, we now turn to look at how transport is considered in the health sector. Recently, the World Health Assembly recognised air pollution as the largest environmental risk to health. Outdoor pollution, to which transport is a significant contributor, is responsible for 3.7m deaths per year (WHO 2015); beyond the direct, local impact of individual respiratory problems, air pollution is a transboundary phenomenon, impacting on health at global scale through environmental change (European Environment Agency (EEA) 2008). Despite such recognition, health policy has generally focused on cure and care rather than preventative measures – other than those designed to prevent the spread of communicable disease – and this is reflected in spending. According to Gatrell and Elliott (2015), spending on public health does not exceed 7 per cent of all heath spending in any country, and this figure is closer to 5 per cent in the UK. What is more, public health spending is facing cuts in real terms (The King's Fund 2017).

It is true that for many people the perceived risk of the spreading of less serious disease remains a barrier to use of local public transport (Dobbie et al 2010), but as attention about ill health in affluent nations has shifted towards non-communicable disease and mental distress, health policy has moved further towards a model focused on structural and contextual factors (Bambra et al 2010). This has resulted in the broader concepts of wellbeing and quality of life gaining currency. The 2010 Marmot Review of health inequalities marked an influential turning point for health policy in the UK, focusing on the social determinants of health as a means of addressing health inequalities (Figure 8.2). Although issues related to transport, mobility and access are not explicitly mentioned in the social determinants

Figure 8.2: Social determinants of health

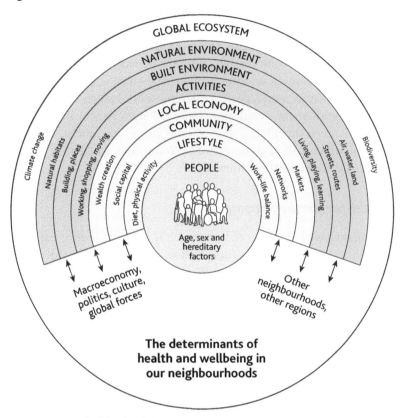

Source: Rao, Prasad, Adshead and Tissera 2007

of health model, it is clear that they intersect with the influences of health behaviours and health outcomes across scales (Marmot 2005). In England, the transfer of responsibility for public health from the National Health Service (NHS) to local authorities in 2013 can be seen as a positive move – it recognises that 'health is about more than medicine' (House of Commons Health Committee 2016: 57) and thus paves the way for a more holistic approach to improving population health across multiple sectors of local government – albeit one that has taken place against a backdrop of real terms spending cuts. The Health Committee stated that health should be a material consideration in all planning and licensing law, presenting a case study of Coventry as a 'Marmot city' actively seeking to consider health outcomes across a range of policy contexts.

Coventry, together with Stoke-on-Trent, Newcastle, Gateshead, Bristol and the county of Somerset, is part of a 'Marmot network' of local authorities. They are committed to a more collaborative, cross-sectoral approach to transport projects, deploying a social determinants of health perspective as a means of addressing health issues. For example, in the 'Cycle Coventry' project (Hands 2015), public health and transport departments worked together, applying for funding from the LSTF for a cycle project designed to have health impacts. In Scotland, the NHS has been involved in setting out a 'Place Standard' in conjunction with urban planning professionals, designed to inform the design of urban environments that support health and wellbeing (Architecture & Design Scotland et al: undated). Transport is mentioned explicitly in four of the 14 criteria – moving around, public transport, traffic and parking, and streets and spaces – as well as impacting on many of the others (Figure 8.3).

Despite these examples and the recognition of the structural influences on health through urban and transport planning, it

Figure 8.3: The Place Standard tool

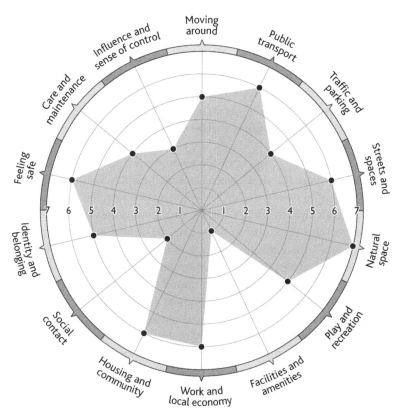

Source: Architecture & Design Scotland et al: undated

remains the case that health promotion is frequently focused around individual responsibility for behaviour change which, in transport terms, predominantly translates into advertising the health benefits of active travel. Incorporation of transport and travel choices into the health promotion agenda can be seen in campaigns such as 'walking for health' and cycle-to-work days. While recognition of the role that public health professionals can play in promoting active travel behaviour has increased, the extent to which this affects macro-level decisions is less clear. Authorities have been all too keen to sanction the development of out-of-town hospitals, for example, necessitating motorised – and often car-based – access by patients, staff and visitors alike (Hamilton and Gourlay 2002). And over time, it is likely that many of the relationships between transport and health will become more acute given that the UK's population (along with those of most other developed countries) is ageing (Chapter 14). As physical mobility reduces, older adults can be more sensitive to their environment (Day 2010) and therefore to the health and wellbeing impacts of their environment, including transport systems. Furthermore, giving up driving in older age is associated with a range of health consequences such as reduced physical activity, isolation and loneliness (Musselwhite et al 2015). As such, it is worth noting the heightened importance of transport and mobility for the health and wellbeing of older populations; a health-promoting transport system has the potential to reduce the healthcare costs associated with an ageing population by helping people maintain or adapt to changing mobilities (see also Johnson et al 2017).

A notable common aspect of the examples we have discussed from both the transport (Healthy Streets) and the health (Marmot Cities and Place Standard) sectors is the level of convergence between transport and health policies around urban planning or a focus on places (Chapter 9). Of course, the relationship between place and public health is long-standing – the expansion of suburbs in the late 19th century, made possible by the advent of efficient commuter railways, was in large part motivated by the will to rid cities of unhealthy, overcrowded conditions (Bruegmann 2006) – although it is perhaps an irony that such responses to historical health issues have resulted in the emergence of car reliant societies and their associated inactivity and obesity crises. In seeking to overcome the disconnect between urban planning and public health that characterised much of the second half of the 20th century, much of the lead in promoting healthy urban environments comes from policy makers' renewed focus on the built environment as a key social determinant of health. Scotland's National Planning Framework, for instance, works over a 20 to 30 year horizon to set spatial priorities that include improving urban accessibility by public and sustainable modes of transport. These come with the expectation that 'significant health benefits could be achieved by substantially increasing active travel within our most densely populated areas' (Scottish Government 2014a: 7). Planning for active travel and walkable places is seen as a way of providing both health and environmental benefits and a suite of policy documents, including the Cycling Action Plan for Scotland (Transport Scotland 2017), the National Walking Strategy (Scottish Government 2014b) and Designing Streets (Scottish Government 2010), propose complementary measures such as 20mph zones in residential and shopping streets, community and workplace walking programmes, and a street–user hierarchy that prioritises pedestrians. Private cars, by contrast, are relegated to the bottom.

Elsewhere in the world, approaches such as compact cities (Jenks et al 1996), placemaking (Friedmann 2010) and car-free cities (Nieuwenhuijsen and Khreis 2016) advocate a holistic way of thinking about urban design, ensuring that all aspects of a place, including transport and mobility, lead to improved quality of life and wellbeing. At the micro-level, DIY Streets, based on the concept of 'home zones', is an example of street redesign to promote active travel and community cohesion (Chapter 9). Architects Gehl[2] and 8:80 cities[3] have used transport and mobility as mechanisms to foster positive health and community outcomes across larger areas. While much of transport planning has, at least until recently, focused on meeting the demand created by necessarily car-based trips, designing places that make such trips optional, capable of substitution by local, walking and cycling alternatives, can be health-promoting on a number of levels because they not only encourage physical activity but also engender social interaction in pleasant environments that can be good for mental wellbeing. Viewing the challenge of an ageing society as an opportunity to improve things for everyone (in much the same way as 'Design for All' – see Design for All Foundation: undated), 8:80 cities is based upon the premise that places designed for both eight and 80 year olds are inclusive and accessible urban environments which can be health-promoting across the life course. The significance of this approach is that it draws attention to both the need and scope for considering multiple perspectives when designing places.

Although approaches such DIY Streets and those from Gehl and 8:80 cities are welcome, we sound a note of caution against the risk of assuming a simple, environmentally deterministic relationship between the built environment and behavioural choice. Such assumptions can ignore complex influences on daily travel practices, where the 'choice' to walk or drive is related to more than preference. Plausible alternative options to any given car journey may well be influenced by urban planning, but they are also products of economic development agendas, the demands of the private market, fraught relationships around 'choice' of school or healthcare, family obligations and other considerations. Is it realistic to assume that re-designing the built environment will in and of itself lead to short-term changes in travel behaviour against a backdrop of 'car-culture'? Certainly it can be difficult to ascertain the direct, short-term health effects of street level interventions such as DIY Streets (Curl et al 2015), for example, a point to which we return. Indeed, we would suggest that to achieve a truly sustainable and thus healthier transport system, there is a need for more equitable cross-sector planning.

An agenda for change: towards a healthy transport system

So far in the chapter we have seen how transport and health policies have evolved from a traditional focus on negative health externalities in transport and 'risk factors' in health, towards a more holistic vision of how mobility can contribute, positively and negatively, to wellbeing. From a transport perspective, health is increasingly considered as part of wider social and economic impacts of transport schemes, beyond journey times and savings and accident reduction. Public health professionals have advocated the importance of contextual influences on health outcomes while, in parallel, attention towards health inequalities, obesity and a strained National Health Service has driven the promotion of 'healthy' transport modes up the policy agenda. In combination, these factors have led to the beginnings of a more holistic approach and a rejuvenated dialogue between health and transport (Rao et al 2007, Koohsari et al 2013) largely centred around the intersection with urban planning, in the UK and globally.

Despite this increased awareness, the reality is that health is not the driving force behind transport investments, and health investment is predominantly focused on health care and cures rather than investing in addressing the causes of health issues. Indeed, a recent report by the Chartered Institute of Highways and Transportation (CIHT) (2016) on relationships between policy and planning in transport and health outlined five key findings:

• Opportunities for connections between transport and health are missed because of lack of strategic direction or joint working.

- Both monetary and non-monetary health impacts of transport investment need to be considered to influence funding.
- Health and wellbeing are not considered sufficiently in local planning systems.
- The importance of mode choice for mental wellbeing needs to be considered.
- The health and wellbeing benefits of walking are not adequately considered.

The same report also offers a number of suggestions for improvements and approaches to appraisal which would better integrate transport and health decision making as well as outlining some good practice examples. We would echo the CIHT's sentiment, emphasising the ongoing desirability of promoting transport and health policy strategies capable of delivering greater health benefits for all, while mitigating negative impacts. In this section we outline some promising areas for action.

Governance and a hierarchy for health

If improving quality of life or wellbeing should be the ultimate aim of any public policy, from a transport perspective this means recognising the impacts that transport planning decisions can have on health and wellbeing. Improvements in this regard can be made by transport policy makers and practitioners seeking to work more collaboratively with other sectors, including health and welfare, to understand transport needs in a given area but also how these transport needs can be met in a way that minimises harm and promotes benefits to health. Unfortunately, despite examples of best practice such as Marmot Cities (see also Davis and Annett 2013), siloed thinking, where decisions made by one government or council department are not necessarily the most sensible from the point of view of population wellbeing, is still the norm. A good example comes from South Gloucestershire, near Bristol. The voluntary recreational running group 'parkrun' has documented public health value (Stevinson and Hickson 2014), but the local council recently attempted to offset maintenance costs by charging the group for the use of a (public) park. Factoring public health benefits (and, potentially, reduced healthcare costs) into its thinking may have changed the nature of the council's decision, although the fact that budgets were so constrained as to make consideration of charging the runners an option in the first place perhaps demonstrates the difficulties faced by local authorities trying to provide even basic local services in times of austerity.

Accessibility planning has demonstrated scope for cross-sectoral practices and, in many cases, nurtured discussion between local authority departments which may previously have had little interaction. Nevertheless, accessibility is still often seen as fundamentally a transport issue, and in some cases the process has been used to deposit a 'shopping list' of transport requirements from other sectors, rather than provoke any serious consideration by planning departments around the location of services. Accessibility as a concept cannot realise its full value unless it is understood – and thus 'owned' – by policy makers from a spatial planning perspective as much as a transport perspective; mobility is not the only solution to addressing inaccessibility. We recognise that moving beyond siloed thinking is extremely difficult in the British governance machine, especially in the context of restricted public spending where each separate institution, department or agency has its own limited budget and associated 'key performance indicators' (KPIs). In this sense it is unlikely that an aspiration of collaborative working will ever in itself be enough, and that some form of integrated framework is likely to be required; achieving the stated KPIs of such a framework depends upon people working beyond their immediate silos. One possibility would be to institute a social determinants of health framework (Figure 8.3) across different governance sectors, with health and wellbeing at the top of the hierarchy of requirements, perhaps based on a Health in All Policies (HiAP) approach for which the Local Government Association (2016) has already published guidance.

Evidence to support assessment and investment

It is all very well calling for more collaborative working, but even clearly identified frameworks are unlikely to be able to invest in necessary policy interventions without changes to existing project appraisal processes. In part this is due to the limited availability of relevant data which makes it difficult to measure the health impacts of transport schemes (Cavoli et al 2015), but it is also due to the appraisal frameworks used in the health and transport sectors which do not favour cross-sector benefits.

In transport appraisal, health and wellbeing are either secondary considerations or only considered when the effects of any given project can be estimated in monetary terms, for example with accidents or journey time reduction (Chapter 6). We noted that recent guidance on monetising physical activity does not go far enough in considering other health impacts or in assessing the physical activity impacts of all modes, and in any case the everyday importance of walking and cycling as modes of transport remains underestimated and thus, potentially, undervalued. For instance, National Travel Survey (NTS) data on short walks – that is, those under one mile – are gathered by asking respondents to record these on one day as opposed to over a longer reporting period (seven days) for other modes (NatCen 2017). Given the NTS's role in informing government policy, it is easy to imagine how any underestimation of walking could lead policy makers to under-recognise and underfund its potential as a means of transport. A recent positive development is the RSPH's (2016) report on the impact of commuting on health and wellbeing, which called for these things to be considered in the franchising and tendering processes for food sold at public transport stations. The report's focus also flags to us the need for all modes of transport to be assessed on a level playing field, because applying such an approach only to public transport, while ignoring it for roads (for example, at motorway service stations), will only serve to perpetuate existing structural problems.

The health sector relies heavily on evidence from randomised control trials to support investment in drugs and applies this approach to appraising the health benefits of investment in non-medical health interventions. Randomised control trials are generally impossible (or at least, unethical) when thinking about impacts of transport or the built environment on health, and causal pathways are complex, meaning that often the outcomes of such studies are disappointing. To us, this should not undermine investments in transport or housing on health grounds, but instead underpin the case for new approaches to appraisal and evaluation that can account for complexity and diverse causal pathways (Rutter et al 2017). Multi-criteria analysis, drawing upon both quantitative and qualitative data, and allowing more meaningful appraisal of policy options in the context of intended outcomes, might be one such approach (Chapters 6 and 11).

Considering the context: multimodal, place-based planning

Broadly speaking, active travel campaigns from the health sector tend to focus on individuals making 'healthy' behavioural decisions or creating a built environment conducive to active travel. But a focus on individual behaviour change ignores the impact of the built and social environment as well as contextual constraints on travel time such as shift working or family responsibilities. The onus of responsibility cannot solely be on the individual to change their behaviour when structural and environmental factors lead to macro-level car dependency in many circumstances. Active travel may not always result in positive health outcomes, for example, depending on the quality of environment in which that travel takes place. Jones et al (2016) found that cycling among older adults was associated with positive health outcomes when it took place in pleasant environments associated with recreational travel, but not necessarily when cycling on roads associated with cycling for transport. Conversely, a focus solely on the built environment can be critiqued for being environmentally deterministic (Andrews et al 2012) and ignoring individual, societal and cultural influences on travel behaviour. As made clear in Chapter 5, the most successful behaviour change strategies will be participatory and take account of the broader, structural context as well as individual or environmental factors. This requires a detailed and nuanced understanding of how daily travel practices are influenced by a range of social, material and economic circumstances, and a recognition that these cannot necessarily be influenced by a short-term focus on individual behaviour or micro-level environmental change; bringing about significant behaviour change requires fundamental cultural, political and institutional changes at multiple scales (see Schwanen 2016 in the context of energy and transport).

We return here to the potential benefits of place-based planning and design strategies. Such approaches can be more inclusive by considering how a place works and what is required for change, rather than a siloed focus on particular modes of transport or types of building; places are produced both by people and their surrounding environment. Declining car ownership among those with higher incomes (Delbosc and Currie 2013), declining car adoption among younger adults (Hopkins and Stephenson 2014, Minton and Clark 2018) and car-free living in central areas of larger cities (Melia 2014) mean that there is a potential appetite for multimodal travel which can support healthier modes of travel as part of a journey (Chapter 14). Multi-modality, including emerging forms of transport such as car- and bike-sharing, also offers the potential to improve accessibility and health outcomes for those who do not have access to a private vehicle (Clark and Curl 2016). Still, considering the context in which such transport schemes operate is crucial if potential health benefits are to be realised. This will also be true for emerging transport technologies. Electric vehicles (EVs) or driverless cars have the potential to address health problems through, for example, improved safety, increased accessibility for those who cannot drive themselves (including and encouraging multi-modality), or reducing pollution and congestion in certain circumstances. Yet health problems could also be exacerbated, through urban sprawl, increased car dependence, reduced physical activity and higher levels of exclusion and isolation for those without a car (Chapter 15).

Proponents of any place-based approach also need to be sensitive to the reality that many of the negative transport impacts on health and wellbeing are felt most harshly by people living in more deprived areas who are the least likely to have contributed to the problems in the first place. (Broadly speaking, this applies globally, with the poorest countries contributing the least to pollution.) In order not only to improve health and wellbeing, but also to reduce health inequalities, it is important to consider the distributional impacts of transport and health policies. We have already noted that those who cannot afford cars are more likely to suffer most from the mode's externalities while being excluded from the benefits of personal motorised travel. It is perhaps not surprising that rates of active travel are highest in more deprived areas – as a matter of necessity rather than choice – and public transport can be perceived as unsafe, dirty and unpleasant (RSPH 2016). In this context, targeting individual behaviour change to effect modal shift away from the car is likely to have limited impacts (Goenka and Andersen 2016). In any case, increasing rates of car ownership in deprived areas of cities such as Glasgow (Curl et al 2018) suggest that the car is both necessary – to reach jobs, services and leisure opportunities – and desirable, and among the poorest communities car ownership (or at least access to a car) is likely to lead to positive wellbeing and quality of life outcomes. Thus while initiatives designed to reduce the dominance of the car are required at an aggregate level, targeting active travel programmes at those who are often already engaged in higher levels of active travel and most likely to suffer adverse health consequences from others' use of the car may not be the most appropriate policy response.

Conclusions

Mobility and accessibility provided by transport systems are important for positive health, wellbeing and quality of life, especially for marginalised populations and in an ageing society. But the transport systems that we use to facilitate mobility often have adverse consequences for these same things. These adverse impacts are felt by everybody: even those who choose car-free, active lifestyles are vulnerable to pollution, noise and accidents as a result of how we structure our transport systems. Polarised arguments 'for' or 'against' the car are neither constructive nor realistic – car use can be associated with positive health outcomes for individuals, but these positive outcomes are rooted in the level of car dependence at a societal level. People without access to a private car are often disadvantaged in terms of access to economic, social and leisure opportunities, while at the same time suffering the negative health consequences of others' driving. The challenge is to limit the adverse health impacts or car reliance at a societal level while ensuring that the difficulties faced by those already at risk of exclusion are not exacerbated.

Transport has huge potential to address many contemporary health problems and health inequalities, but this requires more radical, holistic policies. 'Healthy' modes must be the obvious, easy and normal choice, prioritised by transport policy and urban planning, not an afterthought, simply 'nice to have' or a luxury for more affluent communities who can afford to live in places which allow them access to walkable, cyclable neighbourhoods served by high-quality public transport. Rather than a focus only on changing the behaviour of individuals, we need to build sustainable cities that lead neither to car dependence nor exclusion for those who do not have a car. Policy needs to consider car dependent practices (Mattioli et al 2016) and the relationships between transport and health at different scales, from individual, through city and region, to global.

Notes

[1] The four strategic objectives were listed as: Boosting economic growth, Building a one-nation Britain, Improving journeys and Safe, secure and sustainable transport.

[2] http://gehlpeople.com/

[3] www.880cities.org/

References

Andrews, G, Hall, E, Evans, B, and Colls, R (2012) 'Moving beyond walkability: on the potential of health geography', *Social Science & Medicine* 75(11): 1925–32.

Architecture & Design Scotland, NHS Scotland and Scottish Government (undated) *Place Standard. How good is our place?* www.placestandard.scot Accessed 19 September 2018.

Bambra, C, Gibson, M, Sowden, A, Wright, K, Whitehead, M and Petticrew, M (2010) 'Tackling the wider social determinants of health and health inequalities: evidence from systematic reviews', *Journal of Epidemiology and Community Health*, 64(4): 284–91.

Banister, D (1997) 'Reducing the need to travel', *Environment and Planning B: Urban Analytics and City Science*, 24(3): 437–9.

Bruegmann, R (2006) *Sprawl: A compact history*, London: University of Chicago Press.

Byard, R (2019) 'Deep venous thrombosis, pulmonary embolism and long-distance flights', *Forensic Science, Medicine and Pathology*, 15(1): 122–4.

Cavoli, C, Christie, N, Mindell, J and Titheridge, H (2015) 'Linking transport, health and sustainability: better data sets for better policy-making', *Journal of Transport and Health*, 2(2): 111–19.

Chartered Institute of Highways and Transportation (2016) A transport journey to a healthier life: a discussion paper on how transport policy and procedure can contribute to the health and wellbeing agenda. www.ciht.org.uk/media/4476/ciht_healther_life_a4_proof_v2_linked.pdf Accessed 23 August 2018.

Chatterjee, K, Clark, B, Martin, A and Davis, A (2017) *The commuting and wellbeing study: understanding the impact of commuting on people's lives.* UWE Bristol, UK. https://travelbehaviour.files.wordpress.com/2017/10/caw-summaryreport-onlineedition.pdf Accessed 23 August 2018.

Clark, J and Kearns, A (2015) 'Pathways to a physical activity legacy: assessing the regeneration potential of multi-sport events using a prospective approach', *Local Economy: The Journal of the Local Economy Policy Unit*, 30(8): 888–909.

Clark, J and Curl, A (2016) 'Bicycle and car share schemes as inclusive modes of travel? A socio-spatial analysis in Glasgow, UK', *Social Inclusion*, 4(3): 83–99.

Curl, A, Clark, J and Kearns, A (2018) 'Household car adoption and financial distress in deprived urban communities: a case of forced car ownership?' *Transport Policy*, 65: 61–71.

Curl, A, Ward Thompson, C, Aspinall, P, Thompson, C and Aspinall, P (2015) 'The effectiveness of 'shared space' residential street interventions on self–reported activity levels and quality of life for older people', *Landscape and Urban Planning*, 139: 117–25.

Davis, A and Annett, H (2013) 'Transport, travel and health in public policy: a journey begun', in J-P Rodrigue, T Notteboom and J Shaw, J (eds) *The SAGE Handbook of Transport Studies*, London: SAGE, pp 311–28.

Davis, A and Adrian Davis Associates (2015) *A healthy relationship: public health and transport collaboration in local government.* pteg, Leeds.

Day, R (2010) 'Environmental justice and older age: consideration of a qualitative neighbourhood based study', *Environment and Planning A: Economy and Space*, 42(11): 2658–73.

Delbosc, A (2012) 'The role of well-being in transport policy', *Transport Policy,* 23: 25–33.

Delbosc, A and Currie, G (2013) 'Causes of youth licensing decline: a synthesis of evidence', *Transport Reviews,* 33(3): 271–90.

Department for Environment Food and Rural Affairs (2016) *Emissions of air pollutants in the UK, 1970–2015: DEFRA National Statistics Release.* www.gov.uk/government/uploads/system/uploads/attachment_ data/file/579200/Emissions_airpollutants_statisticalrelease_2016_ final.pdf Accessed 23 August 2018.

Department for Infrastructure (2018) *Cycling in Northern Ireland 2016/17.* www.infrastructure-ni.gov.uk/system/files/publications/ infrastructure/cycling-in-northern-ireland-2016-17.pdf Accessed 23 August 2018.

Department for Transport (2013) *WebTAG: social and distributional impacts worksheets.* www.gov.uk/government/publications/webtag- social-and-distributional-impacts-worksheets Accessed 23 August 2018.

Department for Transport (2016) *Reported road casualties in Great Britain: main results 2015.* www.gov.uk/government/uploads/system/ uploads/attachment_data/file/533293/rrcgb-main-results-2015.pdf Accessed 23 August 2018.

Department for Transport (2017a) *Transport energy and environment statistics.* Table ENVO401. www.gov.uk/government/collections/ energy-and-environment-statistics Accessed 23 August 2018.

Department for Transport (2017b) *Annual report and accounts 2016–17.* www.gov.uk/government/uploads/system/uploads/attachment_ data/file/635176/dft-annual-report-and-accounts-2016-to-2017- web-version.pdf Accessed 23 August 2018.

Department for Transport (2017c) *Impact of the Local Sustainable Transport Fund: summary report.* www.gov.uk/government/uploads/system/ uploads/attachment_data/file/648822/local-sustainable-transport- fund-impact-summary-report.pdf Accessed 23 August 2018.

Department for Transport (2018) *Transport statistics Great Britain.* www. gov.uk/government/statistics/transport-statistics-great-britain-2018 Accessed 26 February 2019.

Design for All Foundation (undated) *What is Design for All?* http:// designforall.org/design.php Accessed 13 September 2018.

DHC, University of Aberdeen and Integrated Transport Planning Ltd (2013) Going smarter: monitoring and evaluation of the Smarter Choices, Smarter Places Programme. Final Report to the Scottish Government. Derek Halden Consultancy, Edinburgh.

Dobbie, F, McConville, S and Ormston, R (2010) *Understanding why some people do not use buses*. Transport Research Series. Scottish Government, Edinburgh.

Douglas, M, Watkins, S, Gorman, D and Higgins, M (2011) 'Are cars the new tobacco?' *Journal of Public Health*, 33(2): 160–9.

Downs, A (2004) *Still Stuck in Traffic: Coping with Peak-hour Traffic Congestion*, Washington, DC: The Brookings Institution.

Duarte, A, Garcia, C, Giannarakis, G, Limão, S, Polydoropoulou, A and Litinas, N (2010) 'New approaches in transportation planning: happiness and transport economics', *Netonomics*, 11(1): 5–32.

Dunlop, S and Swales, K (2012) 'Measuring wellbeing in Scotland : the Oxfam Humankind Index', *Fraser of Allander Econonomic Commentary*, 36(1): 81–8.

Ellaway, A, Macdonald, L and Kearns, A (2016) Are housing tenure and car access still associated with health? A repeat cross-sectional study of UK adults over a 13-year period. *BMJ Open*, 6(11): e012268.

European Environment Agency (2008) *Air pollutants and global effects*. www.eea.europa.eu/publications/2599XXX/page009.html Accessed 26 January 2017.

Friedmann, J (2010) 'Place and place-making in cities: a global perspective', *Planning Theory & Practice*, 11(2): 149–65.

Frumkin, H (2002) 'Urban sprawl and public health', *Public Health Reports*, 117(3): 201–17.

Gamble, T, Walker, I and Laketa, A (2015) 'Bicycling campaigns promoting health versus campaigns promoting safety: a randomized controlled online study of "dangerization"'. *Journal of Transport and Health*, 2(3): 369–78.

Gatrell, A (2011) *Mobilities and Health*, Surrey: Ashgate.

Gatrell, A (2013) 'Therapeutic mobilities: walking and "steps" to wellbeing and health', *Health Place*, 22: 98–106.

Gatrell, A and Elliott, S (2015) *Geographies of Health: An Introduction*, Oxford: Wiley-Blackwell.

Giles-Corti, B, Vernez-Moudon, A, Reis, R, Turrell, G, Dannenberg, A, Badland, H, Foster, S, Lowe, M, Sallis, J, Stevenson, M and Owen, N (2016) 'City planning and population health: a global challenge', *The Lancet*, 388: 2912–24.

Goenka, S and Andersen, L (2016) 'Our health is a function of where we live', *The Lancet*, 387: 2168–70.

Goldacre, B and Spiegelhalter, D (2013) 'Bicycle helmets and the law', *BMJ*, 346: f3817.

Goodwin, P (1995) 'Car Dependence', *Transport Policy*, 2(3): 151–2.

Hamilton, K and Gourlay, M (2002) *Missed hospital appointments and transport.* www.kingsfund.org.uk/sites/files/kf/UEL-missed-hospital-appointments-transport-Kerry-Hamilton-Marion-Gourlay-Kings-Fund-December-2002.pdf Accessed 23 August 2018.

Hands, A (2015) 'A26 Cycle Coventry – healthy transport in a Marmot city', *Journal of Transport & Health,* 2 (Supplement): S18.

Health and Social Care Information Centre (2017) Statistics on obesity, physical activity and diet. www.gov.uk/government/uploads/system/uploads/attachment_data/file/613532/obes-phys-acti-diet-eng-2017-rep.pdf Accessed 23 August 2018.

Hopkins, D and Stephenson, J (2014) 'Generation Y mobilities through the lens of energy cultures: a preliminary exploration of mobility cultures', *Journal of Transport Geography,* 38: 88–91.

House of Commons Health Committee (2016) *Public health post-2013: Second Report of Session 2016–17.* www.publications.parliament.uk/pa/cm201617/cmselect/cmhealth/140/140.pdf Accessed 23 August 2018.

Jenks, M, Burton, E and Williams, K (1996) *The Compact City: A Sustainable Urban Form?* London: E & FN Spon.

Johnson, R, Shaw, J, Berding, J, Gather, M and Rebstock, M (2017) 'European national government approaches to older people's transport system needs', *Transport Policy,* 59: 17–27.

Jones, T, Chatterjee, K, Spinney, J, Street, E, Van Reekum, C, Spencer, B, Jones, H, Leyland, L, Mann, C, Williams, S and Beale, N (2016) *cycleBOOM. Design for lifelong health and wellbeing. Summary of key findings and recommendations.* www.cycleboom.org/summary-report/ Accessed 23 August 2018.

Kjellstrom, T, van Kerkhoff, L, Bammer, G and McMichael, T (2003) Comparative assessment of transport risks – how it can contribute to health impact assessment of transport policies. Bulletin of the World Health Organization 81, pp 451–7. www.ncbi.nlm.nih.gov/pubmed/12894331 Accessed 23 August 2018.

Koohsari, M, Badland, H and Giles-Corti, B (2013) '(Re)Designing the built environment to support physical activity: bringing public health back into urban design and planning', *Cities,* 35: 294–8.

Local Government Association (2016) *Health in all policies: a manual for local government.* www.local.gov.uk/health-all-policies-manual-local-government Accessed 14 September 2018.

Lucas, K and Jones, P (2009) *The car in British society.* RAC Foundation, London. www.racfoundation.org/wp-content/uploads/2017/11/car_in_british_society-lucas_et_al-170409.pdf Accessed 11 September 2018.

Macintyre, S, Hiscock, R, Kearns, A and Ellaway, A (2001) 'Housing tenure and car access: further exploration of the nature of their relations with health in a UK setting', *Journal of Epidemiology and Community Health*, 55(5): 330–1.

Macintyre, S, Ellaway, A, Der, G, Ford, G and Hunt, K (1998) 'Do housing tenure and car access predict health because they are simply markers of income or self esteem? A Scottish study', *Journal of Epidemiology and Community Health*, 52(10): 657–64.

Marmot, M (2005) 'Social determinants of health inequalities', *The Lancet*, 365: 1099–104.

Marmot, M, Allen, J, Goldblatt, P, Boyce, T, McNeish, D, Grady, M, Geddes, I. (2010) *Fair society, healthy lives: strategic review of health inequalities in England post-2010*. London: Marmot Review Team.

Martin, A, Goryakin, Y and Suhrcke, M (2014) 'Does active commuting improve psychological wellbeing? Longitudinal evidence from eighteen waves of the British Household Panel Survey', *Preventive Medicine*, 69: 293–303.

Mason, P, Curl, A and Kearns, A (2016) 'Domains and levels of physical activity are linked to adult mental health and wellbeing in deprived neighbourhoods: a cross-sectional study', *Mental Health and Physical Activity*, 11: 19–28.

Mattioli, G, Anable, J and Vrotsou, K (2016) 'Car dependent practices: findings from a sequence pattern mining study of UK time use data', *Transportation Research Part A: Policy and Practice*, 89: 56–72.

Melia, S (2014) 'Carfree and low-car development', in S Ison and C Mulley (eds) *Parking: issues and policies*, Bingley: Emerald Group, pp 213–33.

Metz, D (2008) 'The myth of travel time saving', *Transport Reviews*, 28(3): 321–36.

Minton, J and Clark, J (2018) 'Driving Segregation: Age, gender and emerging inequalities', in A Curl and C Musselwhite (eds) *Geographies of transport and ageing*, Palgrave Macmillan.

Muirie, J (2017) *Active Travel in Glasgow: what we've learned so far*. Glasgow Centre for Population Health, Glasgow.

Musselwhite, C, Holland, C and Walker, I (2015) 'The role of transport and mobility in the health of older people', *Journal of Transport and Health*, 2(1): 1–4.

NatCen (2017) National Travel Survey. http://natcen.ac.uk/our-research/research/national-travel-survey/ Accessed 23 August 2018.

Newman, P and Kenworthy, J (1999) *Sustainability and Cities: Overcoming Automobile Dependence*, Washington, DC: Island Press.

Nieuwenhuijsen, M and Khreis, H (2016) 'Car free cities: pathway to healthy urban living', *Environment International*, 94: 251–62.

Nordbakke, S and Schwanen, T (2013) 'Well-being and mobility: a theoretical framework and literature review focusing on older people', *Mobilities*, 9(1): 104–29.

Office for National Statistics (2012) *First annual ONS experimental subjective well-being results*. www.bl.uk/collection-items/first-annual-ons-experimental-subjective-wellbeing-results Accessed 13 July 2019.

Office for National Statistics (2014) *Commuting and personal well-being, 2014*. webarchive.nationalarchives.gov.uk/20160105231823/http://www.ons.gov.uk/ons/rel/wellbeing/measuring-national-well-being/commuting-and-personal-well-being--2014/art-commuting-and-personal-well-being.html Accessed 23 August 2018.

Public Health England (2016) *Working together to promote active travel: a briefing for local authorities*. www.gov.uk/government/uploads/system/uploads/attachment_data/file/523460/Working_Together_to_Promote_Active_Travel_A_briefing_for_local_authorities.pdf Accessed 23 August 2018.

Rao, M, Prasad, S, Adshead, F and Tissera, H (2007) 'The built environment and health', *The Lancet*, 370: 1111–3.

Royal Society for Public Health (2016) *Health in a hurry: the impact of rush hour commuting on our health and wellbeing*. www.rsph.org.uk/our-work/policy/championing-the-publics-health/health-in-a-hurry.html Accessed 23 August 2018.

Royal Town Planning Institute (2013) *State of the nation report 2013: transport. Evidence of the Royal Town Planning Institute to the Institution of Civil Engineers*. www.rtpi.org.uk/media/10712/rtpi_evidence_to_ice_state_of_the_nation.pdf Accessed 23 August 2018.

Rutter, H, Savona, N, Glonti, K, Bibby, J, Cummins, S, Finegood, D, Greaves, F, Harper, L, Hawe, P, Moore, L, Petticrew, M, Rehfuess, E, Shiell, A, Thomas, J and White, M (2017) 'The need for a complex systems model of evidence for public health', *The Lancet*, 390: 2602–04.

Schmitz, H (2011) 'Why are the unemployed in worse health? The causal effect of unemployment on health', *Labour Economics*, 18(1): 71–8.

Schwanen, T (2016) 'Geographies of transport I: reinventing a field?', *Progress in Human Geography*, 40(1): 126–37.

Schwanen, T and Ziegler, F (2011) 'Wellbeing, independence and mobility: an introduction', *Ageing and Society*, 31(5): 719–33.

Scottish Government (2010) *Designing Streets. A Policy Statement for Scotland.* www.gov.scot/publications/designing-streets-policy-statement-scotland/ Accessed 13 July 2019.

Scottish Government (2014a) *Ambition-Opportunity-Place. Scotland's Third National Planning Framework.* www.thenbs.com/PublicationIndex/documents/details?%20Pub=ScotGov&DocID=306935 Accessed 13 July 2019.

Scottish Government (2014b) *Let's get Scotland walking. The National Walking Strategy.* www.gov.scot/Resource/0045/00452622.pdf Accessed 23 August 2018.

Sinclair, F and Sinclair, S (2001). *Access all areas: an assessment of social inclusion measures In Scottish local transport strategies.* Centre for Research into Socially Inclusive Services, Edinburgh.

Social Exclusion Unit (2003) *Making the connections: final report on transport and social exclusion.* www.ilo.org/wcmsp5/groups/public/---ed_emp/---emp_policy/---invest/documents/publication/wcms_asist_8210.pdf Accessed 23 August 2018.

Stevinson, C and Hickson, M (2014) 'Exploring the public health potential of a mass community participation event', *Journal of Public Health*, 36(2): 268–74.

Sustrans (2012) Locked out. Transport poverty in England. www.sustrans.org.uk/sites/default/files/images/files/migrated-pdfs/Transport%20Poverty%20England%20FINAL%20web.pdf Accessed 23 August 2018.

Sweet, M (2014) 'Traffic congestion's economic impacts: evidence from US metropolitan regions', *Urban Studies*, 51(10): 2088–110.

Tainio, M, Woodcock, J, Brage, S, Götschi, T, Goodman, A, Kelly, P and de Nazelle, A (2017) Research into valuing health impacts in transport appraisal. Final report. www.gov.uk/government/uploads/system/uploads/attachment_data/file/639211/research-into-valuing-health-impacts-in-transport-appraisal.pdf Accessed 23 August 2018.

The King's Fund (2017) Chickens coming home to roost: local government public health budgets for 2017/18. www.kingsfund.org.uk/blog/2017/07/local-government-public-health-budgets-2017-18 Accessed 23 August 2018.

Tomaney, J (2015) 'Region and place III: well-being', *Progress in Human Geography*, 41(1): 99–107.

Transport for London (2012) *Guidance on the assessment of pedestrian guardrail.* Roads Directorate. http://content.tfl.gov.uk/guidance-on-assessment-of-pedestrian-guardrail.pdf Accessed 23 August 2018.

Transport Scotland (2017) *Cycling action plan for Scotland 2017–2020. Cycling as a form of transport.* www.transport.gov.scot/media/10311/transport-scotland-policy-cycling-action-plan-for-scotland-january-2017.pdf Accessed 23 August 2018.

Transport Scotland (2018) Active travel task force report. www.transport.gov.scot/media/42284/active-travel-task-force-june-2018.pdf Accessed 23 August 2018.

Umberson, D and Montez, J (2010) 'Social relationships and health: a flashpoint for health policy', *Journal of Health and Social Behavior,* 51(1) (Supplement): S54–66.

Urry, J (2007) *Mobilities,* Cambridge: Polity Press.

Welsh Government (2016) *An active travel action plan for Wales.* https://beta.gov.wales/sites/default/files/publications/2017-09/active-travel-action-plan.pdf Accessed 14 September 2018.

World Health Organization (1997) *WHOQOL: measuring quality of life.* www.who.int/mental_health/media/68.pdf Accessed 23 August 2018.

World Health Organization (2015) *Global status report on road safety 2015.* http://apps.who.int/iris/bitstream/10665/189242/1/9789241565066_eng.pdf?ua=1 Accessed 23 August 2018.

World Health Organization (2018) *WHO launches global action plan on physical activity.* www.who.int/topics/physical_activity/en/ Accessed 23 August 2018.

9

Connecting places: towards a participatory, ordinary urbanism

Geoff Vigar and Georgiana Varna

Introduction

Transport is common sense; we all know what it entails. For most people it is a mode – cars, buses, trucks, trains, trams, ships, aeroplanes – for moving people and goods from A to B, connecting the places where we work with those in which we entertain, consume and sleep. This is what we've been taught, and how modernist planning conceived of the modern, functional city, by creating a clear demarcation between zones and responding to the growth of the car with a new system of highways and motorways to connect these zones. But as the 21st century dawned, the ecological, social and health implications of automobility were becoming all too apparent. Coupled with evidence of the self-fulfilling prophecy of 'predict and provide' planning, these implications suggested that new approaches were needed, at least in the relatively low urban growth scenarios dominating western cities. Such approaches became variously labelled a 'new realism' (Goodwin et al 1991) or sustainable mobility (Banister 2008).

In this context, our chapter examines the opportunities and pitfalls of integrating transport planning with urban design and place-making strategies, policies and actions, using design thinking as a way to address many of the 'intractables' associated with implementing transport policy. We argue that it is necessary to focus on the substance and consistency of macro-level strategy as well as concentrated efforts to implement creative and consistent micro-level interventions. We position our argument alongside the contemporary emphasis on smart cities, aiming to reinsert into current debates a more 'ordinary' approach that celebrates the significance of intervention in 'ordinary neighbourhoods' through the deployment of 'ordinary technologies' that are useful in creating more liveable cities – technologies as ordinary as benches and quality pavements. This is not to say that various forms of 'smartness' and increasingly open data are not of use to planning processes, but we do believe the task at hand involves better situating these data as just one form of knowledge among many.

As such, we suggest that planning is a form of knowledge in action, and more attention needs to be paid to the ways in which knowledge is developed, used and deployed. In doing so, and to better secure citizen buy-in to the transformation of public space – whether a public square, a highway or a plot of land – we argue for an approach centred on co-design. This involves engaging local communities through participatory methods, from the agenda-setting stage, through deciding what knowledge might count in a process, all the way towards the development and implementation of spatial interventions (see Chapter 11 for a discussion of citizen involvement in macro-scale projects). In our view, the traditional investigation tools of the 'orthodox' school of transport planning, which remain prevalent in much contemporary practice, should sit in the background (Kębłowski et al 2015). Not least this is because a focus on 'smartness' and big data can fall into a 'generalisation trap' that merely locks in an existing, socially unjust and ecologically inadequate status quo (Schwanen 2016). Such data-driven methods tend to look backwards, at trends in the past, thereby having limited traction when the aim is a transition to a different future (Wright and McCarthy 2005). Design thinking, by contrast, offers an alternative, future-orientated approach to counter the planning orthodoxy that subverts people's everyday needs to the paradigms and embedded routines of local authority planning and transport departments. At some point since the publication of the Buchanan report (Ministry of Transport 1963), UK land use and transport planners (and we note their continued bizarre separation) chose to implement only the half of the report concerned with traffic flow, and neglected the other critical half that spoke of 'environmental areas' and their limits. We suggest it is high time to reassert the significance of this other half and ditch the obsession with traffic flow and congestion, and we show how this might be done.

The macro-level: mobility strategies for the 21st century liveable and sustainable city

The 20th century saw the emergence and embedding of 'predict and provide' as an overarching paradigm for UK transport planning (Vigar 2002), underpinned by neo-classical, 'orthodox' thinking (Kębłowski et al 2015). The desire to provide more space for private cars in cities became allied to a fervour for new technology in which 'outmoded' technologies such as buses, trams and bicycles simply did not fit.

The resultant paradigm of urban modernism was arguably of greatest salience in the mid-1960s, paradoxically at a time when cars were still a minority form of urban transport, but they were seen to be the future (Gunn 2010, Parsons and Vigar 2017).

As concern for the impact of car use on public spaces increased, seminal reports such as Buchanan's set out alternatives and highlighted how to accommodate the increasing demand for car use, but also showed how to limit and manage the impacts. Underpinning Buchanan's report was the idea that a city or town was made up of 'urban rooms' and that the first task of the planner was to set environmental limits within them: 'There must be areas of good environment – urban rooms – and there must be a complementary network of roads – urban corridors – for effecting the primary distribution of traffic to the environmental areas' (Ministry of Transport (1963): para 101).

In central retail areas, such ideas built on a practice of pedestrianisation implemented in many plans of the 1940s and 1950s, and of course this is now commonplace. But Buchanan was also concerned with setting environmental limits *across* the various 'urban rooms' of the city, including residential neighbourhoods and suburban retail centres where he recognised that car traffic would have to be tamed for reasons of liveability. While in the Netherlands such ideas ultimately led to the development of the *Woonerf* principle, where cars are 'guests' in urban neighbourhoods, planners in the UK did not follow such a path. Indeed, as we have noted, the elements of Buchanan's thinking taken into practice in British cities related mainly to urban road building, with less attention paid to the alternatives.

The impacts of subsequent urban motorway building led to a counter-movement, which came from outside mainstream research and established practice communities. Through the work initially of North American authors, different evaluations of what mattered in cities emerged, and with them a set of alternatives that valued attention to the public realm and its everyday use by people. Large-scale urban motorway projects were abandoned and, latterly, concern for those not able to access cars also led to greater attention to public transport as a solution. Nevertheless, beyond a few exemplar cities where alternative solutions were attempted, 'predict and provide' continued in the minds of many professionals and citizens as an intuitive means of tackling congestion (Chapter 7). It would take an increasingly well-developed understanding of the limitations of this approach (Goodwin et al 1991) and the growing coherence of alternatives (Banister 2008) to bring serious challenge to established ways of thinking.

Through the work of Jane Jacobs (1961), Richard Sennett (1974), Edward Relph (1976) and William H. Whyte (1980, 1988), the public space discourse was brought to a new level, and the combined weight of these authors' contributions emphasised its importance to a whole range of urban agendas including the emancipation of marginal groups, the forging of individual and group identities and the promotion of political action, not to mention the overall reorganisation of society. Lefebvre's slogan, the 'right to the city', coined just before the revolutionary events in Paris of May 1968, drove debate about just who produces the 'urban values' that come to matter in the production of the built environment. Perhaps most critically in relation to mobility concerns, since the late 1960s Jan Gehl and his team (Gehl 1987, Gehl and Gemzøe 2000, 2004) have undertaken innovative design-led, place-focused work in Copenhagen.

Despite initial public opposition to the feasibility of restrictions on private vehicles, a focus on designing central Copenhagen in ways that valued pedestrian movement and the importance of public space for human-scale interaction and dwelling emerged. Gehl's practice and teachings have subsequently spread to various cities worldwide. These provide innovative examples of how to re-think and re-shape cities based on the principles of making them liveable, that is, walkable, bike-able, enjoyable. *Life between buildings: using public space* (Gehl 1987) paved the way towards a deeper understanding of the role of public space in creating vibrant urban environments. By gradually applying his ideas and methods in the urban laboratory provided by the Danish capital, he has succeeded in radically changing it from a typical car-dominated western city of the 1960s and 1970s, into one often ranked as one of the world's most liveable cities (for example, Metropolis 2016, Monocle 2017). Writing with his business partner Lars Gemzøe at the turn of the century, Gehl declared that the city's transformation has been so radical that what has emerged is a completely new urban phenomenon, not just a revival of older traditions (Gehl and Gemzøe 2000: 20). Through detailed empirical work across several decades and geographical locations, they are able to demonstrate that:

> In a society in which increasingly more of daily life takes place in the private sphere – private homes, at private computers, in private cars, at private workplaces and in strictly controlled and privatized shopping centres – there are clear signs that the city and city spaces have been given a new and influential role as public space and forum. (Gehl and Gemzøe 2000: 20)

Despite the growing prevalence of exemplars such as Copenhagen, many UK towns and cities are struggling to implement planning and transport strategies that deliver 'liveable' urban qualities. The embeddedness of the car in everyday life and the resilience of predict and provide thinking has made taking back road space for non-car uses difficult beyond central area pedestrianisations. Following John Friedmann, we suggest that one of the problems here is that planning has lost sight of the places that form the backdrop to much of people's lives and that form the beginning and end of many of their journeys, namely neighbourhoods: '...ordinary neighbourhoods... *need to be brought back into view*, so that planners and local citizens can engage in a joint search for genuine betterment in the physical conditions of neighbourhood life' (Friedmann, 2010: 162, emphasis added).

Colin Buchanan might find it odd that his ideas of 'environmental areas' and the creation of 'environmental limits' therein did not gain traction alongside plans for new capacity, as was intended. Despite the publication of his report, the demands of everyday streets remained subverted to the embedded routines, practices and regulatory demands of local authority highways departments. This won't change so long as we predominantly regard the street as a highway rather than focus on the many uses to which a street might be put, and continue to overlook its multiple meanings for the people who use it on a day-to-day basis and as one vital piece of a larger place-making strategy.

Today the benefits from adopting new thinking are built not just on the long-standing debates highlighted earlier but also on increasing evidence about the positive impacts of place-making approaches. Exemplar successes in cities such as Copenhagen, Barcelona and Bogota are hailed as examples of good urbanism; they are the 21st-century cities we look up to. Such cities prioritised high-quality public spaces across the city, well connected by walking and cycle networks and affordable, efficient public transport. Urban development schemes were implemented with an emphasis on design quality, delivered through public-private partnerships where a strong and confident local government was a constant feature, and with the consistent support of a ruling governance regime irrespective of the electoral cycle. Existing neighbourhoods were retrofitted to prioritise active travel and active use of the street. Critically, these things have had economic benefits, too.

In the UK, this way of thinking was originally embodied in experiments with home zones in the 1980s and more broadly the urban renaissance movement and its Urban Task Force (UTF), chaired by Lord Rogers (UTF 1999, 2005). Supported by the Commission for Architecture and the Built Environment (CABE) and focused on the poor quality of many of Britain's towns and cities, it tried to ignite a more place-quality focused development process. Although these approaches did lead to the creation of a series of new, higher quality places across the country (Carmona et al 2002, Hatherley 2010), they came to an end with changes to the planning system post-2010 that brought about a focus on development viability in the wake of the Global Financial Crisis and an abandonment of state-led regeneration effort. It is also true that they had not been without criticism, with much 'urban renaissance' development arguably failing to heed the lessons of the mainland European exemplars it championed. Newly built neighbourhoods often found themselves with the worst of all worlds, subject to maximum parking standards but without quality, affordable public transit and no safe cycling network to speak of. In such cases, public space was once more forgotten, giving the pedestrian the feeling of having to use leftover space without coherence that failed to add to the quality of life of the residents.

Towards the end of the 2010s, after almost a decade of austerity urbanism, planning's role is seen increasingly as providing confidence to the market, and positive planning in neighbourhoods seems a world away. In this rather bleak context we point to hopeful signs that local action can be ignited directly by citizens, rather than by local government, leading to a process of change (Davoudi and Madanipour 2015). Could the neighbourhood void highlighted by Friedmann be picked up in part by citizens themselves? Might citizens opt for redesigned streets and public spaces when given the authority, more so than when imposed by 'expert' planners and engineers? We investigate this possibility through the lens of two case studies, one in the UK (Newcastle's DIY Streets) and one in Belgium (Ghent's Living Streets). The first is at the neighbourhood scale and the second is at the scale of the city. They have mixed outcomes but both suggest that different approaches to planning have much to offer. We conclude by speculating on how such approaches might be scaled-up.

The micro-level: streets, neighbourhoods, places

DIY streets[1]

Newcastle is a city in North East England, situated in the wider Tyne and Wear conurbation that has a population of 1.1 million. In 2014, the City Council successfully bid for £5m from central government to improve cycling levels in five neighbourhoods. Newcastle has a trip rate for cycling in line with the UK average of under 2 per cent of all journeys. A team at Newcastle University and the cycling charity Sustrans designed an intervention in one of these five neighbourhoods, and it is this we report on here. The neighbourhood has income levels below the national and city averages and is ethnically mixed, with a high dependence on public transport and walking and with levels of cycling lower than the Newcastle average. The project focused on a part of the neighbourhood containing two schools and one of the area's main thoroughfares, a car-dominated street where parking on pavements is institutionalised and where public space is limited and underused. The street has two key civic institutions for residents and the nearby community, a library and swimming pool. A health centre and an allotment area lie adjacent to the library and pool, suggesting a large and varied group of stakeholders uses the area, creating the potential for some sort of vibrant civic hub to be developed.

Initially Sustrans had struggled to find local people willing to participate, with conventional modes of engagement (leaflet drops, questionnaires, consultation events) failing to generate community interest. Following engagement with university researchers, the brief was recast. Rather than leading the engagement attempts with transport and mobility issues, a community conversation about the place was instigated, making the process more open-ended. Much participatory practice can fail if it is narrowly instrumental in its conception because citizens immediately find themselves polarised in terms of their opinions, and battle-lines are drawn (Chapter 11). The aim here was to move towards a co-designed model of the built environment where expertise lay in asking the right questions, rather than providing the answers, to assist the community in 'finding answers for themselves' (Watson 2014: 69). This was especially challenging given the lack of any residents' association or similar organisation locally; as much as the process was designed to elicit their views and ideas, it was to 'ignite' citizens (Hajer 2003) to notice their environment could be made to be different and, in turn, that resources to campaign for change could be developed.

Three principles guided the approach to engagement. First, the team[2] sought to engage citizens in an *inspirational* participatory process developed from design thinking, using interesting and playful activities. Second, the approach was *ethnographically driven*. It had to describe the 'here and now' before developing concrete future stages (Blomberg and Karasti 2013: 88). Such description involved 'intermediate interventions' (mock-ups, provocations) to 'disrupt' the present and make more visible the requirements of the future

(Blomberg and Karasti 2013: 90). Third, effort went into creating roles for each participating resident to play (Sanoff 2006). The team deployed interconnected and complementary activities associated with participatory design, including making, telling and enacting (Sanders 2013a):

- *Making* refers to the use of our hands to embody/express ideas in the creation of physical artefacts such as collages, mappings, mock-ups and small-scale models (Sanders 2013b). If utilised in the early stages of the design process, artefacts will likely describe experiences and narratives.
- *Telling* refers to a verbal description of the present situation through stories, moviemaking and storyboards. There may be certain limitations within this activity with regard to the ability of people having the verbal vocabulary to express their own tacit knowledge (Sanders 2013a, 2013b), and so the process benefits from skilled facilitation and the use of visual props.
- *Enacting* temporary settings allows expression of ideas of potential futures to disrupt assumptions and to defy conventions about place. (Tardiveau and Mallo 2014)

Making and enacting are in our view more engaging than traditional forms of telling (through talk and text) used in planning and transportation strategy-making, as they involve a degree of action in themselves. More traditional forms can exclude certain groups without verbal and argumentative confidence and those who find such approaches just plain boring! Table 9.1 describes the methods deployed over a period of one year to underwrite the co-production process.

While social media was used as one communication platform, most other interventions were low-tech with models made traditionally in workshops, often using found and recycled materials. Most of the outcomes were also very 'ordinary' – a zebra crossing, improved pavements, traditional benches, a pocket park of wooden planters and seating. A later phase is planned to include a play space, which is likely to build on more futuristic conceptions. Overall, though, what we would argue was an extraordinary process – it has much in common with others of its ilk but is a world away from the popular practitioner and academic discourse around transport planning (and, for that matter, smart cities and big data as paradigms to shape urban futures) – produced very ordinary, but extremely valuable outcomes. The area now affords easier mobility in more pleasant

Table 9.1: Principles and methods of co-production

Methods	Activities
1 Sensory mapping This entailed building a physical model portraying the street. It was more recognisable than a scaled plan but included fantastical elements that were 'mysterious and elusive' (Gaver et al 2004: 55) aimed at disrupting existing ways of seeing and evoking an imaginary feel for the street.	Making/ Telling
2 Temporary public space Temporary public spaces were built to enact ideas from method one. The space enabled participants to respond in both verbal and embodied ways which were observed and noted by the core Team.	Telling/ Enacting
3 Street trial Mobile furniture was inserted into the environment as 'provocative artefacts ... to understand the [urban environment and]... to expose both the possibilities and constraints on future design directions' (Blomberg and Karasti 2013: 101).	Telling/ Enacting
4 Focus group/Constituted group Large photographs and playing cards were used to facilitate a discussion in a focus group and to prompt ideas shared during previous events. Through sketching over the photographs, ideas were rendered tangible and users imagined how the place might look. The focus group crystallised into a residents' association, with a greater degree of legitimacy in speaking for the neighbourhood than the team initially leading the process.	Telling/ Making
5 Proposing and Acting (building and gardening) The outcomes were highway design proposals (new road crossings, better pavement surfaces) and a pocket park. The latter was a result of seeding a residents' association who then secured central government funds. The group helped to build and subsequently maintain a garden.	Making/ Enacting

Source: Adapted from Mallo and Tardiveau 2017

surroundings, particularly for those on foot. Better cycle provision has been implemented near the schools, even if it was not possible to remove pavement car parking to facilitate a segregated cycle lane due to wider public resistance. Whether this results in an improved modal share for active travel it is too early to say. Nevertheless, the spatial improvements to the public realm led to more convivial and vibrant public spaces that encourage street-level interaction, with observations showing high levels of usage of the benches and the pocket park where none existed previously. Indeed, the Pocket Park has become a focal point for community life and particularly celebrations, such as Christmas (Figure 9.1).

Despite some shortcomings, if judged against the overall programme's intentions we would suggest that these deeper forms of

Figure 9.1: The refashioned public space

Source: A Tardiveau

engagement work in favour of active travel. The open-ended nature of the discussion was critical to generating community buy-in, as were the inspiring methods. The successful *Woonerfs* of the Netherlands were similarly those that had community buy-in from the start, even though they were largely an expert-led process. In paying heed to Friedmann's (2010) call cited earlier for attention to neighbourhoods, we argue that the right tools and language are needed to engage citizens in the planning and future management of their built environments. While the intervention does show the need for certain skills – of facilitation and process design – and technical competencies such as highways regulation and design, it also demonstrates how the ideas of sustainable places and place-making might start at home, at people's front doors and in their very local public places. Indeed, the residents' group that emerged from the process now feels empowered to speak for what it now considers *its own place*. A group has emerged with an explicit focus on caring for a place that might in future yield more projects of social and ecological value, tackling the pavement parking and creating cycle space for example, as well as maintaining what is already there. In this sense, the project demonstrated both that a feeling of community and associated social capital can be brought into being through minor spatial interventions (and the social capital is crucially important, especially in areas such as this where it is low to begin with; see Semenza et al 2006).

Ghent's Living Streets

Ghent is the second city in Flanders, Belgium, with a population of around 225,000, in a larger city region of around 400,000 people. A survey undertaken in 2000 found that over 60 per cent of reported trips were made by car as the main transport mode (45 per cent as a driver and 15 per cent as a passenger), while cycling and walking each accounted for around 15 per cent of trips. Public transport usage was very low: buses had a modal share of 3 per cent, the train 2 per cent and the tram just 1.5 per cent[3] (Witlox and Tindemans 2004). The use of bicycles is low compared to neighbouring Netherlands, where the top municipalities score between 35 and 40 per cent and even the lowest boast between 15 and 20 per cent (Ministerie van Verkeer en Waterstaat 2009). This is in part explained by the lack of attention given to cycling as a practice by policy makers in the 1970s and 1980s in Belgium, and indeed most of Western Europe, compared with the Netherlands (Veraart et al 2016). In order to increase cycling and walking, a few policy initiatives were undertaken from the end of the 1980s, namely the Loop Plan (1987), the Bicycle Action Plan (1993) and the Ghent Mobility Plan (1997, renewed in 2003 and 2014). The latest Mobility Plan, with a time horizon of 2030, is seen as 'a driving force for a sustainable and accessible city,' aiming at transforming the city into a sustainable, clean, healthy, vibrant and dynamic urban centre (Stad Gent 2014).

The plans of current mayor Daniël Termont include reducing car use to 27 per cent by 2030 and extending the 35ha pedestrian area introduced by his predecessor by a further 15ha. These are supported by over 70 per cent of Ghentians (Rutter 2016). A citizen's cabinet comprised of 150 local residents is also being created to advise the deputy mayor and mobility minister, Filip Watteeuw (Rutter 2016). Institutional support on the place-making side is provided by the city planning department, whose main tasks are to guide private development, draw up masterplans, manage streets and public spaces and undertake street-regeneration projects at a neighbourhood scale. Unfortunately, the economic crisis led to a two-thirds reduction in the funding that the city spends on public spaces, and there is growing concern that urbanism is now all about negotiation, with a lack of focus on quality. Voices in the architecture community argue that the city often invests in areas with strong social networks, and that those (many) neighbourhoods in which there are weaker social ties are left behind as a result.[4] In this context, the Living Streets project was born.

In 2013, a group of enthusiasts concerned with mobility issues and the sustainable development of Ghent had the idea of transforming entire streets into temporarily car-free zones, breathing life into car-dominated environments by engaging citizens in shaping their places. The main aim of the Living Streets Project was to work with communities to design safe, attractive, enjoyable streets and public spaces. As the initiators describe it:

> 'The Living Street is an experiment in which residents take over their street and convert it into the street of their dreams. By temporarily banning or partially banning cars from the street (or a section of it) and finding another place for parked cars (for example, in a local car park), space is created for greenery, encounters and social living.' (From leefstraat.be)

The project focuses on the 'ordinary street' as the quintessential space of the community, underused and undervalued following decades of car dominance. Given back to the people on a temporary basis, the streets became: 'living laboratories in which desirable streets of the future can be envisioned with a threefold objective: experimenting with the sustainable mobility of the future; creating a new approach to urban space; and reinforcing social links by multiplying interactions among citizens' (Living Streets Newsletter 2016: 1).

The project was started in 2013 with two streets made car-free for one month (June), and continued in 2014 with ten streets transformed for four months (May, June, September and October). In 2015 the project expanded to include 16 streets. In 2016 there were 19 streets that participated, of which three actively involved children in the streets' redesign in order to focus on providing an enjoyable play space.

In the beginning both local inhabitants and public officials were very sceptical. In particular, the police, and the health and safety and fire departments, would not allow the project to proceed due to the complex set of regulations governing street use. The city's traffic engineers also voiced strong opposition because of the potential for closing streets to vehicles affecting the city's road traffic network. After a long process of negotiation, the activists persuaded the city to agree to the project, although on the condition that they would gather the signature approval of all the inhabitants of the street concerned. It was for this reason that in the first year only two streets had consensus (a primary cause of some of the locals' resistance was the concern that parking spaces would be too far from their homes). Initial fear of change was overcome by the activists' good facilitation skills and by a different process design; rather than imposing a certain view and asking the people to subscribe to it, they presented the whole situation as an experiment and offered the people the option to stop it at any point if they were unhappy. In the words of one of the project coordinators:

> 'The street has become a big playground and also a meeting place for people that before wouldn't interact with each other. Especially older people and children love it! It took a lot of knocking on each house and asking people and then bringing people together; at the beginning there was a lot of reticence as people are afraid of new things. But we presented it as an experiment and told them if you don't like it, we stop it. In the end, it's all about changing mindsets, at the city level as well.' (Living Streets project coordinator)

The project leaders had one person named as the champion for each street, and with the help of donations from local companies bought green carpets and wooden pallets and encouraged the locals to take ownership and change their street as they saw fit (Figure 9.2).

The initiators are confident that Living Streets has been a success since the first year, with the experiment transforming previously unused streets into lively and convivial spaces, strengthening the multi-ethnic local community and helping build interactions among the Turkish, Bulgarian and Belgian inhabitants. Significant also is the increasing number of streets that have joined, and an increased support of the city's inhabitants and leaders. Fundamentally, similar to the Newcastle experiment, the project brought the ideas of sustainable and liveable cities to the inhabitants' doorsteps. More broadly, the project has now been adopted as a European initiative, with projects under way to support the creation of living streets in Brussels, Turin and Rotterdam. Each city pays €15,000 towards the associated costs, with the EU contributing an additional €30,000, and the funds can be used for either a temporary or permanent redevelopment of the street (Van Garse 2016). Key ingredients of the success of Living Streets so far have been the passion and committed energy of the project initiators, and the undertaking of the whole project as an experiment of a truly co-productive nature. It remains to be seen how the lessons from Ghent will translate to other cities in Europe and how Ghent will itself resolve its still strong car dependency culture.

Figure 9.2: An example of a Ghent Living Street before and after transformation

a) Before

b) After

Source: Lab van Troje, www.livingstreet.org

Towards an ordinary urbanism?

In this chapter we have argued for the need to link transport concerns with the process of urban and neighbourhood place-making, with participatory design thinking at the heart of the process. Such an approach can help overcome many of the barriers to implementing sustainable transport policies if done well. In so doing we can arrive at strategies for urban neighbourhoods that are more equitable, democratic and sustainable, echoing the success of global exemplars. But we also note that the skills and resources needed to do so have to function alongside a degree of 'letting go' on the part of central and local government in terms of the ways it typically makes and funds transport policy interventions.

There is contrasting evidence of the willingness of citizens to embrace elements of sustainable mobility (for example, Bratzel 1999) where they see much of this agenda as a restriction on their current mobility practices centred on the use of private cars. While traditional methods of engagement and ways of thinking don't seem to help much here, we have shown through two illustrative examples how open-ended and/or inspirational participatory approaches borrowed from design disciplines can have greater utility than methods and 'knowledge' centred on (social) science traditions. These traditions tend to look backwards at how the world recently was, and are less suited helping citizens imagine transitions to more sustainable mobility and more liveable urban futures. To realise such things, we need creative imagination at the centre of any approach – *a vision of what might be* (see Wright and McCarthy 2005) – or, as the initiators of the Ghent Living Streets project put it, 'the power of "What If"?' In this way, the design process becomes the research process, and it must allow for ambiguity in a way that traditional transport methods do not. Telling, making and enacting are vital, and using physical artefacts, storytelling, sketches and mock-ups (and possibly 3D models and virtual objects) as provocations is a significant part of the process. This open-ended and iterative approach allows citizens to respond to designs, informing and refining the proposals, standing in some contrast to traditional linear processes of transport modelling, land-use planning and for that matter consultation (Chapters 6 and 11).

The materiality of such interventions is critical for participatory processes to succeed and can help dismantle established power relations (Askins and Pain 2011). One role of engineers and planners in a strongly participatory process is to provide their knowledge of models and their limitations, of antecedent and precedent in terms of what might be possible. But since theirs is just one set of knowledges in a widely distributed urban intelligence, further roles are to facilitate and stimulate citizens to think about possible futures while providing a range of technical and best-practice knowledge that helps them do so (Vigar 2017). This 'letting go' of their traditional forms of practice is widely acknowledged to be difficult, but if cities are to 'Copenhagenise', putting sustainability and place-making at the centre of their city visions, relying solely on traditional transport and urban planning approaches is unlikely to help all that much. Transitioning to a radically different mobility system requires demonstrations of what might be possible, both at the city scale and in neighbourhoods, in the context of local circumstances and priorities. It needs planning and urban design processes to work properly together with the people that live in a certain area – their dreams, aspirations and needs – to enable 'the social life of small urban spaces' (Whyte 1980) to flourish. And as urban communities are increasingly diverse in an age of unprecedented transnational migration, the success of such experiments rests on negotiation and compromise, as the Ghent experience showed its initiators:

> 'Dreams vary among residents and streets. And where dreams vary finding compromises is key. In general, these dreams relate to the desire to have a safer place for children to play and meet and to transform the mainly grey, car-centred and anonymous streets into more liveable, enjoyable and colourful places. The dialogue that arises among citizens is key. By identifying each others' needs and dreams, a mutual understanding is created and this can lead to a plan for their Living Streets that enjoys wide-spread support'.
> (Living Streets Newsletter 2016)

Similar to what Jan Gehl and his team did in Copenhagen in the 1960s – starting to slowly close down car parks in the city centre while building bike lanes and improving the pedestrian environment – the Newcastle team and the Ghent activists started small. In Ghent the experiment took off and more and more people joined; in Newcastle it remains to be seen how it can be replicated and expanded. Fundamentally Copenhagen succeeded because there was a strong, well-articulated vision and desire for a better city, consistently promoted by Jan Gehl and his team, which endured over time. The willingness to experiment, to do things differently, was also important, as was political support for the project regardless of electoral or economic cycles (see also Melia 2015). Just as the Ghent project showed, there needs to be some degree of flexibility from the local authorities and *trust* that people can and will make their environment better if helped and given the power to do so. Although the 'smart city' might appeal as a paradigm of 21st-century urban development, decades of top-down modernist planning prioritising the car have left us in desperate need of ordinary things: benches, crossings, well-kept pavements, car-free areas and cycle paths all greatly helping to connect, strengthen and enliven communities.

Thus we argue for a focus on 'ordinary urbanism'. Such an approach has many intellectual antecedents. It is present in the work of critical pragmatism, the temporary urbanism movement, and the radical futures work of architect Buckminster Fuller who asserted that change did not come from fighting the existing rationality but by building a new mode that renders the existing obsolete. Boyd (2013) sees modern manifestations in the Occupy movement, old and new utopian thinking, and transport-related direct action in the form of Critical Mass and Park[ing] Day. In many of the exemplars cited earlier, what Boyd terms 'prefigurative intervention' is present: build an alternative to demonstrate this approach works. The experimental transformation of the streets in places such as Ghent, as well as those of longer-standing exemplars such as Bogota, Copenhagen and Amsterdam, support such ideas. There are some critical voices that argue these lead to environmental gentrification, forcing the priorities of hipsters on less vocal majorities. But such experimentation can be grounded in broadly-based participatory democratic forms – as in the case of streets renaissance in New York[5] and in our examples mentioned earlier – underpinned by local leadership capable of providing the framework within which such experimentation can emerge.

Many will point to the evisceration of local government in the UK as an insurmountable barrier for the implementation of such an agenda. Austerity has been used to drive an ideology that implies a new contract between the local state and citizens where citizens are required to do more for themselves. If this contract is to endure, then everyone needs to adjust to this new situation. The question is whether it implies more or less room for open inquiry, prototyping, and reflection on existing practices from local authority staff and others. City plans still have to be made, after all, but the rise to prominence of public health arguments against contemporary transport planning and built environment forms suggest that the money for such initiatives might equally come from other budgets, not just transport (for example, Davis and Parkin 2015; Chapter 8).

In the final analysis, the interventions described earlier are, in transport planning terms, incredibly modest; they are also, however, eye-opening for how we might begin to transform our streets and public spaces with little financial resource but with great positive outcomes for mental and physical health, social and community capital and consequently our day-to-day life (Semenza et al 2006). Considerable money is spent, and many people are employed, in the transport realm often in a very path dependent way with little preconception of how budgets could be deployed differently. Indeed, significant resource is wasted each year on defending policies and plans that have not been developed adequately with the participation of interested citizens and which lead to a great deal of protest. Localism may offer a further possibility as citizens in England come to use the new tools offered by central government to lead interventions in their neighbourhoods with local government as junior partners. In doing so we suggest that Friedmann's demand to look first at the neighbourhood is the starting point. As Jane Jacobs (1961) proclaimed, the urban street is the fundamental aspect of city life; we might do well to adopt this as the overarching principle for future urban transport planning.

Notes

[1] This section draws heavily on the work of Daniel Mallo and Armelle Tardiveau at Newcastle University, to whom we are indebted.

[2] The initial team comprised five staff from Newcastle University and two from Sustrans. Residents were co-opted into this group variously from the start and this was confirmed by stage four of Table 9.1.

[3] This is similar to the modal split within the Ghent city area as a whole: 60 per cent car rides (43 per cent car drivers and 16 per cent car passengers), 17.5 per cent on foot, 14 per cent by bicycle, 3.5 per cent by bus, 2.5 per cent by train and 2 per cent by tram (Coninx 2014).

[4] Information derived from research by Georgina in 2015, consisting of interviews undertaken in Ghent with architects, activists and planners involved in the Living Streets project.

[5] See www.pps.org/projects/new-york-city-streets-renaissance/

References

Askins, K and Pain, R (2011) 'Contact zones: participation, materiality and the messiness of interaction', *Environment and Planning D: Society and Space*, 29(5): 803–21.

Banister, D (2008) 'The sustainable mobility paradigm', *Transport Policy*, 15(2): 73–80.

Blomberg, J and Karasti, H (2013) 'Ethnography: positioning ethnography within Participatory Design', in J Simonsen and T Robertson (eds) *Routledge International Handbook of Participatory Design*, New York: Routledge, pp 86–116.

Boyd, A (2013) 'Don't wait for the revolution, live it', www.yesmagazine.org/issues/love-and-the-apocalypse/don-t-wait-for-the-revolution-live-it-andrew-boyd Accessed 5 June 2016.

Bratzel, S (1999) 'Conditions of success in sustainable urban transport policy: policy change in "relatively successful" European cities', *Transport Reviews*, 19(2): 177–90.

Carmona, M, Magalhães, C and Edwards, M (2002) 'What Value Urban Design?' *Urban Design International*, 7: 63–81.

Coninx, W (2014) *Living Streets Ghent: Working with Communities to Design Safe, Attractive, Enjoyable Streets and Public Space*, presentation available at https://mobiliteit.stad.gent Accessed 5 July 2018.

Davis, A and Parkin, J (2015) 'Active travel: its fall and rise', in H Barton, S Thompson, S Burgess and M Grant (eds) *The Routledge Handbook of Planning for Health and Well-Being: Shaping a Sustainable and Healthy Future*, Abingdon: Routledge.

Davoudi, S and Madanipour, A (2015) (eds) *Reconsidering Localism*, London: Routledge.

Friedmann, J (2010) 'Place and place-making in cities: a global perspective', *Planning Theory and Practice*, 11(2): 149–65.

Gaver, W, Boucher, A, Pennington, S and Walker, B (2004) 'Cultural probes and the value of uncertainty', *Interactions*, 11(5): 53–6.

Gehl, J (1987) *Life Between Buildings: Using Public Space*, New York: Van Nostrand Reinholdt.

Gehl, J and Gemzøe, L (2004) *Public Spaces Public Life – Copenhagen 1996*, Copenhagen, Denmark: The Danish Architectural Press and The Royal Danish Academy of Fine Arts School of Architecture Publishers.

Gehl, J and Gemzøe, L (2000) *New City Spaces*, Copenhagen, Denmark: The Danish Architectural Press..

Goodwin, P, Hallet, S, Kenny, P and Stokes, G (1991) *Transport: the New Realism*. Transport Studies Unit, University of Oxford, Oxford.

Gunn, S (2010) 'The rise and fall of British urban modernism: planning Bradford, circa 1945–1970', *The Journal of British Studies*, 49(4): 849–69.

Hajer, A (2003) 'Policy without polity? Policy analysis and the institutional void', *Policy Sciences*, 36(2): 175–95.

Jacobs, J (1961) *The Death and Life of Great American Cities*, New York: Random House.

Kębłowski, W, Bassens, D and Van Criekingen, M (2015) *The Differential Performativity of Academic Knowledges in Urban Transport and Mobility Policy and Practice: A View from Brussels.* Working paper, Vrije Universiteit Brussel.

Living Streets Newsletter (2016) Issue 1, Spring. www.leefstraat.be/en/publicaties/ Accessed 5 July 2018.

Mallo, D and Tardiveau, A (2017) *The Craft of Participatory Design: Inspirational Methods in the Co-Production of Urban Space,* Unpublished.

Melia, S (2015) *Urban Transport Without the Hot Air: Sustainable Solutions for UK Cities,* Cambridge: UIT Cambridge.

Metropolis (2016) *The 10 Best Cities to Live In (2016).* www.metropolismag.com/cities/the-best-cities-to-live-in/ Accessed 24 April 2018.

Ministerie van Verkeer en Waterstaat (2009) Cycling in the Netherlands. www.rijksoverheid.nl/onderwerpen/fiets Accessed 16 July 2019.

Ministry of Transport (1963) *Traffic in Towns:* A Study of the Long Term Problems of Traffic in Urban Areas, London: HMSO.

Monocle (2017) Quality of Life Survey: top 25 cities, 2017. https://monocle.com/film/affairs/quality-of-life-survey-top-25-cities-2017/ Accessed 24 April 2018.

Parsons, R and Vigar, G (2017) '"Resistance was futile!" Cycling's discourses of resistance to UK automobile modernism 1950–1970', *Planning Perspectives,* 33(2): 163–83.

Relph, E (1976) *Place and Placelessness,* London: Pion Limited.

Rutter, T (2016) 'Car-free Belgium: why can't Brussels match Ghent's pedestrianised vision?' *The Guardian* 28 November 2016. www.theguardian.com/cities/2016/nov/28/car-free-belgium-why-cant-brussels-match-ghents-pedestrianised-vision Accessed 5 July 2018.

Sanders, E (2013a) 'Prototyping for the Design Spaces of the Future', in L Valentine (ed) *Prototype: Design and Craft in the 21st Century,* Bloomsbury Sanoff.

Sanders, E (2013b) 'Perspectives on Design in Participation', in C Mareis, M Held and G Joost (eds) *Wer Gestaltet die Gestaltung? Praxis, Theorie und Geschichte des Partizipatorischen Designs,* Bielefeld: transcript Verlag.

Sanoff, H (2006) 'Origins of community design', *Progressive Planning,* 166: 14–7.

Schwanen, T (2016) 'Geographies of transport I: reinventing a field?' *Progress in Human Geography,* 40(1): 126–37.

Semenza, J, March, T and Bontempo, B (2006) 'Community-initiated urban development: an ecological intervention', *Journal of Urban Health: Bulletin of the New York Academy of Medicine,* 84(1): 8–20.

Sennett, R (1974, republished 1992) *The Fall of Public Man*, New York: W. W. Norton & Company.

Stad Gent (2014) *Mobility Plan Ghent 2030*. https://mobiliteit.stad. gent/sites/default/files/media/20141022_DO_mobilityplan%20 Ghent%202030.pdf Accessed 5 July 2018.

Tardiveau, A and Mallo, D (2014) 'Unpacking and challenging habitus: an approach to temporary urbanism as a socially engaged practice', *Journal of Urban Design*, 19(4): 456–72.

Urban Task Force (1999) *Towards an Urban Renaissance: The Urban Task Force,* London: Spon.

Urban Task Force (2005) *Towards a Strong Urban Renaissance*, London: Spon. http://image.guardian.co.uk/sys-files/Society/ documents/2005/11/22/UTF_final_report.pdf Accessed 4 April 2016.

Van Garse, S (2016) *Eerste leefstraat in Brussels gewest*. www.bruzz.be/ nl/actua/eerste-leefstraat-brussels-gewest Accessed 5 July 2018.

Veraart, F, Knuts, S and Delheye, P (2016) 'Cycling claims a comeback', in R Oldenziel, M Emanuel, A de la Bruheze and F Veraart (eds) *Cycling Cities: the European Experience*, Eindhoven: Foundation for the History of Technology.

Vigar, G (2002) *The Politics of Mobility*. London: Spon.

Vigar, G (2017) 'The four knowledges of transport planning: enacting a more communicative, trans-disciplinary policy and decision-making', *Transport Policy*, 58(C): 39–45.

Watson, V (2014) 'Co-production and collaboration in planning – the difference', *Planning Theory & Practice*, 15(1): 62–76.

Whyte, W (1980) *The Social Life of Small Urban Spaces*, Washington DC: Conservation Foundation.

Whyte, W (1988) *City. Rediscovering the Center,* New York: Doubleday.

Witlox, F and Tindemans, H (2004) 'Evaluating bicycle-car transport mode competitiveness in an urban environment. An activity-based approach', *World Transport Policy & Practice*, 10(4): 32–42.

Wright P and McCarthy J (2005) 'The value of the novel in designing for experience', in A Pirhonen, P Saariluoma, H Isomäki and C Roast (eds) *Future Interaction Design*, London: Springer.

10

The journey experience

Juliet Jain and William Clayton

Introduction

Travel can be fun, exciting, dull or boring. It can also be hard work; the word *travel* originates from *travail* meaning painfully difficult or laborious effort. However, as Latour (1997) argues, the physical *effort* of moving has been smoothed out by the transport system, and this impacts on the journey experience and brings about the possibility of other activities taking place while travelling. Given that globally billions of people spend a significant part of their life travelling for a multitude of reasons, the impact of journey experience on travellers' ability to use their time for personal and work activities and influence their overall wellbeing should be of concern to travel providers and policy makers.

The experiences discussed in this chapter are rooted in the prosaic journeys of commuting, work-related travel, or accessing other personal activities, rather than specific leisure journeys (for example, a steam train trip). Specifically, we are concerned with how the journey experience is shaped through the interaction between travellers and their mode of transport, other objects and technologies they encounter on their journey, and other travellers. (And here we focus in particular on the 'powered' modes – see, for example, Middleton 2018 and Simpson 2017, 2018 on the journey experiences of walkers and cyclists.) Our approach emphasises the idea that travellers 'craft' their experience in response to the travel context (for example, bus passenger or car driver) and the 'tools' they have to hand (for example, books, phone, or laptop). The crafted journey experience is not just the concern of the 'equipped' individual traveller, however, particularly on public transport systems. It has a wider political and commercial concern in terms of transport planning, provision, management and investment, including infrastructure and vehicle design, engineering and innovation, as these all impact on the travel environment and thus travellers' experiences and time use. For example, UK digital policy making at the time of writing is concerned with delivering 5G along key transport networks to offer continuous digital connectivity, while at the same time ministers are pushing Train Operating Companies (TOCs) to offer free Wi-Fi to rail passengers (Department for Culture, Media and Sport (DCMS) and HM Treasury 2017). Policy makers are making assumptions about people's technology use and desires, and the trajectory of future digital expectations.

Despite this, conceptually transport policy has been more concerned with vehicle flow and speed than enhancing the experience of travel per se. For many policy makers, travel time is conceived principally in economic terms, meaning that the focus of investment is almost always on *making journeys quicker* (Chapters 2 and 6). A good example of this issue is the debate around investment into HS2, the new high-speed rail link in the UK between London, Birmingham and the north of England (Chapter 11). To summarise a complex and ongoing debate, the economic perspective suggests that travel time does not have any intrinsic economic value, and therefore any travel time savings can be converted into benefits to the economy by increased productivity. Based on economic calculations of time saved, a higher speed rail route is presumed to reduce time lost to the country's productive output at the aggregate level, although perhaps saving time is less of an issue if journeys can be productively used (Banister 2011).

Our chapter proceeds as follows. We first consider the debates around travel time values that have framed research examining 'travel time use'. Second, we explore the evidence demonstrating how work can be undertaken on the move, and different types of mobile working environments. The third part of the chapter looks at activities that appear to be the antithesis of work (for example, sleeping), and why these might be important to health and wellbeing (Chapter 8). Our conclusions draw together these elements to raise questions about how the experience of travel might be considered in relation to issues of wellbeing and work–life balance, particularly in the digital age.

Changing paradigms – time on the move

Work time has an economic value and, as we have seen in earlier chapters, the economic value of travel time savings is an important element of cost–benefit calculations for new or improved transport infrastructure investment. Transport investment decisions have focused on the economic benefits of saving time for those travelling in the course of their work, and how much other travellers are willing to pay (for example, in increased fares) to save travel time. Generally, these calculations make an assumption that travel time cannot be used for economic output, or at least not at an equivalent level of productivity as in the work place, and although there are formulae for calculating productivity on the move, these have yet to create an agreed value to inform transport policy (Wardman and Lyons, 2016).

It was research in the United States that first prompted others to challenge this economic paradigm and investigate how time was used while travelling and the related journey experience. Significantly for this discussion, Mokhtarian and Salomon (2001) argued that travel could have a 'positive utility' beyond mere access to destination activities. They found, firstly, that travellers gained pleasure from travelling, and as such that travel might be undertaken for its own sake. They also discovered that the journey could offer value to the individual traveller by providing time either to do something (for example, listen to music, make a phone call) or to relax or think. This second finding gave rise to a new and ongoing research debate around travel time use and the journey experience. Questioning the potential productivity of travel time was central to the ideas of Lyons and Urry (2005), as this directly challenged transport policies driven by the economic assumption that travel time itself had zero value. Their argument was specific to a changing economic and technological landscape and made reference to 'knowledge work', where increasing numbers of people are employed in jobs that have work which can be completed anywhere rather than in a fixed location to access equipment or people. Lyons and Urry (2005) suggested that this work could be completed while travelling, thus potentially changing the value of travel time.

While the focus on productive time was important for challenging the economic paradigm of travel time savings, understanding the journey experience solely on these terms would be limiting. Alongside the opportunity to make travel time productive work time, Holley et al (2008) noted that some travellers value their travel time even when they are sleeping/snoozing, and argue that resting or having a break from work could be beneficial to destination productivity or prompt creative outcomes from having an idle mind. Insights from other research consider the meanings attached to journeys and modes themselves (car, bus, train), whether travel time is used productively en route or not. For example, autobiographical accounts of driving reveal how repeated journeys can generate place attachment with the passing landscape, invoke memories of driving and enable a change in mental state (Edensor 2003, Pearce 2000). Developing such ideas in tandem with those around productive travel time, Jain and Lyons

(2008) advanced new categories as part of a broader typology: the first, *transition time,* is the chance to shift between different roles (for example, parent and employee). The second, *time for,* can be 'me-time' – doing nothing or doing something for personal pleasure (for example, listening to music, reading, and so on) – or work-related time (for example, reading documents) (see also Clayton et al 2017; Chapter 8).

In such ways travel time can be enlivened or made restful by looking out of the window, thinking about the day ahead, or reading. But there are other factors that contribute to the shaping of the journey experience that link to the travellers' physical and mental comfort. Mokhtarian et al (2015) investigated the factors that made travelling tiring or pleasant using data from the French national travel survey. They found, for example, that although listening to music can reduce the feeling of fatigue, it does not necessarily improve the perception of the journey being pleasant. This suggests that activities can be a response to the journey being perceived as pleasant/unpleasant at the outset, rather than a causal outcome of the activity; commuter stress is often linked to overcrowded trains and the lack of personal space, but listening to music or using the phone can help alleviate it (Evans and Wener 2007, Berry and Hamilton 2010). Shaping an experience with activity may only be partially successful at making the journey more pleasant or may even fail, depending on the changing circumstances of the journey.

This idea is explored by Bissell (2008) in his discussion of passenger 'comfort'. The marketing of cars, flying and train travel often emphasises the comfort of their offer – design of the seat or bed, amount of leg room, and so on. To sit comfortably suggests immobility, but Bissell argues that bodies are constantly readjusting themselves to achieve comfort. In this sense, sitting becomes work in itself. Part of sitting comfortably is distributing those things you need for the journey around you, or having your clothing adjusted, as Hughes et al (2017) note when observing that hoods and hats are used to block out others in the attempt to sleep while travelling. Car driving may be turned into a relaxing experience, but there is evidence to suggest that longer-distance car commuting can be particularly stressful and physically uncomfortable (Lyons and Chatterjee 2008).

Discomfort or an adverse affective environment, having something to do or feeling bored, all shape the journey experience because they in turn shape the experience of time. Observations of rail travellers unpacking and deploying artefacts for entertainment, work and nourishment at different times along the journey led Watts (2008) to argue that passengers 'craft' travel time. The experience of time passing rarely coincides with the regulated divisions of clock time; depending on the activity being undertaken, time can speed up or slow down. In crafting travel time, passengers are changing their experience of time passing, and Watts (2008) notes how time spent engaged in activity can compress time, but tiredness and boredom can stretch time. In testing out the impact of activities on the experience of journey time, Watts and Lyons (2011) constructed individually tailored 'travel remedy kits' for a small number of travellers to explore how the deployment of specific tasks, breaks, music, refreshments and things to look out for through the window could reconfigure their experience. They proposed that if planning for the journey could reduce those points at which time stretches out, then the journey experience could be individually managed to individuals' needs (although having lots to do may not necessarily improve the experience, as we discuss later).

Thus while time is attributed economic values in transport planning, travellers experience it in a variety of ways that impact on the perception of their journey experience. Two travellers on the same journey could have two very different journey experiences in the way that they have (actively or inactively) crafted their travel time. It may be that one wanted to work but found the (dis)comfort of the surroundings unconducive because of noise levels or crowding. The other, by retreating under headphones, was able to relax and become comfortable, and experienced the journey in a more positive way. The following sections look more closely at how time is crafted in different ways and how the design of environments, as well as socio-demographics, journey purpose, journey duration and mode of travel can all shape the perception of the experience.

The productivity paradigm

Travellers may use a range of spaces, fixed and mobile, to work. Roadsides and service stations are temporary work-stops for business travellers who drive (Hislop 2012). Airports are modern meeting rooms and temporary office spaces for international travellers, often with special provision for those travelling in executive or business class (Urry 2007). In many countries, larger railway stations also provide special facilities for business class travellers, and indeed most travel time use research has focused on the railway. The train is assumed to offer a better working environment than other modes, especially where a table is provided, and journey durations are often long enough to allow work to be done (Lyons et al 2007). By comparison, a bus journey is likely to offer limited space, be shorter and feature more frequent interruptions from passengers getting on and off, and may therefore be perceived as being less conducive to productivity (Clayton et al 2017). Travelling by coach, flying and driving have received less attention in terms of work-related activities while travelling, but Jain's (2011) account of coach commuting suggested a mix of leisure, personal care and work occurring during the journey. There are currently limitations on mobile technology use on aeroplanes, but this is changing.[1] Many airlines cater for the business traveller by shaping a connected work environment and a rest space, but for the majority the constraints of the 'economy' space may limit possibilities. Focusing on elite travellers, Budd (2013) demonstrates how the interior design of private business aircraft is shaped to facilitate the continuation of business on the move, and that the fast-tracking of business travellers through airports results in less wasted time. Cars too are important workspaces, as we go on to discuss.

The transience of moving through travel networks (bus, coach, train and air) requires travellers to have packed (or purchased) 'resources' for different places and times along the route in order to craft their travel time to successfully meet planned expectations. Yet doing more may not always equate to being more satisfied with the journey experience, but a symptom of boredom, which re-iterates the idea that time doing something may pass more quickly. Clayton et al (2017) found that while younger bus travellers had more with them (mobile phones, personal music players, portable games consoles and the like) and engaged in more tasks than older passengers, they were nonetheless more likely to be bored. It would seem this is often the same on trains as well (Lyons et al 2016, Frei et al 2015). It may be that young people would just prefer to be elsewhere, and that the travel environment is not a good substitute environment for using digital devices (Clayton et al 2017). Awareness of demographic difference in terms of how the journey is experienced, and the potential for technology to enhance opportunities, are important in relation to debates about reducing car use. For instance, the peak car debate has hypothesised that the ability to use digital technology on the move is one factor that is making young people more attracted to public transport than car travel (Kroesen and Handy 2015, Le Vine et al 2014; Chapter 14).

Rail passengers seem to be rather habituated in their time use. Lyons et al (2007, 2013, 2016) have tracked the changing time use of rail passengers over a period of ten years, paying specific attention to 'the Information Age' element of travel time use.[2] Their results demonstrate that few rail passengers spent a lot of time planning their time use for the journey, while the majority state they give it little attention as they tend to use their time in the same way. Business travellers are more likely to spend time planning for their journey than commuters, and leisure travellers plan the least; there is a positive association between planning and viewing travel time as 'worthwhile' (Lyons et al 2016). In the digital age, many travellers are equipped with devices that are not exclusive for travelling (for example, a smartphone), and combined with mobile data for Internet access travellers can have more reactive approach to time use than in the past.

Politically, at least in the UK, providing rail passengers with improved continuous connectivity is seen as increasingly important (Steer Davies Gleave 2016), and investment in free Wi-Fi and improved mobile connectivity is considered of value to the economy by enhancing the opportunity for increased productivity. At present, however, there is little evidence available as to the impact of free Wi-Fi on the journey experience and travel time use. Data from surveys in the US analysed by Banerjee and Kanafani (2008) suggest that on longer journeys passengers are prepared to pay for access to Wi-Fi, but not for journeys less than 80 minutes. These authors propose that the train has potential as an office environment, but recognise this could adversely affect other passengers less interested in working on the train. Dong et al (2015) note in their work also from the US that Wi-Fi could encourage more rail trips.

What people do on the train in the UK increasingly utilises mobile technologies, but activities can be broadly grouped into one of two categories: work activities (phone/text, email, other work activities) and leisure/personal activities (sleeping, looking out of the window, making personal calls/texting, using social networking sites, watching a film, and so on.) (Lyons et al 2016). Table 10.1 presents time use data from 2014 (comparison data across the three years can be found in Lyons et al 2016). It is perhaps not surprising that business travellers are most likely to work while travelling, but this does not preclude them using travel time for leisure and relaxation. Likewise, some leisure travellers engage with work. Some commuters also work during their trips to and from their place of employment, but other activities might improve the experience of the daily routine as discussed earlier. Throughout this discussion of productive travel and working on the move, it remains important to consider that a sizeable proportion of commuting travellers will have an occupation that involves work which *cannot* be undertaken while commuting.

Arguably how people work on the train is more complex than sitting down and undertaking a specific activity, and the data in

Table 10.1: Percentage of passengers indicating any time spent on activities

Time use	All 2014	Commuter 2014	Business 2014	Leisure 2014
Sleeping/snoozing	10.1	11.7	9.7	8.5
Reading for leisure	40.5	45.4	32.0	38.0
Working/studying (reading/writing/ thinking)	21.2	23.9	45.2	8.9
Talking to other passengers	11.6	6.5	9.4	18.2
Window gazing/people watching	43.7	37.2	40.3	52.5
Listening to music/radio/podcast	14.6	20.2	10.6	9.5
Watching a film/video	2.6	3.7	2.7	1.2
Text messages/phone calls – work	12.8	15.0	30.1	3.5
Text messages/phone calls – personal	27.6	30.5	24.8	25.4
Checking emails	25.1	30.4	41.4	12.8
Internet browsing	18.0	23.1	17.0	12.5
Accessing social networking sites	12.2	15.5	9.7	9.3
Eating/drinking	13.0	9.4	18.9	15.0
Caring for someone travelling with you (including children)	2.1	0.8	0.2	4.2
Playing games (electronic or otherwise)	4.5	5.5	3.1	3.8
Being bored	8.4	9.5	6.5	7.8
Being anxious about the journey (for example, delays or where to get off)	14.2	14.4	12.7	14.6
Planning onward or return journey	5.8	4.5	7.2	6.9
Other	0.0	0.0	0.0	0.0
Sample size	27,812	12,644	4,191	10,978

Source: Developed from Transport Focus 2014

Table 10.1 should be interpreted accordingly. They are likely to engage with multiple tasks, and seamlessly slip between work and 'leisure' activities (Lyons et al 2007). The activity of looking out of the window is complex to categorise, as while it may be enjoying (or otherwise) the scenery, it might also be facilitating thinking through a problem or idea, as 'Steve', quoted in Watts and Lyons (2010: 113), describes:

> 'My ideal office is on the train... especially if I've got things to work out [and I'm] at that point when you're just getting creative with it. It's my most creative place to work because it's that, you get a bit stumped, and you get to look out of the window for half an hour... see things...'

Activities such as thinking are also difficult to value in economic terms as there may not be an obvious work output. The blurring of time on a work trip that starts early in the morning or returning in the evening is not uncommon, and films, books, and personal calls, texts and social media will interweave with working activities. (Lyons et al 2007, Gripsrud and Hjorthol 2012).

In Norway, commuters are more likely than their counterparts in the UK to work during train journeys because they can count that time towards their working hours. In this context, commuters and business travellers find the on-board Wi-Fi an essential aid to their working on the move (Gripsrud and Hjorthol 2012), and there is an expectation that the rail industry should create an environment that is conducive to using time productively (see also Bjørner 2016). While this may include at a minimum a seat, and at a maximum space to work (for example, tables), electrical sockets and continuous mobile connectivity, in the UK there persists a more basic challenge in managing the demand on the network to provide reasonable capacity for everyone at peak times. Interestingly, though, even with significant growth in patronage, satisfaction with travel time use in Britain has remained static. There was also an increase in the passengers reporting that they could make worthwhile use of their travel time between 2004 (24.4 per cent) and 2010 (36.7 per cent), although not between 2010 and 2014 (30.6 per cent), against the backdrop of a decline in overall satisfaction with the rail service from 2010 to 2014 (Lyons et al 2016).

The opportunity to use travel time productively is an important but perhaps underutilised selling point for train travel over driving. But the car can also function as a 'second office' for those who travel a lot for work, and again working on the move in a car is not recognised in the calculations for travel time savings. Holley et al (2008) use their participant Oscar's experiences to illustrate how travel in the course of work can be used for both work and relaxation in the car. Oscar views the interstitial time of driving between the stores he oversees as a release from the demands of work (a third category of *time out*, alongside 'transition time' and 'time for' in Jain and Lyons' (2008) typology). Oscar doesn't feel obliged to work as he is driving, but sometimes chooses to use that time to make phone calls to his store managers away from pressures to attend to other demands.

Still sitting in the car (or van), this mode presents a specific travel time space as it often operates as a quasi-office for people like Oscar who are employed in jobs that require travel between multiple locations (Hislop 2012). Travelling sales personnel, and those working between regional locations, are indicative of this group of people.

Taking an ethnographic approach, Laurier examined how a selection of sales employees experienced life on the road (Laurier 2004; Laurier and Philo 2003). The itinerary shaped how equipment, goods and office work were packed into the vehicle before setting out. Mobile technology for communicating with the office and organising information was essential not only for interacting with clients, but also for managing the reorganisation of time when schedules became disrupted (for example, a car breakdown). Administrative activities were undertaken in the car before and after meetings with clients. These practices were also revealed by Hislop (2012) who noted that 55 per cent of survey participants used their phones while driving either 'quite a lot' or a 'great deal'. While sales operatives and regional managers may be a primary example of such a need for travel time in the car, Ferguson (2009) also demonstrates how the car plays a similar role in social work practice as a quasi-office *and* also as a place to recuperate from the emotional demands of the job, much like Oscar taking a breather between the demands of his stores. Hislop's participants also used the journey to think through issues and problems.

A third important element of time use in car journeys is the relationship between co-present passengers and the driver in the course of work (Box 10.1; see Jain and Lyons 2008, for more information about the focus groups). Callum suggests that being in motion and moving towards a destination creates an atmosphere that can focus the interaction – in this instance working as a team preparing for a meeting – although the intimacy that Ray indicates he dreads at the end of this interaction may equally be instrumental in developing relationships. For instance, Ferguson (2009) identifies that sitting side by side in the car can facilitate a different type of relationship between two people than the one played out in an office or other setting. He argues in the context of social workers and their clients (often children or young people) that the driver and passenger have greater parity because conversations are not being conducted face-to-face across a desk. This idea of power relations changing when driving may affect the way in which a team of colleagues interact when travelling, which might be why Callum finds it a useful opportunity to travel to meetings with work colleagues.

Box 10.1: Talking shop

Callum: I find if I'm with work colleagues you can prepare for the meeting and often I rely on that someone being in the car with me to actually prepare for that meeting, so we're having a pre-meeting in the car and that's valuable. In a way, you feel as you're drawing closer to your destination you're mentally tuned into that meeting so that can be useful. But travelling on your own... no.

Ray: I'd much, much rather travel on my own. The enjoyable factor is much greater [but] that's just me. I don't like having to hold conversations with people, maybe work colleagues that you see... every day, you know all about them, there's nothing new to discuss apart from work and I don't want to be discussing work when I'm travelling, so I prefer to be alone.

Callum: I disagree. I think when you're in a car it's a very confined space and you share more and it breaks down barriers and you share things that you wouldn't do in a work environment. And when you're flying as well.

Ray: Yes, but in a car it's a bit difficult.

Callum: We're not talking secrets here, mind.

Ray: Much more intimate in a car, you can't avoid having conversations. If you don't feel you're being rude or whatever.

Source: previously unpublished research undertaken for Jain and Lyons 2008

Despite the examples of the car being used as a place of work and interaction, there are challenges in terms of safety and driver attention that should not be ignored. Technology has moved on, with cars becoming more equipped with devices that connect to the Internet, and this might potentially compromise driver attention at critical moments (see Basacik et al 2011 for a discussion about smartphone use). At the same time, the progressive automation of vehicles might provide an opportunity for drivers to become quasi-passengers and to do other activities while the vehicle drives itself (Chapter 15). The impacts of automation and the need for 'driver' attention is an area ripe for investigation and speculation as to the possibilities of the driver-passenger experience. Of particular interest, given how young people might currently be moving away from the car in favour of modes in which travel time can be used, will be the extent to which these other modes retain their attraction as cars become more automated in the future. None of this is to say, however, that the availability of such technology will necessarily transform travel into a better experience: Ettema et al (2012) found that working or using ICTs while travelling did not increase customers' satisfaction with the journey, even though they may have chosen a given mode in order to work. What they do argue, though, is that static levels of *journey* satisfaction do not preclude the conducting of activities on the move having a positive effect *after* the journey has been completed.

Quiet time

Travelling is more about 'doing activities' on the move, but also a response to what Bissell (2008) terms an 'affective atmosphere'. In this respect cars are a unique space where the driver can shape this atmosphere with, say, music or silence, or by inviting passengers in to share the space. By contrast, public transport is a space where noise and other people are managed by etiquette and rules, and individual travellers have little control. The rise in mobile phone ownership prompted some UK train operators to create 'Quiet Carriages' – this auditory division between quiet and 'unrestricted' carriages is also found elsewhere in Europe and around the globe (see Hughes et al 2017) – in which, ostensibly at least, phone calls and 'leaking' music are not allowed. There is also an assumption that conversations between passengers are kept to a minimum, and children should remain silent or preferably be seated elsewhere on the train. Uniquely, trains have become a space divided not only by cost (business/first and standard classes) but also on the basis of sound (Hughes et al 2017).[3] While buses and coaches do not have the space to divide auditory experiences, the coach journeys between Oxford and London undertaken by Jain (2011) to study travel time use were remarkably quiet. Aeroplanes have their own etiquette, and the move away from the imposed central in-flight film and towards individualised back of seat entertainment has also changed this experience of travel.

Some passengers find their comfort while travelling is adversely affected by other passengers' noise, especially other people's phone calls (Bissell 2008, 2009). In two light-hearted news reports recounting their experience of 'quiet carriages', Russell (2015) and Shilling (2013) infer that the quiet carriage is a place for work and personal relaxation, where noise can intrude and distract. They found, though, that enforcement is problematic for 'disturbed' passengers, and Hughes et al (2017) report how tensions arising from a transgression can alter the affective atmosphere of the whole carriage. Their research documents the different atmospheres between an early morning commuter train and a homebound journey, which in part is shaped by a greater variety of travellers – day trippers, families, students, as well as commuters – on the evening train. The morning journey is described as a sleepy easing into the day, where hushed conversations receive glances, and passengers become more physically animated as the sun rises and the train travels closer to Sydney. On the return journey, there is palpable tension between regular passengers and animated casual travellers engaged in a loud group conversation. It is some time before a passenger indicates this transgression, only to be subjected to ridicule by the offenders. Similar observations of early morning quiet moving into more animated activity as the journey progressed were made by Lyons et al (2007) in the ethnographic observations of first-class passengers travelling on the 6.30 am train from Newcastle to London. Arguably, early morning travel is more likely to be quiet as there are fewer passengers, and fewer work calls are likely to be made before 8.30 am.

In a contrasting approach, Lawrence (2015) investigated the differences in time use and journey experience between quiet coach passengers (n=192) and other passengers (n=180) through an on-board paper survey of passengers travelling between 9.30 am and 12.30 pm, and 3.30 pm and 6.30 pm on Great Western Railway services to and from London. The social demographics of the sample show little difference in the use of the quiet carriage, other than a larger number of older (65+) passengers as compared to younger travellers (18–25). Fewer frequent travellers used it, but those on days out or visiting relatives and friends were proportionally more likely to sit in a quiet carriage. Of the quiet coach sample, however, 20 per cent were travelling for work and 6 per cent for business, whereas in the non-quiet coaches 24 per cent were travelling for work and 12 per cent were travelling for business. In terms of activities undertaken, those in non-quiet coaches were more likely to be working, checking emails, making personal and work phone calls, sending personal and work SMS messages (texts), and accessing social networking sites. Similar numbers in both carriage types were reading for leisure and window gazing/people watching, with a marginally higher number of passengers (2 per cent) 'sleeping/snoozing' or 'doing nothing/just passing the time' in the quiet carriage.

Interpreting his findings, Lawrence (2015) suggests that for many travellers, quiet carriage activity may facilitate 'transition' time or 'time out' rather than work-related productivity – for some who want to work while travelling by train, the quiet coach can be restrictive unless particular 'quiet' activities have been planned for the journey – and as such argues that some people may purposefully seek time away from technology in this zone. This is an interesting notion, as it upends any assumed economic productivity gained from providing a quiet environment in which to work, and yet at the same time has demonstrable value to the passengers that use it. There is a potential tension here in conceptualising what constitutes a 'good' environment in which to work, especially for train operators in developing innovative environments if a stronger focus is made of supporting travel time as productive time. If travel time is used for noisy work (for example, phone call time) and quiet work (for example, writing a document or answering emails), then different zones may continue to have a role. Alternatively, it could be seen as the passenger's responsibility to create quiet time by being equipped with noise cancelling headphones. On other modes, such as commuter coaches or aircraft, the sound environment will need to be considered in different ways. Could there be more opportunities for marketing different styles of environment based on the auditory experience?

Relaxation, sleep and anti-activity

The ability to recharge one's batteries while travelling was put forward as one of the potential benefits of travel time by Holley et al (2008). At first glance, rest or sleep may seem at odds with the notion of productivity, but resting while travelling certainly has the potential to boost destination productivity, which is why airlines provide lie-flat beds in business class. More generally, resting while travelling could lead to greater productivity on arrival that outweighs any output of working while travelling. As yet, researchers have not tested this hypothesis but there is some evidence to suggest that people vary their activities between 'work' and 'relaxation' both within journeys and on different journeys, especially using return journeys as 'downtime' (Holley et al 2008, Lyons et al 2007, Jain and Lyons 2008, Gripsrud and Hjorthol 2012). Ettema et al (2012) argue that talking to others on the return commute makes people feel more relaxed and more enthusiastic, and suggest that this may be the result of a changed mind-set due to the nature of activities – that is, leisure not work – they know lie ahead.

The idea of 'anti-activity', suggesting the need not just to *mentally* switch off while travelling, but to *literally* switch off devices that coerce attention, is becoming a societal challenge in terms of managing work-life balance and personal wellbeing. Anti-activity could be anything that is not associated with paid work or the demands of domestic life, and as such travel time can be appropriated for leisure activities. While Table 10.1 showed few people watch films while travelling, listening to music or other audio is an activity used to make travel spaces more comfortable (even passengers on a crowded commuter train may use technology to make the travel time more pleasurable). Escaping to a quiet railway carriage might be an attempt to create a relaxed atmosphere, and food and drink may be part of the re-energising process (Watts and Lyons 2010). But it is sleep that is the ultimate anti-activity, removing travellers from their surroundings, compressing time and consequently totally reconfiguring the journey experience. Sleep on the move is a topic that is under-researched, and there is little evidence from passenger modes (train, coach, bus, air) regarding the frequency or role of sleep. Provision for sleep has nonetheless been commodified as part of the experience of overnight services on longer-distance sleeper trains and long-distance business class flights. In the UK, Stagecoach provided a Scotland to London overnight coach service ('Megabus Gold') with beds, but more often overnight coach services require passengers to sleep sitting upright. Sleeping overnight effectively saves time for other activities in the waking day, as well as the cost of a hotel, but its benefits with regard to feeling rested or enhancing wellbeing have not been assessed.

While not designed specifically for sleep (that is, not an overnight 'sleeper train' with berths or couchettes), daytime rail travel 'offers the *possibility of* sleep' (Bissell 2009: 429). Routine journeys seem to enable the opportunity to drift off, although as Bissell also points out, railway timetables and the need to alight at the correct station certainly require passenger attention. Passengers may drift between the edge of sleep and a consciousness of station stops to maintain just enough attention to the journey's progress that they know where they are, although many people will have heard or will have their own tales of snoozing on a train, only to wake at the end of the line after falling too deeply asleep. Sleeping on the train (or any other public transport) is a wholly public activity, whereas sleep is usually associated with a very private space.

Potentially there are four different reasons for people falling asleep/snoozing while travelling: tiredness, boredom, blocking out other passengers and/or the impact of motion. Motion it seems is a physical response, where the body is rocked much like a baby into a state of quiescence (Bissell, 2009). Equally, though, the physical design, lighting and audio announcements may create sufficient discomfort to prevent sleep on the move. Many rail passengers are therefore most likely to be 'catnapping' on the move, as opposed to in a deep sleep. In the 2014 National Passenger Rail Survey (NRPS), around 10 per cent of travellers reported that they were sleeping/snoozing for some of the journey, and this had dropped from 14 per cent since 2010 (Lyons et al 2016). This figure may have some variability according to route, journey duration and time of day, as well as being influenced by cultural norms. For instance, research in Japan indicated nearly half of travellers purposefully slept while travelling (Ohmori and Harata 2008).

Implications for the future

In this chapter we have explained that journey experience for individual time use is crafted, with the traveller deploying personal and work activities within the constraints of the travel space and journey duration. The travel environment may play to expectations or serve to disrupt them. It is useful to recognise that all travel is multifaceted in its individual experience, but what are the implications for the travel industry and transport policy? We now address three key issues: i) the challenge of valuing travel time activities, ii) responses to connectivity expectations, and iii) the implications of journey experiences for sustainability.

At the start of the chapter the challenge of valuing travel time activities was explored, but Wardman and Lyons (2016) suggest that where travel time is focused on productivity it is very difficult to quantify if work on the move is equivalent (in quantity and quality) with a place of work. Looking at the journey only from an economic perspective of productivity focuses attention on journeys that are made in the course of work and pushes the need to measure equivalence, rather than understanding any broader, more qualitative personal value the journey experience may facilitate. For instance, measuring value that focuses on work output does not necessarily account for the worker who performs better at his or her destination having had a 'power nap' on the way. Sleep, as discussed, seems counter-intuitive to 'productive' travel time during daytime journeys within the UK, yet for those on sleeper trains or flying internationally it may be an integral part of the business journey experience to arrive refreshed for an immediate business meeting. There may also be lessons to be learnt from the airline industry regarding a holistic view of business travellers' wider needs for longer-distance rail travel (for example, Edinburgh to London) that play into the journey experience. Sleep as a positive use of travel time connects the leisure industry with travel providers as the 'hotel on wheels', and this aspect needs further research, particularly when thinking about new investment in long-distance rail travel in China and the US, or across Europe.

How time is or can be used goes beyond business travel: commuters and others work on the move, as well as squeezing in rest or undertaking personal activities to save time at home. For these travellers, the journey experience in terms of crowding or road congestion may negate any positives that can be gained through activity (or inactivity), although technology is changing possibilities. Rail travellers, for example, are increasingly withdrawing into another world with noise cancelling headphones and watching videos on tablet computers as a way of relaxing on the return commute. At the same time, many work on their way to and from their place of employment, undertake personal tasks and maintain social networks. The implications for travel time use and its relation with the journey experience, therefore, are not necessarily about the provision of a particular environment by the transport operator but how individual travellers can adapt to the existing environment by crafting their own experience with their own resources. Yet comfort and the ability to craft an experience are affected by policy and provision in terms of investment into the physical design of the travel space (for example, power sockets, seat comfort and ergonomics), levels of crowding and the availability of a seat. The recognition of 'experience' as an attractor to sustainable modes is important, and even new faster services such as High Speed 2 (HS2) will still need to focus on these experiential aspects.

Productivity on the move has raised expectations of connectivity in the form of phone calls and the Internet. In the UK, central government transport policy has pushed for train operators to provide free Wi-Fi to passengers, and has proposed improvements to mobile connectivity (see Steer Davies Gleave 2016).[4] The reliability, speed and quantity of data will affect travellers' perceptions of what is possible, and thus their satisfaction with the journey experience if adequately met. Yet Wi-Fi provision comes at a cost to travel providers, and improving Wi-Fi to a sufficient standard may have to be limited to those who are able to pay a higher price for their travel (for example, in business class); Steer Davies Gleave (2016) confirms that only business travellers are prepared to pay the for the best connections. Heavy investment in 5G coverage has the potential to be something of a game-changer, but in the UK at least, maximising the benefit of such technology will require the better alignment of digital policy and transport policy (and operation). It may be, for example, that greater opportunity for productivity on the move creates an opening for working practices to change, particularly for the commute, where commuters are less inclined to pay a high price for peak-time connectivity. We have already highlighted how in Norway employees can use their commuting travel time as part of their working day. While some people in Britain already have this possibility, most are bound by specific working hours that impact on peak travel demand.

Greater flexibility, and travel environments that properly enable work on the move, could enable a redistribution of peak travel over a wider timeframe. Once again transport cannot be seen in isolation, but in the context of broader employment trends and work practices that connect into what is possible in changing behaviours.

At the same time, being continuously connected may have negative social implications in terms of work–life balance and wellbeing. When do people have 'down time' or find time for themselves? Research into travel time use conducted prior to the advent of smartphones suggested that many people welcomed the time gap between work and home to gear up or unwind, or have 'me-time' (Jain and Lyons 2008). If the commute were work time, there could be implications regarding how far people would travel. Equally, if improved digital connectivity enabled the completion online of personal tasks, would the need to get home by a certain time be less relevant? These questions pick up concerns expressed around long-distance high-speed connections such as HS2 becoming commuter routes, but perhaps should also be framed around social wellbeing and the impact of long-distances commuting on social relationships, health and community.

Finally, the journey experience, connected or disconnected, relates to wider issues of sustainability. Notably, how will different modes compete on journey experience in the future? Peak car debates demonstrate that the journey experience is an important factor that makes public transport increasingly attractive over the car for some young people, at least for the moment, even if they simultaneously have a lower boredom threshold than other age groups. For the time being there is little evidence to show how improvements to the journey experience by train may be attracting large numbers of people from the car, but Dong et al (2015) suggest that enhancements such as free Wi-Fi may encourage around 2.7 per cent of existing passengers to travel more frequently by train in the future. The possibilities for 'drivers' of autonomous vehicles (AVs) to use their time differently remain to be seen, even if much is being speculated (see Singleton 2018), but AVs could well compete with the equivalent attractions of being a passenger on a train (Chapter 15). This would be especially true if the road networks have better digital connectivity to high-quality information highways compared to rail routes, or if AVs provide a quieter, uncrowded and comfortable space in which to relax.

Overall, a strong research interest in the journey experience has developed within transport and mobilities studies, and this has provided evidence about what people do and how they go about it while on the move. Our discussions in this chapter demonstrate that travellers work within the travel system to extract personal value where they can – working, sleeping, thinking, and so on – but such personal values are not accounted for in the existing mechanisms for evaluating travel time. There is less evidence to demonstrate the wider direct impact of the journey experience, good or bad, on, for instance, modal choice or commuting distances or when to travel. Digital technology will have a wide-reaching impact connecting the journey experience to a range of other transport issues and implications from how policy joins technology and mobility through to how distance is not removed by technology but enhanced. Critically, evaluating travel time values for cost–benefit analysis potentially moves the debate beyond travel time savings to consider how travel time value could be enhanced by digital connectivity (and associated travel environment features) to improve the opportunity for productivity. At the same time, policy makers still need to consider how the emergence of creativity through thinking or daydreaming could be effectively be captured, let alone the benefits of having a bit of a quiet rest from everything!

Acknowledgements

We are grateful to Dr Iain Weir for producing Table 10.1, and to Transport Focus in providing the NRPS data to UWE.

Notes

[1] Indeed it is. One of your probably-too-hyper-mobile editors was working on an aeroplane reading through a draft of this very chapter that he downloaded using the on-board Wi-Fi.

[2] The questions developed for the Autumn 2004 National Rail Passenger Survey (NRPS) were part of the EPSRC project Travel Time Use in the Information Age 2004–2007. Some of these questions subsequently were included in the Autumn 2010 and 2014 NRPS.

[3] Although not everywhere: in Japan, for instance, the quiet culture is for the whole train, with rail passengers engaging only with silent activities such as Internet browsing and texting, and generally not talking with other passengers (Ohmori and Harata 2008).

[4] In other countries, mobile data coverage is significantly better than Britain, and as such this proposal may appear strange to non-British readers.

References

Banerjee, I and Kanafani, A (2008) *The Value of Wireless Internet Connection on Trains: Implications for Mode-Choice Models.* UC Berkeley, University of California Transportation Center. http://escholarship.org/uc/item/8kf2t753 Accessed 4 July 2018.

Banister, D (2011) 'The trilogy of distance, speed and time', *Journal of Transport Geography*, 19(4): 950–59.

Basacik, D, Reed, N and Robbins, R (2011) *Smartphone use while driving: A simulator study*. Transport Research Laboratory, Technical report 1. Berkshire, UK.

Berry, M and Hamilton, M (2010) 'Changing urban spaces: mobile phones on trains', *Mobilities*, 5(1): 111–29.

Bissell, D (2008) 'Comfortable bodies: sedentary affects', *Environment and Planning A: Economy and Space*, 40(7): 1697–712.

Bissell, D (2009) 'Travelling vulnerabilities: mobile timespaces of quiescence', *Cultural Geographies*, 16(4): 427–445.

Bjørner, T (2016) 'Time use on trains: media use/non-use and complex shifts in activities', *Mobilities*, 11(5): 681–702.

Budd, L (2013) 'Aeromobile elites: private business aviation and the global economy', in: T Birtchnell and J Caletrio (eds) *Elite Mobilities*, Abingdon: Routledge, pp 78–98.

Clayton, W, Jain, J and Parkhurst, G (2017) 'An ideal journey: making bus travel desirable', *Mobilities*, 12(5): 706–25.

Department for Culture, Media and Sport and HM Treasury (2017) *Next Generation of Mobile Technologies: A 5G Strategy for the UK.* https://assets.publishing.service.gov.uk/government/uploads/system/uploads/attachment_data/file/597421/07.03.17_5G_strategy_-_for_publication.pdf Accessed 4 July 2018.

Dong, Z, Mokhtarian, P and Circella, G (2015) 'The estimation of changes in rail ridership through an on board survey: did free Wi-Fi make a difference to Amtrak's Capitol Corridor service?', *Transportation*, 42: 123–42.

Edensor, T (2003) 'Defamiliarizing the mundane roadscape', *Space and Culture*, 6(2): 151–68.

Ettema, D, Friman, M, Gärling, T, Olsson, L and Fujii, S (2012) 'How in-vehicle activities affect work commuters' satisfaction with public transport', *Journal of Transport Geography*, 24: 215–22.

Evans, G and Wener, R (2007) 'Crowding and personal space invasion on the train: please don't make me sit in the middle', *Journal of Environmental Psychology*, 27(1): 90–4.

Ferguson, H (2009) 'Driven to care: the car, automobility and social work', *Mobilities*, 4(2): 275–93.

Frei, C, Mahmassani, H and Frei, A (2015) 'Making time count: traveler engagement on urban transit', *Transportation Research Part A Policy and Practice*, 76: 58–70.

Gripsrud, M and Hjorthol, R (2012) 'Working on the train: from "dead time" to productive and vital time', *Transportation*, 39(5): 941–56.

Hislop, D (2012) 'Driving, communicating and working: understanding the work-related communication behaviours of business travellers on work-related car journeys', *Mobilities*, 8(2): 220–37.

Holley, D, Jain, J and Lyons, G (2008) 'Understanding business travel time use and its place in the working day', *Time & Society*, 17(1): 27–46.

Hughes, A, Mee, K and Tyndall, A (2017) '"Super simple stuff?": crafting quiet in trains between Newcastle and Sydney', *Mobilities*, 12(5): 740–57.

Jain, J and Lyons, G (2008) 'The Gift of Travel Time', *Journal of Transport Geography*, 16(2): 81–9.

Jain, J (2011) 'The classy coach commute', *Journal of Transport Geography*, 19(5): 1017–22.

Kroesen, M and Handy, S (2015) 'Is the rise of the e-society responsible for the decline in car use by young adults? Results from the Netherlands', *Transportation Research Record: Journal of the Transportation Research Board*, 2496(1): 28–35.

Latour, B (1997) 'Trains of thoughts: Piaget, Formalism and the Fifth Dimension', *Common Knowledge*, 6(3): 170–91.

Laurier, E (2004) 'Doing office work on the motorway', *Theory, Culture & Society*, 21(4–5): 261–77.

Laurier, E and Philo, C (2003) 'The region in the boot: mobilising lone subjects and multiple objects', *Environment and Planning D: Society and Space*, 21(1): 85–106.

Lawrence, D (2015) *Life in the 'quiet carriage': An exploration of the impact of the quiet carriage on rail traveller utility.* Unpublished MSc Dissertation, Centre for Transport and Society, University of the West of England.

Le Vine, S, Latinopoulos, C and Polak, J (2014) 'What is the relationship between online activity and driving-licence-holding amongst young adults?', *Transportation*, 41: 1071–98.

Lyons, G and Chatterjee, K (2008) 'A human perspective on the daily commute: costs, benefits and trade-offs', *Transport Reviews*, 28(2): 81–198.

Lyons, G, Jain, J and Holley, D (2007) 'The use of travel time by rail passengers in Great Britain', *Transportation Research Part A Policy and Practice*, 41(1): 107–20.

Lyons, G, Jain, J and Weir, I (2016) 'Changing times – a decade of empirical insight into the experience of rail passengers in Great Britain', *Journal of Transport Geography*, 57: 94–104.

Lyons, G, Jain, J, Susilo, Y and Atkins, S (2013) 'Comparing rail passengers' travel time use in Great Britain between 2004 and 2010', *Mobilities*, 8(4): 560–79.

Middleton, J (2018) 'The socialities of everyday walking and the "right to the city"', *Urban Studies*, 55(2): 296–315.

Mokhtarian, P and Salomon, I (2001) 'How derived is the demand for travel? Some conceptual and measurement considerations', *Transportation Research Part A*, 35(8): 695–719.

Mokhtarian, P, Papon, F, Goulard, M and Diana, M (2015) 'What makes travel pleasant and/or tiring? An investigation based on the French National Travel Survey', *Transportation*, 42(6): 1103–28.

Ohmori, N and Harata, N (2008) 'How different are activities while commuting by train? A case in Tokyo', *Tijdschrift voor Economische en Sociale Geografie*, 99(5): 547–61.

Pearce, L (2000) 'Driving North/Driving South: Reflections upon the Spatial/Temporal Co-ordinates of "Home"' in L Pearce (ed) *Devolving Identities: Feminist Readings in Home and Belonging*, London: Routledge.

Russell, G (2015) 'I ditched the quiet carriage in favour of crunchy crisps, kids and conversation'. 28 May 2015. *The Guardian*. www.theguardian.com/commentisfree/2015/may/28/i-ditched-the-quiet-carriage-in-favour-of-crunchy-crisps-kids-and-conversation Accessed 4 July 2018.

Shilling, J (2013) 'Was I wrong to shush a little girl in the quiet coach?' 15 August 2013. *The Telegraph* www.telegraph.co.uk/women/mother-tongue/10245132/Was-I-wrong-to-shush-a-little-girl-in-the-quiet-coach.html Accessed 4 July 2018.

Simpson, P (2017) 'A sense of the cycling environment: felt experiences of infrastructure and atmospheres', *Environment and Planning A: Economy and Space*, 49(2): 426–47.

Simpson, P (2018) 'Elemental mobilities: atmospheres, matter and cycling amid the weather-world', *Social and Cultural Geography*, Online early.

Singleton, P (2018) 'Discussing the "positive utilities" of autonomous vehicles: will travellers really use their time productively?', *Transport Reviews*, 39(1): 50–65. www.tandfonline.com/doi/abs/10.1080/01441647.2018.1470584

Steer Davies Gleave (2016) Mobile Connectivity Research Study. www.gov.uk/government/uploads/system/uploads/attachment_data/file/518976/mobile-connectivity-research-study_SDG-report-with-appendices.pdf Accessed 29 June 2017.

Transport Focus (2014) *National rail passenger survey – NRPS – autumn 2014 – main report*. www.transportfocus.org.uk/research-publications/publications/national-rail-passenger-survey-nrps-autumn-2014-main-report/ Accessed 9 October 2018.

Urry, J (2007) *Mobilities*, Cambridge: Polity.

Wardman, M and Lyons, G (2016) 'The digital revolution and worthwhile use of travel time: implications for appraisal and forecasting', *Transportation*, 43(3): 507–30.

Watts, L (2008) 'The art and craft of train travel', *Social & Cultural Geography*, 9(6): 711–26.

Watts, L and Lyons, G (2010) 'Travel remedy kit', in M Buscher, J Urry and K Witchger (eds) *Mobile Methods*, Abingdon: Routledge, pp 104–18.

11

Public engagement and consultation: decide, announce and defend?

Tom Cohen and Dan Durrant

Introduction

Any volume that addresses the topic of transport policy needs to confront the issue of the citizen's role in its formulation. This is first for the somewhat hackneyed reasons that citizens will experience many, and often most, of the consequences of the policies adopted, and that they will also pay a large proportion of the costs of implementation and, where relevant, maintenance. But a more pragmatic reason is that citizens often feel frustrated by and excluded from the decisions of transport policy makers. Likewise, planners and policy makers must also at times feel a degree of frustration with publics that are diverse in their interests, views and demands and whose concerns are often not expressed in the more familiar language of transport planning and policy. The tendency to see particularly local protest as self-interested and illegitimate among the promoters of infrastructure has been identified in a whole body of literature on the issue (McAvoy 1998, Cotton and Devine-Wright 2011, McClymont and O'Hare 2008, Devine-Wright 2013). The term NIMBY ('not in my back yard') comes with the implication of a lack of willingness to accept individual losses in order to achieve collective benefits. Set against this, though, the ideal of a disinterested professional able to apply neutral measures to derive objectively the best course of action has also become increasingly hard to sustain in the face of a number of criticisms. For example, 'rent seeking' (Flyvbjerg et al 2003) behaviour, where certain groups and actors advance their own interests in providing and producing transport infrastructure ahead of the public interest, combines with tendencies towards 'strategic misrepresentation' (Flyvbjerg 2008), in particular the distortion of estimates of that infrastructure's costs, timescales and eventual benefits. In this chapter, we aim to look beyond the unproductive dichotomy between the ill-informed and self-interested NIMBY and the shadowy technocrat.

We seek to explore some of the reasons behind the latter and the contributions the former might make to decision making.

That transport policy making is a potential minefield is not in doubt. Many countries struggle to resolve the issues of siting transport infrastructure, with high-speed rail (HSR) often particularly controversial (Della Porta and Andretta 2002, Leheis 2012, Minn 2012, Novy and Peters 2012, OMEGA Centre 2013a, 2013b; Salet et al 2013, Schmidt-Thome and Mantysalo 2013). The UK has a long and not altogether glorious history in this area. The Roskill Commission introduced new methods for accounting for some values, yet ultimately failed to resolve other value conflicts (Hall 1980). The Channel Tunnel Rail Link, later renamed as High Speed 1 (HS1), appeared to show a more consensual, less disruptive approach that could achieve results (Faith 2007), albeit after an adversarial and highly disruptive approach had been exhausted. Lengthy inquiries such as that on Heathrow's Terminal 5 are often held up as emblematic of failings in this area, regardless of whether they are reflective of a wider problem or simply outliers (Marshall and Cowell 2016), creating a preference among policy makers for rapid implementation over more open participatory styles of decision making.

All of this may help to explain the remarkable persistence of 'decide, announce and defend' (DAD), a much-criticised approach to transport decision making. This persistence may surprise some given the increasing expectation and, more significantly, legal requirement that consultation and participation be a feature of any attempt to implement policy. On the other hand, transport planning can still often be the site of clashes between competing forms of expertise, local knowledge, politics, and the interests of those affected. There is increasing understanding of and ability to measure the breadth of the distribution of benefits and burdens of transport infrastructure, with costs imposed on, for example, taxpayers and local environments, and benefits accruing to places and property owners able to capitalise on new connectivity (Chapters 2 and 6). This brings into play an increasing number of stakeholders and constitutes new publics or groups formed around a specific interest in the consequences (either detrimental or beneficial) and the issues that proposals generate. The desire to see new transport infrastructure delivered in the face of the uncertainties generated by such a clash can lead to a reversion by planners and policy makers to more closed technocratic strategies to manage this uncertainty. This tendency rests on the residual power of expertise. Given the technical nature of many transport issues, and the resources available to those interested in producing new transport infrastructure, it is often hard for those on the outside of the process to match the information produced by advocates of a particular project. Those who oppose a particular transport project may find it hard to counter the reams of technical and environmental evidence produced to justify it. There is often a clear imbalance of power with one side more familiar with the rules of the game, and having access to considerably more financial resources and often simply time.

John Dewey (1927), in his exploration of democratic decision making in plural, complex, technological societies, saw the formation of publics in response to the issues generated by new technologies or infrastructures as a beneficial process. It both constrained the consequences of the type of technological decision making seen in transport planning within socially acceptable limits, and created a forum for a more equal deliberation between the different forms of knowledge described earlier. We take in this chapter Phase One of High Speed 2 (HS2), running between London and the West Midlands, as a case in point (Figure 11.1). As a high-profile project it illustrates the ways some of these issues manifest themselves in a large and controversial piece of new transport infrastructure. Beyond its visibility, HS2 provides an example of an approach to transport decision making that we argue is increasingly unsuitable in an era when publics are informed and enabled by new technologies which further undermine claims to a monopoly on expertise. It may be the case that HS2 is something of an outlier – we would not wish to claim this approach is characteristic of *all* transport decisions – yet the persistence of the approach and its application to such a prominent project suggest it remains a default option.

In the remainder of the chapter, we examine, first, the framing (Schön and Rein 1994) of the project and the problem it was intended to solve before identifying some of the issues generated and the formation of publics in response to these issues. In many ways, the approach taken is a classic example of DAD, albeit with specific reasons as to why this may be the case. In the second half of the chapter we explore how this process of public formation might have been anticipated and used more constructively to ameliorate some of the conflict and improve the quality of decisions. We identify a number of potential innovations in the institutional design of the planning process, and suggest how emerging 'mini-publics' may enable the type of deliberation required to achieve these goals. Some or a combination of these techniques may, we conclude, have improved the quality of decisions and at the very least offer some scope for addressing the issues identified in this case study.

Figure 11.1: The proposed HS2 route

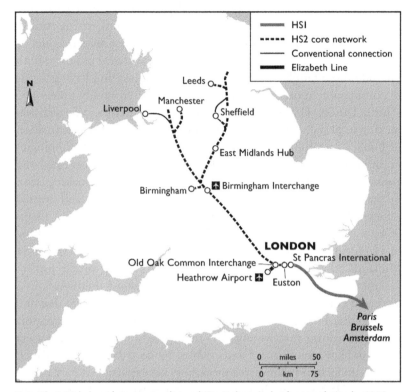

Note: The initial phase, between London and Birmingham, is due for completion by 2026. The full 'Y' is due to be finished by 2033.

Source: Editors

HS2

HS2 is a costly and disruptive project and so would always have generated opposition. Yet in response to what has indeed been a vociferous campaign against it, the UK government's approach has been to defend the initial proposals for the route and its key features such as the direction, very high running speeds and Euston terminus. We must concede that this approach has been successful thus far given Phase One was granted Royal Assent in 2017. It is, however, important to note that consent and design are just the first part of what will be a long process of construction and implementation and, with this in mind, we reserve the right to withhold judgement on the ultimate success of the government's strategy.

The origins of HS2 can be traced back to a report produced by the consultancy Atkins and commissioned by the Strategic Rail Authority

(SRA) in 2002. Justified as a means of addressing projections that capacity on the West Coast Mainline would be reached by 2016 leading to overcrowding at peak times, the report concluded that HSR was the only mode of transport capable of addressing this level of demand (Atkins 2003). The timing of the emergence of the idea is in itself significant. The SRA was established by an incoming Labour government to regain some public control after what was criticised as a chaotic and ideologically driven privatisation of the railways by the previous Conservative administration (Wolmar 2005). The period ended in 2006 with what was effectively the renationalisation of rail infrastructure under Network Rail. Critics have argued a lack of management of the relationship between the SRA and the Train Operating Companies (TOCs, established under privatisation to run rail services, but not to own the infrastructure or rolling stock) led to the TOCs proposing costly schemes that would depend on public funding as they would be unlikely to attract private finance (Wolmar 2005). Indeed, it had been the unsuccessful proposals for high-speed rail (HSR) on the East Coast Mainline from the TOC Virgin Rail that had stimulated the SRA's interest in HSR and led to the commissioning of the Atkins report. The aim of this initial influential report was: 'to establish whether there is a transport and business case for constructing a new high-speed line (HSL) in the *UK from London to the North*' (Atkins 2003 para 1.1, emphasis added).

This constructed a particular framing of the problem and crucially of the solution being high-speed lines from London that has persisted as the concept developed to the point where it became accepted as government policy. While it would not be true to claim that the challenges of engaging with the groups and communities affected were not considered in the Atkins report, they are certainly secondary to the technical analysis, and envisaged as something to be resolved at a later stage in the process. Somewhat revealingly, though, thought is given to how the proposals should be communicated in the form of a section on the 'Communications Strategy' in which it states: 'It will be important for the SRA to be clear about what message it is presenting and how much involvement stakeholders can realistically have in the decision-making process as consultation raises expectations among groups or individuals who have engaged' (Atkins 2003: 8–2). This strategy of managing expectations and a 'realistic' approach to the involvement of stakeholders in the decision-making process appears to be one of the features of the Atkins report that has shaped the character of that process and the approach to consultation.

In the period between this genesis of the project and the establishment in 2009 of HS2 Ltd (a company wholly owned by the Department for Transport (DfT) with the remit of developing high-speed connections between London and the north of England), there was some public debate. From the perspective of achieving a more participative process, however, the failing of this period was that this was a debate largely directed towards politicians and policy makers. The lobbying organisation Greengauge 21 was established and supported by the prominent consultant Jim Steer (who had been part of the SRA team that originally commissioned the Atkins report), but little of the organisation's work sought to engage the wider public. The model of high-speed rail developed was much more ambitious than the eventual proposals for HS2. This was promoted as just one part of a complete UK high-speed network. What may have been desirable in this period, prior to a government commitment to develop the project, would have been some of the features of the later debates. These include the examination of alternative policy options (Theiss and Kersley 2013) and approaches for a more participative form of decision making (Right Lines Charter 2011a) from other think tanks and civil society groups. Yet, for these groups, generally dependent on the support of their own membership, it is often easier to justify allocating limited resources once the wider public is engaged with the issues.

One other consequence of the way in which the project developed was that opponents' perceptions that many of the decisions had been made prior to public consultation, were largely borne out. Certain key features of the decision – such as the need for HSR, the need to address capacity from London and the desire for the highest possible running speeds – were effectively written into the governing documents of HS2 Ltd, having been accepted on the basis of the Atkins report and subsequent lobbying. As the consequences of these decisions became apparent in later, more public, phases of the project development, they served to fuel the criticisms from HS2's many opponents that any consultation was tokenistic. These criticisms may help to explain a number of subsequent attempts to reframe the project. First was a fairly short-lived claim that there were environmental benefits from what was portrayed as a lower-carbon form of travel. This was quickly dropped due to the difficulty in demonstrating that there would be a significant modal shift away from air travel on the relatively short connections proposed. Furthermore, there was evidence that much of the carbon reduction attributable to any shift from the private car would be negated by choices on HS2's speed and energy sources (Greengauge 21 2012). While increasing capacity on the rail network has always remained a strong justification for the project, under the Coalition government (2010–2015) HS2 was also branded an 'engine for growth', linking it to economic development in the North. This is a framing that has persisted largely by ignoring uncomfortable questions about the extent to which the evidence supports benefits to regional economies of rapid transport links to much larger global city economies such as that of London (Tomaney and Marques 2013; Chapter 2).

Prior to the publication of the preferred route in 2010 there was a process of testing various route options which was intentionally hidden from public scrutiny. The justification behind this was the quite reasonable assumption that conducting such a process in the public eye would lead to considerable damage to property values along the routes under consideration. This had been the case in the design of HS1 (Faith 2007). In a country such as the UK, with a dense network of urban areas and relatively developed transport infrastructure, completely new routes are less common than upgrades and enhancement of existing networks. While these projects can create considerable disruption, it is rarer to see the long narrow swathe of property blight caused by a scheme such as HS2. In the surprisingly limited academic literature there is evidence of the perception that 'participation causes blight' (Heap quoted in Hagman 1972), and as such it is difficult to be critical of HS2 Ltd and the DfT for their lack of transparency in this area even if it does feed into and fit with a pattern of such criticism. Where there may be a stronger case to answer is in the lack of appreciation of the tensions between good decision making in the form of a transparent consideration of alternatives, and the potential harm caused to property values or any attempt to remedy it. It appears that a lack of transparency has been the default option. Solutions that might have allowed for a more transparent appraisal of route options such as the Property Bond proposed by HS2 Action Alliance (HS2AA, one of the leading opposition groups) were never fully explored. The proposal appears to have been rejected on economic grounds without a full consideration of the political benefits of a system that would allow property owners to purchase a bond that would underwrite any loss in value resulting from the planning or operation of HS2. This could have effectively removed the risk of blight, allowing for a more public examination of different route options.

Consultation, opposition and participation

The current proposals for HS2 were not formally made public until the release of the High Speed Rail Command Paper (DfT 2010) which sets out the initial design of the route. It had an impact in the areas directly affected and saw the constitution of a public made up of interested local actors in the form of 72 local action groups (LAGs) along the route of Phase One. Some early alterations to the proposals did take place, notably additional tunnelling (the 'Gillan Tunnel' named after Cheryl Gillan, the Conservative MP for Chesham and Amersham), although these are more reflective of the influence of certain powerful and well-connected interests than a participative approach to designing and deciding where HS2 should be built. Much of the wider public debate did not begin in earnest until after the 2010 general election, when the Coalition confirmed its commitment to adopt the previous government's scheme largely unaltered. In 2011, the DfT ran the first national consultation. The consultation itself made little pretence at neutrality. It was conducted in the form of a long document extolling the virtues of the scheme, tending to play down its potential weaknesses. It posed a series of six leading questions, the first being: 'Do you agree that there is a strong case for enhancing the capacity and performance of Britain's inter-city rail network to support economic growth over the coming decades?' (HS2 Ltd/DfT 2011: 23).

As can be seen in this case there was an attempt to conflate something about which there could be expected to be broad agreement, 'economic growth', with acceptance of the scheme. While a majority of respondents to the first question voiced opposition to the scheme, its framing as a driver of economic growth served only to make the task of analysing responses particularly hard. Other features of the document such as the carefully worded statement about taking all perspectives into account and statements such as, 'no final decisions will be taken until everyone has had the opportunity to have their say,' (HS2 Ltd/DfT, 2011: 6) were undermined by ministerial comments dismissing opponents as a 'vocal minority' driven by 'purely local interests' (Hammond quoted in Millward, 2011) and the heavy-handed approach of the communications consultants employed by HS2 Ltd. This was an ill-judged campaign that sought to portray opponents as 'posh people standing in the way of working–class people getting jobs' (Lord Bethell quoted in Doward 2013), based upon the fact that one of the more vociferous groups of opponents were residents of the Chiltern Hills, an affluent area designated as an Area of Outstanding Natural Beauty (AONB) in Buckinghamshire, to the north-west of London.

Despite, or more likely because of, the controversy of the project, there has been considerable interest in participating in the process. The initial consultation, for example, was described as 'one of the biggest and most wide-ranging ever undertaken by the Government' (BBC 2010: unpaginated). This public interest has taken a number of forms worthy of further examination. First, there has been the organised participation of larger regional- and national-level NGOs characterised by a mix of public advocacy, formal contacts with ministers and key decision makers and behind-the-scenes lobbying. By contrast, the 2010 announcement of the route saw the formation of the plethora of LAGs along the line of the proposed route. These groups would ultimately coordinate their activities under a number of different umbrella organisations, with HS2AA and Stop HS2 becoming the most prominent. This pattern of differing approaches and objectives at different levels has been observed in other prominent, controversial HSR projects (Della Porta and Andretta 2002), with some degree of tension between the different levels. In the case of the larger NGOs, despite the way in which they sought to establish a set of principles and standards for HS2 and the way it was planned, designed and implemented (Right Lines Charter 2011b), the overall impact seems to have been relatively limited. This is not to say that the local-level opposition to the project has been any more successful, at least if this is measured in terms of tangible alterations to the project, but they may have proved successful in shaping some of the public debate.

One such area where opponents feel they have been successful has been in attaching controversy to the project. This is largely borne out by even a cursory analysis of media debates in which the project is invariably referred to as 'the government's *controversial* high-speed rail scheme'. Opponents have also mounted what has been quite an effective attack on the economic justification for the project. They successfully brought the often obscure functioning of transport appraisal mechanisms such as cost–benefit analysis and the role of travel time savings within it, and, even more importantly, the assumptions that underpin them, into the public realm (Chapter 6). This has led to a number of notable embarrassments for the project promoters such as the controversy over a report issued by consultants KPMG into the wider economic impacts of the project. As a key part of the political 'fightback' against criticism of the project over the summer of 2013, the report attempted to assess the agglomeration and transport cost advantages, reaching a conclusion that 'investment in HS2 could generate £15 billion of additional output a year for the British economy in 2037' (HS2 Ltd 2013: 15). The method behind the report was rapidly dismissed by both academics (Overman 2013) and prominent journalists (Peston 2013), and heavily criticised in a special hearing of the normally supportive Transport Select Committee conducted after the public controversy had developed.

A number of factors has aided opponents of the project, one being the growing legal requirement for consultation, transparency and access to information in decision making. This is enshrined at an international level in the Aarhus Convention (1998), which came into force in 2001 and of which the UK is a signatory. The UK is further bound by the incorporation of the principles of the Convention into the EU Environmental Impact Assessment Directive (EU Directive 2014/52: articles 18–21). Based on the three pillars of access to information, participation in decision making and access to justice, Aarhus offers a rights-based approach to achieving the 'goal of protecting the right of every person of present and future generations to live in an environment adequate to health and well-being' (Wates 2005: 2). It has been seen as focusing on procedure over substantive standards, failing to support the more radical potential of participatory decision making (Lee and Abbot 2003) and favouring the large transnational non-governmental organisations (NGOs) involved in its drafting (Wates 2005). Despite these weaknesses, Aarhus has been well received by NGOs and governments (Lee and Abbot 2003) and is seen as driving the adoption of procedural environmental rights in Europe and Central Asia (Wates 2005). It is important in that it sets out the legal basis for the participation of civil society and '*the public affected* or likely to be affected' (EU Directive 2014/52: articles 18–21, emphasis added) and establishes a distinctive role in environmental decision making for NGOs (Lee and Abbot 2003).

HS2 Ltd has always been keen to ensure compliance with the Aarhus Convention. There appeared to be some uncertainty over the extent to which existing UK consenting procedures were compliant, and it has been suggested that their very narrow timescales may be in breach of the Convention (Campaign to Protect Rural England (CPRE) 2013). If anything, this uncertainty appears to have produced a tendency to over- rather than under-consult, with eight different consultations on Phase One between the main consultation launched in February 2011, and 2014 when the project began its process through Parliament as a Hybrid Bill. This is a process that again allows for a reasonably broadly defined group of individuals whose interests are affected to speak directly to the MPs and then the Lords who make up the select committees charged with making a recommendation on the project to Parliament. While there is no suggestion this was a deliberate tactic, responding to all these consultations placed considerable burdens on those affected and added no small cost to the project. There was an ongoing programme of 'Community Forums' at three-monthly intervals intended to allow the communities affected to voice their concerns and gain information about the project. As it rapidly became apparent that these were not envisaged as any form of meaningful participation or as a means of empowering those communities affected to shape the decisions about the project, they often descended into fractious affairs. Having committed to this level of engagement, however, HS2 Ltd found it difficult to withdraw from what was a costly and demanding process. There were undoubtedly some benefits from these Forums, as the issues surrounding some local road realignments in rural areas may have been explored in more detail than with a less involved process of consultation. But in the urban areas such as west Euston, where there was to be considerable demolition, and also in areas such as the Chilterns where there was also an impact on the rural environment alongside compulsory purchase of properties, many of the substantive issues were beyond the remit of the Forums, which led to further frustration.

The Forums were by no means the only engagement with groups and individuals who felt their interests were affected by HS2. There was a programme of bilateral meetings over specific issues which often allowed groups to challenge many of the technical parameters of the project when these had controversial consequences. These included issues such as station design and the extent of proposed tunnelling, with some groups seeking to extend this to protect a greater area from the noise generated by the operation of the railway. Alongside this process, the Freedom of Information Act was used extensively as a means of accessing material that HS2 Ltd or the DfT were reluctant to disclose. This in itself generates costs for the project, as the average cost of handling an FoI request in the UK was recently estimated at £293 (Colquhoun 2010). This may also be a reflection of a lack of trust and the perception by LAGs that incomplete information was being provided. Ultimately, there was also a number of largely unsuccessful judicial reviews instigated by groups of opponents to the project. The one area where there was some success is that the consultation over the compensation scheme was declared 'so unfair as to be unlawful' (Ousley 2013: 1), an indication of the risks incurred by project promoters through a failure to consult properly.

As a case study of participation in transport decision making, HS2 reveals the extent to which requirements to consult are enshrined in law and convention. It is no longer viable not to consult, not to allow access to information or to assume the promoters of transport schemes will be immune from legal challenge. In many ways HS2 Ltd consulted extensively, investing considerable resources in the process, but herein lies the key issue. While there is a duty to consult, the extent to which any such exercise seeks genuinely to share power with those affected is much harder to determine or police. A large and well-resourced consultation exercise can still be tokenistic, particularly when much has already been decided outside that process. In this case some of the issues may be to do with the process itself. The Hybrid Bill makes Parliament the consenting body, unlike the relevant minister where other planning legislation is concerned. This has the advantage that those whose interests are affected can speak directly to the MPs making the decision and who have quite considerable discretion to amend the proposals. But, where there is cross-party support, as in this case, there is little prospect of either cancellation or significant modification. In the event, the amendments to the proposals were relatively minor, with increased tunnelling in some areas along with increased noise abatement measures and some amendments to the compensation process (Butcher 2018).

Is a better process possible?

From a certain perspective, one acknowledged in the introduction, the consultation process for HS2 could be regarded as a success: the project has gained consent in a relatively short time in the face of a well-organised and vocal opposition. But critics would argue, and we would concur, that this is a product of a process stacked in its favour. Political commitment from all the major parties to the project from the early stages has resulted in something of a foregone conclusion. Nevertheless, this process has been one of acquiring consent, albeit one that has either ignored or side-lined a number of important questions which, if given fuller consideration, might have produced a less controversial design and could also have allocated the scheme's benefits and burdens differently. These include decisions about technical issues such as running speeds, given that many of the benefits of speed are predicated on the controversial claims on the value of travel time savings. The benefits here may be aggregate and abstracted but the burdens have a distinctly human quality with the loss of housing and land of recreational value along the route. Some losses would undoubtedly occur anyway, but the planning of HS1 shows these can be minimised (Faith 2007); there is, after all, a connection between the current design of the route that limits mitigation options and the intended speed of operation (Durrant 2015). A more considered process would also include the question of whether or not Euston station is the ideal London terminus and, if it is, whether there are less disruptive ways of constructing it or ways of bringing regeneration benefits. Such a process might also address questions of the potential for mechanisms to resolve issues associated with property blight in a way that permits a more transparent consideration of route options.

This list could continue, including, for example, other impacts that have been claimed for HS2, such as the rebalancing of the economy. In fact, it is quite possible that starting here would not lead to the identification of HS2 even as a candidate intervention. This broader discussion is, however, connected to a wider debate concerning the UK's lack of a national strategy relating to infrastructure, transport or land use (Atkins et al 2017). There may well be value elsewhere in taking our hypothetical question back a few stages to ask how we might deliberate at a national level on these issues. We could, for example, productively engage with the question of whether a highly controversial link from the UK's dominant urban economy is really the most beneficial way to begin what may become a national HSR network (even though the economic appraisal concluded this to be the case). But we must be pragmatic: the scheme has been conceived and has, since its conception, had powerful backers. It would now be of largely academic value to ask more philosophical questions such as whether HS2 is the best way of promoting economic growth. The questions that we must ask of citizens in the circumstances are *whether HS2 or some recognisable variant of it should be built and, if so, how*.

An important theme in this discussion is the role of expertise. Arriving at a conclusion in any of these areas requires an understanding of what is technically, legally and economically feasible. Like Dewey (1927), we reject as simplistic the notion that such debates should be seen as pitching an uneducated polis against a technocratic elite. First, experts seldom agree as can be seen in the often-formidable expertise in the ranks of HS2's opponents. Second, there is often a moral dimension to many of these questions given they are about the allocation of benefits and burdens, and this can limit the value of technical expertise. For example, is it just to demolish a real person's house or destroy their livelihood on the basis of notional aggregated benefits? If the answer is yes then what is a just level of compensation for an individual's loss, and are economic measures of this, such as market value, sufficient?

Another point to acknowledge is that any suggested alternative planning process must take place within the legal context that now governs all such major schemes. This means that the participatory approach we construct sits within processes dictated by the Aarhus

Convention (1998) and associated regulation. Many of the features of the process undergone by the government would still be required. Specifically, conventional exercises such as national and local consultations are a given and so it falls to us to attempt to make our proposed participatory process both congruent with this wider set of activities and something that could enhance or add to them. We are loath to attribute instrumental benefits such as savings in time and reductions in costs to an enhanced process, however. This is not because we do not believe that it should not be possible to achieve some of these; it is simply that, given the scale and nature of the project, it is impossible to offer certainty that controversies might not appear in other ways or at other times. What we would argue very strongly, though, is that considerable time and resources have already been committed to a process that appears to have achieved very little in a positive sense. Those involved have not felt adequately informed, reassured or listened to while alternative designs that could be less contentious and arguably meet a broader spectrum of transport needs appear not to have been fully explored. Just as large infrastructure projects create opportunities for innovations in the technologies of engineering, project management and finance, so too should they be treated as opportunities for experimentation in applying well-established technologies of participation.

What a better process might look like

There are very many participatory methods and, while we are not seeking to make the case for one over the others, it is nevertheless important to identify which would be most likely to produce a more satisfactory outcome in a case such as HS2. One helpful typology of engagement methods is provided by Rowe and Frewer (2005) (though its age naturally makes it weaker on electronic participation; something we address later). They begin by identifying three broad categories of engagement: communication, consultation and participation. As with Arnstein's (1969) oft-cited 'ladder of participation' (Figure 11.2), this represents a transition from more passive engagement (communication) to more empowered, active citizen involvement in decision making (participation). *Participation* is clearly the appropriate form of engagement for this exercise as it is the category that explicitly involves dialogue. Indeed, much of our criticism of the methods employed to date in the development of HS2 centres on the absence of meaningful dialogue.

Rowe and Frewer (2005) present a set of criteria that can be used to derive a context-specific shortlist from the fuller set of participatory

Figure 11.2: Arnstein's ladder of participation

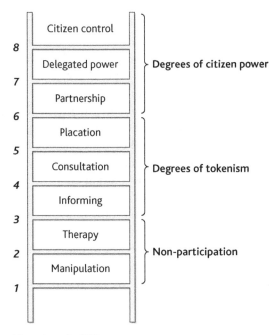

Source: Adapted from Arnstein 1969

methods. Their first concern is with participant selection. Here, a primary goal is to achieve an acceptable level of *representativeness* (socio–demographic and spatial) in the sense that the process is credible: a spectator looking at those involved should be satisfied that the participants represent the community as a whole (Pitkin 1972). This is a key tension within proposals given the different scales at which the consequences manifest themselves. HS2, for example, is conceived as a national project and justified at least in part by its claimed contribution to GDP as a measure of national prosperity. Likewise, the scheme's costs are to be borne by taxpayers across the country. By this measure 'the community' should be seen as the UK as a whole. Yet some areas will clearly gain more than others: the economic benefits will be felt more in some parts of Birmingham than, for example, in Cornwall or the Hebrides. Moreover, there is a significant local impact, some of which is profound for those facing demolition of their homes and businesses, years of construction traffic and disruption and the loss of valued environments. Some of this impact may be offset in the long run by the local benefits of increased transport accessibility and the associated uplift in property value (at least for owners of land and property), but other areas such as the

Chilterns will bear considerable environmental costs with few or no compensating benefits.

A process based on dialogue would obviously need to bring these interested parties at different spatial scales into effective discussion with each other, but at the same time we need to avoid giving the impression that the process is closed. A possible compromise would be to invite interested people to put themselves forward, to be selected using random stratified sampling on socio-demographic grounds as used in recruitment for citizens' juries (Coote and Lenaghan 1997). As necessary, targeted recruitment could be used to strengthen the cohort where self-nomination had not provided a sufficient number. It would almost certainly be the case that those putting themselves forward have an 'agenda' but, as Flyvbjerg's (2008) criticisms show, many parties will have their own agendas. The fact that some individuals are willing to participate ought to be all the more reason to involve them. Ultimately the challenge is not to avoid interests but to balance them.

Rowe and Frewer's (2005) second concern is with *facilitation* – the involvement or not of a facilitator. We suggest that this would, on balance, be a useful addition for reasons of efficiency and for the management of any discord. A competent facilitator can keep the group 'on task', which will generally save time; s/he would also be able to identify and work constructively with conflict, provided s/he avoided appearing to favour any particular course of action. This is not to say that conflict must be stifled, however; a facilitator can ensure there is value in conflict as a means of exposing and understanding issues and strongly held positions while minimising any harm that might arise. The actions of a facilitator are unlikely to be truly neutral but, where the subject is contentious, his or her presence is likely to be of benefit to the deliberative process (Landwehr 2014).

Their third criterion contrasts *open and closed questions*. A closed question limits participants to a set of fixed responses, compared to more open mechanisms that allow the creation of new answers and, perhaps, new questions. Our review of the history of HS2 strongly suggests that the latter is appropriate here. Moreover, the questions we believe should be posed of participants – should HS2 or a recognisable variant of it be built and, if so, how? – can only be properly addressed if participants are free to develop fresh ideas. Even so, some aspects of HS2 could be addressed through closed questions, and we discuss later the possibility of using deliberative polling (DP) in this regard (see further on).

Rowe and Frewer's (2005) fourth criterion concerns the importance of *face-to-face interaction* which they contrast with other methods such as polls and discussions conducted online or by telephone. Here, a scheme of HS2's size implies a multiplicity of participation activities, and the answer to this question can be a combination of face-to-face deliberative exercises with other, possibly online, mechanisms (Grönlund and Strandberg 2014). One model would have at its core a deliberative process taking place in person, surrounded by other (self-nominated) interested stakeholders, monitoring proceedings online, posing questions and making comments. The advantages of such 'distributed' dialogue – low costs of participation and the removal of barriers for those who might struggle to attend in person – could therefore be captured at the same time as harvesting the benefits of face-to-face deliberation.

Finally comes the *aggregation of views*: is this structured (for example, through voting or surveys that allow quantitative findings) or unstructured? Here, we need to remember that the participatory process we envisage will be part of a wider planning exercise which it must inform. The more policy makers can be told about what participants think, the better, provided some of the more nuanced conclusions of the deliberation are not lost in the process. This points to a well-designed use of polling or surveys as part of the reporting process.

Towards a method

Using our answers to the questions posed by Rowe and Frewer's (2005) typology produces a shortlist of 'matching' participatory methods: planning cell and DP. A similar shortlisting exercise conducted using the database of methods maintained by Participedia (2013) produces a distinct but complementary set of 21st century town meeting, citizens' summit, multi-criteria decision analysis (MCDA) and public debate. That the last of these should arise is interesting given that the French *débat public* came about following opposition to a high-speed rail scheme (Marshall 2016). It is no coincidence that all of these methods fit under one or other definition of 'mini-publics'. According to Ryan and Smith (2014: 20) these involve 'a *broadly* inclusive and representative sub-group of an affected population engag[ing] in structured deliberation enabled by independent facilitation… with the aim of aligning decision making with the considered views of citizens.' We now explore some of these methods to establish how they might assist with the task of developing a more constructive and productive means of involving publics in the HS2 decision-making process.

Deliberative polling

The real value (in this particular case) of DP lies in its approach to recruitment and its use of before-and-after surveys to capture movement in opinion. With respect to the former, the divisive character of major infrastructure projects such as HS2 makes it necessary to be able to demonstrate an unimpeachable approach to the gathering of participants. Advocates of DP emphasise its rigorous recruitment method in order to create a 'microcosm' (Fishkin and Farrar 2005: 68) of the wider community, which it achieves through stratified random sampling. They also emphasise the practice of remunerating participants for their time, which encourages seldom-heard members of the public, for example those on lower incomes or with limited time, to take part. Fishkin and Farrar (2005) in fact pick out these two characteristics as being points that DP has in common with the democratic processes of ancient Athens. The recruitment process used in DP is, according to Ryan and Smith (2014), presented by its originators as the basis for believing that it is the only *true* mini-public, others falling short of the ideal because of compromises in the way they assemble participants.

The before-and-after survey is a distinctive aspect of DP designed to demonstrate the effect of the deliberative process upon participants' views. This can be seen as built-in evaluation in that it helps to show the impact of the exercise. From the point of view of controversial projects, it could prove extremely useful in providing an audit trail to support policy makers as they make decisions. We suggest that these characteristics – the recruitment of a (representative) microcosm and the use of metrics that track changes in opinion – make DP a method worth considering for the most contentious questions relating to HS2. And, given the spatial inequalities associated with the scheme, a mini-public drawn from across the country might be entrusted with issues that have so far proved divisive because of the very polarised likely distribution of benefits and costs.

The 21st century town meeting

This kind of town meeting (America Speaks 2010) is distinctive in its use of technology to support deliberative gatherings of as many as 5,000 people (Lukensmeyer and Brigham 2005, Nabatchi 2010). While the core of the meeting is a conventional table at which citizens discuss topics with the aid of a facilitator, the use of networked computers enables the rapid collation of views which are then interpreted by the 'theme team' for dissemination to the assembled participants, which 'build[s] collective ownership of the entire group's work' (Lukensmeyer et al 2005: 159). Voting keypads are also used to enable the views of the large number present to be gathered in real time for consideration and further debate. Over the course of the meeting, participants discuss various aspects of the question they have gathered to address, with the facilitation team noting points of agreement as they arise. A useful case study can be drawn from Washington, DC: there, the mayor established a two-yearly cycle involving a 21st century town meeting to inform his strategic plan. He used the meeting to inform the revision of the plan, then presented it back to citizens two months later (Lukensmeyer et al 2005).

Though this method stops short of involving people online – it demands the physical presence of participants – its use of information and communication technology (ICT) appears to overcome a key problem with many forms of mini-public, namely an unavoidably small number of people taking part. Small numbers risk both resentment on the part of keen applicants who are turned away and the possibility that conclusions reached through a deliberation exercise are not representative of the wider community. Recruitment methods as discussed in the context of DP can help to avoid accusations of a skewed participant group, but this does not address the fact that consultation exercises relating to HS2 and the like must allow those with a pre-existing interest to participate. Given that this group is unlikely to mirror the socio-demographic profile of the country, making it as large as possible is likely to provide some defence against a claim of unrepresentativeness.

Multi-criteria decision analysis

Unlike the other models discussed here, MCDA is not in itself a form of mini-public, nor is it inherently participatory, although it has been advanced as a means of balancing multiple stakeholder (or actor) interests (Macharis and Baudry, 2018). The term describes a broad suite of different appraisal methods that can be tailored to the needs of the institutional framework in which they operate, including use behind closed doors by technocrats. The essential characteristics of MCDA are the use of scores against well-defined performance criteria and of weights that enable those scores to be aggregated into a single total for each option under examination (Department for Communities and Local Government (DCLG) 2009).

There is a history of the use of the method in the appraisal of transport projects (Macharis et al 2009), and it has already been suggested as one mechanism for capturing the wider benefits of HS2 (Hall, 2013). Indeed, a form of it is now being used as the DfT's recommended approach to appraisal (DfT 2018; Chapter 6).[1] Where the benefits lie in this case is in the ability of the tool to be used in a participatory format, something tried in other equally controversial decision-making contexts (Stirling and Mayer 2001). 'Standard' MCDA can be expanded to enable the distinct viewpoints of stakeholders or stakeholder groups to be made explicit, with the aim of enabling the methodical consideration of strength of feeling as part of working towards a decision. Macharis and Baudry (2018) term this application 'multi-actor, multi-criteria analysis (MAMCA)'; it has also been described as 'participatory MCA'.

MCDA can include both the monetised and non-monetised costs and benefits in a single analysis, and given that much of the rationale for HS2 is couched in economic terms it would seem perverse to suggest any participatory method that would not fully include the evidence from economic appraisals. But such processes need to be set in a broader context so as not to crowd out other technical appraisal techniques such as the assessment of environmental impact. Beyond this they also need to include many of the non-monetisable impacts, such as the disruption to local communities. While reliance by some proponents on a 'stakeholder concept' (Macharis and Baudry 2018) may not always resolve questions of how those who qualify as having a stake are identified, the potentially transparent nature of MCDA – the different priorities attached to various impacts are rendered explicit by the process – and the fact that it produces an audit trail that can be examined and interrogated by non-participants, recommend it as a potential aspect of the HS2 deliberation process.

A combination of methods?

Having identified a range of mini-publics that might offer useful mechanisms for deliberating on the HS2 question, it is not necessary at this stage to come down firmly in favour of a particular method. As we have argued, in fact, a combination of methods is likely to be appropriate in order to deal with the range of spatial scales, the variety of questions that may need to be posed concerning the scheme at both a strategic and a local level, and the diversity of those who might participate, be they currently engaged in the HS2 process or not. But this leaves hanging the question of, *then* what? A major concern of researchers working on mini-publics is that most of the exercises have been designed to enable the testing of the method with no expectation of real impact upon policy decisions. Niemeyer (2014: 194) identifies a range of potentially positive impacts of mini-publics, but 'for any of these mechanisms to work, mini-publics would need to achieve considerable democratic status, well beyond what is ordinarily the case thus far'. Whether a deliberative process of the sort we are discussing would be given a meaningful status in the overall decision-making process is outside our control, although we can say that for it to take place without being embedded in the wider decision-making system would be at best wasteful and, quite possibly, worse.

Conclusions

The proposals here are clearly out of time and the reasons HS2 Ltd chose not to explore forms of democratic innovation in the planning process, while touched upon, are ultimately beyond the scope of this chapter. Given the apparent success of DAD in the case of HS2, the central question is what might ultimately bring about change. In the case of HS2 it does not seem that the level of public opposition has led to the shift towards more deliberative methods that has been seen in France (Leheis 2012, Marshall 2016), although interest in these mechanisms is growing among policy makers in the UK (Atkins et al 2017). In setting out alternatives our aim has been less to critique current practice than to inform future approaches. In restricting ourselves to a discussion of how this might have worked in shaping the current proposals, and in highlighting the empirical evidence that mini-publics can offer a viable solution to similar issues, we have tried to avoid allegations that the value of deliberative methods exists only at the level of political theory. Furthermore, we have sought to avoid over-claiming for these techniques. It is clear that no process could avoid some of the conflicts inherent in a project such as HS2, but it is equally clear that they could have been addressed in a better, arguably more productive, way. Put simply, no process designed and operated by real people with conflicting aims would see all opposition disappear. It may, however, be possible to challenge and even reframe the problems it is conceived to resolve. After all, a 'realistic' approach does not have to be one that systematically excludes the perspectives of those affected.

Some of the solutions could already be on the table: the property bond may have fared better had its value in terms of allowing open decision making been acknowledged and appreciated. Compensation, the protection of property values and, perhaps more importantly, the homes and livelihoods of those non-property owners threatened by HS2, are areas where the current institutional design merits improvement. Face-to–face deliberation may have been a more suitable mechanism given that it can provoke sensitivity to issues of justice and to the plight of others. It could have supplemented and made up for the obvious limitations of market mechanisms. The evidence that opponents of the project can still offer viable solutions breaks down the somewhat unhelpful distinction between the objective expert and the self-interested NIMBY. It may well be the case that some of the interests that drive opponents are local in that they reflect concerns with the immediate area, community or even individual property. But to seek to exclude or marginalise such concerns removes an important source of challenge from the decision-making process. Such publics are in many ways compelled to participate, and such participation ought to have the effect of raising standards of decision making while challenging the planners and promoters of transport infrastructure to minimise local impacts.

Some may feel that this raises the bar too high, grants too much power to opponents and undermines the role of expert evaluation of issues such as the economic or environmental impacts. This may be so. But we would argue it is important to set a high bar for new transport infrastructure. Even the less environmentally damaging forms still demand considerable resources, can inflict harm on those who live nearby, threaten private property rights and quite often require some form of fiscal support. Such projects, particularly the most disruptive, ought not to be undertaken lightly, or on the basis of inaccurate or optimistic appraisal (Chapter 7). Indeed, this leads us back to the second half of the false dichotomy we identified at the start of this chapter: the role of expertise. We do not seek to rule out projects that are disruptive or have high costs, nor to dismiss the considerable expertise and knowledge represented by disciplines such as transport planning and engineering. Put simply, we are arguing for a more effective process of decision making that brings this expertise into *meaningful* dialogue with those who have to bear the burden generated alongside the collective benefits of transport infrastructure.

Note

[1] WebTAG, as it is known, is a form of MCDA (albeit a very loose one because it stops short of deriving a single score).

References

Aarhus Convention (1998) *Convention on access to information, public participation in decision-making and access to justice in environmental matters.* www.unece.org/fileadmin/DAM/env/pp/documents/cep43e.pdf Accessed 5 July 2018.

America Speaks (2010) *21st century town meeting, America speaks. Engaging citizens in governance.* http://americaspeaks.org/services/21st-century-town-meeting/ Accessed 9 September 2013.

Arnstein, S (1969) 'A ladder of citizen participation', *Journal of the American Planning Association*, 35(4): 216–24.

Atkins (2003) *High speed line study: summary report.* https://webarchive. nationalarchives.gov.uk/+/http:/www.dft.gov.uk/pgr/rail/ researchtech/research/hspeedlinestudysummaryreport.pdf Accessed 18 February 2019.

Atkins, G, Wajzer, C, Hogarth, R, Davies, N and Norris, E (2017) *What's wrong with infrastructure decision making? Conclusions from six UK case studies.* London: Institute for Government. www. instituteforgovernment.org.uk/sites/default/files/publications/ Infrastructure%20report%20%28final%29r.pdf Accessed 1 November 2017.

BBC (2010) 'London-to-Birmingham high speed train route announced', www.bbc.co.uk/news/uk-politics-12035524 Accessed 18 October 2018.

Butcher, L (2018) *High Speed 2 (HS2) Phase 1.* Commons Briefing Paper CBP 316. London: House of Commons Library. https:// researchbriefings.parliament.uk/ResearchBriefing/Summary/ SN00316 Accessed: 2 June 2019.

Campaign to Protect Rural England (2013) *HS2 bill timescale could breach international law.* www.cpre.org.uk/media-centre/latest-news-releases/item/3479-hs2-bill-timescale-could-breach-international-law Accessed 4 April 2014.

Colquhoun, A (2010) *The cost of freedom of information.* Constitution Unit, University College London. www.ucl.ac.uk/constitution-unit/ sites/constitution-unit/files/cost-of-foi.pdf Accessed 2 June 2019.

Coote, A and Lenaghan, J (1997) *Citizens' Juries: Theory into Practice,* London: Institute for Public Policy Research.

Cotton, M and Devine-Wright, P (2011) 'Discourses of energy infrastructure development: a Q-method study of electricity transmission line siting in the UK', *Environment and Planning A: Economy and Space*, 43(4): 942–60.

Della Porta, D and Andretta, M (2002) 'Changing forms of environmentalism in Italy: the protest campaign on the high speed railway system', *Mobilization: An International Quarterly*, 7(1): 59–77.

Department for Communities and Local Government (2009) *Multi-criteria analysis: a manual.* Communities and Local Government, Wetherby.

Department for Transport (2018) *Transport Analysis Guidance. The transport appraisal process.* www.gov.uk/government/uploads/system/uploads/attachment_data/file/712965/webtag-transport-appraisal-process-may-2018.pdf Accessed: 2 June 2019.

Devine-Wright, P (2012) 'Explaining "NIMBY" objections to a power line: the role of personal, place attachment and project-related factors', *Environment and Behavior,* 45(6): 761–81.

Dewey, J (1927) *The Public and its Problems.* London: George Allen and Unwin Ltd.

DfT (2010) *High Speed Rail.* Department for Transport, London.

Doward, J (2013) 'High-speed rail opponents "portrayed as posh nimbys" by peer's lobbying firm', *The Observer,* 6 March, www.theguardian.com/uk/2013/apr/06/high-speed-rail-hs2-nimbys Accessed 31 March 2013.

Durrant, D (2015) 'The controversial discourse on speed in the case of HS2', *Proceedings of the Institution of Civil Engineers – Urban Design and Planning,* 168(5): 241–50.

Faith, N (2007) *The Right Line: The Politics, the Planning and the Against-the-odds Gamble Behind Britain's First High-Speed Railway,* Kingston: Segrave Foulks.

Fishkin, J and Farrar, C (2005) 'Deliberative polling: from experiment to community resource', in J Gastil and P Levine (eds) *The Deliberative Democracy Handbook: Strategies for Effective Civic Engagement in the Twenty-first Century,* 1st edn, San Francisco: Jossey-Bass, pp 68–79.

Flyvbjerg, B (2008) 'Curbing optimism bias and strategic misrepresentation in planning: reference class forecasting in practice', *European Planning Studies,* 16: 3–21.

Flyvbjerg, B, Bruzelius, N and Rothengatter, W (2003) *Megaprojects and Risk: An Anatomy of Ambition,* Cambridge: Cambridge University Press.

Greengauge 21 (2012) *High Speed Rail: the carbon impacts of HS2.* www.greengauge21.net/publications/the-carbon-impacts-of-hs2/ Accessed 5 July 2018.

Grönlund, K and Strandberg, K (2014) 'Online deliberation: theory and practice in virtual mini-publics', in K Grönlund, A Bächtiger and M Setälä (eds) *Deliberative Mini-publics: Involving Citizens in the Democratic Process,* Colchester: ECPR Press, pp 93–113.

Hagman, D (1972) 'Planning (condemnation) blight, participation and just compensation: Anglo-American comparisons', *Urban Lawyer,* 4(3): 434–62.

Hall, P (1980) *Great Planning Disasters,* Oakland: University of California Press.

Hall, P (2013) 'High Speed Two: the great divide', *Built Environment*, 39(3): 339–54.

HS2 Ltd (2013) *HS2 regional economic impacts*. Ref: HS2/074. https://assets.kpmg/content/dam/kpmg/pdf/2013/09/hs2-regional-economic-impact-1.pdf Accessed 2 June 2019.

HS2 Ltd/DfT (2011) *High Speed Rail: investing in Britain's future. Consultation.* February 2011. www.gov.uk/government/consultations/high-speed-rail-investing-in-britains-future-consultation Accessed 5 July 2018.

Landwehr, C (2014) 'Facilitating deliberation: the role of impartial intermediaries in deliberative mini-publics', in K Grönlund, A Bächtiger and M Setälä (eds) *Deliberative Mini-publics: Involving Citizens in the Democratic Process*, Colchester: ECPR Press, pp 77–92.

Lee, M and Abbot, C (2003) 'The usual suspects? Public participation under the Aarhus Convention', *The Modern Law Review*, 66(1): 80–108.

Leheis, S (2012) 'High-speed train planning in France: Lessons from the Mediterranean TGV-line', *Transport Policy*, 21: 37–44.

Lukensmeyer, C and Brigham, S (2005) 'Taking democracy to scale: large scale interventions–for citizens', *The Journal of Applied Behavioral Science*, 41(1): 47–60.

Lukensmeyer, C, Goldman, J and Brigham, S (2005) 'A town meeting for the twenty-first century', in J Gastil and P Levine (eds) *The Deliberative Democracy Handbook: Strategies for Effective Civic Engagement in the Twenty-first Century*, 1st edn, San Francisco: Jossey-Bass, pp 154–63.

Macharis, C, de Witte, A and Ampe, J (2009) 'The multi-actor, multi-criteria analysis methodology (MAMCA) for the evaluation of transport projects: theory and practice', *Journal of Advanced Transportation*, 43(2): 183–202.

Macharis, C and Baudry, G (2018) 'The Multi Actor Multi Criteria Analysis framework', in C Macharis and G Baudry (eds) *Decision-making for Sustainable Transport and Mobility: Multi Actor Multi Criteria Analysis*, Cheltenham: Edward Elgar Publishing, pp 2–27.

Marshall, T (2016) 'Learning from France: using public deliberation to tackle infrastructure planning issues', *International Planning Studies*, 21(4): 329–47.

Marshall, T and Cowell, R (2016) 'Infrastructure, planning and the command of time', *Environment and Planning C: Politics and Space*, 34(8): 1843–66.

McAvoy, G (1998) 'Partisan probing and democratic decision making: rethinking the Nimby syndrome', *Policy Studies Journal*, 26(2): 274–92.

McClymont, K and O'Hare, P (2008) '"We're not NIMBYs!" Contrasting local protest groups with idealised conceptions of sustainable communities', *Local Environment*, 13(4): 321–35.

Millward, D (2011) 'High speed rail campaign mocks rich opponents of scheme'. *The Telegraph*, www.telegraph.co.uk/news/8585304/High-speed-rail-campaign-mocks-rich-opponents-of-scheme.html Accessed 2 June 2019.

Minn, M (2012) 'The political economy of High Speed Rail in the United States', *Mobilities*, 8(2): 185–200.

Nabatchi, T (2010) 'Deliberative democracy and citizenship: in search of the efficacy effect', *Journal of Public Deliberation*, 6(2), Article 8.

Niemeyer, S (2014) 'Scaling up deliberation to mass publics: harnessing mini-publics in a deliberative system', in K Grönlund A Bächtiger and M Setälä (eds) *Deliberative Mini-publics: Involving Citizens in the Democratic Process*, Colchester: ECPR Press, pp 177–202.

Novy, J and Peters, D (2012) 'Railway station mega-projects as public controversies: the case of Stuttgart 21', *Built Environment*, 38(1): 128–45.

OMEGA Centre (2013a) *Project Profile: TGV Méditerranée* www.omegacentre.bartlett.ucl.ac.uk/wp-content/uploads/2014/12/FRANCE_TGV_MED_PROFILE.pdf Accessed 23 November 2017.

OMEGA Centre (2013b) *Project Profile: Netherlands HSL-Zuid.* www.omegacentre.bartlett.ucl.ac.uk/wp-content/uploads/2014/12/NETHERLANDS_HSL_ZUID_PROFILE.pdf Accessed 23 November 2017.

Ousley, Justice (2013) R (On the application of Buckingham County Council and others) -V- Secretary of State for Transport High Court (Administrative Court) 15 March 2013 Summary to assist the media.

Overman, H (2013) *The regional economic impacts of HS2*. LSE Spatial Economic Research Centre Blog. 13 September 2014. http://spatial-economics.blogspot.co.uk/2013/09/the-regional-economic-impacts-of-hs2.html Accessed 16 April 2014.

Participedia (2013) *Participedia. Strengthen democracy through shared knowledge.* https://participedia.net/ Accessed: 1 November 2017.

Peston, R (2013) 'What KPMG ignored when arguing for HS2'. Robert Peston, BBC Economics Editor's Blog, 11 September 2013, www.bbc.co.uk/news/business-24047047 Accessed 16 April 2014.

Pitkin, H (1972) *The Concept of Representation*, Berkeley and London: University of California Press.

Right Lines Charter (2011a) *Note of expert seminar on public engagement and High Speed Rail.* Original website now disabled, but see www.civicvoice.org.uk/uploads/files/Right_lines_Charter_FOR_WEBSITE.pdf Accessed 16 July 2019.

Right Lines Charter (2011b) *Right lines charter: a charter for doing High Speed Rail well* www.civicvoice.org.uk/uploads/files/Right_lines_Charter_FOR_WEBSITE.pdf Accessed 16 July 2019.

Rowe, G and Frewer, L (2005) 'A typology of public engagement mechanisms', *Science, Technology & Human Values*, 30(2): 251–90.

Ryan, M and Smith, G (2014) 'Defining mini-publics', in K Grönlund A Bächtiger and M Setälä (eds) *Deliberative Mini-publics: Involving Citizens in the Democratic Process*, Colchester: ECPR Press, pp 9–26.

Salet, W, Bertolini, L and Giezen, M (2013) 'Complexity and uncertainty: problem or asset in decision making of mega infrastructure projects?', *International Journal of Urban and Regional Research*, 37(6): 1984–2000.

Schmidt-Thomé, K and Mäntysalo, R (2013) 'Interplay of power and learning in planning processes: a dynamic view', *Planning Theory*, 13(2): 115–35.

Schön, D and Rein, M (1994) *Frame Reflection: Toward the Resolution of Intractable Policy Controversies*, New York: Basic Books.

Stirling, A and Mayer, S (2001) 'A novel approach to the appraisal of technological risk: a multicriteria mapping study of a genetically modified crop', *Environment and Planning C: Government and Policy*, 19(4): 529–55.

Theiss, D and Kersley, H (2013) *High Speed 2: One track mind? Considering the alternatives to HS2.* New Economics Foundation, London.

Tomaney, J and Marques, P (2013) 'Evidence, policy and the politics of regional development: the case of high-speed rail in the United Kingdom', *Environment and Planning C: Politics and Space*, 31(3): 414–27.

Wates, J (2005) 'The Aarhus Convention: a driving force for environmental democracy', *Journal for European Environmental and Planning Law*, 2(1): 2–11.

Wolmar, C (2005) *On the Wrong Line: How Ideology and Incompetence Wrecked Britain's Railways*, London: Aurum.

12

Remote, rural and island communities

David Gray

Introduction

> "The troubles of the rural buses really stem
> from the growth in the number of private
> motor cars now on our roads."

> "A lot of people who have the car are
> prepared to give a lift into the town on market
> days to their neighbours or friends."

Assuming a favourable policy environment – and various chapters in this book have shown how in the UK this can never be taken for granted – journey makers in large towns and cities can have a range of different transport modes to choose from because population size and density creates sufficient demand to sustain them. In less densely populated areas, relative remoteness, journey distance and settlement size and distribution can combine to constrain journey-making options and increase journey-making time and cost. Sometimes people in rural areas have no option but to travel by car – either their own or someone else's – and, indeed, often they choose to even when alternatives are available. Car dependence and the cost and perceived unsuitability of public transport in meeting the accessibility needs of journey makers is often called the *rural transport problem.*

Transport matters in rural areas. In our most remote and peripheral communities, relying on the presence of lifeline services and the resilience of the transport system in often harsh environments, transport is typically the most salient local concern. Issues such as the condition of the trunk road, the absence or disappearance of bus services, the reliability of air services, the convenience of ferry timetables (or the ferries themselves) or the perceived deterioration of rail services are often highly politicised (Commission for Integrated

Transport 2001). The two opening quotes illustrate important elements of the contemporary rural transport problem: the inability of public transport to provide a viable alternative to the car, reinforcing rural car dependence and, for those without direct access to a car, reinforcing a reliance on lifts from family, friends, neighbours and carers. The following quote hints at the tantalising prospect of technology and new forms of transport ownership, organisation and coordination providing the silver bullet(s) to help solve the problem: "There are a good number of new forms of transport coming into being with which we are not very familiar." While these three quotes help us frame the issue of the rural transport problem today, they are actually taken from a UK Parliamentary debate on the issue held in 1962 (Hansard 1962). The challenges around providing cost-effective alternatives to the car in remote, rural and island areas have been taxing policy makers and transport planners for decades.

In more than half a century of trying, then, why haven't we been able to solve the rural transport problem? In this chapter, I will use the north of Scotland as a case study to reflect on the enduring nature of the issues at play, and why rural transport has posed such a challenge to transport planners and policy makers. I will look back at some of the 'new forms' of transport that have been tried (often with limited success) and consider the extent to which rural transport is subsidised and, indeed, whether such subsidy that is provided is actually spent on the right things. I'll show that it is possible to reduce per-passenger subsidy costs and will explore the opportunities offered by technological, institutional and social innovation. After devoting much of the chapter to the limitations of alternatives to the car, the I'll turn my attention to the most important rural transport mode and will discuss experiences of private car users and passengers. Of importance here are the relative impacts of fuel price rises and infrastructure investments on rural car use, as well as how norms, expectations of rural journey makers have changed over time. I'll conclude by suggesting that policy makers abandon their current approach to the rural transport problem – a failed, 60-year-old paradigm – for a more radical stance that focuses on increased capital investment to support innovation that complements, or in some instances replaces, rural bus services.

The rural transport problem

Why is it so difficult for bus, and historically rail, services to provide viable alternatives to the car in rural areas? In large part, it is a question of geography. I'll illustrate using the two extreme examples of Aberdeenshire and the Isle of Lewis; much of the rest of rural and island Scotland sits somewhere in between. Rural Aberdeenshire has a population of 220,000 distributed across 6,313 km² (34.8 people per km²). Most of the population is located on the fertile plains of the north and east, while the western interior is mountainous. Even in the relatively densely populated farming areas like Formartine or Buchan, it can be difficult to provide public transport because the population is distributed across an intensely cultivated agricultural landscape of farms, hamlets, villages and small towns (Figure 12.1). Households are connected by hundreds if not thousands of miles of A and B roads, unclassified roads and farm tracks, rendering it impossible to serve everyone with an accessible bus route that gets people to where they want to go, when they need to get there, in a reasonable amount of time.

An added complication is the number of competing urban centres. Would a journey maker from Kinnadie, for example, prefer to visit a large supermarket in Peterhead (10 miles) or Ellon (10 miles), or a smaller outlet in Mintlaw (4 miles)? Or would a member of the same household prefer a bus service that can allow them to access one of the universities in Aberdeen (27 miles)? Or health appointments at Aberdeen Royal Infirmary (26 miles)? Or family in Turriff (20 miles)? Or employment in Dyce (25 miles)? There are lots of competing destinations in different directions, few of them close by, all requiring

Figure 12.1: Rural population distribution: the agricultural landscape of Aberdeenshire

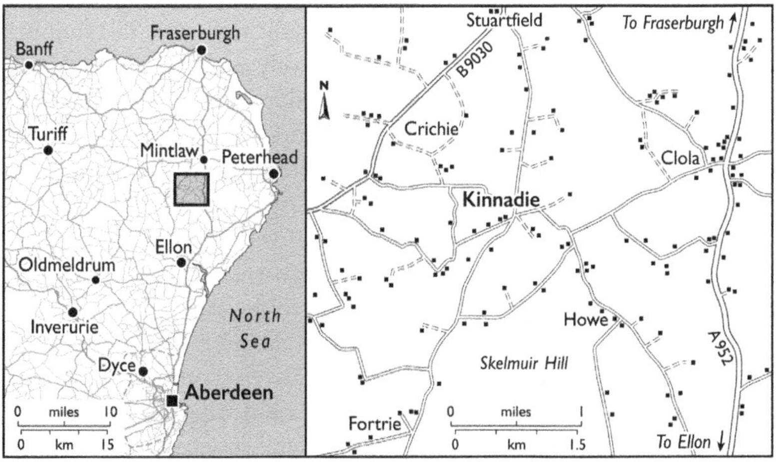

Source: Author

different bus routes and/or lengthy journeys. Kinnadie is also 2 miles from the nearest bus route (the 68 from Ellon to Fraserburgh), although households in this locality are able to call upon demand-responsive transport (DRT), the Central Buchan A2B (available anytime on Monday to Saturday between 8.00 am and 6.30 pm), which can transport passengers within a limited local area, including connecting to timetabled bus services in Mintlaw (Aberdeenshire Council 2018). In practice, it would be possible to make all the journeys listed earlier by public transport. But with the exception of visiting the small supermarket in Mintlaw, all trips would be time-consuming and would require at least one change of vehicle.

From Aberdeenshire, we learn that a landscape where the population is distributed widely and evenly presents challenges for transport planners. Those living close to major road corridors will have an acceptable bus service, with high frequency, evening and weekend coverage and tolerable travel times. Those living at a distance from these 'thick routes' will be much more constrained in their travel opportunities, reliant on DRT or the car (either their own or a lift in someone else's). Not all rural and island areas are the same, however, and in some it is actually quite easy to plan a public transport service that should, in theory, provide an effective alternative to the car.

The Isle of Lewis, the largest of the Western Isles with a population of 18,000 located within 1,770 km^2 (10.2 people per km^2), is a good example. We saw earlier that higher population densities tend to support the provision of public transport alternatives, and at first glance – with a third of the population of Aberdeenshire and 25 per cent of the population density – we might expect that planning public transport on Lewis would be extremely challenging. In reality the opposite is true, because its geography makes it well-suited to running a network of bus services. Firstly, the relatively small rural population is clustered into a number of crofting townships on the fertile Machair land around the edge of the island (Figure 12.2). The interior is comparatively empty of people. Township clusters lie quite close together and are linked by a small number of roads, which mean that the rural population can be served by a relatively small number of bus routes. Secondly, there is only one major urban centre, Stornoway, so the majority of passengers will want to go to the same place to access shops, services, health care and recreation. There is little destination competition. And thirdly, the island is relatively compact, so only a small number of journey makers will face a bus trip of more than an hour to reach the capital, and there are several services a day on each route, six days a week.

Figure 12.2: Rural population distribution: the crofting landscape of the Isle of Lewis

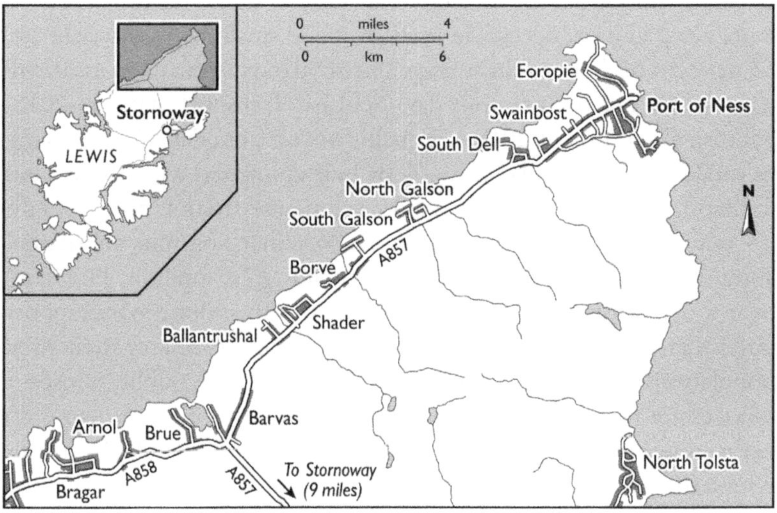

Source: Author

Thus while it is difficult to provide a viable alternative to the car in agricultural Aberdeenshire, it is easy, at least in theory, in crofting Lewis. With such ideal geographical conditions for planning bus services, it might be expected that bus services are popular, sustainable and perhaps even commercially viable. Yet this is not so. All services in the Western Isles are supported by the local Council (the *Comhairle nan Eilean Siar*), which spends a total of £6.3 million on school, integrated and public transport; around 50 per cent is dedicated to the last of these. Passenger numbers on public daytime and evening bus services are very low, with some evening services recording an average of only two or three passengers per run. The *Comhairle* cannot justify the cost of supporting services that carry only a handful of passengers, and is engaged in redesigning its public transport operations to achieve more ambitious affordability targets. A 'thinning' of daytime and evening timetables is being considered, along with the discontinuation of some non-statutory services. There is also recognition of the need for a more collaborative approach with operators and local populations, including the enhanced use of community-provided, demand-led services and smaller vehicles.

Consequently, even in a rural region where bus services should work, they are apparently failing to meet the needs of journey makers. Across the country, on any given day only 1 per cent of adults in remote rural areas – that is, small communities living more than 30-minutes' drive from a settlement of 10,000 people or more – and 1 per cent in remote small towns will use a bus. Patronage is only a little higher (5 or 6 per cent) in more accessible rural areas and small towns. By contrast, 55 per cent of those adults surveyed in Scotland's large urban areas will have used a bus the previous day (Scottish Transport Statistics 2018, Scottish Government 2018a). Equally, only 2 per cent of those living in rural households travel to work by bus, compared with 18 per cent for Scotland as a whole (Scottish Government 2018a). Unsurprisingly, it's not just the *Comhairle nan Eilean Siar* that commits substantial amounts of money – Aberdeenshire spends £7.5 million, Highland over £5 million and Orkney more than £2 million – to support buses that, in reality, serve only a very small proportion of their rural populations (Scottish Government 2018a). Where public transport services are running close to empty, subsidy costs of more than £50 per passenger journey are not uncommon, especially on DRT services where the additional cost of service coordination needs factoring in.

Rural authorities across Scotland are judging that such figures are not sustainable during times of austerity and reductions in public spending, and like the *Comhairle* are taking action to address their spending on public transport. The result has been that rural and island bus networks have shrunk more significantly than the Scottish average over the last ten years (Table 12.1): in Highlands and Islands, for example, the number of network kilometres reduced by 23 per cent between 2006/07 and 2016/17, and the number of annual bus passenger journeys fell by 20 per cent. Across Scotland as a whole the numbers are 15 per cent and 17 per cent, respectively. In this context, a vicious circle of decline is created, where a contracting network becomes even less able to take passengers where they want to go, when they need to be there, in an acceptable amount of time. Journey makers are required to find alternatives, which leads to further reductions in passenger numbers and still higher per-passenger journey subsidy costs

Table 12.1: Scottish Bus decline, 2006/07–2016/17

	Annual bus journeys	Network annual km
Scotland	−17%	−15%
Highlands and Islands	−20%	−23%
North East	−9%	0
South East	−6%	−7%
South West & Strathclyde	−27%	22%

Source: Scottish Government 2018a

on marginal services. These are then themselves withdrawn, resulting in another contraction in network coverage.

Among the benefits ascribed by numerous authors to the UK-wide introduction of free bus travel for older people and other eligible groups, is the demand for bus use it has stimulated (Chapter 14). Like their equivalents in England, Wales and Northern Ireland, the Scottish Government (2018a) invests heavily in its Concessionary Fares scheme, to the tune of £260 million per year. But a free bus pass is only useful if potential journey makers have services to use it on. Eligible passengers living in Edinburgh use their bus pass *ten times* more than their equivalents in Orkney (Table 12.2). Similarly, cardholders in Aberdeen City will make three times more journeys than their counterparts in neighbouring Aberdeenshire. Indeed, the councils with the lowest use of the concessionary fares schemes are all rural or island authorities (*Comhairle nan Eilean Siar*, Dumfries and Galloway, Highland, Moray, Orkney, the Scottish Borders and Shetland). Ironically, then, a potentially significant source of additional subsidy for rural bus services cannot be taken advantage of because there are not enough services available, increasingly as a result of reductions in subsidy from other sources, in the first place. It is incontrovertible that the Concessionary Fares scheme, the primary mechanism for supporting alternatives to car travel for eligible groups in Scotland,

Table 12.2: Lowest to highest journeys by free bus pass in Scotland. Data shown for 14 of the 32 council areas.

Ranked (lowest to highest)	Journeys per capita, over 60s
Orkney Islands	3.83
Comhairle nan Eilean Siar	3.98
Shetland Islands	4.47
Highland	5.51
Moray	5.79
Dumfries & Galloway	6.06
Scottish Borders	6.08
Aberdeenshire	6.47
Aberdeen City	19.77
Renfrewshire	20.48
Midlothian	20.71
Dundee City	24.61
Glasgow City	26.72
City of Edinburgh	35.26

Source: Figures derived from Scottish Transport Statistics, Scottish Government 2018a

is inequitable, biased as it is against those living in remote, rural and island areas.

Providing alternatives to the car

The idea of a rural transport problem first came to national prominence in the 1960s, with the high-water mark being the publication of *The Rural Transport Problem* (Thomas 1963). The issue re-emerged in the 1980s. This 'second era' of the rural transport problem attracted more sustained interest from policy makers and academics whose interests can be grouped into three overlapping areas:

- the piloting of community and other forms of innovative rural transport, particularly in the English shires, in the late 1970s (see Balcombe 1979, Banister 1982, Nutley 1988, Banister and Norton 1988);
- the emergence of interest in wider rural accessibility (see Moseley 1979, Banister 1982, Cloke 1985); and
- the impact of bus deregulation in the 1980s, which brought about a contraction of rural networks as the practice of cross-subsidising expensive country routes with the profits from lucrative urban ones came to an end (see Farrington 1985, Bell and Cloke 1991).

Throughout the 1990s, community transport and other innovations piloted in the 1970s and 1980s were increasingly seen as the solution to the decline of the rural big bus, not least because they had the added benefit of door-to-door route flexibility and service availability (see Mageean and Nelson 2003). Demand responsive dial-a-ride services emerged and quickly became popular with passengers; the services were typically supported and/or provided by local authorities (to meet public transport or social care needs), health boards (to provide transport to hospitals or other NHS facilities) or community groups (with the emergence of Community Transport as a new phenomenon). Ring-and-ride services ranged from the use of off-peak taxis, to minibuses (often owned and operated by community groups and purchased through Community Transport schemes), to tendered mid- and full-sized buses owned by bus companies (see Laws et al 2009).

By the late 1990s a more sophisticated appreciation of the heterogeneity of rural areas – and thus the solutions necessary to address their transport problems – had emerged (CfIT 2001), along with a better understanding of the relationship between accessibility and social inclusion (Farrington and Farrington 2005, Preston and

Raje 2007, Lucas 2012; Chapter 4). Subsequent work around the notion of accessibility planning (see Halden 2011, Curl et al 2011) refocused attention on reducing the need to travel, but using modelling to take a more systematic and analytic approach to reducing the number of necessary destinations and improving the level of local service/employment availability (Gray et al 2008). Other research (Gray et al 2006, for example) has acknowledged the importance of social networks in supporting informal lift-giving (see further on), and there is a significant amount of contemporary interest in how technological innovation and integration with other modes can support last-mile solutions (Chapter 15).

Especially in the context of reduced public spending (and even in better times the often 'stop-start', short-term nature of government funding arrangements throughout the UK), a significant oversight in previous academic research has been its tendency to pay little heed to the long-term cost of recommended approaches capable of enhancing access and mobility. This at least partly explains why, even when realised in combination, mobile facilities, DRT, accessibility planning and the like have failed to provide a lasting, 'silver bullet' solution to the rural transport problem. Indeed, many 'successful' projects have struggled to endure beyond the pump priming phase. Dial-a-ride services, for example, were typically supported by time-limited Bus Innovation or Community Transport grants from central government. Although popular with passengers they were expensive: with their additional control and planning costs, limited passenger numbers and variable vehicle occupancy, DRT schemes often cost more to run than conventional big buses (there are anecdotes emerging from local authorities of demand responsive services costing over £100 per passenger journey). When central government funding ran out the schemes became a burden for rural councils. While some, such as Aberdeenshire, persist with DRT schemes and recognise the cost and commitment required to maintain them, services in other areas were discontinued where no additional local funding could be secured to support them. This is the same kind of central versus local funding issue identified earlier, in relation to the Concessionary Fares scheme.

One of the problems in attempting to manage the cost of public transport services was/is the competitiveness of tender prices. In remote, rural areas, both DRT and conventional bus services are often operated by small taxi or bus companies whose core business lies elsewhere (typically in providing school transport or private hire). Many are reluctant to tender for the additional business and do so on an inflated take-it-or-leave-it basis. Lack of tender competition thus increases the cost of providing services to transport authorities. Worse still, in some areas, de facto cartels exist with operators seemingly disinclined to compete for tenders on each other's routes. In this absence of competition there is no hope of driving down tender prices, reinforcing the perception that the free market system is failing and not cost-effective away from lucrative metropolitan networks. This said, technology will almost certainly assist in managing costs. 'Big data', smart solutions – such as Mobility as a Service (Chapter 15) – are likely to play an important role in making services more attractive to passengers and reducing per-passenger subsidy costs. Again, though, geography is important, if only because the extent to which we can simply transfer metropolitan practice to the rural context will be limited by the availability of sufficient 4G/5G bandwidth and broadband connectivity. EU projects such as Improving Transport and Accessibility through New Communications Technologies (ITRACT) (2015) found that smart mobility solutions had limited impact in rural areas where online access is not widespread or reliable enough.

In any case, the problems are not solely related to cost. Successive generations of government at all spatial scales have failed to coordinate sufficiently their provision of public transport, school transport, community transport and vehicles operated by social services and health care providers.[1] Community transport cannot duplicate or compete with registered bus services, but otherwise there is very little active institutional coordination of transport services provided for (on the face of it) different purposes, leading to inefficiency and duplication of services, vehicles and drivers. The different eligibility rules of the different institutional transport providers also mean that some vulnerable social groups benefit from a number of free transport services, while others (such as young people and job seekers) only have access to public transport and have to pay for it. Others still, as we have seen, have access to public transport for free, but where services are very limited this will be of little or no use. The main barrier to better coordination, at least in Scotland, remains institutional. Organisations with separate budgets, transport resources and particular transport requirements have been reluctant to collaborate in planning their activities. Significant factors are the lack of political will within disparate public sector organisations, and that for some, while transport facilitates what they do (for example, provide healthcare), it is not their 'core business'.

One example of a 'non-smart' initiative that has increased passenger numbers, reduced per-passenger subsidy costs and negotiated the local institutional context is the Glenelg and Arnisdale shared taxi scheme. This was established following the withdrawal of a link service that connected the Highland communities of Glenelg and Arnisdale with the coach services that run between the Isle of Skye and Inverness/Glasgow. Highland Council stopped the service because of unsustainably high per-passenger subsidy costs, even though it was regarded as an important source of mobility and access to the local community. In response to significant local opposition to the loss of the service, Highland Council engaged Robert Gordon University to develop a low-cost alternative. The solution was characterised by five key features:

- The scheme is managed and operated by the community through a constituted bus users' group (BUG).
- The BUG receives a small fixed grant of £3,000 to support the scheme every year. When the money runs out, the service stops or the community engages in fundraising to supplement the grant.
- The fare structure is organised to encourage vehicle sharing. A flat rate of £5 is charged for each passenger, while the taxi company receives a fixed fare of £15 per trip. If only one person uses the service, the BUG must cover the £10 shortfall from its grant. If three passengers make a trip, the BUG breaks even, and if four or more make a journey then the BUG generates additional revenue.
- The taxi is contracted on a 'call-off' rather than a 'stand-by' basis. Most demand responsive services are tendered on a stand-by basis, so that the operator gets paid regardless of whether or not there are any passengers. By contrast, the BUG only pays for a minibus when it requires one.
- While it is possible to purchase tickets via a website, the majority of tickets issued are paper and issued in the local shop to minimise reliance on ICT in an area where there is poor broadband and 4G connectivity.

In its first year, the service reduced per-passenger subsidy costs by 80 per cent and tripled passenger numbers. It has now been operating for three years and recently carried its thousandth passenger. I would stress that the Glenelg and Arnisdale scheme was the right solution for the right community. It may work in other localities or it may not, depending on the local geography, operating requirements and/or other particular factors. One such factor here was the way in which the call-off contract was able to be negotiated. Such contracts are not popular with transport operators because they are far less lucrative than stand-by equivalents, but the BUG was able to secure one because of local family connections with the operator. It is important to reinforce that it is not always possible to transfer innovative practice from one locality to another, and that as such a detailed appreciation of the heterogeneity among places will always be necessary (see also MAMBA 2018, G-PaTRA 2018).

Rural car dependence

So far in the chapter I have confined my discussion to the rural transport problem as it relates to public transport. Yet remote, rural and island communities are highly *car dependent* (Goodwin 1995, Gray et al 2001, Lucas and Jones 2009), and many more people than in towns and cities choose to make their journeys by car even when there is adequate public transport available. The most salient fact about car dependence in rural areas concerns people who do *not* own a car and who live in deep rural areas and remote rural areas – typically the elderly. Such people will still make more journeys by car than by big bus, demand responsive minibus, community transport, subsidised taxi and social service minibus combined. It is the same for those in one-car households who do not drive or have access to the vehicle for much of the day – young people and stay-at-home parents, for example. A lift in someone else's car – whether from a friend, family member, carer, work colleague, neighbour or someone from a local community group – is the most common form of public transport (in its widest sense) and one, with the exception of modest fuel price rebates in some areas, which is unsubsidised (See Gray et al 2006).

Informal lift-giving is invisible public transport, and its importance is rarely recognised or acknowledged by policy makers, transport authorities or, for that matter, academics. It is reliant on informal networks of people who know each other ('social capital' as it is more formally called – see Putnam 2000). In very isolated communities where people have very limited spheres of activity and are more likely to encounter each other in a shop, bank, pub, community centre or another social arena, these social networks are strong and extensive, and it is logical that informal lift-giving would be particularly prevalent, especially since conventional public transport might be infrequent if it exists at all. The Hansard (1962) quotes at the start of the chapter suggest that informal lift-giving has been commonplace in rural areas for decades, and indeed there is a sense in which the emergence of shared transport, vehicle pooling and associated lift-giving technology in urban areas is merely taking advantage of a suitable technological platform to mimic long-standing informal practice in small tight-knit rural and island communities.

While all remote, rural and island areas are highly car dependent, the nature and extent of this dependence varies across different ruralities in the same way that local authorities' capacity to plan bus networks depends upon the geography of the places they are trying to serve. For example, a common misconception is that people living in very remote communities make lots of long journeys. But it is not necessarily the case that car dependence intensifies with increasing distance from a metropolitan area. Indeed, the least car dependent rural communities in Scotland – measured in terms of car and multi-car ownership, modal share, annual kilometres travelled by car and expenditure on fuel – are remote small towns like Stornoway, Thurso, Kirkwall and Lerwick (Scottish Government 2018a). These towns are compact, where many journeys can be made on foot, and thus for a significant number of residents there is often no reason (or opportunity) to make longer car journeys to a nearby larger or competing urban centre because there simply isn't one.

Still, one doesn't have to travel very far from a town like Lerwick to find highly car dependent households. Gulberwick is 3 miles outside Lerwick. There are no shops, services, employment, schools or healthcare in Gulberwick, so almost every trip involves getting in a vehicle – invariably a car – and travelling 3 miles. Car dependence in Gulberwick is therefore greater than in Lerwick, despite their proximity. Gulberwick's growth in recent decades has followed a broader process of decentralisation that has created attractive but highly car dependent semi-rural and suburban settlements reinforcing the trend for people to live at increasing distances from where they work, shop, socialise and take recreation. Scaling up this Shetland example to city regions across Scotland, our most car dependent localities are actually 'accessible rural areas', that is, commuter towns and peri-urban developments within relatively easy driving distance of the country's big cities. Thus the most car dependent rural communities in Scotland are not those in the far north of Sutherland (where most car journeys are short and local); they are the small towns, villages and housing developments that lie close to Glasgow, Edinburgh, Aberdeen, Perth, Dundee and Inverness.

Of course, this trend of travelling to shop and enjoy recreation is not confined to accessible rural areas, and I relate here an anecdote to illustrate not only that people living in deep rural communities make such journeys, but also how rural car use and journey-making patterns are not static and evolve over time. As you would expect, such evolution is related to the changing norms and expectations of journey makers themselves, and the extent to which particular transport issues command local attention at any given point. In the winter of 1997, I conducted a focus group in the village of Kinlochbervie, in the northwest Highlands. I was working on a research project exploring car dependence in rural Scotland, precipitated by concerns about the rising cost of petrol and diesel (Gray et al 2001). Kinlochbervie is one of the most isolated communities on the UK mainland, and fear of the impact of high forecourt prices was *the* local issue. At the focus group, I was confronted by a group of local councillors and community councillors who had me metaphorically pinned up against the wall for two hours. I was someone from 'The Centre', a captive audience, and I was obliged to listen to their concerns – delivered passionately and, at times, angrily – about high fuel prices devastating their way of life. For me, it was a memorable and at times intimidating session, but one which generated some remarkable qualitative data: "I believe... this is going to be the straw that breaks the camel's back. It is as simple as that. It will decimate rural areas;" "You'll be more effective than the Duke of Sutherland in clearing the Highlands." For the people of north-west Sutherland in 1998, transport and the spectre of rising fuel prices mattered fundamentally.

Ten years later, I visited Kinlochbervie again. I was returning to some of the places visited during the car dependence study to try and track down people I'd interviewed to see what had changed. Unsurprisingly, I was nervous about going back; it was the first half of 2008 and the UK was in the midst of another fuel price spike. I moderated several interviews and focus groups and waited for the inevitable tongue-lashing. It never came. What emerged instead were anecdotes of people from Durness and Kinlochbervie jumping into their cars and driving the 104 miles to Inverness of an evening, going to the cinema, enjoying a meal, stocking up with provisions and fuel at Tesco and driving back the same night. A 208-mile round trip to enjoy the same experience that those living in much less isolated localities take for granted.

Again, these interviews elicited some remarkable data, but for entirely different reasons than the first time around. An apparently frivolous evening out in Inverness would simply not have been contemplated in 1997, and certainly not in 1989, when I first ventured to the region to carry out PhD fieldwork and when miles and miles of roadworks impeded progress around Wester Ross. In 2008, the price of fuel was never raised as an issue by the Sutherland interviewees, even though the issue was exercising the rest of the UK at the time (and barring a few exceptions like motorway service stations the price of fuel in deep rural areas is usually the highest in the country). Similarly, the price of diesel and petrol has never been raised as a concern at Board meetings of the Highlands and Islands Transport Partnership (HITRANS) since my appointment to it in 2010.

Why has the price of fuel receded as a key local issue in Kinlochbervie and other, similar places? My sense is that the explanation lies in two interrelated factors. Firstly, the perception of the likely impact of fuel price increases in 1998 proved to be out of step with the subsequent reality. People coped and adapted. Regular long-distance travellers in the Highlands were early adopters of fuel-efficient diesel vehicles, for example. By 2008, a decade of fuel price fluctuations in the far North West had come and gone without any significant or widespread impact on journey making or quality of life. In fact, I would argue that the economic impact of fluctuating fuel prices was insignificant, relatively speaking, compared to the second key factor, namely the impact on journey making of three and a half decades of trunk road improvements and bridge building. Those roadworks that disrupted travel in the late 1980s were part of what turned out to be around 35 years of road infrastructure improvements, largely funded by the EU through its various regional support programmes. The 200-mile round trips from north-west Sutherland are only possible because of the consequent reductions in journey time. The decade since those lively 1998 focus groups had witnessed significant improvements to the road linking Ullapool with the far North West, reducing travel times significantly and enhancing accessibility by car. As road infrastructure improved and journey times to places like Inverness fell, people's journey-making norms and expectations evolved dramatically over a relatively short timescale.

If one wanted to sample what life was like before large-scale road improvements, one could compare the experience of negotiating the A897 between Melvich and Helmsdale and the A832/A890 between Garve and Kinlochewe. The former is almost 40 miles of single-track road with passing places, on which motorists can just about manage an average speed of 35 mph, so long as they do not meet too many vehicles coming the other way or get delayed behind the many timber lorries that use the road. The latter is a much-improved wide-carriageway road, which is relatively straight and fast and where motorists can easily average 45 mph. It is now possible to drive the 50 miles between Kinlochewe and Inverness in about the same time (1 hour 7 minutes) as one can travel the 40 miles between Helmsdale and Melvich. Or put another way, increasing the average speed from

35 to 45 mph has reduced the journey time between Kinlochewe and Inverness by 40 minutes for a return journey. Scottish Transport Appraisal Guidance (Scottish Government 2018b) advises that the value of such a 40-minute journey time saving to a commuter is £6.60. To a business (which operates a delivery van, for example), the value of that journey time saving is around £10. If the cost of fuel increased substantially by 30 per cent (from around £1.20 to £1.55 per litre), the additional fuel cost for a Ford Transit for that journey would be in the region of £5.60. There is critique elsewhere in the book (Chapter 6) of overly simplistic transport appraisal mechanisms that rely too heavily on travel-time valuations, but it is possible using this example to see how such valuations provide at least a starting point for discussion about the long-term economic impact of road improvements in the Highlands and Islands relative to fluctuations in fuel prices.

Equally significant was the reduction in journey times realised by the bridge building programme that accompanied the road improvements. Notable construction projects included the Cromarty (1979), Kessock (1982), Kylesku (1984), Dornoch (1991) and Skye (1995) bridges (Figure 12.3). Those travelling into Inverness from the north and west benefited from one or more of these bridges. The combination of the Kessock, Cromarty and Dornoch bridges themselves cut the journey time between Dornoch and Inverness by at least 40 minutes each

Figure 12.3: Recently constructed bridges in the Highlands and Islands

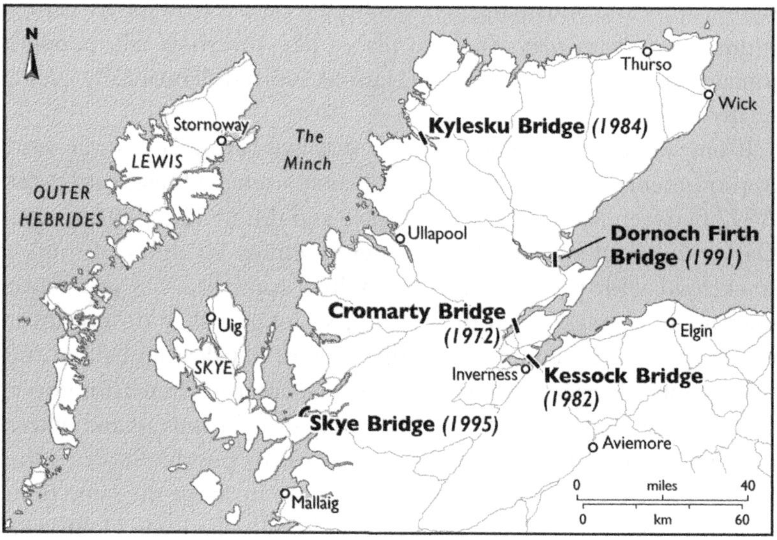

Source: Author

way, giving a return journey time saving of an hour and 20 minutes. Such changes have brought substantial economic benefits for those living in the northern and western Highlands and have brought communities like Dornoch within commuting distance of Inverness. Road and bridge improvements have transformed where people can live and work and – as in the Kinlochbervie example – how and where people can shop, socialise and take recreation. Improvements have also made the region more accessible for tourism and have underpinned developments like the North Coast 500, the self-described 'ultimate road trip' around the north of Scotland sponsored by Edinburgh's Aston Martin dealership (North Coast 500 2018).

The impact of road and bridge improvements in the Highlands and Islands goes beyond a question of whether transport 'matters': investment in transport infrastructure has changed fundamentally the way that life is lived in this part of the world. Of course we should be wary of assuming that all of this has been for the better, and certainly there have been disadvantages and unintended consequences. For example, the local community on Skye is beginning to complain that the opening of the Skye Bridge has rendered the island too popular with tourists, overheating the local economy. Shorter journey times to major urban centres and greater car dependence are a threat to local shops, banks and other services in many smaller settlements across the Highlands. What is more, while historically remote rural communities were tight-knit, comprised of households with very localised and overlapping spheres of activity, an expansion of these spheres would be expected to undermine social capital and weaken local cultural identity and sense of place (Gray et al 2006). An increase in in-migration, at least partly a result of better transport links, would be likely to exacerbate this trend, although the economic, social and cultural impact of large-scale road and infrastructure improvements on deep rural and island communities is to date under-researched.

Prospects for the future

Over the past half-century we can discern something of a mixed picture in Scotland's rural, remote and island areas. One the one hand, the rural transport problem remains unresolved, while on the other fairly substantial road investment has had dramatic effects on the way of life for those with access to a car. What, then, of the next three or four decades? It would seem hard to escape the conclusion that unless there are some radical changes around how we support and subsidise rural public transport, the Hansard quotes at the start of this chapter will still be relevant in ten or 20 years' time. We need to learn from decades of failure.

The first point to make is that currently we spend nothing on the most common form of rural public transport – *someone else's car.* One answer might be to be more imaginative with the eligibility of concessionary travel. Although to prevent an increase in car use in urban areas there would need to be some restriction, such as the distance an individual lives from a functioning bus route, being able to use a smart card to purchase fuel for the person who provides the lift would be a start. Capping the amount of funds an individual can receive annually would iron out the current inequity between eligible pass holders in rural and urban areas without increasing overall Scottish Government expenditure on the concessionary fares scheme. The second, related, point is that we should focus more on capital expenditure rather than revenue expenditure, because it would seem to provide much better value for money in the long term. It may well be that one source of this enhanced capital expenditure were a reduction in local authority support for big bus services, but the potential to unlock significant sums for investment would only really be attainable as the result of a concerted effort between the range of transport-providing institutions (local authorities, the Scottish and UK governments, health providers and so on) to coordinate their activities and identify both economies of scale and targeted priorities.

It is not often said in relation to rural and remote areas – the focus of attention is usually on urban and inter-urban travel because of the capacity to address at-source air pollution – but there is a clear case for sustained investment in the support infrastructure for electric and other zero emission vehicles, vessels, trains and aircraft. In remote and particularly in island regions, EVs make very good sense. On Scotland's islands, for example, where there is a limited road network and relatively short journey distances, motorists are very unlikely to exceed 60 miles per day, so range and range anxiety are not issues. More generally, people living in very remote localities tend to make two kinds of journeys: lots of short, local trips and the occasional very long outing. There are no range issues with the former, and although Scotland is beginning to develop a proper, strategic, region-wide charging infrastructure along key trunk roads, further capital investment in rapid chargers will all but eliminate range problems for travel over longer distances. Rather than being seen as principally an urban mode of transport, electric and zero emission technology is well aligned to the journey-making patterns of isolated localities. It also addresses the problem of Scotland's remote and island communities facing the highest fuel prices in the UK, especially where electricity is generated locally from renewable (often wind) sources.

Some deep rural authorities have already begun to capitalise on what they see as strong opportunities from EVs and alternative-fuel vehicles. Indeed, this partly explains why Orkney has the highest proportion of electric cars in the private vehicle fleet of any UK local authority area (Orkney Renewable Energy Forum (OREF) 2018). Orkney also generates 120 per cent of its energy demand from wind at peak times, so the Islands are looking at transport (including buses and ferries) as a way of absorbing this excess – zero emissions technologies offer energy management efficiencies in places where there is a substantial amount of community wind generation, but little smart infrastructure to smooth out the peaks and troughs in generation. There is also an entrepreneurial cluster engaged in developing land and marine renewables energy that has turned its attention not only to EVs but also hydrogen fuel cell (HFC) technology for ferries. With a recent history of supporting energy innovation, institutional inertia is not likely to be a barrier to the continued uptake in alternative-fuel modes of transport in Orkney, but encouragingly there are signs this might also be the case elsewhere in the Highlands and Islands. Electric buses are already in operation and HITRANS is looking at the business case for replacing diesel powered trains with battery or fuel cell powered train/tram hybrids on the Inverness to Kyle of Lochalsh line. There is also interest in electric aircraft to provide a more cost-effective option for inter-island flights.

Further into the future, autonomous vehicles (AVs) also have the potential to be truly transformational for remote, rural and island areas. We know that conventional rural public transport often provides poor value for money because there are too few passengers and rarely enough fare box revenue to cover the cost of service. AVs allow the removal of the highest running cost – the driver – and operating several electric or fuel cell powered smaller AVs instead of one big bus could potentially deliver the responsiveness and flexibility that rural journey makers crave, at a fraction of the cost. AVs could also have particular application in areas like social care (in regions which have a rapidly ageing population). For example, there are plans to embed AVs into a smart sheltered housing project development in Orkney, where AVs will be trialled alongside health and wellbeing sensor and remote monitoring technology. Cruise ship destinations like Orkney and Shetland are also becoming victims of their own success, where during peak season thousands of passengers visit world-famous archaeological sites like Scara Brae and the Ring of Brodgar on a daily basis, causing a massive logistical headache for the local authority. AVs allied to smart routing systems could help manage and optimise the flows of people around popular tourist attractions, reducing the reliance on diesel buses.

Ultimately, the most remote regions in the country are characterised by a limited road network, a low population and a small number of common destinations, and as such are an ideal living lab for developing, testing and refining AV technology in the real world. As one part of a broader approach to tackling the challenges of the rural transport problem, capital investment can usefully be focused on research and development to make AV operations safe, reliable and resilient with the aim of making such technology commonplace beyond our cities and inter-urban routes.

Note

[1] School buses are available for use by adults in many rural areas. In Scotland, non-pupils can use school transport if it is a registered service, but local authorities only tend to register services for secondary school transport and these are not popular with adults. Anecdotally in the Highlands and Islands, the modal share for non-pupil journeys made by school transport is negligible.

References

Aberdeenshire Council (2018) Central Buchan A2B website. www. aberdeenshire.gov.uk/roads-and-travel/public-transport/a2b-dial-a-bus/central-buchan/ Accessed 6 August 2018.

Balcombe, R (1979) *The rural transport experiments: a mid-term review Supplementary Report 492*. Transport and Road Research Laboratory, Crowthorne.

Banister, D (1982) 'Community transport for rural areas: panacea or palliative?', *Built Environment*, 8(3): 184–9.

Banister, D and Norton, F (1988) 'The role of the voluntary sector in the provision of rural transport services – the case of transport', *Journal of Rural Studies*, 4(1): 57–71.

Bell, P and Cloke, P (1991) 'Deregulation and rural bus services: a study in rural Wales', *Environment and Planning A: Economy and Space*, 23(1): 107–26.

Cloke, P (ed.) (1985) *Rural Accessibility and Mobility*. IBG Rural Geography Study Group, Lampeter.

Commission for Integrated Transport (2001) *Key issues in rural transport*. CfIT Rural Working Group. Commission for Integrated Transport, London.

Curl, A, Nelson, J and Anable, J (2011) 'Does Accessibility Planning address what matters? A review of current practice and practitioner perspectives', *Research in Transportation Business & Management*, 2: 3–11.

Farrington, J (1985) 'Transport geography and policy: deregulation and privatization', *Transactions, Institute of British Geographers*, NS10: 109–19.

Farrington, J and Farrington, C (2005) 'Rural accessibility, social inclusion and social justice: towards conceptualisation', *Journal of Transport Geography*, 13: 1–12.

Goodwin, P (1995) 'Car dependence', *Transport Policy,* 2(3): 151–2.

Gray, D, Shaw, J and Farrington, J (2006) 'Community transport, social capital and social exclusion in rural areas', *Area*, 38(1): 89–98.

Gray, D, Farrington, J and Kagermier, A (2008) 'Rural Transport', in R Knowles, J Shaw and I Docherty (eds) *Transport Geographies: Mobilities, Flows and Spaces*, Oxford: Blackwell, pp 102–19.

Gray, D, Farrington, J, Shaw, J, Martin, S and Roberts, D (2001) 'Car dependence in rural Scotland: transport policy, devolution and the impact of the fuel duty escalator', *Journal of Rural Studies*, 17: 113–25.

G-PaTRA (2018) *Green Passenger Transport in Rural Areas. Interreg North Sea Region Programme* http://northsearegion.eu/g-patra/ Accessed 6 August 2018.

Halden, D (2011) 'The use and abuse of accessibility measures in UK passenger transport planning', *Research in Transportation Business & Management,* 2: 12–19.

Hansard (1962) *Rural transport*. House of Commons Debate on Rural Transport, 11 May. Volume 659, column 794–887. Available at https://api.parliament.uk/historic-hansard/commons/1962/may/11/rural-transport Accessed 1 June 2019.

ITRACT (2015) *Improving Transport and Accessibility Through New Communication Technologies. Interreg North Sea Region Programme* www.itract-project.eu Accessed 6 August 2018.

Laws, R, Enoch, M, Ison, S and Potter, S (2009) 'Demand responsive transport: a review of schemes in England and Wales', *Journal of Public Transportation*, 12(1): 19–37.

Lucas, K (2012) 'Transport and social exclusion: where are we now?', *Transport Policy,* 20: 105–13.

Lucas, K and Jones, P (2009) *The car in British society*. RAC Foundation, London. www.racfoundation.org/wp-content/uploads/2017/11/car_in_british_society-lucas_et_al-170409.pdf Accessed 11 September 2018.

Mageean, J and Nelson, J (2003) 'The evaluation of demand responsive transport services in Europe', *Journal of Transport Geography*, 11(4): 255–70.

MAMBA (2018) *Maximised Mobility and Accessibility of Services in Regions Affected by Demographic Change. Interreg Baltic Area Programme.* www.nordregio.org/research/mamba-maximised-mobility-and-accessibility-of-services-in-regions-affected-by-demographic-change/ Accessed 6 August 2018.

Moseley, M (1979) *Accessibility: The Rural Challenge*, London: Methuen.

North Coast 500 (2018) *The ultimate road trip.* www.northcoast500.com Accessed 6 July 2018.

Nutley, S (1988) '"Unconventional modes" of transport in rural Britain: progress to 1985', *Journal of Rural Studies,* 4(1): 73–86.

Orkney Renewable Energy Forum (2018) www.oref.co.uk/electrical-vehicles/ Accessed 6 August 2018.

Preston, J and Rajé, F (2007) Accessibility, mobility and transport-related social exclusion, *Journal of Transport Geography*, 15(3): 151–60.

Putnam, R (2000) *Bowling Alone: The Collapse and Revival of American Community*, New York: Simon & Schuster.

Scottish Government (2018a) *Scottish Transport Statistics, No 36, 2017 Edition.* www.transport.gov.scot/publication/scottish-transport-statistics-no-36-2017-edition/_Accessed 6 August 2018.

Scottish Government (2018b) Scottish Transport Appraisal Guidance (Scot-TAG) www.transport.gov.scot/our-approach/industry-guidance/scottish-transport-analysis-guide-scot-tag/ Accessed 6 August 2018

Thomas, D (1963) *The Rural Transport Problem*, London: Routledge.

PART III

New policy imperatives

13

Disruption and resilience: new realities?

David Dawson and Greg Marsden

Introduction

Even as recently as the late 1980s, the British public was being sold the vision of a transport system that would be expanded to cater for the future growth that would come with rising prosperity (Department of Transport (DoT) 1989). Fast forward to today and we see systems that are run at, or over, their capacity with limited reserve or redundancy (Mattsson and Jenelius 2015; Chapter 1). Frequently vulnerable to even the smallest of breakdowns and accidents, we have a system that is seen to be unreliable and increasingly in peril. This matters to passengers and businesses, and therefore on occasion to politicians (House of Commons 2009, Confederation of British Industry (CBI) 2014, Transport Focus 2015a, 2015b). Road traffic congestion alone has been estimated to cost the economy billions of pounds a year (Centre for Economics and Business Research (CEBR) 2014). The focus of policy today is on managing rather than accommodating demand, improving the efficiency of journeys, investing in pinch point congestion remediation and creating a more 'informed traveller' (Department for Transport (DfT) 2015, Transport Systems Catapult (TSC) 2015, National Infrastructure Commission (NIC) 2016). All of this is a recognition that delays and disruption have increasingly become part of the normal experience of travelling and that, in the face of anticipated traffic growth (DfT 2015; although see also Chapter 7), this is set to become worse. While in this chapter we focus on how the UK is approaching managing increasing disruption, this is a problem being faced by many cities and countries where the growth in demand for transport is outstripping or has outstripped the supply of infrastructure and services.

Understanding disruption

Disruption is such a common term in discussing transport today it is tempting to presume that those using it share some common understanding. We would suggest that how we understand and represent disruption is critical to how the problem is defined, what the solutions are seen to be and, therefore, what is in and out of scope. What are the competing interpretations of disruption? Mattsson and Jenelius' (2015) recent review characterises transport disruption in terms of the transport system's *reliability* and *vulnerability*. Figure 13.1 illustrates their distinction between the two concepts, which is developed from a risk perspective. Frequently occurring events that impact the reliability of the system such as road traffic incidents or over-running engineering works are deemed to have less of an impact (that is, the upper left section of Figure 13.1). These are the business of day-to-day operations, of communicating with travellers where they might be expected to be familiar with what to do when disruption happens. On the other hand, low-frequency, high-impact events

Figure 13.1: Risk curve showing the current distinction between reliability and vulnerability of the transport system with some selected examples of disruption

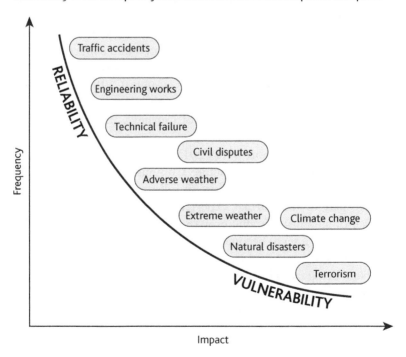

Source: Adapted from Mattsson and Jenelius 2015

such as extreme weather or acts of terrorism are seen to be different and demonstrate system vulnerability because they are unknown, unexpected and therefore are often combined with limited historical experience and thus limited understanding of how best to adapt when they occur (the lower right of Figure 13.1).

Intuitively attractive though such a schema is, we should question the origins of terms such as reliability, vulnerability and impact. Disruption is a social construct and is conditioned by the nature of the systems that are available, how they are being used, who is using them and in which cultural context(s). Consider a scenario where the fastest journey time between two cities used to be two hours but was subsequently cut to 90 minutes by a motorway. Two hours used to be a good journey time, but now, occasionally experiencing a two-hour journey is seen to be a delay. A particular (improved) level of performance becomes the norm. This can also work the other way. The M25 is now so regularly congested that very few people will see the inability to travel at 70 mph during the peak as a disruption, reserving those assessments for days when the Dartford Crossing is closed, for example, and when journey times rocket beyond those typically experienced. So, disruption needs to be seen in the context of some reference point, which itself is dynamic over time. What we perceive as disruption today, may in fact be acceptable in the future (if we stood in 1970 and looked at the delays experienced today that would be evident). Goodwin and Lyons (2010: 8) suggest that many people in the UK now see congestion as a 'fact of life'.

Hendrik Vollmer, a sociologist of disasters, focuses his insights (although not specifically considering travel) around disruption on the 'coordination of activities and expectations' within a collective entity (2013: 2). One of the reasons that disruption is so prevalent in our discourse today is that our extensive transport networks have encouraged the development of hugely complex activity patterns and supply chains. We have developed associated societal expectations around these activity patterns being usually possible on our networks. Individuals and businesses map out their own tight webs of arrangements, but it is only when things go wrong that we are exposed to the realities of just how complex and interdependent these arrangements are, and how reliant we have become on a particular view of how the system should work (Graham 2010).

The notion of impact itself also requires some further thought. Do we take this to be the sum total of all of the impacts of an event? The welfare cost of road congestion (for example, costs of lost time, additional fuel, accidents and disruption to socio-economic activities) on a 'normal' day is estimated to be around £60 million although this is spread over a very large area (DfT 2011). After the rail line collapse at Dawlish in the south west of England in 2014, daily economic losses were estimated to be around £600,000 (House of Commons 2014). Clearly these impacts were more tightly focused around one geographic area. Even here though, there will be differences between who is impacted. Consider flooding in a city. There will be some people who can't get out but were, in any case, not planning to go out or for whom rearranging activities would be straightforward. For others, that may mean the loss of work or missing a marriage celebration or other major life event which would be very significant. During the closure of large parts of European airspace following the Icelandic ash cloud of 2010, those most significantly affected were stranded away from home. Others were unable to leave on flights for business or leisure and had to postpone or cancel trips (Guiver and Jain 2011). Many, though, would not have been planning to fly and would only have been affected by shortages of goods that were beginning to manifest themselves just as air space was reopened. The impacts are not evenly felt.

We suggest therefore that frequency of occurrence and duration seem reasonable metrics to use to think about different disruption events, at least in the short run. Impact is much more problematic as a category and we return to this later in the chapter, in thinking about the different response options that exist.

Regular disruptions

Transport system (un)reliability, as captured by the upper left of Figure 13.1, is a well-established field of study. Although debate continues about how best to measure unreliability and how travellers conceptualise and value it (Carrion and Levinson 2012), it is estimated that the cost of lateness is valued at more than three times the normal in-vehicle journey time (Abrantes and Wardman 2011). The conceptualisation of regularly occurring congestion dominates the way in which network providers assess the performance of their assets. For example, on the rail network, the public performance measure (PPM) shows the percentage of trains arriving at their terminating station 'on time'. Rail franchise operators promise certain performance thresholds and have to refund season ticket holders if they fail to meet these thresholds.

It is interesting to further unpick the performance measure as a means of understanding the difficulty of relating what is essentially an engineering-based measure of system performance with the expectations of the travelling public. Network Rail, the owner and operator of Britain's railway infrastructure, classifies a train as late if it is more than five minutes past its scheduled arrival time if it is a commuter service, and ten minutes if it is a long-distance service. In addition, a train is 'significantly late' if it arrives more than 30 minutes beyond its scheduled arrival time. Again, customer compensation payments begin to kick in on significantly late trains. (By contrast, if a Japanese train is over a minute late an official apology is made to travellers as this is deemed unacceptable (JR-Central 2014).) Behind the PPM there is a complex system for agreeing the source of unreliability between Network Rail and the train operating companies (TOCs). This can involve annual payments of around £600 million per year.

While such a system of compensation appears to have the interests of the traveller at heart, this is not always the case. Any system of performance management will create the potential for perverse incentives. Here, once trains are beyond a given lateness threshold there is little incentive for the operator to ensure that the delayed travellers are taken to their destinations as quickly as possible because TOCs want to ensure one delay does not have a knock-on effect on other services. This might involve terminating a heavily delayed service short of its destination so it can pick up a (partial) return journey on time. Interestingly, while 12 per cent of train passengers report reliability as the biggest source of dissatisfaction with the rail service in Britain, 56 per cent report this to be how the train companies deal with delays (Transport Focus 2015b).

The rail sector, then, provides an excellent window on some of the tensions between how system operators measure performance and why that might not always match passenger expectations. The road sector, adversely, is almost absent of any clear performance benchmarks which mean anything to its users (Box 13.1). In England, for example, greatest attention is given to the Strategic Road Network (SRN) which is now managed by an arms-length government owned company, Highways England. The company is subject to some regulatory scrutiny, but travellers do not know what the SRN is and are in any case interested in the door-to-door journey experience rather than what happens on only one part of the network. The lack of insight into door-to-door journey reliability is even more apparent when we consider multi-modal journey making across all of the networks, which if the notion of 'Mobility as a Service'[1] takes off will become more important as an issue but also easier to track. We do not currently have a way of assessing and informing travellers about the likely and actual current reliability and performance of a set of multi-modal transport options (TSC 2015).

Box 13.1: Definition of reliability on the Strategic Road Network

'The measure of reliability... is the Planning Time Index (PTI). The PTI tells us about the predictability of travel times during the daytime (6 am–8 pm), and aims to measure the additional time compared to free flow conditions that drivers need to leave on individual road sections (broadly defined as sections of road between adjacent junctions on the network) to ensure that they arrive on time. This measure is the ratio of the 95th percentile travel time to the free flow travel time. The PTI can also be presented as a percentage...

Reliability on the SRN as a whole is calculated by averaging the PTI across individual road sections, weighting by traffic flows for each section. The PTI does not represent the reliability of start to end journeys, across several road sections.'

Source: DfT 2016

Infrequent disruptions

We turn now to the bottom right-hand end of the curve in Figure 13.1, the more infrequent disruptions.[2] In the UK, natural disasters are not a major source of concern (with perhaps the exception of the impacts from those elsewhere such as the Icelandic Ash Cloud). There are then three separate but related bubbles of climate change, extreme weather and adverse weather. In the UK, as elsewhere, there has been a recent increase in concern from the government and key bodies regarding the resilience of transport infrastructure in the face of weather-related threats (HM Government 2011; DfT 2011, 2014; Highways England 2016; Network Rail 2014a, 2015; Committee on Climate Change (CCC) 2016). The increase in interest is motivated by the need to protect the economy and its future growth, and a focus on immediate emergency response and addressing infrastructure asset vulnerabilities are the prominent strategies for achieving this (for example, RSSB 2016). Tackling long-term (that is, greater than 20 years) strategic challenges (for example, uncertainty, climate, resilience, adaptation) alongside near-term operational requirements (for example, maintaining functional assets and services, capital and maintenance costs) is difficult in organisations whose typical foresight and management structure is based around five-to-ten-year periods.

We know the future of our weather and climate is uncertain, but it is now widely acknowledged that the climate is changing as a result of anthropogenic activities and that this will amplify existing risks to natural and human systems, as well as create new ones (Intergovernmental Panel on Climate Change (IPCC) 2013). Jaroszweski et al (2010) list seven sources of disruption that are expected to become more common in the transport system: an increased number of hot days, fewer cold days, more intense rainfall, more pronounced seasonal changes, drought, an increase in the number of extreme events and coastal flooding. Notwithstanding these likely future trends, it seems we are already used to the impacts of intensive weather events. A survey of 2,700 people in six cities and surrounding travel to work areas found that 60 per cent of respondents had had their daily activities disrupted by bad weather in the past six months with only 6 per cent reporting that this had never happened to them (Anable and Budd 2014). Finding data on disruption at the system level is more difficult but, again, the regulatory requirements of the rail system in the UK do shed some light on the issue. Network Rail reports that for the period 2006/07 to 2014/15 compensation payments to the operators attributed to weather reached more than £50 million per annum. As Figure 13.2 shows, there were significant impacts on train performance 'from the severe weather events during 2007, 2012 and 2013 from rainfall, and 2009 and 2010 from snowfall. In terms of the proportion of delay minutes, weather and seasonal events on average caused 12 per cent of all delays experienced during this period' (Network Rail 2015: 9).

Dawlish diversions and difficult decisions

Still, while significant and highly concentrated in time (and often space) when they do occur, weather events only account for 12 per cent of all compensation-related delays on the railway. Put another way, 88 per cent of delays are not weather-related, and so might sit towards the top left (or more regular disruption) part of Figure 13.1. Although the current and future justification of resilience expenditure needs to be seen in this context (for example, additional adaptations or increased running costs), weather-related impacts can have significant social and political implications. The rail network in the far south west of England provides a good example. Consisting of one main line and several branch lines, the network has relatively low usage

Figure 13.2: Distribution of Network Rail Schedule 8 payments attributed to weather, 2006/07–2014/15

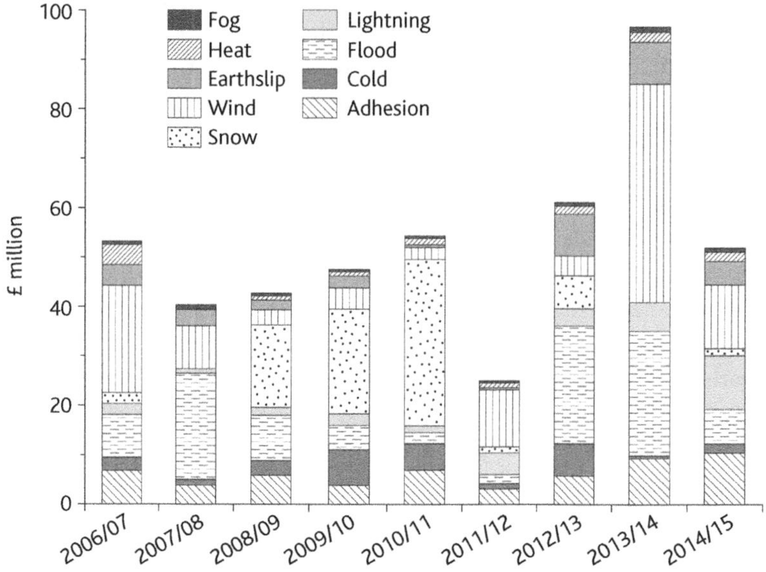

Source: Network Rail 2016

compared to other regions (Office of Rail and Road (ORR) 2016), albeit with patronage growth of nearly twice the national average over the last 10 years. Investment has not kept pace with this increased patronage, however: while on average transport investment in England has gone up, the southwest region has seen a 13 per cent fall (Cornwall Council et al 2013) and now suffers from one of the lowest transport expenditures per head in the entire UK (HM Treasury 2016).

The south west's is also a network that is prone to disruption during extreme weather events. The 'notorious' Dawlish-Teignmouth coastal section between Exeter and Plymouth is a key example, being subject to frequent closures and breaches due to wave action. Not counting one-off investments in structural improvements, Network Rail typically spends around £1.8 million per year on defence maintenance (Network Rail 2014), and the 4.2km-long stretch of line remains one of its most expensive sections of track to maintain. Two of the most notable disruption events, both undermining the route's defences and leaving track hanging in thin air, occurred on 5 October 1846 (shortly after it was initially opened) and on 4 February 2014 (Figure 13.3). Between these two extremes is a long succession of low-, medium- and high-impact overtopping events nearly every winter (Dawson

Figure 13.3: Sea wall breaches on the Western Route at Dawlish

a) There is no illustration of the 1846 event, the earliest being of the breaching in February 1855

Source: Fyfe 2013

b) The most recent breach in February 2014

Source: Network Rail 2014b

et al 2016). With no alternative route, south and west Devon and all of Cornwall are left without a rail connection when the line at Dawlish closes.

Temporarily 'cutting off' the region from the rest of the rail network has raised questions regarding the future of the line, as some consider it a basic right to have a rail network that is not severed during high seas (House of Commons 2015). Yet arguments about the necessity and merits of an alternative route are not new, and have broken out several times over the past 170 years. Ever since the first severance event in 1846 opinions about the route's alignment have been mixed, but the idea that an alternative should be built to provide additional resilience was quick to emerge: 'As a main trunk line from London to Penzance it is utterly preposterous, and is now so considered by every man between those termini' (*The Times* 1846: 5). In 1939 construction actually began on an alternative route further inland, but the outbreak of the Second World War stopped all work for good (Kay 1993). Making matters worse, an already-existing alternative – at least for Plymouth and Cornwall, if not for south Devon – a route to the north of Dartmoor was closed in 1968 because it was deemed too expensive to keep open. Regular skirmishes between representatives of the far south west and the government (*The Guardian* 1986 and *Western Morning News* 1996 cited in Dawson 2012, House of Commons 2015) finally resulted in a DfT commitment to provide significantly enhanced resilience measures with the Secretary of State for Transport, Chris Grayling, assuring people in the region that 'sorting out the route through Dawlish is my number one national rail priority' (DfT 2018: unpaginated). A diversionary route remains firmly off the table, dismissed by Network Rail (2014c) as unaffordable on the basis of a business case that curiously seemed to omit reference to social and economic benefits that might accrue from building the new line (Chapter 6).

The Dawlish example, although somewhat unusual in its geography, highlights some critical issues for policy and, by extension, travellers:

- There are some parts of the network that are vulnerable to weather events and which it is either impossible or deemed impracticably expensive to protect.
- Despite the social and political demands for investment in protection or in alternative infrastructure, the (official) economic case for investing in facilities to cater for low-frequency, high-impact events is often weak.
- There is, therefore, a requirement to manage a significant and growing set of weather-related network disruptions and it is not

possible to guarantee the uninterrupted performance of the network to travellers.

Table 13.1 and Figure 13.4 quantify the extent of the transport network that intersects with areas of potential flood risk, coastal and fluvial, based on known geological indicators (British Geological Survey (BGS) 2016). Although a rather crude indicator in that the elevation of the actual transport links in relation to the flood maps is not accounted for, it allows us to make some first-order observations about the future flood risk to UK transport systems. For example, there are around 35,000km of road in potential flood zones, and nearly 70 per cent of these are classed as minor (local) roads that are under local authority ownership. Nearly a quarter of the rail network is in an area of potential flood risk.

We can therefore expect an increase in the number of sections of the transport system that are flooded or inundated by rivers or the sea. While flood-related disruptions will not occur every year in exactly the same places and with the same level of severity, there are some parts of the network that will be affected more often, and worse, than others. Mapping exercises to improve on that undertaken by the BGS, with greater spatial resolution and network elevation information (for example, Light Detection and Ranging, or LIDAR), are an important first step to help identify the areas that are likely to see the effects of climate change earliest. At this stage, however, despite the potential extent of the disruptive threat, there are very few examples of transport vulnerability and impact analysis being linked to future climate projections to allow analysis of the probability and frequency of future climate change-related events on the networks (Dawson et al 2016). We can make an educated guess that these events will constitute a very sizeable fiscal challenge given the combination of ongoing requirements for rebuilding works[3] as well as preventative measures such as better sea defences (as in the case of Dawlish) and

Table 13.1: Estimated UK transport network located within potential coastal/river flood risk areas (see Figure 13.4)

Type	Length (km)	Risk of flooding (km)	Network at risk
A roads	46,678	6,557	14%
B Roads	29,806	3,233	11%
Minor Roads	266,246	26,358	10%
Motorway	3,621	506	14%
Rail	16,057	3,889	24%

Sources: BGS 2016; Ordnance Survey 2017

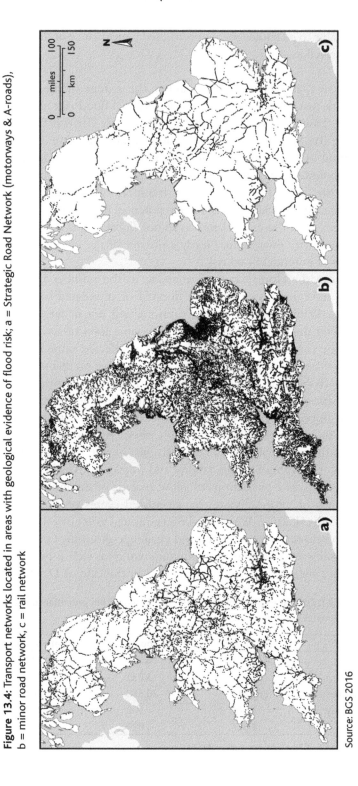

Figure 13.4: Transport networks located in areas with geological evidence of flood risk; a = Strategic Road Network (motorways & A-roads), b = minor road network, c = rail network

Source: BGS 2016

many hard and soft flood prevention schemes across the country.[4] We should remember, of course, that flooding does not relate to all seven of Jaroszweski et al's (2010) potentially more likely sources of disruption to impact transport networks.

It is interesting in this context to note that the increased risk of future disruption does seem to be understood by the public. In a study of areas affected by flooding, 66 per cent of respondents agreed that disruption to transport systems was going to increase in the future with only 6 per cent having an opposing view (Marsden et al 2016). At the same time, though, having an awareness that disruption is likely to increase is not the same as accepting that as a traveller one should be impacted by it. Exploring rail passengers' experiences of weather-related disruption on the rail network, Transport Focus (2015c: 1) concluded that 'passenger expectations are high and possibly unrealistic,' noting that there was a presumption that there should be 'a normal service even in extreme weather.' Moreover, the researchers found travellers believe that because 'snow, heavy rain and high winds happen every year,' the industry should invest and plan to negate these effects: '[t]o the extent that passengers consider practicality and safety at all, they tend to assume that the right level of investment and planning can overcome the problems' (Transport Focus 2015c: 1).

As the evidence from existing disruptive events and from forecasts of the increase in the number of future events suggests, the case for investment cannot always be made and even if it could, it is difficult to imagine sufficient public finance being made available to tackle the scale of network problems that exist and that will emerge. Already difficult decisions over scheme prioritisation will intensify as politicians are presented with an increasing number of calls on budgets we are told are perennially stretched. An alternative position is to plan to respond to incidents as they arise and place the costs of not adapting on the users as well as the operators, although fixing things 'in a hurry' will be sub-optimal from a capital spend efficiency perspective. There would also be a need for a much greater emphasis on engaging with how traveller disruption is managed, and how best to mitigate the impacts of network disruption to the broader social systems that transport underpins.

Social disruption

As we set out earlier in the chapter, while what breaks is typically a piece of infrastructure or a vehicle, what is impacted is the system of social coordination that depends on that infrastructure or vehicle.

Looked at through this lens, we can understand more about how disruptions are experienced. Figure 13.5 shows a hypothetical timeline of a disruption from the perspective of the engineering performance of a piece of infrastructure. It highlights some distinct phases of the recovery process which have different implications for travellers and different response options. The initial stage immediately following, for example, a line or road closure is a period of significant uncertainty. Many people are in the middle of a journey somewhere and there is a priority to understand how long the period of disruption will be and what the options are to complete or cut short the journeys they are conducting. This is the bread and butter of transport operators and network providers as such events, which are fixable within hours, occur on a daily basis. Here, developments in real-time information and effective use of social media and better operator communications with travellers are increasingly important (Transport Focus 2015c). In work examining the behavioural response to the Forth Road Bridge Closure in Edinburgh in late 2015, Shires et al (2016) found that people on average accessed five different sources of information to help their travel decisions. Social media, radio and operator websites were the most helpful resources, indicating a search for up-to-date information but also highlighting the need to ensure good planning across all of the actors involved in such events, as there is no 'single source of truth'.

Figure 13.5: Timeline showing disruption performance levels over the duration of a disruption event

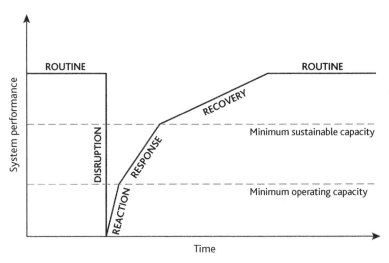

Source: Adapted from Hay 2013

For events where the recovery period is extended to days or months (for example, extended snow and ice events, flood recovery or loss of infrastructure such as bridges), there is both the possibility and necessity to look beyond information as a solution. Much attention is paid to the ability of people to change mode or route. Of course, this can work but only if the other networks are able to cope with a surge in demand. Because such large-scale events mean the loss of a critical link or the partial or total loss of capacity on some parts of the network, there is limited additional capacity for re-routing and changing transport mode. This is particularly true given how under-constructed – in relation to both the country's population and the standards of comparably advanced European countries – and therefore busy the UK's transport networks are (Chapter 1), and thus how little spare capacity there is to soak up diversions. So long as this fundamental problem remains unaddressed (and, in reality, to a lesser extent even if it were), a different form of social adaptation is required.

In research conducted by one of the authors (Marsden et al 2016), significant evidence of adaptation in time and space was found that included travellers starting/ending activities later, rearranging activities and/or conducting them more locally. During the closure of the Forth Road Bridge crossing due to structural failure for several weeks, there was a 12 per cent reduction in the number of days people travelled into work, with around three quarters of this being made up by working from home and most of the rest by people working more intensively over fewer days using flexitime (Shires et al 2016). Across all of the work conducted in this area there has been a relationship between the extent to which employers are accommodating about not coming in to work and the degree to which employees decide to work from home, as shown in Table 13.2. While not all jobs/employers are amenable to homeworking or flexitime, the ability for some people to avoid travelling is especially important in areas already prone to

Table 13.2: How employer attitude to changing working patterns impacts on travel choices

		Employer attitude	
Survey	% Response	Very accommodating	Very unaccommodating
Flooding	% Carried on	55	67
	% Work from home	12	0
Winter weather	% Carried on	30	40
	% Work from home	24	18

Source: Shires et al 2016

daily congestion given that during major disruption events parts of the network are not available.

The social response then is not simply defined by individuals, but it is more broadly about the social norms which are in – or come into – operation during major events (we are back to Vollmer's (2012) notion of expectations). This may explain why employers would not be tolerant of repeated small amounts of lateness (focus group discussions have highlighted instances of people losing their job due to repeated public transport unreliability), but why lateness during days of bad weather is seen differently. A further example of societal adaptation was in 2009 when a major flooding event in Cumbria led to the loss of a bridge in Workington, severing the town for months and leading to a very long diversion of around 50 miles by car. Rail service connections remained available, and it was also possible to cross from one side of the town to the other on foot. Some of the innovative social responses to this disruption included reassigning people to different doctors' surgeries, setting up a pop-up supermarket on one side of the river and allowing council workers to work from the nearest available office (Guiver 2012). Of course, such adaptation is not without challenge to those affected but it does demonstrate a range of adaptive strategies that can be, and are, deployed. The challenges, then, are to be able to mobilise such strategies across government, transport operators, businesses and other organisations such as schools and hospitals.

Finally, in Figure 13.5 it is presumed that the routine after such an event looks exactly like the routine before such an event. In infrastructure terms that may be true (although often improvements are made) but in social terms it is not. Even during periods of significant disruption where alternative modes are not in good condition, people experiment with new ways of doing things because they have to. This might be re-timing their trips, working from home a bit more or changing mode. For periods of extended closure with long diversionary routes it may mean changing job. Evidence from the closure of the Forth Road Bridge shows that 8 per cent of travellers reported being not at all or very unlikely to return to their previous frequency of travel; 7 per cent reported being not at all or very unlikely to return to the previous timing of travel; and 6 per cent reported being not at all or very unlikely to return to the previous mode of travel. As things stand, though, we know comparatively little about the long-term impacts of disruptions at an individual, community or business level (Parkes et al 2016; Shires et al 2018). We have limited information, for example, about how often or how bad disruption would need to be for companies to consider relocating or not investing in a particular area.

It is not clear what levels of additional stock-holding may be needed to insulate a company against disruptive events. And we need to find out much more about the real costs to travellers, although we can say that these are all unlikely to be represented solely by additional economic costs of lengthened journey times and journeys foregone. It will be necessary to seriously think about how far, when, where and to whom a process of 'externalising' the cost and responsibility for adaptation from transport providers/the government to others (some of whom are public sector and many of whom are not) is desirable, especially since, as we have noted, it is likely to result in poor value-for-money each time repair work is necessary (see also Chapter 4 on this question of externalities impacting disproportionately on certain journey makers).

Conclusions

Growing demand and limited capacity expansion, even with smarter control systems, means our networks are increasingly susceptible to impacts from day-to-day disruptions. If over the last 50 years the UK had invested the same proportion of GDP in its infrastructure as some European peers did in theirs, it is likely there would be a more robust network with more high-quality alternative options and fewer capacity constraints. Even with the recent ramping up of infrastructure investment, for various reasons the notion of solving rather than postponing or limiting even routine congestion seems some way off. In essence, current policy continues to be one of managing a deterioration in network conditions in most places, and the social response is to adapt to this over time as some sort of new, if not desirable, normal. There is of course much to be done to improve the flows of information, the treatment of passengers and the connectivity between modes so that travellers can make better on-the-spot decisions. But given the lack of spare capacity in most of our networks at key times of the day, better decisions might actually mean not travelling at all and being more flexible in re-timing activities, using virtual alternatives and picking more local opportunities.

Although less frequent in nature, there is a substantial amount of weather-/climate-related disruption occurring on our networks and this too is set to grow. The extent to which the network and its services might be impacted is so widespread and the costs of attempting to prevent such disruption so large that it is unimaginable that we could protect all of our network from all such events. In some ways, the political challenge that this presents is similar to that of day-to-day disruption. At some point it seems that it will be necessary to acknowledge that congestion cannot be fixed in the same way that our networks cannot be fully protected, and that we will have to find other ways to organise to cope with this. Presently we have a government and regulatory system that seek to offer some guarantee of a nominal level of service, but with future increases in demand, capacity constraints and external vulnerabilities it is one which they seem unlikely to be able to fulfil. Such a mismatch creates anger and resentment among travellers.

In other important ways, climate-related disruption is different in how it directly confronts our current decision-making paradigms. The impacts of low-frequency climate-related events can be significant, even disastrous, in local terms but they are often insignificant relative to the regular congestion caused by more frequent reliability issues. And it is the impacts of these day-to-day events that dominate the case for investment in transport improvements. Our vignette of the Dawlish rail diversion highlights the need to understand much more about the wider socio-economic impacts of low-frequency but high-impact events. The damage to small businesses, community cohesion or longer-term inward investment might all present a different set of arguments and rationales for investment than the current paradigm with its emphasis on daily time savings (Chapter 6). As the anticipated number and variety of major disruption events grows over time, so too will the evidence base to challenge conventional approaches. There are, of course, areas in the UK – such as England's far south west – where there is a mismatch between the intensity of day-to-day congestion (low) and the vulnerability to climatic events (high), and it is here that the current definition of 'transport need' to promote growth will be deemed weakest. As there will be fewer resources available to upgrade the resilience of the existing network as part of other capacity upgrades, we suggest that these spatial inequalities will become more significant over time.

It is also necessary to think ahead about information and accountability. Recent moves have, for example, strengthened the need to formalise assessment of the performance of the SRN. We are rapidly moving (or have already moved) from an era where information about the performance of the transport network is largely held by the operators and regulators of different parts of the infrastructure. As we highlighted earlier, travellers are often multi-modal and are certainly uninterested in which side of a geographical boundary they are on when their journeys are disrupted. The advent of smartphone technology and apps that track where, when and how people travel, mean that it will be individuals and software companies that aggregate real-time feeds from individuals experiencing the performance of the transport system, from door to door, by any mode or combination of modes (Docherty et al 2018; Chapter 15). Such knowledge could be used to challenge existing unimodal practices of planning and promote investment in the development of more effective multi-modal and cross-boundary operation of the network in the interests of travellers. By inference, greater multi-modality and integrated network analysis and planning should also promote greater resilience with the caveat that there needs to be some redundancy somewhere in the system for information about alternatives to be useful. It will also, over time, become easier to trace the impact of disruptive events on the number and purpose of journeys, allowing greater understanding of who and where is most affected.

Our assessment of the current position of policy and practice on managing disruption is of an incremental muddling through. Infrastructure improvements will happen, but slowly, and the risks of disruption will grow rather than diminish. In the meantime, travellers and businesses will continue their own ongoing adaptations such that these become less painful for many. Fundamentally, it seems to us that the greatest capacity to adapt to frequent and infrequent disruptions will generally exist where the distances between activities are shorter; the range of alternatives (routes and modes) for making the journey the greatest; the potential for re-timing or relocating activities the most well-rehearsed; and the orchestration of these events the most well developed. This sounds a bit like the sorts of measures that might be adopted for more sustainable urban mobility systems for every day of the year...

Notes

1. 'Mobility as a Service' is a system where people would pay for access to a range of mobility options rather than owning their own vehicle. The service provider would arrange both the integration of the mobility options and the pricing (Chapter 15).

2. We do not focus here on terrorism which is, fortunately, very infrequent. We of course acknowledge this does not make it insignificant. The additional time and resources required to oversee safe check-in at airports, for example, affects millions of journeys every year.

3. Rebuild costs for a typical rail section can be up to £100 million/km, or £14 million/lane km on roads (HM Treasury 2010).

4. Hard engineered flood projection costs range from £0.5–£11 million/ km (Environment Agency 2015).

References

Abrantes, P and Wardman, M (2011) 'Meta-analysis of UK values of travel time: an update', *Transportation Research Part A: Policy and Practice*, 45(1): 1–17.

Anable, J and Budd, T (2014) *Work Package 1 Questionnaire Survey – Descriptive Statistics*. Disruption Project Working Paper. University of Leeds, UK.

British Geological Survey (2016) *Geological indicators of flooding*. www. bgs.ac.uk/products/hydrogeology/indicatorsOfFlooding.html Accessed 29 October 2016.

Carrion, C and Levinson, D (2012) 'Value of travel time reliability: a review of current evidence', *Transportation Research Part A: Policy and Practice*, 46(4): 720–41.

Centre for Economics and Business Research (2014) *The future economic and environmental costs of gridlock in 2030*. A report for INRIX, July 2014. CEBR, London.

Committee on Climate Change (2016) *UK Climate Change Risk Assessment 2017: Synthesis report: priorities for the next five years*. CCC, London. www.theccc.org.uk/wp-content/uploads/2016/07/UK-CCRA-2017-Synthesis-Report-Committee-on-Climate-Change. pdf Accessed 8 October 2010.

Confederation of British Industry (2014) *Taking the long-view: A new approach to infrastructure*. CBI-URS Infrastructure Survey 2014 www.cbi.org.uk/media/3590298/cbi_urs_infrastructure_survey.pdf Accessed 15 January 2015.

Cornwall Council, Devon County Council, Plymouth City Council, Somerset County Council and Torbay Council (2013) *The case for greater investment across the south west peninsula railway network*. www.plymouth.gov.uk/sites/default/files/TheSouthWestSpine.pdf Accessed 11 July 2018.

Dawson, D (2012) *The impact of future sea-level rise on the London-Penzance railway line*. Unpublished PhD Thesis, University of Plymouth.

Dawson, D, Shaw, J and Gehrels, R (2016) 'Sea-level rise impacts on transport infrastructure: the notorious case of the coastal railway line at Dawlish, England', *Journal of Transport Geography*, 51: 97–109.

Department for Transport (2011) *Winter Resilience in Transport: an assessment of the case for additional investment*. DfT, London. https:// assets.publishing.service.gov.uk/government/uploads/system/ uploads/attachment_data/file/4557/an-assessment-of-the-case-for-additional-investment.pdf Accessed 8 October 2018.

Department for Transport (2014) *Transport Resilience Review: A review of the resilience of the transport network to extreme weather*. DfT, London. https://assets.publishing.service.gov.uk/government/uploads/system/uploads/attachment_data/file/335115/transport-resilience-review-web.pdf Accessed 8 October 2018.

Department for Transport (2015) *Road Investment Strategy: for the 2015/16 – 2019/20 Road Period*. DfT, London. www.gov.uk/government/publications/road-investment-strategy-for-the-2015-to-2020-road-period Accessed 8 October 2018.

Department for Transport (2016) *Travel time measures for the Strategic Road Network, England: January to March 2016*. Statistical release. DfT, London. https://assets.publishing.service.gov.uk/government/uploads/system/uploads/attachment_data/file/523918/travel-time-measures-srn-march-16.pdf Accessed 8 October 2018.

Department for Transport (2018) *Transport Secretary Chris Grayling commits to delivering a modern railway in the south-west resilient to extreme weather.* www.gov.uk/government/news/transport-secretary-chris-grayling-commits-to-delivering-a-modern-railway-in-the-south-west-resilient-to-extreme-weather Accessed 11 July 2018.

Department of Transport (1989) *Roads for Prosperity*. Cm 693. DoT, London.

Docherty, I, Marsden, G and Anable, J (2018) 'The governance of smart mobility', *Transportation Research Part A: Policy and Practice*, 115: 114–25.

Environment Agency (2015) *Cost estimation for coastal protection – summary of evidence Report –SC080039/R7*. EA, Bristol.

Fyfe, P (2013) 'Illustrating the accident: railways and the catastrophic picturesque in the Illustrated London News', *Victorian Periodicals Review*, 46(1): 61–91.

Goodwin, P and Lyons, G (2010) 'Public attitudes to transport: interpreting the evidence', *Transportation Planning and Technology*, 33(1): 3–17.

Graham, S (2010) 'When infrastructures fail', in S Graham (ed) *Disrupted Cities. When Infrastructure Fails*, London: Routledge, pp 1–26.

Guiver, J (2012) *Travel Disruption: Three Case Studies*. UCLAN Discussion Paper. Preston, UK.

Guiver, J and Jain, J (2011) 'Grounded: Impacts of and insights from the volcanic ash cloud disruption', *Mobilities*, 6(1): 41–55.

Hay, A (2013) 'Resilience: a developing planning tool', *Infrastructure Asset Management*, 1(4): 130–4.

Highways England (2016) *Climate Adaptation Risk Assessement*. https://assets.publishing.service.gov.uk/government/uploads/system/uploads/attachment_data/file/596812/climate-adrep-highways-england.pdf Accessed 1 June 2019.

HM Government (2011) *Climate Resilient Infrastructure: Preparing for a changing climate*. Cm 8065. https://assets.publishing.service.gov.uk/government/uploads/system/uploads/attachment_data/file/69269/climate-resilient-infrastructure-full.pdf Accessed 11 July 2018.

HM Treasury (2010) *Infrastructure Cost Review: Technical Report*. https://assets.publishing.service.gov.uk/government/uploads/system/uploads/attachment_data/file/192589/cost_study_technicalnote211210.pdf Accessed 11 July 2018.

HM Treasury (2016) *Public expenditure statistical analyses (PESA) 2016*. https://assets.publishing.service.gov.uk/government/uploads/system/uploads/attachment_data/file/539465/PESA_2016_Publication.pdf Accessed 11 July 2018.

House of Commons (2009) *The effects of adverse weather conditions on transport*. Fourth Report of the Transport Committee, House of Commons Session 2008–09, HC328. https://publications.parliament.uk/pa/cm200809/cmselect/cmtran/328/328.pdf Accessed 11 July 2018.

House of Commons (2014) Committee holds fourth evidence session on investing in the railway. www.parliament.uk/business/committees/committees-a-z/commons-select/transport-committee/news/investing-railway-ev4/ Accessed 11 July 2018.

House of Commons (2015) Investing in the railway. Seventh report of the Transport Committee of House of Commons session 2014–15, HC257. https://publications.parliament.uk/pa/cm201415/cmselect/cmtran/257/257.pdf Accessed 11 July 2018.

Intergovernmental Panel on Climate Change (2013) 'Summary for Policymakers', in T Stocker, D Qin, G-K Plattner, M Tignor, S Allen, J Boschung, A Nauels, Y Xia, V Bex and P Midgley (eds) *Climate Change 2013: The Physical Science Basis. Contribution of Working Group I to the Fifth Assessment Report of the Intergovernmental Panel on Climate Change*, Cambridge and New York: Cambridge University Press.

Jaroszweski, D, Chapman, L and Petts, J (2010) 'Assessing the potential impact of climate change on transportation: the need for an interdisciplinary approach', *Journal of Transport Geography*, 18(2): 331–5.

JR-Central (2014) *JR-Central Japan Railway Company Annual Report 2014*. https://global.jr-central.co.jp/en/ Accessed 1 October 2018.

Kay, P (1993) *Exeter – Newton Abbot: A Railway History*, Sheffield: Platform 5.

Marsden, G, Shires, J, Anable, J and Docherty, I (2016) *Travel Behaviour Response to Major Transport System Disruptions: Implications for Smarter Resilience Planning*. Discussion Paper 16–09. University of Leeds, UK.

Mattsson, L-G and Jenelius, E (2015) 'Vulnerability and resilience of transport systems – a discussion of recent research', *Transportation Research Part A: Policy and Practice*, 81: 16–34.

National Infrastructure Commission (2016) *The impact of population change and demography on future infrastructure demand*. www.gov.uk/government/publications/the-impact-of-population-change-and-demography-on-future-infrastructure-demand Accessed 11 July 2018.

Network Rail (2014a) *Weather and climate change resilience: how our routes are mitigating the impact of weather and climate change to maintain an efficient service*. www.networkrail.co.uk/publications/weather-and-climate-change-resilience/ Accessed 14 November 2014.

Network Rail (2014b) *Dawlish Railway information*. www.networkrail. co.uk/timetables-and-travel/storm-damage/dawlish/ Accessed 10 April 2014.

Network Rail (2014c) *West of Exeter Route Resilience Study*. www.networkrail.co.uk/publications/weather-and-climate-change-resilience/west-of-exeter-route-resilience-study/ Accessed 14 November 2014.

Network Rail (2015) *Climate Change Adaptation Report 2015*. Network Rail, London. https://cdn.networkrail.co.uk/wp-content/uploads/2016/11/Climate-Change-Adaptation-Report-2015_FINAL.pdf Accessed 8 October 2018.

Network Rail (2016) Public performance measures 2016. www.networkrail.co.uk/about/performance/ Accessed 29 October 2016.

Office of Rail and Road (2016) *Regional Rail Usage (Passenger Journeys) 2014–15 Annual Statistical Release*. http://orr.gov.uk/__data/assets/pdf_file/0006/20697/regional-rail-usage-2014-15.pdf Accessed 29 October 2016.

Ordnance Survey (2017) *Integrated Transport Network (ITN) [GML2 geospatial data]*. Scale 1:1250, Tiles: GB, Updated 22 May 2014, Ordnance Survey (GB), using EDINA Digimap Ordnance Survey Service, http://digimap.edina.ac.uk, Accessed 30 November 2017.

Parkes, S, Jopson, A and Marsden, G (2016) 'Understanding travel behaviour change during mega-events: Lessons from the London 2012 Games', *Transportation Research Part A: Policy and Practice*, 92: 104–19.

Shires, J, Ojeda Cabral, M and Wardman, M (2018) 'The impact of planned disruption on rail passenger demand', *Transportation*. Online early.

Shires, J, Marsden, G, Docherty, I and Anable, J (2016) *Forth Road Bridge Closure Survey: Analysis of Commuter Behaviour: Final Report, May 2016*. www.disruptionproject.net Accessed 1 October 2018.

The Times (1846) Regional News. *The Times*, London, 31 October, p 5.

Transport Focus (2015a) *Road user needs and experiences: Summary Report*. March 2015. www.transportfocus.org.uk/research-publications/publications/road-user-needs-and-experiences-summary-report/ Accessed 11 July 2018.

Transport Focus (2015b) National Rail Passenger Survey: Autumn 2015 Main Report. www.transportfocus.org.uk/research-publications/publications/national-rail-passenger-survey-nrps-autumn-2015-main-report/ Accessed 11 July 2018.

Transport Focus (2015c) *Reacting to extreme weather on the railways*. July 2015. www.transportfocus.org.uk Accessed 1 October 2018.

Transport Systems Catapult (2015) *IM Traveller Needs and UK Capability Study, supporting the realisation of Intelligent Mobility in the UK*. TSC, Milton Keynes.

Vollmer, H (2013) *The Sociology of Disruption, Disaster and Social Change: Punctuated Cooperation*, Cambridge: Cambridge University Press.

14

Changing demographics

Charles Musselwhite and Kiron Chatterjee

Introduction

Across the globe we live in an ageing society. Western countries especially are seeing rapid ageing due to a combination of people living longer because of better health and social care, and lower birth rates. This results in both a higher number and a higher percentage of people in their later years. There are now 840 million people over 60 across the world, representing 11.7 per cent of the population. In 1950, there were only 384.7 million people aged over 60, representing 8.6 per cent of the global population (UN 2015). Projections suggest that by 2050 there will be 2 billion people aged over 60, representing 21.2 per cent of the global population (UN 2015). The rate of increase in older people is faster in wealthier countries. For example, 25 per cent of the UK's population is likely to be over 60 by around 2030 (Office for National Statistics (ONS) 2013). Figure 14.1 illustrates the ageing of the UK population. It shows historical change between 1980 and 2014 as well as projections to 2050. There has been a large increase in the number of people aged 60 and over since 2000, and the number of people aged 75 and over increased from 3.2 million in 1980 to 5.2 million in 2014 and is set to increase to 11.6 million by the middle of the century. By contrast, the number of under-thirties has been fairly stable since 1980, although there was a decline between 1980 and 2000 which has now reversed (with a significant contribution from inward migration). Numbers are set to increase into the future, albeit at a lower rate of increase than older adults, and thus most of the projected growth in the population is expected to be of those aged 60 and over.

In this chapter, we examine trends in the travel behaviour of both younger and older adults, along with reasons for these trends and implications for transport policy and provision. With the average age of the UK population increasing, it is of course important to look at the travel behaviour of older people and how it is changing, but the

Figure 14.1: UK population composition estimates and projections by age group, 1980–2050

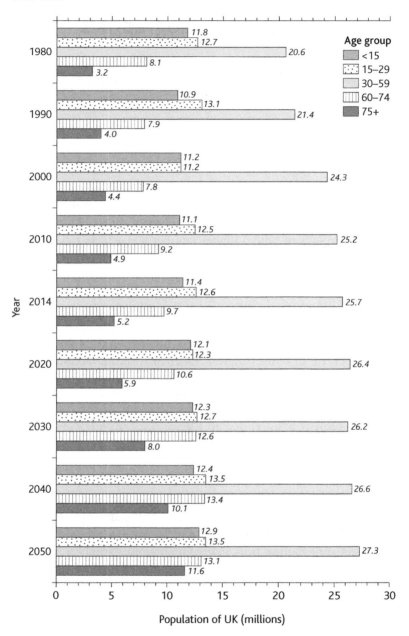

Sources: ONS 2013, 2015a, 2015b

travel behaviour of young people is also significant as patterns that develop in their early years are likely to be highly formative in shaping travel throughout their life course (Beuret 2016).

Car use by older people and young adults

Older people today are fitter and more active than in previous generations. Coupled with an increasingly hypermobile society, where connections with families and friends and accessing shops and services are more dispersed across space than ever before, a large increase in mobility has resulted among this age group. Much of this increase is geared around private mobility, and there has been a sharp increase in driving licence holding and miles driven by the over-60s. In Great Britain in 1975, only 15 per cent of people aged over 70 held a driving licence; by 2014, this had risen to 62 per cent (Department for Transport (DfT) 2015; Figure 14.2). Overall, fewer females hold licences than males, but there has been a greater than average increase in female licence holders in this age bracket, from 4 per cent in 1975 to 47 per cent in 2014. This compares with 32 per cent of males holding a licence in 1975 and 80 per cent in 2014 (DfT 2015).

Figure 14.2: Percentage of driving-licence holders by age categories in Great Britain, 1975–2013

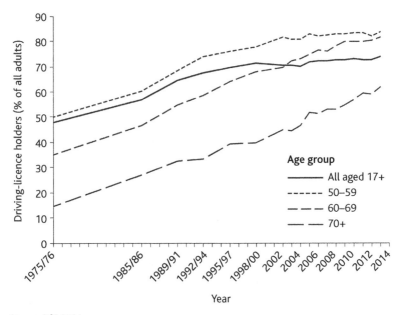

Source: DfT 2014

Across all modes, miles travelled tend to fall in later life, although in many wealthy countries distance driven is increasing year on year for older people against a backdrop of declining distance driven for the population as a whole. Since 1995, Britain has seen an 8 per cent reduction in the number of miles driven across all age groups, whereas for those aged over 70 the figure is a 77 per cent increase (DfT 2015). Noticeably, in the UK and many other high-income countries, the percentage of overall distance travelled as a passenger in a car increases for over-70s (DfT 2015), while the percentage of their distance travelled as a driver falls. In addition, miles travelled on buses increases for this age group. Females travel fewer miles per person across all ages and are much more likely to be multimodal throughout life, having higher percentages of their travel than men as car passengers, bus users and walkers (Chapter 4). This is even more pronounced in later life. As would be expected, miles travelled commuting to and from work or for work purposes falls dramatically – the over-70s travel only 95 miles per person per year against an average across all ages of 1,899 miles per person per year. At the same time, the over-70s are more likely than average to travel further on shopping trips (1,094 miles per person per year against the average across all ages of 769 miles per person per year) (DfT 2015).

Nevertheless, access to transport is a particular barrier for older people in relation to leisure travel. For example, 12 per cent of older people would like to visit family more often, 10 per cent would like to visit friends' homes more often and a further 10 per cent would like to meet friends elsewhere more often (DfT 2001). Visiting friends and relatives is slightly lower than average for the over-70s (1,112 miles per person per year for the over-70s against 1,297 miles per person per year across all ages) but is much lower than that of 50–59-year-olds (1,412 miles per person per year) and 60–69-year-olds (1,605 miles per person per year). This suggests an age effect which could get worse with time; people's expectations of leisure travel in later life are growing, and they could be frustrated if they are unable to undertake this.

In some contrast to the trends among older people, there has been a decline in car use among the younger population. This was examined in a study commissioned by the DfT (Chatterjee et al 2018). In Figure 14.3 we see that the trend of reduced licence holding for young adult men can be traced back to the early 1990s. The peak for 17–20-year-old men occurred in 1992/94 at 55 per cent, after which licence holding steadily declined until 2004 (29 per cent), rose again until 2007 (41 per cent) and declined once more until 2014 (34 per

Figure 14.3: Percentage of men with a driving licence by age group in England, 1975/76–2014

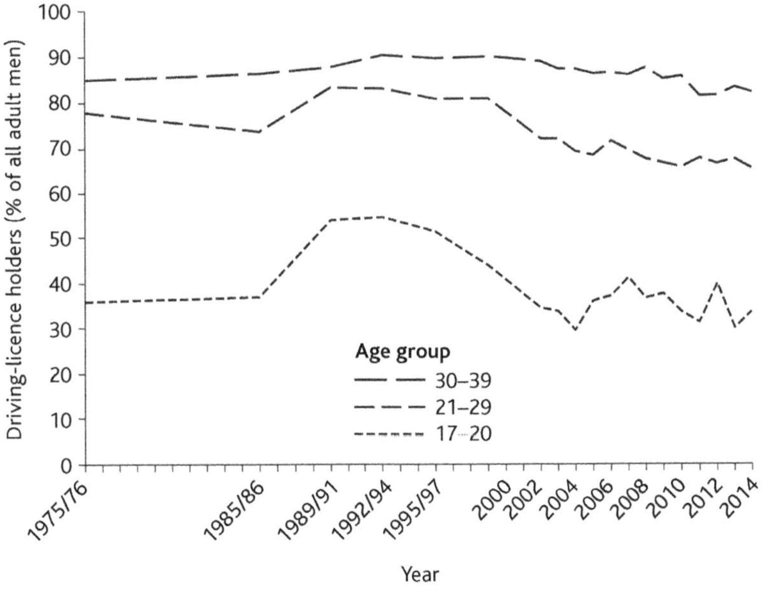

Source: DfT 2005

cent). The decline for women (Figure 14.4) has been more modest and can be traced back to the late 1990s. The overall outcome across both genders is that less than a third (29 per cent) of 17–20-year-olds held a full driving licence in 2014 compared to nearly a half (48 per cent) in 1992/94. Less than two thirds (63 per cent) of 21–29-year-olds had a full driving licence in 2014, compared to three quarters in 1992/94.

The reduction in licence holding has been accompanied by other changes in travel behaviour, identifiable from the National Travel Survey (NTS) (Chatterjee et al 2018):

- In 2010–14 less than half (47 per cent) of 25–29-year-olds were car drivers compared to 54 per cent in 1995–99.
- Over the same period, there has been a 20–30 per cent decrease in the total number of trips made by all modes among young adults.
- There has been a large reduction in how much young men drive (in terms of both trips and distance) of about forty per cent, and a more modest reduction for young women, which has led to the gap between young men and women's car travel almost disappearing.
- Mode share of trips by public transport increased by six percentage points between 1995 and 2012 for 21–29-year-olds, with a five

Figure 14.4: Percentage of women with a driving licence by age group in England, 1975/76–2014

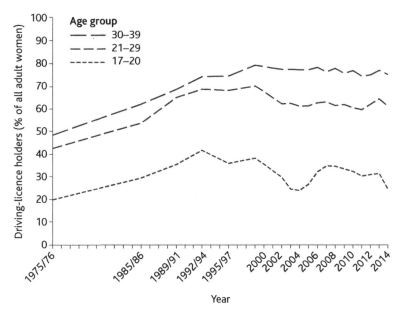

Source: DfT 2015

percentage-point reduction as car driver and a two percentage-point reduction on foot. The absolute number of additional public transport trips was modest, however.

These trends mean that men born from about 1980 onwards (referred to as Generation Y or Millennials) have reached 30 years of age with substantially lower licence rates and car driving mileage than previous cohorts. This cohort effect is also apparent for women but smaller in magnitude. These trends of lower car use are specific to young adults aged 17 and over and do not apply to pre-driving age young people, for whom there has been little change in travel behaviour including the amount they are driven by car. The trends are particularly striking for young men, although over the last 20 years there has been a reduction in trip making and car use for all working age men.

Factors underlying these shifting patterns

Older adults are more mobile and in particular are driving more than ever before, while young adults, men in particular, are driving less now than they did 20 years ago. The same phenomenon has been seen in other industrialised countries (Delbosc and Currie 2013, Institute for Mobility Research 2013). Why is this? Explanations are offered for the reduced driving of young adults in the DfT study (Chatterjee et al 2018), and it would appear that several factors are at play. The first is linked to demographics. There has been a long-term trend for later marriage and parenthood (Campbell et al 2014), and given that those with children are more likely to drive a car (Berrington and Mikolai 2014) these changes have contributed to reduced licence holding and car use of young adults. Moreover, the share of migrants in the total population of young people has risen sharply since the turn of the millennium (Vargas-Silva and Markaki 2015) and this is likely to have also contributed to reduced car use because newcomers are less likely to have a driving licence than those born in the UK (Berrington and Mikolai 2014). Older people are more likely than previous generations to have connections with family and friends that span large geographical distances, including internationally. Achieving 'co-presence' with such people requires higher mileage to be travelled.

A second factor is changes in people's living situations. Compared with previous generations, young people tend now to stay for a longer period with their parents (ONS 2015b), and are more likely to live in shared or rented accommodation (Dorling 2015) and in urban areas (Chen et al 2014). In turn, young people living in rented accommodation and in more urbanised areas are less likely to drive (Berrington and Mikolai 2014). It is less clear what effect living with parents has, but in combination these trends are considered to have contributed substantially to reduced car use and increased patronage on public transport. Older people, conversely, are more likely than the general population to be living in areas with a dispersed population (Mitchell 2018). Such areas are less well served by public transport and have fewer shops and services spread across a wider geographical area, meaning that cars are more likely to be required for accessibility (Chapter 12).

A third factor is people's socio-economic situation. For the young, this has changed considerably over recent decades. Increased participation in higher education (Higher Education Funding Council for England (HEFCE) 2013), a decline in young people's disposable income (Kingman and Seager 2014), a growth in low-end service jobs (McDowell 2014) and the rise of precarious employment (Standing 2013) are likely to be key contributors to a reduction in car use. These trends are more pronounced for young men than women, with the latter increasingly likely to be in full-time employment in their late twenties. This increases their likelihood of driving, and in turn this partly explains why the decline in car use has been more striking for young men. Older people, on the other hand, are more affluent than previous generations and as such more likely to be able to afford to run a car, although there is a growing divide between the rich and poor in later life and it is incorrect to think of all older people as well-off. Especially in areas of limited public transport provision, this divide can make a big difference to mobility and accessibility. Changes in retirement law have also led to more older people working, a trend that is set to continue into the future, and helps to explain why those aged 60–69 are travelling more miles, especially by car, than previously.

Another factor is the increasingly ubiquitous presence of information and communications technologies (ICTs) in everyday life. ICTs enable an increasing number of people to conduct activities and access goods, services, facilities and social networks without the need for physical mobility of their own. At the same time, they can stimulate mobility by making it easier for people to travel more to distant locations (online booking, and so on), and modify the way in which people travel by making them more aware of options or changing the relative attractiveness of transport modes (see Lyons 2015). The future effects of ICTs are uncertain. One review concluded:

> ...so far ICT usage either has no net impact on the amount of physical mobility that one performs, or... ICT and physical mobility may on balance be positively related (in economic terms, complementary), or even have a mutually modifying relationship (through modal shifts, changes in trip timing, or use of travelling time). (Pawlak et al 2015: 44)

This said, aggregate trends in travel and time use can be informative, because patterns of trip making are a potential indicator of the influence of ICTs. As we have seen, there have been contrasting trends by age group in the last 20 years (Chatterjee et al 2018), with young adults on average making fewer trips and spending more of their time at home, and trip rates remaining stable for those aged 60 and above. Two different interpretations can be offered for this. One is that the ability to undertake more activities at home may have caused less need and desire for travel. The other is that barriers to travel such as costs have led to young adults adapting their behaviour to undertake more activities at home; under this interpretation, the increasing amount of time spent at home is not a cause of reduced travel but a consequence of transport constraints. Either way, ICTs appear influential in reducing travel among young adults by facilitating a greater range of home-based activities. Older adults, meanwhile, are less likely to use the Internet for shopping, for accessing services and information and for social networking than other age groups (Ofcom 2017), and it appears for now at least that ICTs have not impacted upon the extent of their travel.

The fifth factor we identify is changing values and attitudes. After the Second World War, car use came to represent a symbol of independence and transition to adulthood, and this role has still been found to have some resonance in research with young people. At the same time, it may be that the cultural significance of the car and driving is at least in part being displaced by other items/activities (Delbosc and Currie 2014), although there is little academic research to confirm this. Evidence from a large sample in the United States has found a weaker 'auto orientation' – described as 'propensity to value the freedom and independence gained from owning cars and to disagree with the concept that borrowing or sharing a car is just as good as owning one' (Coogan et al 2016: 5) – for Millennials than other age groups. Older people appear still strongly to value the car as an expression of freedom, independence and remaining active (Musselwhite and Haddad 2010), but evidence is also limited as to whether this is changing over time. It is known that pro-environmental attitudes and behaviours tend to increase with age (Thornton 2009), but, interestingly, not in relation to mobility; for example, turning the television off and re-using carrier bags because of environmental concerns increases with age but walking, cycling or using public transport environmental reasons does not (Chatterton et al 2009; Chapter 5).

The sixth issue is the difficulty of learning to drive. This has increased after the introduction of a theory test in 1996 (Noble 2005) and increases in the costs of learning to drive and buying and insuring a car (Le Vine and Polak 2014) have also played a role in the reduced driving of young adults. Increases in insurance costs have been large for 'at-risk' driving groups at both ends of the age spectrum, but older motorists have been more able and willing to pay for these. The cost of motoring is strongly linked to our seventh and final factor capable of explaining the changing travel patterns of young and older adults, namely the existence (or otherwise) of alternatives to driving. Reductions between 2001 and 2011 in driving to work and increases in public transport use among young adults aged 16–34 occurred to the greatest extent for those living in London and in more densely populated areas (Chatterjee et al 2018). Indeed, over this time period the difference between the commuting mode choices of young adults in these areas and their peers living elsewhere widened. Possible reasons for this include: (i) improved public transport in London; (ii) employment in large cities being increasingly located in areas better served by public transport and more constrained for car commuting; (iii) housing costs and design in large cities making it prohibitive and inconvenient for young people to own and use a car; and (iv) young people who prefer and can afford an urban lifestyle (possibly because they choose not to own a car) increasingly concentrating in large cities. Further research is required to examine these hypotheses.

For older drivers, rising costs of car-use (such as escalating insurance bills) have not deterred car travel to the same extent as among younger people, despite the availability of free off-peak bus transport – the concessionary travel scheme – for the over-65s.[1] There is compelling evidence that use of the bus system increases with 'free' travel for older people, with around 60 per cent of older people reporting an increase in their bus use due to free travel (Baker and White 2010, Mackett 2013a, 2013b). In surveys, Hirst and Harrop (2011) found 74 per cent of their older respondents in Manchester said that having a pass enabled them to engage in new pursuits and visit new places, and Andrews (2011) found that 74 per cent of his respondents thought their free bus pass improved their quality of life. While becoming eligible for a free bus pass is associated with increased use of public transport (Webb et al 2011), this has not reduced the amount of driving among the older population; perhaps without the introduction nationwide of free bus travel, car use would have increased even further within this age group.

Due to population ageing and the financial crisis in 2008, there is currently significant interest in inter-generational justice (Higgs and Gilleard 2010, Houston and Tilley 2016) and a debate has ensued as to whether younger people would benefit from a concessionary travel pass of their own. Arguments for such an intervention are often positioned against the older people's scheme with a value judgement that the young are more in need and more worthy – for example, they are poorer as a cohort and need access to education, training and jobs, which older people do not, and while ability to pay is not a major barrier to many older people's mobility, cost may have become more significant for some younger people (Houston and Tilley 2016). Constructing the debate in such stark terms is unfortunate given the contributions made to society by older people, who may be working themselves, supporting others to work or performing voluntary and caring duties that require travel. There are also wider benefits for older people resulting from free bus travel, including improved physical health through reduced likelihood of being obese (Webb et al 2011) and social connections that can help ward off loneliness and isolation (Andrews 2011). Indeed, a recent report (Greener Travel 2014) using DfT guidance on economic appraisal found for every £1 spent on free bus passes for older people, £2.87 is returned to the economy (although see Chapter 6 on DfT economic appraisal techniques).

At the same time, the provision of free bus travel for older people is not without its problems. Bus companies are subsidised on a per-journey basis for accepting the concessionary travel pass, but there are no restrictions on how they use this revenue. This diverts a significant amount of money (£1.03 billion in England alone in 2016/17 (DfT 2017)) away from transport authorities being able to use it themselves for other transport investment – infrastructure, for example, or subsidies for other unprofitable public transport services (in the evenings, at weekends, in rural areas) – for the benefit of everybody, including older people. There is also an argument that older people who can afford the bus fare should contribute money towards it, and research has found that some would indeed be willing to contribute to their travel, especially where there are concerns about potential service withdrawal (Musselwhite 2018). It is worth remembering in this context that those in the highest income groups travel more in later life, including on public transport, and hence benefit more from receiving it free than more in-need lower income groups (Houston and Tilley 2016).

Community transport, another alternative to the car, is the provision of off-timetable services for a specialist population (typically those who don't have ordinary access to the bus because of difficulty in accessing conventional bus services), and has grown in prominence over the past 25 years (Chapter 12). It can be anything from an individual with a car through to large enterprises with 50 or so minibuses. Journeys typically suit the practical level of need, providing transport to shops, services and doctors and hospitals, but increasingly 'discretionary' journeys are being provided by some organisations (Musselwhite 2017). Perhaps unsurprisingly, community transport is very well received by people who use it, although there are barriers to use. It is quite common, for example, for people not to know about the existence of a service (Ward et al 2013, Parkhurst et al 2014), and services often only serve a subset of those that would benefit most from it. There can also be a feeling among older people that community transport is a service for someone other than themselves, for example, the infirm or for those with registered disabilities, and even where this is not the case a poor perception of community transport can arise where it is provided in cheap, old-fashioned and uncomfortable mini-buses. Lastly, the legal bureaucracy associated with running a service means it is hard to set up, making it difficult for an individual 'wanting to do something good' for a community. This results in top-down rather than bottom-up provision, favouring larger settlements where there are economies of scale, established providers and many people with resources, skills and expertise to run services.

Age-friendly transport

What emerges from the earlier discussion is that explanations for the decline in young adults' car use and increase in older people's car use lie primarily outside the transport sector. Changes in young people's travel behaviour have been related to the declining significance of many of the traditional markers of adulthood – stable employment, stable relationships and family life, an owner-occupied home in a suburban or ex-urban location and a traditional division of labour within the household. Insofar as the traditional markers of adulthood still represent a desired future for most young people (which can be debated), the realities of the labour and housing markets have made them unattainable for large groups of young adults; aspirations seem to have shifted accordingly for a substantial share of this group of the population. For older people, aspirations and markers for successful and active ageing have shifted to include being highly mobile, especially through private mobility. Since changes in mobility are deep-rooted and social in origin, they are multifarious and interlocking. The effects, therefore, of not having desired mobility can be substantial and can affect many aspects of individuals' lives.

The changes in travel behaviour of young adults are broad and complex and vary substantially within the young population, including between men and women. It is important to recognise the new realities of the lives and travel behaviour of young adults in policy analysis and development, at the very least paying more attention to the needs of the increasing number of people without car access. The participation of young adults in employment and other activities – and thus their current and future life opportunities – depends very much on there being alternatives to the private car. This of course requires consideration of public transport provision, but also other mobility options such as active travel and car and bicycle sharing as well as potential accessibility-based solutions such as superfast broadband.

There is a sense in which these changing patterns of travel behaviour offer a significant opportunity if they contribute to lower car-based mobility as young adults progress through the life course, because they are consistent with long-term goals of reducing adverse impacts of transport use (see, for example, Chapter 3). Interviews with young people indicate that while some are frustrated at not being able to drive, others do not feel the need in the foreseeable future and there is a view that if young adults move to suburbs on starting families – given the scarcity of affordable housing provision in urban areas – they will have become accustomed to using alternatives and be generally satisfied with these (Social Research Associates 2015). This would provide a market opportunity for transport providers, encouraged by local authorities, to develop and offer services such as on-demand public transport, car clubs and bicycle sharing. It is of course also possible that lower ownership and use of cars has adversely affected the quality of life and social mobility of certain groups of young adults by making it difficult to meet with friends and others, to access potential employment or education, or to participate in leisure activities individuals have reasons to value. Research in the United States has identified the increasing prevalence of a group of young adults labelled as 'car-less' – they make fewer trips than other young adults but do not all live in more densely populated areas – who are likely to be restricted in terms of their social participation (Ralph 2016). It should thus not be lost on policy makers that an important objective is to enable young people in all socio-economic and living situations to access relevant destinations in ways that are both environmentally and socially sustainable.

For older people, being mobile as they age is linked to quality of life (Schlag et al 1996). Giving up driving has repeatedly been shown to relate to a decrease in wellbeing and an increase in depression and other related health problems, and even increased mortality. This can be because of a reduced number of out-of-home activities and associated reduction in social networks (Harrison and Ragland 2003, Mezuk and Rebok 2008), an increased dependency on others and a reduction in independence (Rosenbloom, 2001, Siren and Hakamies-Blomqvist 2009), feelings of now being at odds with societal norms of using the car (Musselwhite and Haddad 2010, Schwanen and Zieglar 2011) and the conception of loss associated with the view that using the car is associated with being young and healthy (Musselwhite and Shergold 2013). Ziegler and Schwanen (2011) conclude that driving cessation constitutes a major life event for older people with equivalent long-term consequences for wellbeing as losing one's spouse or job. Those more likely to give up driving include women (Braitman and Williams 2011, Hakamies-Blomqvist and Wahlström 1998), the over-80s (Edwards et al 2009, McNamara et al 2013), those who have been less reliant on the car throughout their lives (Hakamies-Blomqvist and Siren 2003, Rabbitt et al 1996) or who have had chronic or acute health problems (Siren and Haustein 2016) and people with the support of family and friends.

We might well ask, how have we ended up with the car being such a powerful force that giving up driving can be linked with such detrimental outcomes? Decades of investing more in private mobility than public transport and the active modes (Wright and Egan 2000), and clever marketing by car manufacturers aimed at people's practical and emotive needs have resulted in a strong attachment to the car among the older generation. Transport investment has been focused on the strategic road and rail networks with a view to supporting the economy, and this tends to marginalise the important unpaid work contributed by older people (Parkhurst et al 2014). People in the UK aged 65–74 are those most likely to be involved in voluntary activities, a mobilisation essential to notions of civic engagement and the 'big society' favoured by successive Western governments as a way of meeting needs at a time of austerity budgets for the public sector (Hennessy et al 2014). In addition, older people support others, for example by looking after grandchildren enabling their son or daughter to work, yet this is not recognised by a narrow economic definition of labour. Finally, older people seem to receive little attention in transport planning surveys, models and analyses (Evans, et al 2012, Parkhurst et al 2014) and as a result their transport needs often receive little attention in transport (and urban and regional) planning documents.

Transport is important in later life because it connects people together with other people and the things that are necessary for a good quality and healthy life. In our hypermobile world, where successive government policies championing the car have made distances between home and work, shops, services and communities longer than ever, the car allows connectivity without recourse to the sometimes considerable physical effort needed to traverse long distances by public transport or the active modes. But the negative aspects of car-dominant policies are more likely to be detrimental to car-less people at the margins, including a considerable number of younger and older people. Hypermobility means people work and live in different places, local communities are severed and broken, and dormitory towns are created where people only sleep and eat. Younger and older people, meanwhile, spend more time closer to home, in and around neighbourhoods that once flourished and were a source of community but can now be quiet, with few or no shops or services and empty of residents during the day.

There is still a long way to go to reverse the damage of decades of car-centric policies, not least in terms of recreating neighbourhoods and communities, making places somewhere people desire to be part of, somewhere where it is worth walking to and within, rather than just being dormitory towns or movement corridors (Chapter 9). There is a need to start visioning what we want from an age-friendly community and place transport and mobility at the heart of that vision. A key means of achieving this would be for transport strategies to adopt a life course approach to understand how policies may impact on different age groups. For example, Local Transport Plans might be required to include evidenced statements as to how particular policies or combinations of policies would affect people at key stages across the life course, with the expectation of a positive impact or a strong justification as to why negative impacts should be accepted (Musselwhite 2016).

Conclusions

In this chapter we have demonstrated that the needs of older people and young adults are not necessarily being met with the legacy transport systems and services and broader societal organisation based around assumption of ubiquitous car access and use. There is a substantial number of older people and a growing number of younger people who are non-drivers and it is paramount that such people are taken into account in future planning. To some extent it is hypothesised that increased use of ICTs is reducing the need for physical mobility, although those who have used cars find it hard to replace the mobility that the car affords through such virtual means. Without proper understanding of the importance of the car to the individual, it is uncertain whether trends in non-car use among younger drivers are impacting upon access to education and job markets and reducing quality of life, especially outside of urban areas where public transport is lacking.

We can paint both a positive and a negative future based on current trends. Given the lower rates of Millennials driving, there is the potential that this will help them as they age. Older people who have had a history of being multimodal throughout their life are healthier and happier when they give up driving. They are much more likely to experiment with different modes post-car, much more likely to walk and more likely to feel their needs are met (Musselwhite and Shergold 2013). In the longer term, we may not see such negative outcomes for future generations with regard to giving up driving in later life since they are less likely to be drivers, or to drive as many miles as the current older population.

Focusing on age has revealed the disconnect between service provision and individual mobility needs, wants and desires. On the one hand, transport policy and practice continues to see transport as a means to an end and as a way of driving the economy. On the other hand, people view the importance of mobility not only in serving practical needs, but also in terms of identity, independence and status. For young people of today, there is a suggestion that the smartphone has replaced the car in meeting some of these needs but it has not yet been understood whether an increasing reliance on virtual services in early adulthood will have a negative impact on later life outcomes. Older people's ability to be mobile signals to the world that they are still fit and engaged, helps them stay connected to communities and in turn helps give them an understanding of their place in society relative to others. A lack of mobility, conversely, appears to be detrimental to physical and mental health. Ultimately, younger and older people, more than other age groups, often require types of mobility not suited to a commuting-dominant model of transport planning, such as off-peak, multimodal journey opportunities. Examining mobility in relation to age suggests a need to look more roundly at how transport matters across the population as a whole, and from the viewpoints of individuals and their relationship with society.

Note

[1] In England, outside of London, eligibility for the scheme was originally for those who were 60 and over but this will rise to those 66 and over as the state pension age for women is gradually increased. Currently, in London, Scotland, Wales and Northern Ireland eligibility is for those aged 60 and over.

References

Andrews, G (2011) *Just the Ticket? Exploring the Contribution of Free Bus Fares Policy to Quality of Later Life*. Unpublished PhD thesis, University of the West of England, Bristol.

Baker, S and White, P (2010) 'Impacts of concessionary travel: case study of an English rural region', *Transport Policy*, 17(1): 20–6.

Berrington, A and Mikolai, J (2014) Young Adults' Licence-Holding and Driving Behaviour in the UK: Full Findings. RAC Foundation, London. www.racfoundation.org/assets/rac_foundation/content/downloadables/Young-Adults-Licence-Holding-Berrington-Mikolai-DEC-2014.pdf Accessed 12 July 2019.

Beuret, K (2016) *Children and Travel. ITC Occasional Paper 9.* Independent Transport Commission, London.

Braitman, K and Williams, A (2011) 'Changes in self-regulatory driving among older drivers over time', *Traffic Injury Prevention*, 12(6): 568–75.

Campbell, M, Robards, J and McGowan, T (2014) *Comparing changing age-specific fertility across the United Kingdom using Lexis diagrams.* ESRC Centre for Population Change Working Paper 50.

Chatterjee, K, Goodwin, P, Schwanen, T, Clark, B, Jain, J, Melia, S, Middleton, J, Plyushteva, A, Ricci, M, Santos, G and Stokes, G (2018) *Young People's Travel – What's Changed and Why? Review and Analysis.* Department for Transport, London. www.gov.uk/ government/publications/young-peoples-travel-whats-changed-and-why Accessed 26 June 2018.

Chatterton, T, Coulter, A, Musselwhite, C, Lyons, G and Clegg, S (2009) 'Understanding how transport choices are affected by environment and health: views expressed in a study on the use of carbon calculators', *Public Health*, 123(1): 45–9.

Chen, Q, Levine, S and Polak, J (2014) *Generation Next: The Changing Travel Habits of Pre-Driving Age Young People in Britain.* RAC Foundation, London.

Coogan, M, Ajzen, I, Bhat, C, Lee, B, Ryerson, M and Schwieterman, J (2016) *Intercity Passenger Rail in the Context of Dynamic Travel Markets.* National Cooperative Rail Research Program (NCRRP) Report 4. Transportation Research Board, Washington, DC.

Delbosc, A and Currie, G (2013) 'Causes of youth licensing decline: a synthesis of evidence', *Transport Reviews*, 33(3): 271–90.

Delbosc, A and Currie, G (2014) 'Using discussion forums to explore attitudes toward cars and licensing among young Australians', *Transport Policy*, 31: 27–34.

Department for Transport (2001) *Older Drivers: A Literature Review.* DfT, London.

Department for Transport (2015) *National Travel Survey.* www.gov.uk/ government/collections/national-travel-survey-statistics Accessed 14 April 2016.

Department for Transport (2017) *Annual bus statistics: England 2016/17.* https://assets.publishing.service.gov.uk/government/uploads/ system/uploads/attachment_data/file/666759/annual-bus-statistics-year-ending-march-2017.pdf Accessed 22 October 2018.

Dorling, D (2015) 'Policy, politics, health and housing in the UK', *Policy & Politics*, 43(2): 163–80.

Edwards, J, Perkins, M, Ross, L and Reynolds, S (2009) 'Driving status and three-year mortality among community-dwelling older adults', *Journals of Gerontology Series A: Biological Sciences and Medical Sciences*, 64A(2): 300–5.

Evans, S, Hills, J and Orme, J (2012) 'Doing more for less? Developing sustainable systems of social care in the context of climate change and public spending cuts', *British Journal of Social Work*, 42(4): 744–64.

Greener Travel (2014) *Concessionary travel costs and benefits September 2014*. www.greenerjourneys.com/bus-pass/research/ Accessed 6 April 2017.

Hakamies-Blomqvist, L and Wahlström, B (1998) 'Why do older drivers give up driving?' *Accident Analysis and Prevention*, 30(3): 305–12.

Hakamies-Blomqvist, L and Siren, A (2003) 'Deconstructing a gender difference: driving cessation and personal driving history of older women', *Journal of Safety Research*, 34(4): 383–8.

Harrison, A and Ragland, D (2003) 'Consequences of driving reduction or cessation for older adults', *Transportation Research Record: Journal of the Transportation Research Board*, 1843(1): 96–104.

Hennessy, C, Means, R and Burholt, V (2014) 'Countryside connections in later life: Setting the scene', in C Hennessey, R Means and V Burholt (eds) *Countryside Connections: Older People, Community and Place in Rural Britain*, Bristol: Policy Press, pp 1–30.

Higgs, P and Gilleard, C (2010) 'Generational conflict, consumption and the ageing welfare state in the United Kingdom', *Ageing and Society*, 30(8): 1439–51.

Higher Education Funding Council for England (2013) *Trends in young participation in higher education*. www.hefce.ac.uk/pubs/year/2013/201328/ Accessed 17 April 2016.

Hirst, E and Harrop, B (2011) *Getting Out and About: Investigating the Impact of Concessionary Fares on Older People's Lives*. Transport Action Group, Manchester.

Houston, D and Tilley, S (2016) 'Fare's fair? concessionary travel policy and social justice', *The Journal of Poverty and Social Justice*, 24(2): 187–207.

Institute for Mobility Research (2013) *Mobility 'Y' – The Emerging Travel Patterns of Generation Y*. Institute for Mobility Research, Munich. http://www.ifmo.de/publications.html?t=6 Accessed 6 April 2017.

Kingman, D and Seager, A (2014) *Squeezed Youth: The Intergenerational Pay Gap and the Cost of Living Crisis*. The Intergenerational Foundation, London.

Le Vine, S and Polak, J (2014) 'Factors associated with young adults delaying and forgoing driving licenses: Results from Britain', *Traffic Injury Prevention*, 15(8): 794–800.

Lyons, G (2015) 'Viewpoint: Transport's digital age transition', *Journal of Transport and Land Use*, 8(2): 1–19.

Mackett, R (2013a) 'The impact of concessionary bus travel on the wellbeing of older and disabled people', *Transportation Research Record: Journal of the Transportation Research Board*, 2352(1): 114–19.

Mackett, R (2013b) The benefits of a policy of free bus travel for older people. In: *Proceedings of the 13th World Conference on Transport Research*, Rio de Janeiro, 15–18 July.

McDowell, L (2014) 'The sexual contract, youth, masculinity and the uncertain promise of waged work in austerity Britain', *Australian Feminist Studies*, 29(79): 31–49.

McNamara, A, Chen, G, George, S, Walker, R and Ratcliffe, J (2013) 'What factors influence older people in the decision to relinquish their driver's licence? A discrete choice experiment', *Accident Analysis and Prevention*, 55: 178–84.

Mezuk, B and Rebok, G (2008) 'Social integration and social support among older adults following driving cessation', *Journals of Gerontology Series B: Psychological Sciences and Social Sciences*, 63(5): 298–303.

Mitchell, C (2018) 'Are older people safe drivers on the roads, testing and training?', in C Musselwhite (ed) *Transport, Travel and Later Life*, Bingley: Emerald, pp 37–64.

Musselwhite, C (2016) Vision for an age friendly transport system in Wales. *EnvisAGE, Age Cymru* 11, pp 14–23.

Musselwhite, C (2017) 'Exploring the importance of discretionary mobility in later life', *Working with Older People*, 21(1): 49–58.

Musselwhite, C (2018) 'Public and community transport', in C Musselwhite (ed) *Transport, Travel and Later Life*, Bingley: Emerald, pp 117–28.

Musselwhite, C and Haddad, H (2010) 'Mobility, accessibility and quality of later life', *Quality in Ageing and Older Adults*, 11(1): 25–37.

Musselwhite, C and Shergold, I (2013) 'Examining the process of driving cessation in later life', *European Journal of Ageing*, 10(2): 89–100.

Noble, B (2005) *Why are some young people choosing not to drive?* Proceedings of European Transport Conference, Strasbourg, France, 18–20 September 2005. http://abstracts.aetransport.org/paper/index/id/2097/confid/11 Accessed 7 March 2016.

Ofcom (2017) Adults' media use and attitudes Report 2017. https://www.ofcom.org.uk/__data/assets/pdf_file/0020/102755/adults-media-use-attitudes-2017.pdf Accessed 23 November 2017.

Office for National Statistics (2013) *Mid-1971 to Mid-2012 Population Estimates: Quinary age groups for Constituent Countries in the United Kingdom.* ONS, London.

Office for National Statistics (2015a) *Annual Mid-Year Population Estimates for the UK.* www.ons.gov.uk/peoplepopulationandcommunity/populationandmigration/populationestimates/bulletins/annualmidyearpopulationestimates/latest Accessed 6 April 2017.

Office for National Statistics (2015b) *2014-based National Population Projections.* www.ons.gov.uk/peoplepopulationandcommunity/populationandmigration/populationprojections/bulletins/nationalpopulationprojections/2015-10-29 Accessed 6 April 2017.

Parkhurst, G, Galvin, K, Musselwhite, C, Phillips, J, Shergold, I and Todres, L (2014) 'Beyond transport: understanding the role of mobilities in connecting rural elders in civic society', in C Hennessey, R Means and V Burholt (eds) *Countryside Connections: Older People, Community and Place in Rural Britain*, Bristol: Policy Press, pp 125–57.

Pawlak, J, Le Vine, S, Polak, J, Sivakumar, A, Kopp, J (2015) *ICT and Physical Mobility: State of knowledge and future outlook.* Institute for Mobility Research, Munich. www.ifmo.de/publications.html Accessed 9 December 2015.

Rabbitt, P, Carmichael, A, Jones, S and Holland, C (1996) *When and why older drivers give up driving.* Foundation for Road Safety Research, Basingstoke, UK.

Ralph, K (2016) 'Multimodal millennials? The four traveler types of young people in the United States in 2009', *Journal of Planning Education and Research*, 37(2): 150–63.

Rosenbloom, S (2001) 'Sustainability and automobility among the elderly: an international assessment', *Transportation*, 28(4): 375–408.

Schlag, B, Schwenkhagen, U and Trankle, U (1996) 'Transportation for the elderly: towards a user-friendly combination of private and public transport', *IATSS Research*, 20(1): 75–82.

Schwanen, T and Ziegler, F (2011) 'Wellbeing, independence and mobility: an introduction', *Ageing and Society*, 31(5): 719–33.

Siren, A and Hakamies-Blomqvist, L (2009) 'Mobility and well-being in old age', *Topics in Geriatric Rehabilitation*, 25(1): 3–11.

Siren, A and Haustein, S (2016) 'Driving Cessation Anno 2010. Which older drivers give up their license and why? Evidence from Denmark', *Journal of Applied Gerontology*, 35(1): 18–38.

Social Research Associates (2015) *On the move: exploring attitudes to road and rail travel in Britain.* Independent Transport Commission, London. www.theitc.org.uk/our-research/research-reports-2/ Accessed 6 April 2017.

Standing, G (2013) 'Why zero-hours contracts remind me of the horrors of 1990s Russia', *The Guardian,* www.theguardian.com/ commentisfree/2013/apr/09/zero-hours-contracts-1990s-russia Accessed 9 April 2016.

Thornton, A (2009) Public attitudes and behaviours towards the environment – tracker survey: A report to the Department for Environment, Food & Rural Affairs. Defra, London. http:// webarchive.nationalarchives.gov.uk/20130123162956/http:/www. defra.gov.uk/statistics/files/report-attitudes-behaviours2009.pdf Accessed 6 April 2017.

United Nations (2015) *World Population Ageing.* United Nations, New York. www.un.org/en/development/desa/population/publications/ pdf/ageing/WPA2015_Report.pdf Accessed 6 April 2017.

Vargas-Silva, C and Markaki, Y (2015) *Geographical Distribution and Characteristics of Long-Term International Migration Flows to the UK.* Migration Observatory, University of Oxford, 4th Revision, 29 May 2015.

Ward, M, Somerville, P and Alamanos, E (2013) *Rural Transport and Older People in Lincolnshire, Final Report.* University of Lincoln and Lincolnshire County Council, Lincoln.

Webb, E, Netuveli, G and Millett, C (2011) 'Free bus passes, use of public transport and obesity among older people in England', *Journal of Epidemiology and Community Health,* 66(2): 176–80.

Wright, C and Egan, J (2000) 'De-marketing the car', *Transport Policy,* 7(4): 287–94.

Ziegler, F and Schwanen, T (2011) '"I like to go out to be energised by different people": an exploratory analysis of mobility and wellbeing in later life', *Ageing and Society,* 31(05): 758–81.

15

Will the 'smart mobility' revolution matter?

Graham Parkhurst and Andrew Seedhouse

'Smart Mobility': the transport sector in transition?

In essence, 'smart mobility' is the belief that by significantly increasing the application of computer science technologies in the transport sector, long-term aspirations for more efficient movement of people and goods, with fewer negative consequences, will finally be realised. In this vein, since 2010, there has been a steady stream of publications from global consultancy firms seeking at once to offer an 'insider's guide' to a revolution in the transport sector identified as highly-lucrative, while showcasing the credentials of key personnel to provide services in that transforming market (for example, Lerner 2011, Graham 2013, Van Audenhove et al 2014, Bouton et al 2015). To this end, Arthur D Little (Lerner 2011) identified 'niches of potential' related to 39 'key technologies' and 36 'potential urban mobility business models' which would, by 2050, be contributing to a market forecast to be worth $829 billion per annum. The same firm, in a follow-up publication three years later (Van Audenhove et al 2014: 7), referred to 'a clear trend' to 'Urban Mobility 2.0,' identifying '[i]mperatives to shape extended mobility ecosystems of tomorrow.' The following year, McKinsey & Co (Bouton et al 2015) titled its offering 'urban mobility at a tipping point'.

These visions of the future show a high degree of conformity around a global perspective in which the industrialising states are assumed to undergo significant urbanisation and economic growth. Further, they share beliefs in a trend away from traditional transport systems to 'mobility services', the latter increasingly combining transport and digital technologies to deliver more personalised and flexible travel options. This integrative platform serves within these visions to underlie a novel mobility 'ecosystem', which is foreseen to nurture two technical transitions: i) the shift from internal combustion engines (ICE) powered by liquid carbon fuels to battery electric vehicles (BEVs), and ii) the adoption of road vehicles which are increasingly driven by robotic systems and digitally connected with other road system 'agents' in a cooperative way. Moreover, within this new ecosystem, levels of sharing of road vehicles not seen in the industrialised states since prior to mass adoption of the private car are predicted to emerge. Taken together, the facets of this new 'smart' mobility are presented as offering cleaner, more efficient, and greater volumes of mobility, while creating significant economic rewards in the process.

Indeed, from transport sector professionals committed to sustainable development and government departments, there is enthusiasm that smart mobility will be a different basis of mobility precisely because it will break the historic association between transport development and both energy consumption and social and environmental costs (Department for Transport (DfT) 2015). Here, rather than underpinning the next wave of capitalism or furthering 'progress', smart mobility is able to underpin more 'liveable', productive cities, in which accessibility needs are met but with urban spaces less dominated by the infrastructure and practices associated with the private car (Skinner and Bidwell 2016). Central to this vision is the idea of the 'better mobility mix' in which informed, rational and pro-social citizens choose the form of travel that is 'optimised' for the situation. In short, the shared 'policy discourse' (Hajer 1995) asserts that the future transport systems in the industrialised democracies should exhibit:

- fewer vehicles on the road networks than now;
- significantly higher average vehicle loading;
- simplified access to information, ticketing and the services themselves, regardless of transport mode or which agency is the supplier;
- vehicles that are powered in a more energy efficient way and which produce fewer in-street emissions; and
- effective 'cohabitation' between motor vehicles other road uses on all but limited-access highways.

With the important exception of 'higher vehicle occupancy', which immediately conflicts with important social norms around personal space and individual agency, and also some difference of views around the sharing of streets, the 'future of urban mobility' would be for many, and in many respects, a positive one. Yet a number of important strategic questions must be answered before it can be ascertained whether, and how, this smart mobility revolution 'matters'. These include: is such a vision underpinned by feasible technological change? Under what circumstances? If it is feasible, by when might it be realised? How widespread and socially inclusive might its influence be: will it be the mainstream mobility experience of most citizens, or confined to a handful of 'world cities'? And most importantly, would the socio-technical changes proposed actually result in the economic and environmental benefits promised?

In seeking to address such questions, we will in this chapter summarise and interrogate the four key technological shifts that underpin the transition to a new mobility, considering in turn connected and autonomous vehicles (CAVs), electric vehicles (EVs), digitally enabled mobility (DEM) and collaborative/shared mobility (CM). We consider the factors that support and constrain the development of these four trends and consider how far each is likely to support or threaten current policy objectives. CAVs are considered in the next section, then EVs in the following section. The emergence of digitally enabled and collaborative mobilities are sufficiently intertwined that we consider them in an integrated third section. Our emphasis is on urban areas, as much of the development and policy focus is currently there, although we draw out implications for suburban and rural areas where possible (Chapter 12). In the final section, we seek to synthesise the smart mobility developments, considering in more detail their interactions and dependences, in order to offer our view about whether the four developments together suggest that more sustainable mobility is now in reach.

Connected and autonomous vehicles

The emergence of CAVs involves a range of technologies. These are divisible into sensing, processing and decision-making systems that provide automated driving or 'self' driving capacity to road vehicles, and communications systems which enable connectivity between vehicles or between vehicles and a road infrastructure management system. Autonomous vehicles do not need to be connected to function, but a number of technical advantages, including data acquisition and processing efficiency, have led commentators to argue they will be (KPMG/Center for Automotive Research (CAR) 2012). One of the key benefits would be the possibility to manage and optimise the movements of individual vehicles and flow of traffic streams, at which point it is in fact more appropriate to refer to 'automated' rather than 'autonomous' vehicles. From the perspective of the individual citizen-motorist, the road system becomes a very different proposition, with 'free will' potentially limited to selecting origin and destination, and perhaps some routing and timing preferences. It also greatly increases potential concerns about cybersecurity, if a whole system, rather than an individual vehicle, might potentially be 'hacked'.

Apparently accepting the view that cybersecurity measures will be effective, the UK government (DfT 2015) has identified a broad range of potential benefits from the adoption of CAVs, including the possibility to enhance the mobility of groups unable to drive themselves, energy-use and emissions reductions, as well as 'freeing up' time spent driving for a more productive journey experience. The most salient political argument to date, however, has been the potential to approach 'vision zero' levels of road safety by eliminating human errors from the driving task, identified as present in over 90 per cent of incidents (Fagnant and Kockelman 2015). (And while we focus here on autonomy in the road passenger transport sector, as a critical subsector for transport policy, automation is already important on railways, in aviation and in the logistics supply chain in the form of automated warehouses. It has potential in container terminals, shipping movements within ports and eventually on the open seas, and as a means of 'last mile' delivery by aerial drone (Paddeu et al 2019). Moreover, automation is well established in transport-sector support systems, from self-service ticket machines through to unstaffed public cycle hire.)

Growing automation is a cross-sectoral technological change that is affecting domains ranging from hazardous industrial activities and precision tasks such as surgery and healthcare, to labour intensive activities such as driving. A recent analysis (Roberts et al 2017) estimated that '60 per cent of occupations have at least 30 per cent of activities which could be automated with already-proven technologies,' though with considerable variation between sectors and roles. Ultimately, if all the technical, regulatory, financial and public acceptance barriers are overcome, professional road transport-driving jobs could disappear. At the same time, a far greater quantity of labour is invested by drivers transporting themselves or others on a personal or voluntary basis or for employer's business during the hours of work. Automated vehicles could eliminate the need for a driver to provide 'escort' trips to deliver others, and it may be possible to put in-vehicle time to a more productive (or 'consumptive') use. It is for this reason that, of the new technologies, automation has the potential to radically influence not just the transport system, but the whole basis of the automobile society.

It is necessary to point out that even just considering technical constraints, the transition to fully automated road vehicles is predicted to take decades. As well as the technical constraints, a significant barrier is the hugely extensive sunk investment in non–automated vehicles and production capacity. The transition has been described in technical capability terms by professional institutions such as the Society of Automotive Engineers (SAE) (2014), which identifies a hierarchy of five levels of automation (Table 15.1). KPMG (2015: 10)

Table 15.1: Society of Automotive Engineers' definitions of automation levels

SAE Level	Narrative definition	Example(s)
5: Full Automation	The full-time performance by an automated driving system of all aspects of the dynamic driving task under all roadway and environmental conditions that can be managed by a human driver	Full end-to-end journey
4: High Automation	The driving mode-specific performance by an automated driving system of all aspects of the dynamic driving task, even if a human driver does not respond appropriately to a request to intervene	Remote Parking; Urban Automated Driving; Low-Speed Autonomous Transport Systems without guideway but off public roads ('pods')
3: Conditional Automation	The driving mode-specific performance by an automated driving system of all aspects of the dynamic driving task with the expectation that the human driver will respond appropriately to a request to intervene	Highway Autopilot; Valet Parking Assist
2: Partial Automation	The driving mode-specific execution by one or more driver assistance systems of both steering and acceleration/deceleration using information about the driving environment and with the expectation that the human driver performs all remaining aspects of the dynamic driving task	Traffic Jam Assist
1: Driver Assistance	The driving mode-specific execution by a driver assistance system of either steering or acceleration/deceleration using information about the driving environment and with the expectation that the human driver performs all remaining aspects of the dynamic driving task	Intelligent Speed Adaptation; Lane Keep Assist; Autonomous Emergency Braking

Source: SAE International 2014

reports a relatively cautious, if still ambitious, prediction indicating that just 2 per cent of the UK vehicle fleet would be fully automated by 2030, although 80 per cent are expected to be connected and 40 per cent achieving SAE Level 3. Approaching half of vehicles would therefore be equipped with features such as automated self-parking for urban areas and a high level of driver assistance on highways, although, critically, not to the extent of releasing the driver from the task of actually driving the vehicle. Highways are seen as the least complex environment in which to provide automation, due to the limited set of vehicle interactions and their exclusive use by motorised vehicle traffic capable of high speeds, followed by urban areas, where there is some segregation of flows on most streets. Road user interactions, particularly in shared spaces, remain problematic, and rural roads, with higher speeds than urban areas and often lacking pavements, represent the toughest challenge. Indeed, such are the complexities of rural environments that it is not certain that the entire existing public road network in all states can be made 'machine readable' (Stilgoe 2017).

Despite the uncertainties about when (and in some quarters *if*) Level 5 operation would be possible, the level of driver assistance features in cars already available to purchase is rising. By 2017, a growing share of new vehicles was already equipped with Level 1 and 2 features, and a small number of models featured aspects of Level 3. While the latter were marketed as 'driver assist' features, there had already been high-profile crashes in which a key factor was the driver using the feature as temporary 'driver-replacement'. Similarly, connectivity was growing, with the European automatic emergency call system (eCall) to be present in all new vehicles sold in the continent from April 2018. The systems of a typical passenger car already collect a large quantity of data, which could provide dynamic information to a road system manager, once the legal, regulatory and infrastructure barriers are overcome.

For whom might CAVs matter most?

Despite strong government and industry support for CAVs, a review of public opinion surveys (Clark et al 2016) found that US, UK and Australian respondents showed polarised attitudes towards autonomous vehicles, with half to two thirds preferring a human-driven car. Notably, preferences were much more favourable in samples from industrialising states, reflecting the lower level of licence holding. By contrast, in the industrialised states at least, driver assistance technologies already have proven appeal for those who have acquired a driving licence and prefer to retain legal responsibility at all times for the motion of the vehicle, but would like to reduce the cognitive and physical load of driving. In addition to reducing the fatigue from driving, these systems are also relevant where drivers have limitations on their physical or perceptual abilities that are not severe enough to prevent them from driving, but could be ameliorated in conditions of, say, poor weather, low light or congested traffic. These features do not so much 'drive' the vehicle but provide information to the driver to ensure turning movements are safe, and provide warnings or apply emergency braking if a collision risk is detected. Fully automatic parking is already available on some models; parallel parking involves a set of manoeuvres that require awkward head-turning movements and distance perception, and thus older and mobility impaired motorists are seen as key beneficiary groups.

Another set of potential motorist-beneficiaries of automation short of completely driverless journeys would be those who travel long distances on motorways. Here, the restricted-access nature of the road, the relatively comfortable in-vehicle conditions and the more limited-range vehicle interactions compared to non-motorway travel mean that fully autonomous driving for specific sections of road in certain conditions is likely to happen early in the technological transition. The attractions of this feature would be to free up the travel time currently spent on driving a vehicle so it can be used for other activities, such as safe communication by telephone or with other vehicle occupants, working, reading, playing games or watching digital media. The demand from businesses in particular for 'part-time' automation is likely to be high, due to the potential for employee time to be used on more productive activities. Here, one early-adopter commercial sector is likely to be roadfreight, through the application of truck platooning (Commission of the European Communities (CEC) 2017), designed to reduce heavy goods vehicle (HGV) fuel consumption, although the challenges of integrating electronically-coupled 'trains' of large vehicles on highways busy with light, faster-moving passenger vehicles have yet to be resolved.

Public transport systems are a third emerging niche. Due to the defined nature of the routes in most current public transport business models, it is likely to be possible for Level 4 automation to be adopted earlier than a 'go anywhere at any time' application. Early experimentation (for example, Citymobil: undated) has focused on small-to-medium (four to twelve seats) vehicles, commonly referred to as shuttles or 'pods', in partly-segregated environments sharing space only with pedestrians, although projects with road-going vehicles are emerging. As pods are battery-electric, the operational distances are generally kept short, and currently speeds in shared spaces are typically kept to a fast walking pace to ensure safe operation. The market niches that have seen greatest focus to date include providing the 'last-mile' extensions from public transport hubs, within 'campus' facilities such as airports and business parks and in pedestrianised urban areas. With the rise in demand for special car access requirements by mobility impaired people, such vehicles could enable full pedestrianisation while retaining access for all.

CAVs and sustainable mobility

The tendency for 'smart mobility' to be presented as much as a business opportunity as a transport efficiency opportunity is particularly true for CAVs. KPMG (2015), commissioned by the British automotive industry representation body The Society of Motor Manufacturers and Traders, identified a potential £51 billion worth of social and economic benefits by 2030 to the UK economy alone, derived from capital investment opportunities, job creation and road safety improvements. The business model under which such benefits would arise is not clearly articulated, although it tends towards one of 'business as usual', with most vehicles provided on owner-user basis. Under these circumstances, some tendencies for more sustainable – if still car-dependent – mobility might arise. For one thing, the speed imperative may fall with autonomous driving. The optimal amount of time may no longer be the minimum travel time, but might instead become the time necessary to undertake a desired activity, such as to sleep seven hours, particularly in the case of a commercial driver requiring a statutory rest break, or matched to the length of a film a family wishes to watch together. The prospect of a greater variety of in-vehicle activities becoming possible may have implications for demand for surface public transport (and even short-haul air travel), but would enable road transport to operate at an energy and emissions-optimal speed. Moreover, the prospect of connected vehicles increases the likelihood that the road network will become an increasingly managed system: travelling at different times and perhaps at different speeds might attract differential pricing to match demand efficiently to capacity.

Many of the socio-economic benefits of CAV use due to greater participation in society and the economy could be largely independent of the model of implementation. A blind person might travel independently to work or meet friends, with only remote surveillance of the vehicle cabin and environs and telecommunication with the occupants to ensure personal security and provide reassurance. Further, the wider adoption of CAVs within the public transport network is seen as an opportunity to reduce the cost of supply: driver labour costs in particular, but also energy consumption, wear and tear, and collision repairs. In the absence of on-board personnel, digital technologies will facilitate access, enable ticket validation and provide remote surveillance. A key potential of this development would be the opportunity to operate more, smaller, vehicles in lower demand-density environments, improving the penetration by public transport of suburbs and rural areas. Survey evidence from Bristol, however, indicated that over half of respondents would not use an automated bus, suggesting that the public remains to be convinced about the trustworthiness of the technology and not having personnel on-board (Clayton et al 2017).

At the same time, substantial risks to sustainable mobility can be identified if CAVs were introduced without an accompanying change in the relationship between the car and society. Removing the limits created by the current legal requirements for driving skills, satisfactory health and physical ability, and being fit to be in charge of a vehicle (sufficient sleep, absence of intoxicants) would be expected to release latent demand, particularly from those who can't drive. Removing other deterrents, such as the requirement to find a parking space, or navigate and drive in unfamiliar locations, would increase demand from those who are uncomfortable with such things. In the highest-traffic scenarios, existing demand may be increased by travellers choosing to 'summon' and 'send' privately owned CAVs to and from their home base to avoid parking constraints and charges at the destination.

It is also likely that an increase in CAV use would be associated with a fall in other types of travel, including walking, which would have health implications. While 80 per cent of trips in the UK of under one mile are walked, there is a growing group, particularly older citizens, for whom walking is very limited. We noted earlier that one of the potential shuttle niches would cater for those with limited independent walking ability, but it might be practically impossible to reserve such a service for those who need, rather than choose, to use it. In a context of rising population obesity associated with declining physical activity (Mytton et al 2018), automated local transit might remove a key opportunity for exercise during the course of the day. If security questions are resolved, busy parents might see CAVs as an ideal way to send children to school, freeing them from the school run. This latter example does remind us, though, that many CAV benefits, such as social inclusion, will only arise once particular thresholds of technological development are achieved, to the extent that minors could travel unaccompanied without any traveller interaction with the vehicle being necessary. In the meantime, there is a risk that private cars with greater driver assistance will sharpen and increase the divide between those with and without car access in society: during the transition, assistance features will only be available to those with driving licences and car access, and these features will enable the 'part-time' driver, multitasking on the move, to travel further to take advantage of opportunities such as optimal employment, lower consumer prices, and attending signature cultural events, while for those without access to automated cars, the horizon, at least in relative terms, will recede.

Electric vehicles

The inclusion of EVs as a feature of a smart mobility revolution may, on the face of it, come as a surprise. Electric power has been the dominant motive force for street and underground rail systems for more than a century, and has a significant share of general rail traffic in many countries, including 100 per cent of rail-km in Switzerland. By contrast, as a road transport power source, electricity has had a niche role since the invention of the motor car, for example for urban delivery rounds for products such as milk delivered to the doorstep. The factors that made electricity of interest to early road motor vehicle producers were similar to those that had appealed in street rail: a relatively simple and reliable technology that avoided explosive liquid fuels and without emissions from the vehicle. More recently these benefits have been accompanied by the additional energy (and therefore carbon) efficiency of EV systems over the ICE, namely reduced energy loss to heat and noise, the high torque meaning gearboxes are not required, virtually zero energy consumption on idle and the potential to recover energy during deceleration. These more advanced automotive technologies do, however, require complex on-board management systems to optimise performance, often married with ICE power sources in hybrid-power configurations. The on-board systems are connected to increasingly sophisticated 'smart charging' facilities to minimise charging time, themselves part of emerging 'smart grids' to ensure that a massively increasing demand for electric power can be met by the most efficient, flexible supply arrangements.

Several 'vehicle-fuel pathways' offer the potential for 'cradle-to-grave' greenhouse gas emissions (GHG) which approach half those of petrol-fuelled ICE vehicles (Elgowainy et al 2016), although the greatest potential lies with HEVs, BEVs and fuel-cell electric vehicles (FCEVs). Moreover, if electricity from renewable energy sources can be sourced, these combinations largely eliminate greenhouse gas emissions from vehicle operation. Hydrogen, whether used directly as an ICE fuel or to power fuel cells to produce electricity on-board, has been for decades the main rival to BEV technology. Recently, in 2015, the first large-volume car manufacturer, Toyota, finally put a hydrogen fuel cell vehicle (HFC) into production. Although HFC technology avoids the refuelling and range problem that has until recently been associated with BEVs (a three-minute hydrogen refuelling can give up to 500 km range), it has a greater problem in requiring a novel supply network, whereas there is an established electric supply grid already. Moreover, there is the need to handle and compress an explosive fuel, although research to develop nanoporous materials to physically absorb hydrogen as an alternative to high compression is ongoing (for example, Noguera-Díaz et al 2016). A more fundamental limitation currently is that HFC technology is mainly reliant on fossil fuel petrol as the raw material in a chemical process to produce hydrogen, whereas electricity is a highly flexible storage medium for energy and has greater current potential for production from renewable sources. Most major automotive manufacturers are now developing BEVs as the 'smart vehicles' of the future, and they are therefore the focus of this section.

Electricity is under development as a transport motive power source in applications ranging from the electric bicycle to the aeroplane. Hybrid human/mechanical power in the e-bike extends both the possibility of cycling to a wider population, and the range of existing utility cyclists. The emergence of electric aircraft is most obvious in the case of drones with a range of applications from remote sensing to deliveries, although commercial, long-range electric passenger aviation remains a very long-term prospect. The limitation on the expansion of the EV road vehicle was the lack of a practical equivalent to the ground or overhead supply infrastructure that make electric railways so effective. It is only in very recent years that this fundamental barrier has started to fall. The EV problem is a nexus of the technical capabilities of on-vehicle storage solutions, the commercial cost of such technologies, the availability of recharging infrastructure and the speed of recharge. For decades, automotive batteries were heavy, low-performance lead-acid capacitors requiring overnight trickle charging. The main weight of a battery delivery vehicle was the batteries. The range of electric cars was typically limited to around 100 km, with a sharp trade-off between range and acceleration or cruising speed.

Such performance would only be adequate for a car used exclusively for short-range journeys, perhaps as the second car in a household. Early adopters were encouraged to modify their driving styles and would need to make alternative arrangements for medium or long-range trips.

Far more appealing in most markets were the hybrid vehicles that originated in Japan in the 1990s, initially using electric power to replace the ICE at low speed, and to assist it at high speed, but subsequently acquiring 'plug-in' capacity. In this more recent guise, a hybrid operates as a rather heavy and complex EV for most trips, but with the capacity to revert back to traditional ICE technology on longer trips, once the battery is exhausted. Of note here is the case of Norway, the BEV market-leading state by far, where, in 2015, EV sales exceeded 15 per cent of market share. This was achieved in the context of taxation policies that meant the 'total cost of ownership' of an electric car had fallen below that of an ICE car, and a number of incentives, which variously include parking fee and toll exemptions and the possibility to use bus lanes (Bauer 2018). The Norwegian case exemplifies at once the impact that a clear set of policies backed by public sector funding can have on consumer attitudes and behaviour, but also the scale of the transition. In 2017, sales of electric and hybrid cars exceeded half of new registrations for the first time (Knudsen and Doyle 2018), but 79 per cent of vehicles sold still contained an ICE. Initiatives to further the consumer appeal of EVs, particularly in states where government fiscal incentives are less (or not) available, fall in to two broad strategies: further enhancement of battery-technology and innovative means of recharging.

By 2017, it could be argued that for the 5 per cent or so of car purchasers seeking an 'executive' model, the EV 'problem' was effectively solved, through the emergence of production cars priced by range, acceleration and other performance features, with a 400km car retailing at around $85,000 and a 600km car nearly twice that price. Moreover, recharging facilities allowed these electric 'supercars' to achieve 50 per cent recharge within 20 minutes and full recharge in an hour. As safety advice for long-distance driving in any case recommends breaks of 15+ minutes every two hours, provided that sufficient recharging facilities were available, the electric car has now become an option for long- as well as short-range trips. The focus of the challenge has thus been shifted from absolute technological limitations to constraints on mass-market commercialisation. By 2018, prospects for a 35–40 per cent cut in the price of lithium-ion batteries seemed high (Lambert 2017, Schmitt 2017). Such a development would facilitate the $35,000 electric car, although this would only represent one further step towards a genuine 'economy' model.

Alternative solutions to the battery range problem have focused on different means of recharging, rather than increasing battery capacity or achieving faster charging rates. A long-established option for vehicles in industrial use is to swap a discharged battery for a charged one. Development of this technology reached a modern high point in 2012 when the US-Israeli firm 'Better Place' began pilots in Israel and Denmark. The technology proved effective, in that a battery swap could be accomplished in less than five minutes, competitive with the time to replenish liquid fuels. Within a year the company was in liquidation, however. Two factors that contributed to the failure were inherent to the business model. First, was a specific incidence of a general problem for transport technologies that major investment is required upfront to establish a network of sufficient scale, in this case to attract users who wished to use electric cars as flexibly as they did ICE cars. Second, was the difficulty of attracting car manufacturers willing to accept battery standardisation to the specification of a small start-up, and in practice only a few agreements were signed (Gunther 2013). Given that much of the charging was in any case expected to have been done at home, the advent of fast-charging facilities at highway rest areas means that the case for the battery-swap approach now seems to have largely disappeared.

Other innovative approaches to charging are still at the developmental and pilot stage, but seek to extend vehicle range on highways through charging on the move. One approach is to take the trolleybus principle and apply it for hybrid-power HGVs on highways, with the trucks using diesel power away from the pantograph. A 2km trial facility already exists on a Swedish highway (Mendelsohn 2016). A number of national highways authorities worldwide have also explored wireless inductive charging technologies for a range of vehicle types. The upfront cost of providing the infrastructure underneath the road surface might be part-justified by the potential to charge for associated services, notably access to a priority lane, but electromagnetic leakage problems would need to be resolved (TRL 2015).

EVs and sustainable mobility

In common with all transport systems, production of and provision for EVs require raw materials. FCEVs are dependent on platinum-derived catalysts, but they are already used within ICE vehicle exhausts, the demand for which can be expected to decline as EV adoption grows

(Blue Quadrant Capital Management 2017), meaning there is unlikely to be a platinum scarcity for FCEVs. The battery-technology of BEVs, instead, is crucially dependent on lithium. While lithium is not a rare commodity, there are logistical constraints on securing sufficient high-quality lithium at a viable price (Narins 2017).

Changing demands for raw materials for automotive production is just one factor that suggests that, while BEVs and rival technologies offer great potential, achieving the theoretically described transition presents major technical and political challenges. In practice, as Greene and Parkhurst (2017) concluded, the international climate change policy commitments for emissions reductions by 2050 will not be achieved without behaviour change measures to mitigate greenhouse gas production as well as technological development (Chapter 3). Paradoxically, however, the whole commercial basis of the technological development is to minimise the necessary behavioural, cultural and economic adjustments. Further complicating matters, without significant behaviour change technology substitution can result in 'rebound' effects, whereby cost reductions lead to higher consumption of the same or other goods and services (Bjelle et al 2018). Direct rebound effects arising from the relatively high EV capital costs but lower running costs compared to ICE vehicles, could lead to higher annual distances travelled and in the short-to-medium-run contribute to rising traffic and congestion, which in turn would slightly worsen the performance of the existing ICE fleet.

Sustainable mobility is not solely about reducing climate change impacts, important though those are. A clear benefit is that toxic exhaust emissions from vehicles are much reduced by a switch to EVs, albeit that 'zero impact' claims require some caveats. For a start, EVs continue to have negative impacts on air quality because of particulate emissions from the wear of vehicle components such as tyres and brake friction surfaces. Being heavier than ICE equivalents, those non–exhaust emissions can potentially be actually higher (Timmers and Achten 2016). In relation to noise pollution, far quieter operation does offer a benefit to the public realm, particularly at slow speeds in urban areas, although both the US and EU have mandated that new EVs from 2019 must emit a sound sufficient to enable pedestrians to be aware that a vehicle is being operated. And EVs require additional 'street infrastructure', in the form of recharging points and cables, so will tend to add to the overall consumption of street space by road vehicles, as well as increasing their visual intrusion. EVs emerge as an important mitigation-technology for some of the negative effects of car use, but do not, in themselves, entail a sustainable transport system.

Digitally enabled collaborative mobility

The sharing of transport assets in time or space by unrelated citizens, formal or informal, on officially regulated transport services or those operating beyond the law, has always been a feature of the personal mobility system. In the industrialised democracies, though, sharing as a formalised, sanctioned practice – that is, promoted or even managed by public bodies and often attracting public funding – has hitherto tended to focus on public transport systems. The growth of smart media and an 'always on' digital infrastructure have revolutionised, in three decades, the way people communicate, socialise and access data-based services, and there is reason to suppose that travel behaviour might be more subject to change now, than in recent times. Several initiatives have emerged to promote and exploit this potential. The public sector has been active in promoting higher-technology integrated ticketing solutions to render collective transport solutions more attractive and easy to use, whereas the private sector has sought to develop 'ridesourcing' and 'Mobility as a Service' solutions, some of which offer the potential of more collaborative, and therefore potentially more sustainable, solutions.

The digital integration of transport through MaaS

At the core of the digital transport revolution is accurate and dynamic (real-time) travel information. From this perspective, the citizen-on-the-move requires information 'now', and expects to get it immediately, whether in the home or another location, or travelling, and often without speaking to another person. It was not so long ago when the location of buses, trains and trams remained the domain of specialist staff in operational depots or call centres, but GPS, enhanced signalling and 4G technology has revolutionised this in a very short timescale. Although real-time information provision remains patchy in extent and reliability, often travellers with the relevant 'app' available on their portable digital technology can be notified if a particular bus is running five minutes late for a usual trip home, or enable the booking of a table seat with a window on a train departing in two hours' time. It is from this 'digital' perspective that the concept of MaaS emerges. The term MaaS is in fact used variously (Jittrapirom et al 2017), with some authors restricting its application to services which may be provided by different operators but bundled together into a service contract with a consolidating organisation (Holmberg et al 2016). Here, though, we use the term more generally, to cover various means by which public transport can be integrated with transport services such as taxis, car share, car hire and cycle hire, to deliver a seamless service for a consumer to access his or her mobility needs.

Such has been the technological development that the barriers today in the transition to effective MaaS solutions are not in reality IT-related but are a manifestation of the governance of mobility policy. It was EU directive 91/440 in 1991 that structured a trend in the industrialised democracies for the state to disaggregate itself from both the direct control and operation of public transport services (the directive itself was specifically concerned with railway services). Great Britain is an extreme case, with its total deregulation of buses outside London, removal of state intervention powers on service coordination, and franchising of trains on the former British Rail network. The outcome of this policy approach is the creation of isolated, closed bus networks and systems at a company level. Passengers are sought as exclusive consumers, with operations, ticketing, fares and information systems deployed to achieve that end; such an approach is directly in conflict with the open and collaborative principles of MaaS. Just the matter of persuading bus companies to work together to provide a simple multi-operator ticket can be a highly complex and protracted process.

Yet public transport consumer mobility needs are rarely *inherently* so exclusive, and nor is such loyalty willingly given. Indeed, a common desire of travellers is to have access to sufficient information about a range of travel modes and service providers, so as to be able to decide which will allow them to reach particular destinations, at the most suitable time, for an acceptable price and at desired levels of comfort and service reliability (Lyons 2006). Central to these motivations is the ability to capture core data in a standard form for comparison of options and product delivery. This, of course, is neither revolutionary nor new. In 2000, the UK launched *Traveline*, a national phone number and Internet service for local passenger transport journey information, delivered through regional consortia on the instruction of the national government. *Traveline* acted as a key conduit for the standardisation of timetable information through a new data standard, transXchange, which has led to a national passenger transport timetable dataset, updated regularly, as an accessible national resource that is at the heart of most British journey planning apps and real-time information systems. Although commendable in a deregulated market (albeit the UK national dataset only exists because of state intervention), after almost 20 years *Traveline* is still largely unable to inform customers how much it will cost to go to town on the bus. While the UK does indeed have a complex structure of ticket types and options within a deregulated market, there is no *technical* barrier which would prevent a process for storing and updating such information. Why this has not happened remains an ongoing matter of debate (with yet another consultation on future data standards, provision and responsibilities underway at the time of writing).

Indeed, alongside information, electronic ticketing is the other key aspect of the digital transport revolution. In the UK, the technical solution to operator-led closed ticketing systems that restrict opportunities for multi-operator products was ITSO, a national standard for multi-operator ticketing (ITSO: undated). ITSO is an open ticketing standard based on global banking data protocols, defining how ticketing messages are exchanged in a secure, encrypted manner, enabling a customer's purchase and use of a product to be identified and associated with payment apportionment. As an open standard, any supplier of ticketing equipment can develop a product and have it certified by ITSO as meeting the requirements to support multi-supplier data exchange. This specific issue of payment validation and apportionment is at the heart of the opportunity for IT to exploit MaaS in a deregulated sector. As we consider later in the section, 'transportation network companies' (TNCs) such as Uber and Lyft successfully exploit the IT infrastructure through providing a shared access and payment platform between the consumer and the provider. Payment is agreed in advance and is unique per trip based on time of day, distance, vehicle type and even the level of demand versus supply at the time of booking. There is limited risk of a customer over-riding without extra payment, as the journey data is captured and remunerated in full.

In a deregulated passenger transport network of driver-only buses with multiple doors and a limited number of revenue protection officers, and non-gated local rail and tram stations, the ability to capture the journey data and reimburse fairly in accordance with an operator's business rules is critical to MaaS acceptance. Assuming both journey and fare information is available, how can barriers be overcome and opportunities realised in multiple closed-system areas? In addressing this question, we need to recognise that the last decade has seen a genuine uplift in the capability of in-vehicle ticketing equipment for taxi, bus and rail systems, all exploiting GPS and 4G communications. Within the bus sector, the transition from solid state electronic ticket machines (ETMs) to on-board computer-based ETMs is almost complete. Three existing IT platforms already exist to exploit these new ETM capabilities using open standards to support multi-operator closed systems: contactless bankcard payment linked to account-based ticketing, barcode ticketing and smartcards.

Contactless payment (cEMV) on buses is currently in the process of being widely introduced across the UK bus networks, as in many other parts of Europe. Eliminating the need to carry cash provides a clear customer advantage, as does the ability to use third party payment apps such as Apple Pay or Android Pay. Still, cEMV does retain inherent challenges for MaaS delivery. First, outside of London, on-bus cEMV is only being used as a payment platform. For a ticket purchase up to £30 in value a paper ticket is issued; lose that paper ticket and there is no 'insurance' – the traveller must pay again. In addition, 'smart ticketing' has not achieved fare capping across modes and operators outside London. Fare capping is a politically desirable and popular charging practice that means no further charges are accrued once a certain amount has been spent in a defined period. While account-based ticketing can be introduced outside London, enabling an individual customer's total spend to be capped at a fixed daily, weekly or other rate, this has in practice only been achieved at the level of a single operator (corresponding to a single 'finance key' embedded within the ETM). So, as of 2018, 'multi-key' capping across a defined area outside London is not available: multimodal and multi-operator tickets are on a fixed-price rather than variable-with-cap basis, meaning they are more likely to be attractive to travellers who are able to plan ahead and have a high level of knowledge about ticketing options.

Barcode ticketing offers a relatively cheap platform for multi-operator product issuing and revenue apportionment by product. ETM infrastructure add-ons are relatively low cost, and products can be hosted as paper tickets or on mobile devices. Like the pre-ITSO days of smart ticketing, however, the bus sector has not agreed to support one particular barcode standard, meaning the ability for the product to be read across multiple operators is not guaranteed. Lastly, smartcard ticketing using a defined standard such as ITSO remains the safest and most secure platform for open area multi-operator ticket retailing, ensuring full product business rules can be applied, data to support accurate revenue apportionment captured and customers supported if a card is lost or stolen. But there are costs associated with the card-based infrastructure and product vending. A hybrid of full ITSO security embedded within a phone app, enabling instant ticket upload, delivering full ITSO messaging to each Terminal using the phone's Near Field Communication capability and available as an open platform for all, is currently being developed between ITSO and a major Internet system provider. If successful it has the potential to deliver a real opportunity for any MaaS or other provider to be able to offer secure multi-operator passenger transport in an open-system environment.

Thus it is not IT that is a barrier to a wider customer proposition of accelerating change in mobility behaviour, but the required adoption of existing standards to provide the core data upon which opportunity is built. With bus patronage in all deregulated areas of the UK in decline for most of the last three decades, and London the only regulated and genuinely integrated area having experienced significant growth, how long can a failed model of ineffective national policy on the application of data standards and weak local governance be tolerated if shared passenger transport is to have a future? After all, it is well established that the introduction of multimodal and easy-to-use ticketing options can increase public transport use, even if part of that increase is often explained by an effective reduction in fare levels if there is a maximum fare price cap (Balcombe 2004), and additional usage alone rarely covers the costs of investing in new ticketing systems (Shergold 2016). Smart ticketing investments do have wider benefits, though, including better system usage data for the operator, and although Shergold did not identify evidence that smart ticketing in itself is the key factor in mode switches from car to public transport, a supporting and facilitating role in modal shift to help promote more sustainable mobility remains very plausible.

A widening range of mobility services

In the highly industrialised states, transport provision has generally exhibited a sharp divide between private and public systems, with public transport services generally running on fixed routes and schedules, using medium or high capacity vehicles, and being professionally managed and delivered. In recent decades, though, these states have seen a growth in both the range and magnitude of mobility options involving both the shared ownership and the shared use of assets such as cars, bicycles and taxis. Digital technologies have underpinned these new ways of owning and using mobility assets, by enabling the provision of information, the completion of transactions, and managing the physical access to assets for a low cost, for example, because operational staff do not need to be present.

In the case of cars, it is possible to categorise a growing diversity of ways in which cars can be owned and used (Table 15.2). Informal sharing remains an important practice in specific communities and types of geographical area, such as among urban minority ethnic groups or in rural areas with limited transport alternatives (Chapter 12). More

Table 15.2: Diversification of car ownership and access niches. New forms shown in italics; disappearing form in brackets.

		Shared with			
		No-one	'Known' others, for example, friends, acquaintances	Strangers	Clients
'Ownership' for periods of:	Hours	Car sharing A2B/A2A	*Ways which combine shared 'ownership' with shared access, often with facilitation through online mobility brokerage platforms*		
	Days	Traditional car hire *P2P car hire*			
	Months/ years	Leasing	Informal car pooling with work colleagues *Formal car pooling with colleagues or near-colleagues*	(Traditional hitch-hiking) *'Lift share': virtual hitch-hiking not-for-profit*	Traditional Taxi *Deregulated 'Smart Taxi'*
	Flexible	*Mobility as a service packages*			
	Full-time	Traditional ownership			

Source: Graham Parkhurst

generally, however, rising wealth has permitted most households to own one or more private cars, and sharing generally became limited to people in the same households, families and friend groups. The decline of casual hitch-hiking is one example of this change. Recent decades have, though, seen the emergence of car-sharing schemes – which provide members with pay-on-use access to cars which are owned by private, public or third-sector organisations, sometimes referred to as 'clubs' – and car pooling – regular arrangements by which car owners driving to a location offer unoccupied seats to people travelling to the same location, such as work colleagues, on a not-for-profit basis (Cairns and Harmer 2011). These practices are now institutionalised as policy measures, enshrined in processes such as the EU Sustainable Urban Mobility Plan initiative (for example, Wefering et al 2014). Rather than being secured through word-of-mouth 'micro-agreements', employees are now encouraged to find car-pooling partners with the aid of geospatially-linked databases of likely suitable colleagues. Preferential parking and other incentives support this 'behaviour change' (Litman 2016). Car sharing instead provides a rational solution for the household which desires some access to a car, without the high cost per journey of hiring a taxi, but does not want to be subject to the social control, precarity and exchange constraints which seeking assistance from a relative, friend or neighbour who has a car might entail, particularly if the need is frequent or routine (Chapter 12).

Two features characterise the resurgence of shared mobility. First, it is not motivated primarily by the limited personal spending power of the traveller. Instead, sharing results from consumer decisions in which cost is only one of a complex range of factors generally linked to new types of lifestyle. For example, Rayle et al (2016) found that 'ridesourcing' services such as Uber and Lyft had a special appeal for a group of generally younger, well-educated urban travellers with a high value of time; 'special' in the sense that the offer was not replicated by other modes. Second, the rise of information technologies applied to the mobility sector has made such services both more attractive to users and possible for providers (Enoch 2015). Labour costs have been avoided, for example, by the provision of automatic rather than staffed cycle hire from docking stations provided in the street. Internet-connected vehicles and docking stations enable real-time information on the availability of assets for hire and booking and payment systems to secure them remotely. The rise of automation may also favour shared mobility if the links between vehicle ownership and use are further weakened by the car becoming more utilitarian and less an expression of socio-economic position and less influenced by emotion (Steg 2005). Chatterjee et al (2018: x) observed that reductions in car use among UK adults born since 1964, compared with those born in the period 1946–1964, have been 'influenced by a long-term increase in the age at which people typically start working, begin relationships and have children.' The same authors concluded, however, that this reduction could only partly be explained by deterrent economic factors such as transport costs, and that attitudinal survey evidence indicated greater acceptance over time of lifestyles not orientated around the car (Chapter 14). It seems, then, that the attitudes and behaviours of current young adults will, overall, reflect weaker attachment to the car in later life as well, although with variation within that group according to lifestyle choices and circumstances, and to some extent showing greater engagement with the car later in the lifecourse.

Will collaborative mobility enhance sustainability?

Given that shared mobility is altering social practices, creating new economic opportunities (while potentially undermining others) and encouraging different ways of being mobile, in most cases with traffic, energy and emissions consequences, does the greater sharing of transport assets necessarily promote more sustainable mobility in its broadest sense? Does it offer the potential for regime change? Or is it, as Martin (2016: 149) suggests, just 'a nightmarish form of neoliberal capitalism'? The most established TNC based on a digital platform is Uber. Like other platform-based companies, Uber has been criticised for its labour conditions (for example, Lawrence 2016), but focusing on transport service considerations, three key concerns have emerged. The first is that Uber may result in a decline in service standards by circumventing regulations which may not concern the traveller at the point of purchase, but exist to protect the public, the public interest or minorities. In practice, whether Uber threatens regulations will tend to depend on the specific local ordinances on taxi regulation. In the UK, for example, Uber operates as a 'private hire' service which is the form of a pre-booked taxi with a less onerous form of regulation. It cannot operate as a 'Hackney Carriage', so does not benefit from using on-street ranks, but at the same time it avoids more onerous regulations such as using fully accessible vehicles, a specific livery or meeting particular emissions standards. Since app-hailing represents greater competition for the street rank than pre-booking by phone, however, it may indirectly make higher-regulation services less viable.

Second is the concern that TNC companies will compete with public transport, on which some citizens, for whom 'ridesourcing' services are not suitable or too expensive, are dependent. A consequence arising might be the need for greater public sector support to maintain public transport networks. Here, the evidence is provisional. Hall et al (2017) concluded that for US metropolitan areas there was considerable variability on the impact of Uber on transit services, but on balance they found a complementary effect. More research into these phenomena is necessary.

Third is the more subtle concern that Uber is conceived by transport sector policy makers and professionals as a shared service, because it may be a factor in some users not owning their own cars, and because it has a shared-ride variant. Bondorová and Archer (2017) report information from Uber indicating that one-fifth of UberPOOL customers in the 33 cities where it was being offered were sharing, rising to half of customers in San Francisco. But the potential for intensive 'synchronous' sharing of flexible route and schedule TNC services remains very much a potential rather than a reality. Uber Pool is not available in all jurisdictions, and then only in certain large cities in those countries in which it is offered. The conceptual attractiveness of an urban mobility future in which sharing becomes the social norm has been demonstrated through scenario modelling studies, but with important caveats. In the case of Lisbon, for example, the International Transport Forum (ITF) (2015) showed that an exclusively-used (asynchronously) shared CAV fleet would only be 23 per cent smaller than an unshared fleet providing for the same level of mobility but traffic and peak congestion would double, due to the repositioning of empty vehicles. A fully synchronously-shared fleet could be much (90 per cent) smaller, but even here, traffic and peak congestion would show modest increases of 6 and 9 per cent respectively.

All of these findings underline the ongoing importance of high-efficiency, traditional public transport routes on principal urban corridors, with users walking modest distances to access the services, implying that to some extent a mixed-mode ecosystem would need to be retained. It is also worth pointing out that all such studies rely on the very important assumption that citizens will share small vehicles with strangers – significant psychological barriers to sharing will remain even if the practical ones are effectively overcome (Merat et al 2017) – and also that the applicability of the shared mobility service models outside of densely populated urban areas will be subject to much greater viability constraints.

Smart mobility: more than an investment opportunity?

In summary, the analyses of the previous three sections indicate that:

- The benefits of CAVs are highly uncertain, both in terms of extent and evolution, and considerable disadvantages are foreseeable, with the balance between the two being highly dependent on the socio-economic and policy context in which CAV technologies are applied.
- Electrification of the road vehicle fleet is a necessary but not sufficient condition for more sustainable mobility, with some unintended consequences and uncertainties in relation to the rate of substitution and importance of rebound effects on traffic and overall energy consumption.
- DEM is technically quite feasible even if it continues to face considerable regulatory, institutional and financial challenges. Enhanced information and easier ticketing options are also desirable from the traveller's perspective, provided the technologies are accessible to all.
- Collective mobility is the development which can potentially have the greatest impact on the sustainability of our future mobility, and indeed of the four is the sufficient condition for sustainability, but at the same time is apparently the perceived transition which is most dependent upon faith: that citizens will alter both their travel and social behaviours to share small vehicles with unacquainted

fellow travellers, even though exclusive-use travel options remain in affordable reach.

The uncertainties that emerge with each of the four technological shifts we have reviewed contrast with the certainty and appeal of the smart mobility discourse; the evidence behind the aspirations is largely based on assumption and scenario. In this context it is tempting to dismiss the claims of smart mobility protagonists as just another example of the conflation of technological innovation with 'progress', and 'progress' with 'improvement' (Bimber 1990). If the rhetoric identifies the 'future conditional' as 'smart' or 'intelligent' then, by implication, traditional mobility arrangements are not only an 'imperfect past', but 'unintelligent' if not 'stupid' and are to be replaced. In the transport sector, however, 'progress' has generally been associated with increases in distance, capacity and speed, and the perceived spatio-temporal shrinking of the globe: in short, technical innovation has underpinned the long-run trends that many commentators now identify as being central to 'unsustainable transport' (Banister 2005).

The enthusiasm for 'smart mobility' also needs to be seen in the context of economic interests, and its emergence in a period of economic decline. Some commentators on recent economic performance regard the decade of austerity which began in 2008–09 as just another low point in the economic cycle, and identify new technologies as a means through which capital can 'reinvent' itself to once again 'create' value, encourage investment and promote growth (Chang 2014), leaving some traditional transport systems redundant in the process. In their place rises the 'platform capitalist' (Srnicek 2017) business model of asset-light, information-rich software, extracting value from knowledge about the locations of travel demand and operators with assets well positioned to serve it, and from the labour involved in the processes of both information creation and provision of the service. The new 'transportation network companies' are perhaps the signature exemplars of this new business model. What remains very uncertain is whether the stock market valuation of Uber – the highest-value private technology company whose worth peaked at nearly €70 billion in February 2017 (Abboud 2017) – reflects long-term viability, enthusiastic (possibly over-enthusiastic) belief in the potential by the investors, or simple speculation, in the context that the company has yet to return a profit.

Other commentators, however, identify a different kind of emergent capitalism, a 'fourth wave', or go so far as to refer to 'post-capitalism' (Mason 2015). This latter thesis posits information technology not simply as 'just another outlet' for moribund capital seeking higher profit, but instead, asserts that the nature of the new technologies themselves are part of a fundamental change in economic behaviours. Indeed, other manifestations of smart mobility, emerging alongside but in contrast to the TNCs, apparently defy established capitalist logic. According to the primacy of the market, there is no economic basis for the sharing of open source and free-to-access geospatial information and travel planning tools via the Internet (Mason 2015). Nonetheless, services such as the journey planner for cyclists 'CycleStreets' are free to use. CycleStreets (undated) has operated for more than ten years as a not-for-profit company. It makes use of voluntary software coding labour, with the only revenues being from donations. And some aspects of smart mobility may literally be a 'driving force' towards post-capitalism. Automation across the economy is predicted to reduce the costs of production by replacing waged labour, but the difference between the value created by human labour and the wages paid to workers has traditionally been an important source of profit, which under automation would disappear. From this perspective, whether goods and services, including transport services, remain viable as for-profit activities in an automated economy will depend on whether investors are willing to accept long-run returns on the value of high investments in automation equipment, or are able to rely on other sources of profit. These other sources of profit might include the value of a brand or, where businesses do indeed manage to exert proprietary rights over datasets, the extraction of value from information.

Hence, the transport sector emerges not only as a hotbed of innovation, but as a key 'foundry' for new economic alchemy. In this context of experimental uncertainty, the role of public policy emerges as critical: there is little doubt that 'smart mobility' will bring important changes and this will include changed networks of policy making, with different actors controlling aspects such as information about travel demands and influencing service delivery in time and space. If the public good is to be protected in this new context there will correspondingly need to be a new regulatory framework with sufficient powers and likely new forms of intervention in the market (Docherty et al 2018). Such a public policy framework needs to be wide-ranging and flexible, too, not least because the simultaneous emergence of the four technological trends creates interactions between them. BEV technology can be more efficient if applied in a CAV context because a managed operating system can maximise battery range and life through optimised driving and charging. DEM services facilitate collective mobility through reducing the transaction costs of payment and increasing the chances that attractive synchronously or asynchronously-shared travel opportunities are included in a MaaS suite. Similarly, DEM services can enhance EV use by providing information and securing access across the recharge facilities of different operators. And potentially most fundamentally, automation, by reducing operating costs and providing a high-quality passenger experience, opens up the possibility that access to a fleet of highly-available taxis may be sufficient to weaken the attraction of car ownership, and in turn that intensive use will result in faster turnover of a (reduced) vehicle fleet, enabling swifter technological upgrade in the future.

The extent and depth of change such development would entail, though, should not be underestimated. While the other three trends can be potentially assimilated within the socio-economic status quo, CM can only play a significant role if along the way it is associated with the scale of traditional light vehicle production being reduced to a fraction of current demand and advertising for personal vehicle ownership, currently one of the highest-spending sectors, largely disappears, along with the service industries dependent on mass car ownership, such as auto-retail, servicing, insurance and valeting. But only in the case of synchronous sharing does that change in ownership behaviour become traffic reducing, rather than traffic generating: without sharing-in-use, vehicle-km travelled must rise in providing an exclusive-use taxi service equivalent to owner-driver trip-making. And here emerges a key and paradoxical discord: if many citizens are already reluctant to share with strangers, research into attitudes – at least current ones – suggests this reluctance becomes clear resistance in the absence of the authority of a human driver due to automation (Clayton et al 2017), and it is debatable whether remote surveillance by camera will be an acceptable alternative to a human presence in the vehicle. Hence, combining psychology and economics, CM emerges as potentially the most divisive, disruptive and challenging of the four phenomena. Mobility policy would be critical in 'cracking' this conundrum, through a package of financial incentives for sharing, traffic management priorities for shared services and appropriate remote security and passenger support facilities. Even so, new small vehicle designs intended for sharing by unacquainted travellers and changes in social norms and expectations are also likely to be critical in enabling this practice.

Meanwhile, in considering for whom the smart mobility revolution could matter, and how it could matter, it is clear that there will be an ongoing need to tackle established, mobility-related social inequalities, for example, in the context of shared-ownership mobility (Clark and Curl 2016). Even if smart mobility results in a fall in operating costs per unit of passenger transport service offered, that may not result in a fall in user costs, particularly if the reductions are reinvested in higher quality, or more extensive, services. Indeed, one pressure for more extensive services will arise from lower density suburban and rural areas within which traditional public transport has shown decline over many years, although it remains unclear how far the efficiencies and cost reductions of collective automated transport would be revolutionary, rather than marginal, outside of the metropolitan areas.

Without an inclusive transport policy and successful promotion of CM, then the possibility of those with sufficient means deserting public transport in favour of personally owned and used electric CAVs opens up a potential nightmare scenario for those dependent on traditional bus services (unless the state then contracts inefficient personal CAV travel for them as well). The wider socio-political consequences of such a scenario can only be telegraphed here, but might include further pressures for low-density development in a context of declining travel costs, and a cranking-up of the public health crisis if transport services are ever-more door-to-door or even terminating within buildings. Despite the many challenges and paradoxes, however, just suppose a different 'psychology of the car' proves possible: the future really could be one mixing 'active' with 'passive' mobility, with the latter provided by quieter vehicles with zero local exhaust emissions, connected so that they become production and consumption spaces on the move, rented by the hour rather than owned, and often also shared, and being reliably, carefully and respectfully self-driven, ending the culture of the car as apparatus for the social display of aggressive or arrogant driving 'prowess'. In short, in smart and revolutionary times, transport policy matters more than ever.

References

Abboud, L (2017) *Uber's $69 Billion Dilemma.* www.bloomberg.com/ gadfly/articles/2017-03-16/uber-needs-to-get-real-about-that-69-billion-price-tag Accessed 3 March 2018.

Balcombe, R (ed) (2004). *The Demand for Public Transport.* TRL Report 593. https://trl.co.uk/reports/TRL593 Accessed 21 March 2018.

Banister, D (2005) *Unsustainable Transport: City Transport in the New Century*, London: Routledge.

Bauer, G (2018) 'The impact of battery electric vehicles on vehicle purchase and driving behavior in Norway', *Transportation Research Part D: Transport and Environment*, 58: 239–58.

Bimber, B (1990) 'Karl Marx and the three faces of technological determinism', *Social Studies of Science*, 20(2): 333–351.

Bjelle, E, Steen-Olsen, K and Wood, R (2018) 'Climate change mitigation potential of Norwegian households and the rebound effect', *Journal of Cleaner Production*, 172: 208–17.

Blue Quadrant Capital Management (2017) *The rise of electric vehicles: is there a future for platinum?* https://seekingalpha.com/article/4077607-rise-electric-vehicles-future-platinum Accessed 23 August 2018.

Bondorová, B and Archer, G (2017) *Does sharing cars really reduce car use?* Briefing Transport and Environment, Brussels. www.transportenvironment.org/publications/does-sharing-cars-really-reduce-car-use Accessed 13 March 2018.

Bouton, S, Knupfer, S, Mihov, I and Swartz, S (2015) *Urban mobility at a tipping point.* McKinsey Center for Business and Environment.

Cairns, S and Harmer, C (2011) *Accessing Cars: Insights from International Experience.* Royal Automobile Club Foundation, London. www.racfoundation.org/wp-content/uploads/2017/11/accessing-cars_international_review-cairns_harmer-dec11.pdf Accessed 13 March 2018.

Chang, H-J (2014) *Economics: The User's Guide*, London: Penguin.

Chatterjee, K, Goodwin, P, Schwanen, T, Clark, B, Jain, J, Melia, S, Middleton, J, Plyushteva, A, Ricci, M, Santos, G and Stokes, G (2018) *Young People's Travel – What's Changed and Why? Review and Analysis.* Report to Department for Transport. UWE Bristol, UK. www.gov.uk/government/publications/young-peoples-travel-whats-changed-and-why Accessed 2 August 2018.

Citymobil (undated) Project website. www.citymobil-project.eu/ Accessed 4 March 2018.

Clark, B, Parkhurst, G and Ricci, M (2016) *Understanding the socioeconomic adoption scenarios for autonomous vehicles: A literature review.* Project Report. UWE, Bristol, UK. http://eprints.uwe.ac.uk/29134 Accessed 23 August 2018.

Clark, J and Curl, A (2016) 'Bicycle and car share schemes as inclusive modes of travel? A socio-spatial analysis in Glasgow, UK', *Social Inclusion*, 4(3): 83–99.

Clayton, W, Paddeu, D, Parkhurst, G and Gomez de Segura Marauri, M (2017) 'Autonomous vehicles: willingness-to-pay and willingness-to-share', in *Universities' Transport Study Group (UTSG) 2018 Conference*, University College London (UCL), 3–5 January 2018. http://eprints.uwe.ac.uk/34007 Accessed 18 July 2019.

Commission of the European Communities (2017) *Community Research and Development Information Service: Sartre Project.* https://cordis.europa.eu/project/rcn/92577_en.html Accessed 4 March 2018.

CycleStreets (undated) About CycleStreets. www.cyclestreets.net/about/ Accessed 3 March 2018.

Department for Transport (2015) *The pathway to driverless cars: summary report and action plan*. DfT, London.

Docherty, I, Marsden, G and Anable, J (2018) 'The governance of smart mobility', *Transportation Research Part A: Policy and Practice*, 115: 114–25.

Elgowainy, A, Han, J, Ward, J, Joseck, F, Gohlke, D, Lindauer, A, Ramsden, T, Biddy, M, Alexander, M, Barnhart, S, Sutherland, I, Verduzco, L and Wallington, T (2016) *Cradle-to-grave lifecycle analysis of U.S. light-duty vehicle-fuel pathways: a greenhouse gas emissions and economic assessment of current (2015) and future (2025–2030) technologies.* ANL/ESD-16/7. Argonne National Laboratory, Argonne, Illinois. https://greet.es.anl.gov/publication-c2g-2016-report Accessed 4 March 2018.

Enoch, M (2015) 'How a rapid modal convergence into a universal automated taxi service could be the future for local passenger transport', *Technology Analysis & Strategic Management*, 27(8): 910–24.

Fagnant, D and Kockelman, K (2015) 'Preparing a nation for autonomous vehicles: opportunities, barriers and policy recommendations', *Transportation Research Part A: Policy and Practice*, 77: 167–81.

Graham, R (2013) *The future of urban mobility: an overview of current global initiatives and future technologies to help meet the challenges of urban mobility*. A Leasedrive White Paper. Leasedrive, Wokingham.

Greene, D and Parkhurst, G (2017) Decarbonizing transport for a sustainable future – mitigating impacts of the changing climate: a White Paper. Conference Proceedings 54, Transportation Research Board, Washington DC. www.trb.org/Main/Blurbs/177088.aspx Accessed 4 March 2018.

Gunther, M (2013) 'Better place: what went wrong for the electric car startup?' *The Guardian*, www.theguardian.com/environment/2013/mar/05/better-place-wrong-electric-car-startup Accessed 4 March 2018.

Hajer, M (1995) *The Politics of Environmental Discourse: Ecological Dodernisation and the Policy Process*, Oxford: Oxford University Press.

Hall, J, Palsson, D and Price, J (2017) 'Is Uber a substitute or complement for public transit?', *Journal of Urban Economics*, 108: 36–50.

Holmberg, P-E, Collado, M, Sarasini, S and Williander, M (2016) Mobility as a Service – MaaS: describing the framework. Final report, MaaS Framework Project. Viktoria Swedish ICT, Gothenburg. www.viktoria.se/sites/default/files/pub/www.viktoria.se/upload/publications/final_report_maas_framework_v_1_0.pdf Accessed 13 March 2018.

International Transport Forum (2015) *Urban mobility system upgrade: how shared self-driving cars could change city traffic.* ITF / OECD, Paris. www.itf-oecd.org/urban-mobility-system-upgrade-1 Accessed 1 August 2018.

ITSO (undated) *The national smart ticketing standard.* ITSO Ltd, Milton Keynes. www.itso.org.uk/ Accessed 9 March 2018.

Jittrapirom, P, Caiati, V, Feneri, A, Ebrahimigharehbaghi, S, González, M and Narayan, J (2017) 'Mobility as a service: a critical review of definitions, assessments of schemes, and key challenges', *Urban Planning*, 2(2): 13–25.

Knudsen, C and Doyle, A (2018) Norway powers ahead (electrically) – over half new car sales now electric or hybrid. *Reuters Autos* 03/01/2018. https://uk.reuters.com/article/uk-environment-norway-autos/norway-powers-ahead-over-half-new-car-sales-now-electric-or-hybrid-idUKKBN1ES1DB Accessed 4 March 2018.

KPMG/Center for Automotive Research (2012) *Self-driving cars: the next revolution.* KPMG. https://assets.kpmg/content/dam/kpmg/pdf/2015/10/self-driving-cars-next-revolution_new.pdf Accessed 2 June 2019

KPMG (2015). Connected and autonomous vehicles – The UK economic opportunity. March 2015 [online] Available from: https://assets.kpmg/content/dam/kpmg/pdf/2016/05/connected-autonomous-vehicles-study.pdf Accessed 2 June 2019.

Lambert, F (2017) *Tesla is now claiming 35% battery cost reduction at 'Gigafactory 1' – hinting at breakthrough cost below $125/kWh.* https://electrek.co/2017/02/18/tesla-battery-cost-gigafactory-model-3/ Accessed 4 March 2018.

Lawrence, F (2016) 'Uber is treating its drivers as sweated labour, says report', *The Guardian*, www.theguardian.com/technology/2016/dec/09/uber-drivers-report-sweated-labour-minimum-wage Accessed 3 March 2018.

Lawrence, M, Roberts, C and King, L (2017) *Managing automation: employment, inequality and ethics in the digital age.* Institute for Public Policy Research, London. www.ippr.org/publications/managing-automation Accessed 3 March 2018.

Lerner, W (2011) *The future of urban mobility*. www.adlittle.com/sites/ default/files/viewpoints/adl_the_future_of_urban_mobility_report. pdf Accessed 18 July 2019.

Litman, T (2016) *Parking management strategies, evaluation and planning*. Victoria Transport Policy Institute, Canada. www.vtpi.org/park_man. pdf Accessed 3 March 2018.

Lyons, G (2006) 'The role of information in decision-making with regard to travel', *IEE Proceedings – Intelligent Transport Systems*, 153(3): 199–212.

Martin, C (2016) 'The sharing economy: a pathway to sustainability or a nightmarish form of neoliberal capitalism?', *Ecological Economics*, 121(C): 149–59.

Mason, P (2015) *Postcapitalism: A Guide to our Future*, London: Penguin.

Mendelsohn, T (2016) *Sweden trials electrified highway for trucks*. https:// arstechnica.com/cars/2016/06/sweden-trials-electrified-highway-for-trucks/ Accessed 4 March 2018.

Merat, N, Madigan, R and Nordhoff, S (2017) *Human factors, user requirements, and user acceptance of ride-sharing in automated vehicles*. Discussion Paper 2017: 10. International Transport Forum. http:// eprints.whiterose.ac.uk/112108/ Accessed 13 March 2018.

Mytton, O, Ogilvie, D, Griffin, S, Brage, S, Wareham, and Panter, J (2018) 'Associations of active commuting with body fat and visceral adipose tissue: a cross-sectional population based study in the UK', *Preventive Medicine*, 106: 86–93.

Narins, T (2017) 'The battery business: lithium availability and the growth of the global electric car industry', *The Extractive Industries and Society*, 4(2): 321–8.

Noguera-Díaz, A, Bimbo, N, Holyfield, L, Ahmet, I, Ting, V and Mays, T (2016) 'Structure-property relationships in metal-organic frameworks for hydrogen storage', *Colloids and Surfaces A. Physicochemical and Engineering Aspects*, 496: 77–85.

Paddeu, D, Calvert, T, Clark, B and Parkhurst, G (2019) *New technology and automation in freight transport and handling systems. A Review for the Foresight Future of Mobility Project*. UK Government Office for Science, London. https://assets.publishing.service.gov.uk/ government/uploads/system/uploads/attachment_data/file/781295/ automation_in_freight.pdf Accessed 2 June 2019.

Rayle, L, Dai, D, Chan, N, Cervero, R and Shaheen, S (2016) 'Just a better taxi? A survey-based comparison of taxis, transit, and ridesourcing services in San Francisco', *Transport Policy*, 45: 168–78.

Roberts C, Lawrence, M and King, L (2017) *Managing automation: employment, inequality and ethics in the digital age*. IPPR. http://www.ippr.org/publications/managing-automation Accessed 2 June 2019.

SAE International (2014) *Taxonomy and definitions for terms related to on-road motor vehicle automated driving systems*. Report J3016_201401. www.sae.org/standards/content/j3016_201401/ Accessed 2 June 2019.

Schmitt, B (2017) 40% Price Drop On Chinese EV Batteries Spells Trouble For Tesla. *Forbes*. www.forbes.com/sites/bertelschmitt/2017/01/19/40-price-drop-on-chinese-ev-batteries-spells-trouble-for-tesla/#2dd4e2636189 Accessed 4 March 2018.

Shergold, I (2016) 'Evidence measure review No. 15: e-ticketing', *World Transport Policy and Practice*, 22(1/2): 142–51. http://worldtransportjournal.com/wp-content/uploads/2016/05/30th-Mayopt.pdf Accessed 2 June 2019.

Skinner, R and Bidwell, N (2016) *Making better places: autonomous vehicles and future opportunities*. WSP Parsons Brinckerhoff.

Srnicek, N (2017) *Platform Capitalism*, Cambridge: Polity Press.

Steg, L (2005) 'Car use: lust and must. Instrumental, symbolic and affective motives for car use', *Transportation Research Part A: Policy and Practice*, 39(2-3): 147–62.

Stilgoe, J (2017) 'Seeing like a Tesla: how can we anticipate self-driving worlds?', *Glocalism: Journal of Culture, Politics and Innovation*, 3.

Timmers, V and Achten, P (2016) 'Non-exhaust PM emissions from electric vehicles', *Atmospheric Environment*, 134: 10–17.

TRL (2015) Feasibility study: powering electric vehicles on England's major roads. Report PR42/15 Highways England, Guildford. https://highwaysengland.co.uk/knowledge-compendium/knowledge/publications/1902/index.html Accessed 2 June 2019.

Van Audenhove, F-J, Korniichuk, O, Dauby, L and Pourbaix, J (2014) *The future of urban mobility 2.0: imperatives to shape extended mobility ecosystems of tomorrow*. Arthur D Little.

Wefering, F, Rupprecht, S, Bührmann, S and Böhler-Baedeker, S (2014) *Guidelines: developing and implementing a sustainable urban mobility plan*. www.eltis.org/sites/eltis/files/sump_guidelines_en.pdf Accessed 13 March 2018.

16

Future mobility

Glenn Lyons

Introduction

Transport is integral to people's daily lives across the planet. It plays a profound part in determining a society's credentials in terms of economic prosperity, wellbeing and social equity, and environmental sustainability. Transport shapes and is shaped by society as populations grow and fulfilment of access to people, goods, services and opportunities is pursued. Should anyone have been in doubt, this book underlines that transport matters. Mattering, however, does not make the role of a transport minister one that is sought after or long held – at least in the UK. Being Secretary of State for Transport has tended to be seen as a mark of a politician who is passing through the role on their way up to higher things or on their descent from frontline politics. Responsibility for transport can be a poisoned chalice for the very reason that transport does matter and because it is a source of both opportunity and threat to society. There is the opportunity to better connect society and help it thrive. Yet there is the threat that the consequences of such connectivity are harmful to society in terms of reshaping it in ways that bring about environmental degradation, social inequity and adverse health consequences. This book elaborates on such opportunity and threat, and explores and critiques aspects of governance and policy making. Critical commentary on where we have been, and on the course that has been charted for developing our transport system, now matters even more. It can help inform the ongoing shaping of transport supply and demand in the face of a deeply uncertain future as we head further into the digital age.

And it is inevitable that the world changes. Change can sometimes appear dramatic. An earthquake that literally shakes up the built environment. A stock market crash. A new president. Or at a personal level, being made redundant, the arrival of your first baby or winning the lottery. But change is often much less dramatic. We may have variations in routine from day to day, but for the most part the world of today seems much as it was yesterday, last month or even last year. There are established norms, rituals, dependencies, procedures, experiences and expectations. Commuting to work, for instance, is seen as a common ritual associated – for many – with being in a private car confronting some degree of inconvenience from other road users; or entering the domain of public transport with its schedules, rhythms of stopping, starting and moving, and stolen glances at other passengers. Change, at a number of levels, is going on but it is what might be termed incremental (and therefore stealthy); and yet sometimes this is powerfully cumulative. The drip-drip of an occasional cyclist fighting through traffic in London becomes, over time, a trickle of cyclists, which becomes, over more time, a steady flow of cyclists, which becomes, over yet more time, a torrent of cyclists.

This closing chapter reflects upon change and the prospect of change in looking to the future of mobility and why transport matters. It highlights that we are confronted by two agendas: (i) a need for policy making and investment to chart a course into a deeply uncertain future; and (ii) a need to consider how well equipped our orthodox approaches in transport analysis are in the face of what appears to be an ever more complex and changing world.

Changes we have seen

According to the ancient Chinese philosopher Laozi (or so it is now paraphrased), 'those who have knowledge, don't predict; those who predict, don't have knowledge.' It is perhaps a reminder that in a complex world, any notion of being able to foretell its future state is illusory. A reminder too that at the same time, many seem drawn towards offering more or less well-informed attempts to do so. There has been no shortage of pundits offering their views on, for example, how far and how fast self-driving cars are set to become a feature of future mobility.

In 1949 the magazine of popular science and technology *Popular Mechanics* ran an article entitled 'Brains that Click' in which it was suggested that '[w]here a calculator like the ENIAC [Electronic Numerical Integrator and Computer] today is equipped with 18,000 vacuum tubes and weighs 30 tons, computers in the future may have only 1000 vacuum tubes and perhaps weigh only 1½ tons' (Hamilton 1949: 258). This quote is 70 years old: not much different in time span to the 60-year appraisal period in which – with apparent authority – we examine the expected return on investing in the transport system based upon assumptions about how the future will unfold. In its time, this future projection was doubtless seen as bold – could computers really reduce in size so dramatically? Today, immeasurably more powerful and versatile than ENIAC, the MacBook weighs less than one kilogram. In more recent times we are experiencing ever more wondrous developments in what has been a rapidly maturing digital age. In the classic science fiction work *The Hitchhiker's Guide to the Galaxy* from 1981, the Babel Fish was a small, yellow fish which when put into your ear could translate from one spoken language to another. In October 2017 – 36 years later – Google announced its new Pixel Buds[1] earpieces which support live translation between 40 spoken languages. Science fact follows science fiction.

In 1998 the UK Labour Government published the first transport White Paper for a generation (Department of the Environment, Transport and the Regions (DETR) 1998). In its follow-up, ten-year plan for investment it was right to remark that 'social and technological changes will also alter patterns of behaviour in unforeseen ways' (DETR 2000: 8). It also commented that '[t]he likely effects of increasing Internet use on transport and work patterns are still uncertain, but potentially profound, and will need to be monitored closely.' In 1998, not even 10 per cent of UK households had access to the Internet (Office for National Statistics (ONS) 2018). The Google domain name had only been registered for a year and the availability of Microsoft Outlook as part of Microsoft Office was only a year old; eBay had not been launched in the UK; and Wikipedia, Skype, YouTube, Facebook and Twitter did not exist (Lyons 2015). Having a mobile phone was not yet the norm, let alone having a smartphone with mobile Internet.

Fast forward to the present day and such things have become features of many people's everyday lives. Ninety per cent of UK households have access to the Internet (ONS 2018). Over three quarters of adults have bought goods or services online in the last year. In the five years from 2013 there was a four-fold increase in the number of *superfast* broadband connections and a near four-fold increase in residential fixed broadband download speed (Ofcom 2018).

Connectivity and access

Why has the previous section focused upon such non-transport technological changes when the chapter concerns mobility? A central tenet of orthodox transport planning has been that travel is a derived demand (Mokhtarian and Salomon 2001). Demand derives from a need or desire to *access* people, goods services and opportunities at alternative locations. Physical mobility is a means of gaining access – it's a form of bridging distance to achieve *connectivity*. Indeed, in recent decades our pursuit of access in order to support economic prosperity and social wellbeing has been dominated by the centrality of the private motor car – the automobility *regime* has significantly defined modern society in many countries (Geels 2012, Geels et al 2012). Yet we are now in a world where digital connectivity has rapidly matured and continues to do so. We are, increasingly, accessing people, goods, services and opportunities using the telecommunications system (Kenyon et al 2002) as well as, or instead of, using the transport system. As such mobility, and especially future mobility, needs to be considered in both physical and virtual forms.

Transport matters but telecommunications also matter. Indeed, the motor age and the digital age have collided and are now merging. Orthodox transport planning and modelling have found it convenient to distinguish between trips and activities and treat them as discrete and separable uses of time. Trips have typically been seen as *means* which carry with them disutility (cost) to reach the *ends* provided by activities which yield utility (benefit). But it has become apparent, increasingly over time, that connectivity in society is changing such that people are both physically moving to gain access and at the same time gaining access while on the move, supported by mobile technologies. Jain and Clayton (Chapter 10) elaborate on the complexities that have become apparent as travel time's use, meaning and value receive growing attention in a mobile world, raising questions over the relative merits of speeding up journeys or improving the journey experience as a means to reduce the 'cost' of travel. Through questions included in the National Rail Passenger Survey over a ten-year period (2004–2014), the nature of travel time use has been empirically tracked (Lyons et al 2016). There has been a growing use of a changing array of mobile technologies. The proportion of rail travellers saying mobile technologies make their travel time use better has more than doubled. From 2004 to 2010 there was a significant growth in the proportion of travellers indicating that they had made *very worthwhile* use of their time on the train. In 2014, over one in four rail passengers indicated that how they could use their time while travelling was an important factor, or the main reason, for choosing to travel by train.

The relationships between (use of) the transport system and the telecommunications system are continuing to evolve, as is the balance between supply and demand. Change can take time. The growth in worthwhile use of rail travel time did not continue on from 2010 to 2014. Lyons et al (2016) suggest that this may because rail has become a victim of its own success – the very appeal of access while on the move has contributed to growing demand and overcrowding. Our transport systems are under pressure to provide more access for growing populations in a world that appears ever more in a hurry. It seems untenable that society's future connectivity needs will be fulfilled by transport systems alone to the extent that they have been in the past.

Transport technologies

Nevertheless, our physical transport systems will continue to play a highly important *part* in the future fulfilment of access needs. What then of developments in transport technologies and services? Are these showing the same degree of *transformational* change that has been illustrated earlier for digital communications? It would be hard to say 'yes'. There is much progress of merit and future potential – but also much hype. As part of informing its second Road Investment Strategy, the UK Department for Transport (DfT) recently completed a study (Kantar Public 2018) examining public reactions to the prospects of four areas of transport technologies and services that some would see as centre stage in future mobility: electric cars, truck platooning, connected vehicles and real-time information, and autonomous pods (and the related opportunity for shared mobility services). Do these collectively mark the coming of a new *regime* for physical mobility? The answer is uncertain. There is now momentum surrounding the electrification of the car fleet in a number of countries with commitments from governments to ban in future new production and sales of traditional internal combustion engine (ICE) vehicles. Volvo pledges that '[e]very new Volvo car launched from 2019 onwards will have an electric motor' (Volvo 2019). It can be expected that vehicles will become more connected and, in turn, that there will be more information available to drivers that supports both safe and efficient driving. What is much less clear, as Parkhurst and Seedhouse discuss in the previous chapter, is how far and how fast we will move into a world of autonomous vehicles (AVs), and with what consequences.

Driverless cars

There are commentators who suggest that a world of driverless cars is rapidly approaching (for example, Arbib and Seba 2017).

Yet beyond technological and legal issues to solve (concerning both vehicles and infrastructure) there are matters of price, consumer demand, market penetration and behavioural response to contend with. Gartner's Hype Cycle depicts a common path followed by emergent technologies (Linden and Fenn 2003). They typically create a crescendo of market noise known as the 'peak of inflated expectations'. This is followed by a descent into the 'trough of disillusionment' before emergence along a 'slope of enlightenment' towards the 'plateau of productivity'. Figure 16.1 charts what Gartner is indicating over time for AVs. As of 2017 they had just passed over the peak with an implied descent into the trough to follow. The 2018 update recognises the different forms of AVs and their respective positions along the cycle. In technological terms, Volvo has made – or had been making – impressive headway with its 'Drive Me' autonomous driving project until a scaling back and delay to its test programme was announced at the end of 2017 (Camhi 2017). In a separate development, on 18 March 2018, Elaine Herzberg was the first pedestrian to be killed (in Arizona, US) at the 'hands' of a vehicle operating in self-driving mode.

Advocacy of the appeal of AVs has included the following: (i) *improved safety* – human error reduced or removed from the driving

Figure 16.1: Compilation of Gartner's positioning of autonomous vehicles on its hype cycle

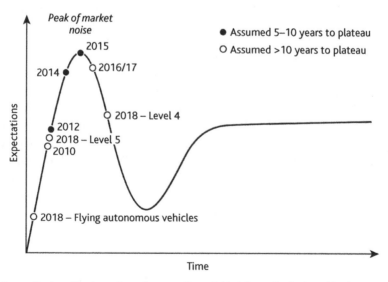

Source: Produced by the author using annually available information in the public domain from Gartner

task leading to fewer accidents, injuries and loss of life; (ii) *improved access to automobility* – those unwilling or unable to drive a vehicle have the opportunity to independently make use of AVs; and (iii) *improved travel time use* – freedom away from the driving task to use travel time for other activities. All three of these prospects could indeed hold great promise, if they are realised, but it remains far too early to judge whether or to what extent this will be the case.

A first order effect of AVs may well be to improve road safety, but it is plausible that a second order effect could be to perpetuate or further extend the sedentary lifestyles already associated with car dependence. Might not a third order effect then be that public health declines through lack of physical activity? As Curl and Clark point out in Chapter 8, transport can make an important contribution to improving *or harming* public health and wellbeing. Improved access to automobility for those unable to drive does not seem possible if Level 4 autonomy (see Table 15.1) prevails as the dominant manifestation of future automobility – a steering wheel remains and the vehicle's user will still be required to be able to drive on occasions. For those who are physically disabled, AV technology may not solve the problem of how they get into and out of the vehicle unaided, although this is not beyond the reach of vehicle design to address. It is not immediately apparent, beyond the rhetoric of 'access for all' offered by proponents of a driverless future, that much attention is being paid to what Middleton and Spinney (Chapter 4) refer to as 'emotional work'. This is the additional (and hidden) effort that some parts of society are subjected to in fulfilling their mobility needs because the design of that system has overlooked them. With regard to improved time use, the Volvo depiction (in its portrayal of a driverless future) of the vehicle occupant reading a book may seem rather incongruent with the experience of many of today's car passengers. Diels (2014) indicates that some 60 per cent of car passengers can experience nausea, with lateral and longitudinal accelerations of the vehicle being important contributory factors. He suggests that car sickness may be less likely to occur if AVs reduce the incidence of such accelerations.

In short, we do not yet know what the future has in store regarding what technological possibility might offer in relation to automobility. Invention is not the same as innovation. The former is what is made possible, the latter is whether, how and to what extent the invention is taken up and applied, and with what consequences. Any vision of future mobility involves a considerable number of assumptions (Parkhurst and Lyons 2018).

From intelligent or smart mobility to effective mobility

New future-facing terms are now in use: 'Intelligent mobility' and 'Mobility as a Service' or MaaS. They seem to have been embraced with remarkable speed. Yet not long ago the transport sector concerned itself with 'Intelligent Transport Systems' (ITS) and 'Advanced Traveller Information Systems' (ATIS). In essence, we are continuing a journey of development in which improved data collection and data processing yield feeds of information into (new) services for transport system operators and users. This is indeed an important journey but it is one of likely evolution rather than revolution, notwithstanding the ever-improving journey planning information at our fingertips. MaaS embodies the notion of subscribing to a single service catering for mobility needs by helping users conveniently access and pay for different modal options for reaching their destinations – as an alternative to the *private* car (Jittrapirom et al 2017). Crucially, however, this is predicated upon there being a suitable quality of transport services available to rival the private car. This is more likely to be the case in urban than in rural areas, but even in cities there can be multiple players that make up the mobility system. Coordinating and harmonising them through a single system remains highly challenging. Pangbourne et al (2018: 44) suggest that '[t]he dominant rhetoric surrounding MaaS is technologically deterministic and highly optimistic.'

We can be at risk of being seduced by the siren sound of technology. What may be technologically *feasible* for future mobility is not necessarily the same as what is *desirable* for future mobility. The latter is more value-laden and different stakeholders – from policy makers, to shareholders to consumers – will have their own interpretations. For instance, with reference in general to whether technology can 'save us', Young (2016: unpaginated) cautions that 'the ultimate end of many products is profit not utility – exchange value not use value.' If stewardship of the future is valued highly then it can be suggested that regardless of technological enablement and sophistication, effective mobility should be taken as that which plays its part in shaping and *supporting* the sort of society we want – economically prosperous but also socially desirable and environmentally sustainable.

We can and should take issue with use of terms such as smart or intelligent mobility and ask how they do, or should, relate to *sustainable* mobility (Lyons 2018a). Are the terms synonymous? Do they overlap or is one subservient to the other? It would make sense for them to be harmonised such that smart (urban) mobility might be defined as 'connectivity in towns and cities that is affordable, effective, attractive and sustainable' (Lyons 2018a: 6). Vigar and Varna (Chapter 9) very aptly argue for the role of urban design and place making within the era of 'smart technologies', emphasising a need for what they call the 'ordinary technologies' such as benches and quality pavements. Docherty et al (2018: 114) caution that without clear governance of what technological possibility has to offer and of the stakeholders involved, there is a risk of 'locking the mobility system into transition paths which exacerbate rather than ameliorate the wider social and environmental problems that have challenged planners throughout the automobility transition.'

By giving more attention to clarifying the end we seek, rather than losing sight of this to instead fixate on a particular means, we recall that motorised mobility is not the only means to realise connectivity in society. Alongside the physical transport system there is also the land use system that can allow connectivity through proximity and thus through greater reliance on walking and cycling. Rode et al (2014) provide an important reminder of the huge significance to their resulting form and function of different accessibility pathways taken by cities. Atlanta and London are comparable in terms of economic output yet the former is seven times less dense than the latter, has very much more dependence on private motorised mobility and over seven times fewer people living within 500m of rail-based public transport. Alongside the transport and land use systems and their interaction, there is now a mature telecommunications system that allows digital connectivity. Taken together, such a 'triple access system' – transport, land use and telecommunications – should be the focus of attention when addressing future mobility (Lyons and Davidson 2016). Indeed, its importance is underlined by the strain under which our transport system is being placed, with, as Dawson and Marsden point out in Chapter 13, limited reserve or redundancy and a susceptibility to disruption. The triple access system offers greater prospect for resilience and an ability to absorb disruption and maintain provision of access.

Deep uncertainty

A changing world is unavoidable. Parts of orthodox transport planning have, however, rather relied upon being able to take a systems approach that can make sense of cause and effect so as to have some meaningful agency in the processes of change. Classically a four-stage model of trip generation, trip distribution, mode split and traffic assignment has been employed to represent the transport system and in particular the road traffic system. Future changes to supply and/or demand are then examined that in turn can inform an economic appraisal of whether or not such change is likely to yield future benefit sufficient to warrant the cost of pursuing the change. A model is by definition a simplified representation of reality. Still, with regard to its construct (and related assumptions), its inputs (and related assumptions) and its application (and related assumptions), there must be sufficient confidence that the model serves a purpose in reasonably representing reality. Phil Goodwin discusses in Chapter 7 how, for some, the enduring application of the approach outlined earlier has been justifiable during a period in history where the incumbent regime of automobility has predominated. Others would contend that its simplicity has failed to take sufficient account of unanticipated and unintended consequences arising from second and third order effects and feedback loops. In the context of our discussion in this chapter, it seems that assumptions taken in pursuit of such an approach – which (implicitly) account for the wider 'system of systems' of which the transport system is a part – are under increasing strain in terms of achieving reasonable representation of reality in a changing world.

Allied to the notion that we may currently be in the midst of a regime transition in mobility (Lyons, 2015) is a sense that we are currently facing deep and STEEP uncertainty. *Deep* uncertainty reflects that while the future is always uncertain, it may be more so now than recognised for some time previously; *STEEP* reflects the multiple and inter-related dimensions of that uncertainty – Social, Technological, Economic, Environmental and Political drivers of change.

Demographic change

Consider just one strand of uncertainty through the lens of society's demographic profile. Nearly one in five people in the UK today are aged 65 or over (ONS 2017). A baby born today has an average life expectancy of 91 (male) or 93 (female), and a one in three chance of living to 100 (ONS 2016; see also Leeson 2014). Someone who is 50 today has an average life expectancy of 86 (male) or 89 (female). Increasing life expectancy relates to mortality. Yet there is also a need to consider *morbidity* – that is, a state of being diseased or unhealthy. Is change in healthy life expectancy keeping pace with life expectancy? As Jagger (2015: 5) suggests, society may either move in a direction of prolonging life in a way that results in more years of unhealthy living 'due to advances in medical treatments and technology keeping alive those who would previously have died,' or in a direction where morbidity is compressed, resulting in more years of healthy living. Her recent evidence review finds that '[i]ncreases in health expectancies in the UK are not keeping pace with gains in life expectancy, particularly at older ages' (Jagger 2015: 4). Thus while people are both living longer and spending more years in good health they are also spending slightly more years in ill health (Public Health England 2017).

Alongside life expectancy and healthy life expectancy is working life expectancy (Mayhew 2009). Individual and societal economic and social wellbeing and associated implications for future mobility depend significantly on how these three interrelate. It would be an easy mistake to assume that the future workforce will be dominated by millennials; the reality is that as many if not more workers are likely to be older workers, where good health allows. Research by Sahlgren (2013: 7) suggests that as a result of reduced physical activity and social interaction, 'being retired decreases physical, mental and self-assessed health.' This points to the prospect that living longer, healthier and happier can come from *choosing* to continue to work in later life – increasing retirement age may represent a positive not only for the Treasury balancing its books but in terms of the wellbeing of people themselves. And there is considerable diversity and uncertainty in where older people will live, how they will live, whether and how they will work and what demands they will in turn place upon the transport system (Shergold et al 2015).

Peak car

Musselwhite and Chatterjee highlight in Chapter 14 the dependence of older people upon the car and the adverse effect of giving up access to the car in a car-centric society. But they also look to the other end of the age spectrum where growing numbers of young people do not have access to driving a car. Young adults in a number of countries around the world are growing less likely to acquire a driving licence (Delbosc and Currie 2013). At least in the UK there may be a number of factors at play here including uncertain income, urbanisation and digitalisation that lessen the need or means to embrace what was once a rite of passage into adulthood. Chatterjee et al (2018: 2) have provided a comprehensive examination of these matters, with strong indications of fundamental changes in travel behaviour taking place: '29% of all 17–20 year olds had a full driving licence in 2014 compared to 48% in 1992/94,' for example. Marsden et al (2018) point to evidence of substantial declines over the last two decades in the average number of commuting trips, shopping trips and indeed overall trips per person.

This trip rate decline is unprecedented. Unprecedented too between 2004 and 2014 in a number of countries was a period of *zero* growth in total car traffic. This has been labelled 'peak car' – a shorthand term for uncertainty over whether the future of car travel is one of grow, peak or plateau (Goodwin and Van Dender 2013).

Hence, while much attention is currently focused upon a driverless future for mobility there is also the prospect of a *drive-less* future. Indeed, deserving of greater attention alongside driverless cars is the prospect that *carless drivers* (that is, pedestrians and cyclists) become a growing feature of future mobility. There has been a 28 per cent increase in pedal cycle traffic in the UK in the last ten years. It is plausible that driverless, drive-less and carless (future) trends will all be at play in combination, although pointing to national statistics always risks overlooking the heterogeneity of society and its mobility needs. Gray reminds us in Chapter 12 of rural transport needs beyond the temptation to fixate upon urban areas. He highlights the perennial challenge of providing viable rural bus services to support people's access needs. In turn, the enduring centrality of one's own car (or someone else's car) is made apparent and he entertains the possibilities for rural access that driverless vehicles may bring.

Scenario planning

When faced with deep uncertainty, our approach to examining future demand needs to change – as is being recognised within a number of transport authorities (Lyons 2018b). Since our modelling and forecasting approach of decades past may no longer be sufficient, scenario planning has an important part to play because it exposes and embraces uncertainty rather than concealing it. The approach is to identify drivers of change that are both important and also highly uncertain and then to develop narrative scenarios of plausible futures that could emerge depending upon how those uncertainties play out (for examples see: Office for Science and Technology (OST) 2006, Zmud et al 2013, Lyons and Davidson 2016, Government Office for Science (GOS) 2019). Policy and investment options can then be tested in terms of their potential risk and yield in the face of uncertainty. Options can be examined in relation to how well they perform in helping to fulfil a vision or strategy in *multiple plausible futures* (for an example of how this is being examined at a national level see Lyons et al 2018).

During 2015/16 through a series of workshops across the UK, 200 transport professionals engaged in considering future uncertainty and in turn reflecting upon the established approaches to transport analysis and policy making and whether or not these were aligned with the circumstances of uncertainty faced (Lyons 2016). They were presented with the results of a scenario planning exercise undertaken by the New Zealand Ministry of Transport (Lyons and Davidson 2016) and asked to consider the plausibility of four different scenarios for transport and society when applied to the UK context. The scenarios have associated estimates of change in total car travel between 2014 and 2042 (vehicle distance travelled), and are based on the playing out of the following two critical uncertainties: (i) what society in future will *want* to do – centred upon the balance of connectivity preference between physical access and virtual access; and (ii) what society in future will be able to *afford* to do – centred upon the relative cost of energy. The estimates of change in total car travel since 2014 ranged across the four scenarios from +35 per cent to −53 per cent. When asked in an exercise to indicate the relative likelihood of each of the scenarios coming to pass, 20 per cent of the collective vote across all workshops went to the scenario with 35 per cent growth in total car travel. The scenario with 53 per cent *reduction* in total car travel was awarded 29 per cent of the likelihood share (the highest of the four scenarios). The latest official Road Traffic Forecasts for England and Wales indicate a growth in car travel from 2015 of between 11 and 48 per cent by 2050 (DfT 2018).

The transport profession, it seems, is collectively alive to the deep uncertainty faced and indeed prepared to contemplate radical change beyond the official position. Such radical change relates to the prospect of a fundamental regime transition now taking place over a period of decades from the motor age as we have known it, to something else. But the further insights from this national study of transport professionals' views are also rather sobering (Lyons 2016). There is a sense of professional impotence, arising from being 'on the back foot' and from a lack of skills within the profession to confront the uncertainty faced. The transport sector is felt to be subject to vested interests, risk aversion and a 'rearview mirror' mentality that results in inertia to change. Transport analysts have become *accountable* to the dogma and procedures of regime compliance instead of *responsible* for stewardship of the future through 'regime testing'.

Biases

Transport analysts (and indeed wider intellectual interest from scholars in both psychology and sociology) preoccupy themselves with trying to make sense of the changing transport system and the changing (and attempts at changing) behaviour of its users. But they are now also confronted with a need to reconsider the attitudes and behaviours within transport analysis itself and the policy-making pathways that are followed. This is really difficult. We are all subject to our own and each others' unconscious biases. These extend beyond, but are also associated with, differences in disciplinary perspectives (such as those between sociologists and psychologists that, as Barr and Preston explain in Chapter 5, bring into question the very basis for defining behaviour). Google Trends offers insights into the popularity of search terms over time and 'Unconscious bias'[2] has seen a seven-fold increase when comparing September 2018 with September 2013. Still, *awareness* of bias does not necessarily mean we are doing anything about it.

Biases include the following: *cognitive fluency* – the more understandable we find something, the more believable we consider it to be; and *confirmation bias* – we are inclined to look for information that supports our existing views rather than actively seek out information that may challenge our views. To these can be added the bias of *false precision*. We look into a deeply uncertain future and yet are prepared to produce analytical results with predictions of outcomes whose precision does not reflect their accuracy: for example, benefit–cost ratios for 60-year scheme appraisals reported to two decimal places. We are also subject to an overarching *blind spot bias* – in other words we tend to believe we are less prone to bias than those around us (Pronin 2007). Such biases may well have contributed to the perpetuation of what are now well-established transport appraisal approaches that favour the centrality of cost–benefit analysis – something which Hickman brings into question in Chapter 6.

A way forward

Where does this brief exploration of issues relating to future mobility leave us? The complexity and challenges could suggest cause for despair. This need not actually be the case, although a different way of thinking is called for. Uncertainty is problematic if an approach of 'predict and provide' is maintained. Instead, uncertainty can and should be turned into an *opportunity* because the future – to at least some significant extent – is ours to shape. We should therefore be shifting our thinking and action towards *decide and provide*: decide what type of society we want and the forms of connectivity that might best support it and then shape our 'triple access system' accordingly.

Human behaviour adapts remarkably well to change. If we shape our future mobility systems then this will in turn shape demand. A decide and provide approach is not to be confused with what Cohen and Durrant (Chapter 11) refer to as 'decide, announce and defend' (DAD), although the scope for misunderstanding is apparent. What they highlight is the important distinction between policy making and investment that avoids, versus that which embraces, meaningful dialogue with the very people beyond the political class and transport profession who are affected by the decisions.

As part of a *participatory* decide and provide approach, there is a need for what might be termed 'responsible innovation'. One of the challenges with mobility is that it is a consumption behaviour. Private sector providers of mobility services and their shareholders understandably have a vested interest in more rather than less mobility, unless less can be offset by higher unit price. There is a *responsibility* to help set a framework for innovation that ensures that its benefits can be enjoyed while unanticipated and undesirable consequences such as rebound effects can be avoided. In this vein, it was welcome to see that the House of Lords' Science and Technology Select Committee (2017: 5) recommended in its examination of connected and autonomous vehicles (CAVs) that 'the Government should bring forward a wider transport strategy that places the development and implementation of CAV in the context of wider policy goals, such as increased use of public transport, and the reduction of congestion and pollution.'

At the end of 2016 the UK Government announced a £500 billion infrastructure investment pipeline, including transport (Infrastructure and Projects Authority 2016). With such record investment that, if made, would shape society for generations to come, investing wisely is an imperative. This must involve incorporating the priorities of flexibility and resilience into the design of infrastructure and services: spending (even) more up front to ensure this, with the prospect of being better placed to account for future uncertainty and thereby secure a dividend in terms of supporting a thriving future society through mobility provision. Future mobility is not rocket science. It is far more complicated than that. But the challenge is there for the taking and marks an important and exciting time for those who are professionally engaged in this domain.

Notes

[1] www.cnbc.com/2017/10/04/google-translation-earbuds-google-pixel-buds-launched.html

² https://trends.google.com/trends/explore?date=all&q=unconscious%20
bias#TIMESERIES

References

Arbib, J and Seba, T (2017) *Rethinking Transportation 2020–2030 – The
disruption of transportation and the collapse of the internal-combustion vehicle
and oil industries*. RethinkX, May. www.rethinkx.com/transportation
Accessed 14 January 2019.

Camhi, J (2017) Volvo scales back self-driving test program. *Business
Insider UK* http://uk.businessinsider.com/volvo-scales-back-self-
driving-test-program-2017-12 Accessed 14 January 2019.

Chatterjee, K, Goodwin, P, Schwanen, T, Clark, B, Jain, J, Melia,
S, Middleton, J, Plyushteva, A, Ricci, M, Santos, G and Stokes, G
(2018) *Young people's travel – what's changed and why? Review and analysis.*
Final Report to the Department for Transport. http://eprints.uwe.
ac.uk/34640 Accessed 14 January 2019.

Delbosc, A and Currie, G (2013) 'Causes of youth licensing decline:
a synthesis of evidence', *Transport Reviews*, 33(3): 271–90.

Department of the Environment, Transport and the Regions (1988)
DETR. *A new deal for transport better for everyone*. Transport White
Paper, Department of the Environment, Transport and the Regions,
London: TSO.

Department of the Environment, Transport and the Regions (2000)
Transport 2010: The 10 Year Plan for Transport, London: TSO.

Department for Transport (2018) *Road traffic forecasts 2018*. https://
assets.publishing.service.gov.uk/government/uploads/system/
uploads/attachment_data/file/740399/road-traffic-forecasts-2018.
pdf Accessed 14 January 2019.

Diels, C (2014) *Will autonomous vehicles make us sick?* www.researchgate.
net/publication/259674103_Will_autonomous_vehicles_make_us_
sick Accessed 14 January 2019.

Docherty, I, Marsden, G and Anable, J (2018) 'The governance of
smart mobility'. *Transportation Research Part A: Policy and Practice*,
115: 114–25.

Geels, F (2012) 'A socio-technical analysis of low-carbon transitions:
introducing the multi-level perspective into transport studies', *Journal
of Transport Geography*, 24: 471–82.

Geels, F, Kemp, R, Dudley, G and Lyons, G (eds) (2012) *Automobility
in Transition? A Socio- technical Analysis of Sustainable Transport*, New
York: Routledge.

Goodwin, P and Van Dender, K (2013) 'Peak car – themes and issues',
Transport Reviews, 33(3): 243–54.

Government Office for Science (2019) *A time of unprecedented change in the transport system*. Final report from Foresight on the Future of Mobility, Government Office for Science, January. https://assets. publishing.service.gov.uk/government/uploads/system/uploads/ attachment_data/file/775077/future_of_mobility.pdf Accessed 12 February 2019.

Hamilton, A (1949) 'Brains that click', *Popular Mechanics*, 91(3): 162–7 and 256–8.

Infrastructure and Projects Authority (2016) *National infrastructure and construction pipeline analysis*. HM Treasury and Cabinet Office. www.gov.uk/government/uploads/system/uploads/attachment_ data/file/574523/2905918_NIC_Pipieline_pdf_v9.pdf Accessed 14 January 2019.

Jagger, C (2015) *Trends in life expectancy and healthy life expectancy*. Future of an ageing population: evidence review, Foresight, Government Office for Science. https://assets.publishing.service.gov.uk/ government/uploads/system/uploads/attachment_data/file/464275/ gs-15-13-future-ageing-trends-life-expectancy-er12.pdf Accessed 14 January 2019.

Jittrapirom, P, Caiati, V, Feneri, A-M, Ebrahimigharehbaghi, S, AlonsoGonzález, M and Narayan, J (2017) 'Mobility as a service: a critical review of definitions, assessments of schemes, and key challenges', *Urban Planning*, 2(2): 13–25.

Kantar Public (2018) *Future Roads: Public Dialogue – Exploring the public's reactions to future road technologies*. Final Report to the Department for Transport, May. www.gov.uk/government/publications/future-roads-public-dialogue Accessed 14 January 2019.

Kenyon, S, Lyons, G and Rafferty, J (2002) 'Transport and social exclusion: investigating the possibility of promoting inclusion through virtual mobility', *Journal of Transport Geography*, 10(3): 207–19.

Leeson, G (2014) 'Future prospects for longevity', *Post Reproductive Health*, 20(1): 11–15.

Linden, A and Fenn, J (2003) *Understanding Gartner's Hype Cycles*. Strategic Analysis Report No R-20-1971. Gartner Inc., Stamford.

Lyons, G (2015) 'Transport's digital age transition', *Journal of Transport and Land Use*, 8(2): 1–19.

Lyons, G (2016) *Uncertainty ahead: which way forward for transport?* Final report from the CIHT FUTURES Initiative, Chartered Institution of Highways & Transportation. https://www.ciht.org.uk/news/ciht-publish-report-uncertainty-ahead-which-way-forward-for-transport/ Accessed 14 January 2019.

Lyons, G (2018a) 'Getting smart about urban mobility – aligning the paradigms of smart and sustainable', *Transportation Research Part A: Policy and Practice*, 115: 4–14.

Lyons, G (2018b) *Handling uncertainty in transport planning and decision making – Report of a roundtable discussion held in London on 20 July 2018*. Project Report. UWE Bristol. http://eprints.uwe.ac.uk/37926 Accessed 14 January 2019.

Lyons, G and Davidson, C (2016) 'Guidance for transport planning and policymaking in the face of an uncertain future', *Transportation Research A: Policy and Practice*, 88: 104–16.

Lyons, G, Jain, J and Weir, I (2016) 'Changing times – a decade of empirical insight into the experience of rail passengers in Great Britain', *Journal of Transport Geography*, 57: 94–104.

Lyons, G, Cragg, S and Neil, M (2018) Embracing uncertainty and shaping transport for Scotland's future. *Proc. European Transport Conference*, Dublin, 10–12 October.

Marsden, G, Dales, J, Jones, P, Seagriff, E and Spurling, N (2018) *All Change? The future of travel demand and the implications for policy and planning. The first report of the Commission on Travel Demand*. www.demand.ac.uk/wp-content/uploads/2018/04/FutureTravel_report_final.pdf Accessed 14 January 2019.

Mayhew, L (2009) *Increasing longevity and the economic value of healthy ageing and working longer*. City University. http://openaccess.city.ac.uk/13667/1/increasinglongevity_report.pdf Accessed 14 January 2019.

Mokhtarian, P and Salomon, I (2001) How derived is the demand for travel? Some conceptual and measurement considerations. *Transportation Research A* 35, pp 695–719.

Ofcom (2018) *Communications market report*. Office of Communications. www.ofcom.org.uk/__data/assets/pdf_file/0022/117256/CMR-2018-narrative-report.pdf Accessed 14 January 2019.

Office for National Statistics (2016) *What are your chances of living to 100?* https://visual.ons.gov.uk/what-are-your-chances-of-living-to-100/ Accessed 14 January 2019.

Office for National Statistics (2017) *Overview of the UK population: July 2017*. www.ons.gov.uk/peoplepopulationandcommunity/populationandmigration/populationestimates/articles/overviewoftheukpopulation/july2017/pdf Accessed 14 January 2019.

Office for National Statistics (2018) *Internet access – households and individuals: Great Britain 2018*. Statistical bulletin. www.ons.gov.uk/peoplepopulationandcommunity/householdcharacteristics/homeinternetandsocialmediausage/bulletins/internetaccesshouseholdsandindividuals/2018 Accessed 14 January 2019.

Office for Science and Technology (2006) *Intelligent infrastructure futures: project overview*. Foresight Programme. www.gov.uk/government/uploads/system/uploads/attachment_data/file/300334/06-522-intelligent-infrastructure-overview.pdf. Accessed 14 January 2019.

Pangbourne, K, Stead, D, Mladenovic, M and Milakis, D (2018) 'The case of Mobility as a Service: a critical reflection on challenges for urban transport and mobility governance', in G Marsden and L Reardon (eds) *Governance of the Smart Mobility Transition*, Bingley: Emerald Points, pp 33–48.

Parkhurst, G and Lyons, G (2018) The many assumptions about self-driving cars – where are we heading and who is in the driving seat? *Proc. of the 16th Annual Transport Practitioners Meeting*, 5–6 July, Oxford. http://eprints.uwe.ac.uk/36997/ Accessed 14 January 2019.

Pronin, E (2007) 'Perception and misperception of bias in human judgment', *Trends in Cognitive Science*, 11(1): 37–43.

Public Health England (2017) *Chapter 1: life expectancy and healthy life expectancy*. www.gov.uk/government/publications/health-profile-for-england/chapter-1-life-expectancy-and-healthy-life-expectancy Accessed 14 January 2019.

Rode, P, Floater, G, Thomopoulos, N, Docherty, J, Schwinger, P, Mahendra, A and Fang, W (2014) *Accessibility in cities: transport and urban form*. NCE Cities Paper 03. London School of Economics and Political Science, London.

Sahlgren, G (2013) *Work longer, live heathier – the relationship between economic activity, health, and government policy*. IEA Discussion Paper No. 46. https://iea.org.uk/publications/research/work-longer-live-healthier-the-relationship-between-economic-activity-health-a Accessed 14 January 2019.

Science and Technology Select Committee (2017) *Connected and autonomous vehicles: the future?* Second Report of Session 2016–17, HL Paper 115, House of Lords. https://publications.parliament.uk/pa/ld201617/ldselect/ldsctech/115/115.pdf Accessed 14 January 2019.

Shergold, I, Lyons, G and Hubers, C (2015) 'Future mobility in an ageing society – where are we heading?', *Journal of Transport & Health*, 2(1): 86–94.

Volvo (2019) https://group.volvocars.com/company/innovation/electrification Accessed 14 January 2019.

Young, D (2016) 'Can technology save us?', *New Philosopher*, 11, February.

Zmud, J, Ecola, L, Phleps, P and Feige, I (2013) *The future of mobility – scenarios for the United States in 2030*. RAND Corporation. www.rand.org/content/dam/rand/pubs/research_reports/RR200/RR246/RAND_RR246.pdf Accessed 14 January 2019.

Index

Printed and bound by CPI Group (UK) Ltd, Croydon, CR0 4YY

23/04/2025

14661023-0005